Australian Society

Australia
1788-1988

Australian Society

Edited by

Keith Hancock

Published in association with
the Academy of the Social Sciences in Australia

The right of the
University of Cambridge
to print and sell
all manner of books
was granted by
Henry VIII in 1534.
The University has printed
and published continuously
since 1584.

CAMBRIDGE UNIVERSITY PRESS

Cambridge

New York   Port Chester   Melbourne   Sydney

CAMBRIDGE UNIVERSITY PRESS
Cambridge, New York, Melbourne, Madrid, Cape Town,
Singapore, São Paulo, Delhi, Tokyo, Mexico City

Cambridge University Press
The Edinburgh Building, Cambridge CB2 8RU, UK

Published in the United States of America by Cambridge University Press, New York

www.cambridge.org
Information on this title: www.cambridge.org/9780521369633

First published 1989
Re-issued 2011

A catalogue record for this publication is available from the British Library

Library of Congress Cataloguing in Publication Data
Australian society/edited by Keith Hancock.
p. cm.
"Published in association with the Academy of the
Social Sciences in Australia."
ISBN 0-521-36161-3
1. Australia - social conditions. 2. Australia - Economic
conditions - 1945-
I. Hancock, Keith Jackson.
II. Academy of the Social Sciences in Australia.
HN843.5.A89 1988
306'.0994-dc1988-20242

ISBN 978-0-521-36161-3 Hardback
ISBN 978-0-521-36963-3 Paperback

Contents

Illustrations

Tables

Figures

Contributors

Glenn Withers is Professor of Economics at La Trobe University in Melbourne. Previously he held appointments at Harvard, Macquarie and the Australian National Universities. He has published on a wide range of topics, including conscription and the economics of the performing arts. Professor Withers is co-Chairman of the National Population Council.

Jacqueline Goodnow has been Professor of Economics at Macquarie University in Sydney since 1975. Her interests have consistently been in the nature of human development and in the social context of families – the latter being the source of her interest in families. **Ailsa Burns** has been a staff member at Macquarie since 1973 and is now an Associate Professor. Her work combines an interest in family patterns and their history with an interest in social policies that affect various family members. **Graeme Russell** is an Associate Professor at Macquarie, where he has worked since 1974. He is particularly interested in the role of fathers and in non-traditional family patterns.

R.G. Brown has been Professor of Social Administration at the Flinders University of South Australia in Adelaide since 1965. His principal research interests are in social welfare policy and historical demography. He has served on the South Australian Social Welfare Advisory Council, the Commonwealth's Social Welfare Commission and the Advisory Committee of the National Population Inquiry.

Brian Crittenden has been Professor of Education at La Trobe University since 1973, having previously been Professor of the Philosophy of Education at the Ontario Institute for Studies in Education. His research interests include the social philosophical issues of educational theory, policy and practice, curriculum theory and moral education. He is a former President of the Philosophy of Education Society of Australasia.

F.L. Jones has, since 1972, been Professor and Head of the Department of Sociology in the Research School of Social Sciences at the Australian National University in Canberra. His main research interests are social mobility and social inequality. He has recently reviewed the labour force experiences of immigrants for the Office of Multicultural Affairs.

W.D. Borrie is Emeritus Professor of Demography of the Australian National University. He was Professor and Head of the Department of Demography in 1951–68, Director of the Research School of Social Sciences in 1968–73, Chairman of the National Population Inquiry in 1971–78 and Director of the Academy in 1979–85.

List of contributors

J.W. Nevile has been Professor of Economics at the University of New South Wales in Sydney since 1965. He has been a consultant to the International Monetary Fund. Most of his published work is in the fields of economic growth, inflation, unemployment and macroeconomic policy. He is a past President of the Economic Society of Australia.

Keith Hancock is a Deputy President of the Australian Conciliation and Arbitration Commission, having taken up this appointment in 1987. Previously he had been Professor of Economics at Flinders University since 1964, and was Vice-Chancellor of that University during 1980–87. His principal area of academic interest was the economics of labour. **Don Rawson** is concurrently a Senior Fellow in Political Science in the Australian National University and Executive Director of the Academy. His principal research interest in recent years has been the political and legal aspects of industrial relations, and he has worked on related topics in the United Kingdom, the United States, Sweden and Canada.

James Crawford, since 1986 Challis Professor of International Law in the University of Sydney, was formerly Professor of Law in the University of Adelaide in 1983–86. He was a full-time Commissioner of the Australian Law Reform Commission in 1982–84 and, since 1984, has been a part-time Commissioner. In 1985–87 he was a Member of the Advisory Committee on the Australian Judicial System which assisted the Constitutional Commission.

Don Aitkin is Chairman of the Australian Research Council and a full-time Executive Member of the National Board for Employment, Education and Training. In 1980–88 he was Professor of Political Science in the Research School of Social Sciences at the Australian National University and before then Professor of Politics at Macquarie University. He has written extensively about the Country Party, Australian electoral behaviour and political institutions. **Francis G. Castles** is a Senior Research Fellow in Political Science in the Australian National University and was formerly Professor of Comparative Politics in the Open University in the United Kingdom. He has written about the development of the welfare state in Scandinavia and Australasia and is a pioneer of the development of comparative public policy as a branch of political science.

J.D.B. Miller, an Emeritus Professor of the Australian National University, had the Chair of International Relations in the Research School of Social Sciences between 1962 and 1987. Previously he was Professor of Politics in the University of Leicester: earlier in his career, he worked for the Australian Broadcasting Commission. His books deal with Australian foreign policy in the context of studies of Australian politics, the Commonwealth in the world, British relations with the Dominions and the European Economic Community.

Preface

The Academy of the Social Sciences in Australia consists of some two hundred Fellows elected by their peers for their eminence in the various social science disciplines. Its main tasks are: first, to encourage scholarship among social scientists (whether or not they are Fellows); second, to educate the wider public about social science – both its capacities and its limitations; and, third, where possible to be of service to governments and others by suggesting sources of authoritative advice. The chapters in this book show the breadth of social science, although not all disciplines are represented.

A volume of essays on social science topics likely to be relevant in 1988 seemed to the Academy to be an appropriate and useful contribution to the bicentenary. I was invited to select the topics and the authors, and I was generally pleased at the willingness of busy scholars to give their time to the project. The Myer Foundation has financially supported the project and I express my warm appreciation of this assistance.

Of course no attempt was made to induce any authors to support or oppose particular views and, undoubtedly, different authors would disagree with each other on various points. I suspect, for example, that several would disagree with Rawson and me about opinions expressed in our chapter about industrial relations. Thus each chapter is to be considered as a self-contained contribution to the overall project.

Are there, despite this, some messages or themes which transcend particular chapters? I believe that there are.

One is the susceptibility of social affairs to profound disturbances whose occurrence and effects may be explicable in retrospect, but are not allowed for in seemingly reasonable predictions. Thus Borrie is (in all probability) correct in perceiving the collapse of fertility rates which has occurred in the 1970s and 1980s as a continuation of a century-long trend. But few, if any, foresaw what has occurred. Social planning (for example, in education and retirement provision) envisaged much higher levels of fertility than now obtain and the community is now digesting the 'mistakes' of the planners. Again, there are persuasive *ex post* explanations for the economic 'bad news' of the years since 1974 (the problem addressed by Nevile); but it was not foreseen and it has profoundly affected the lives of millions of people. And the dramatic changes in family structures and intra-family relations described by Goodnow, Burns and Russell are further evidence of the volatility – within periods much less than an ordinary lifetime – of fundamental social entities.

A second message is closely related. The best-laid plans of social planners often go awry, either in the sense that the anticipated effects do not eventuate or because there are unforeseen and undesired side-effects. This is a message which emerges with particular force (in my view) from the papers of Brown and Crittenden on social welfare and education, respectively. (These authors may or may not agree with me.) It is a warning, too, in the essay of Hancock and Rawson, who suggest that measures recommended by those who call for deep-seated reform of industrial relations are likely to find (if they live for a reasonable time) that the outcomes are different from those contemplated. The problem of planning, of course, is that it involves prediction, which is hazardous. Taken to an extreme, this message would become a recipe for paralysis. 'No policy' is self-contradictory, for a decision to let matters take their own course is itself a policy. If a prescription suggests itself, it is that policies should be incremental and their effects sedulously monitored. This judgement, which many will resist, is reinforced in my mind by William Beaumol's recent exposition (for laypersons) of chaos theory. It is a sobering exposition of the capacity of minor – seemingly trivial – variations in the parameters of the relationships to cause, within measurably short periods, enormous alteration in the outcomes.[1]

Third, there are strong hints of the interrelatedness of social affairs. I say 'hints', because each of the chapters focusses upon a given dimension of our society. But it is clear (for example) that the population story, as told by Borrie, has significant connections with Goodnow, Burns and Russell's picture of the family and *vice versa*; and it is likely that both are interrelated with the social welfare situation described by Brown. The shifts in community values recounted by Jones have, no doubt, contributed to developments in all three areas. Aitken and Castles, in an essay which is more historical than others, argue that political development in Australia has taken a significantly different course from that foreseen by reasonable people in the early decades of the century. They suggest that part of the explanation lies in the industrial relations system – notably, the capacity of workers (through their trade unions) to capture benefits in industrial arbitration. Again the 'flavour' of Australian society, as discerned by Withers, owes something to its ethnic content and hence to immigration policy; and Australia's relations with the rest of the world (the subject of Miller's chapter) impinge in many ways upon its economy, its politics and its values. Many interconnections, obviously, are more subtle and more debatable than these. Even the few examples given, however, point to a major dilemma of social science. The manageability of problems requires that it be subdivided into discrete components each of which has its own forms of expertise. But the boundaries created by the subdivisions inevitably cause distortions. The inescapability of this dilemma is yet another limitation on the predictive powers of social science and hence its capacity to generate reliable prescriptions.

The foregoing, perhaps, are somewhat depressing messages. On the brighter side, an impression emerges of a society which in 1988 is less static, more amenable to diversity, better able to absorb shocks and less derivative than in earlier eras. Even the legal system, discussed in this volume by Crawford, has moved in directions which increasingly distinguish it from its English parent and do so in ways which reflect local perceptions of need and local solutions to it. Withers reminds us that visitors to Australia in bygone years, such as D.H. Lawrence, found it a boring place. Modern visitors can no doubt be found who would have similar reactions, but these would fail to register the greater complexity, pluralism and tolerance of minority groups and interests, let alone the much higher level of cultural achievement.

---

[1]Beaumol suggests that this point has been missed through use of the assumption of linearity. Chaos theory comes into its own when non-linear relations are recognized. The Chaos Phenomenon: A Nightmare for Forecasters. *LSE Quarterly*, Spring, 1987.

For the reasons given earlier, the possibilities of worthwhile prediction may well be few. The available alternative is the continuous up-dating of the present scene – the writing of 'current history'. Not only is the subject-matter of intrinsic interest: the exercise would also facilitate a better understanding of the evolving menu of social and political choice. A *Yearbook of Australian Society* is too much to hope for. A quinquennial review may not be and is perhaps consonant with the rate of social change. Intervals of 200 years are far too long.

The chapters in this book were written during 1986 and 1987. Revisions were made to ensure that the contents were as up-to-date as possible, but events occurring during 1988 could not be taken into account.

1

Living and Working in Australia

Glenn Withers

AUSTRALIAN LEGENDS

Field Marshal Sir William Slim was well-liked as Australia's Governor-General. He attached great weight to meeting the people. On one Outback tour he drove into a small one-pub town, leapt in full uniform from his car, and strode up to a tall, lean, sun-browned stockman who was resting against the verandah post of the pub. 'I'm Slim', said the Governor-General, thrusting his hand forward in greeting. The hand was amiably grasped, accompanied by the laconic query: 'G'day Slim. Slim who?' This sort of story touches a responsive chord in many Australians. There is in many minds an image of the sunburnt country, a land of sweeping plains, of bush-dwellers who tamed a vast continent, a manly, hardy, stoical new breed, independent, equal and free. The image appeals because it establishes Australia as different. And it is a successful image because it has foundation. It is not just a myth. But it is strictly a legend[1] – a partial truth.

A greater truth is that Australia's genuine historical distinctiveness lay in being one of the world's first truly post-industrial societies. Almost from the time of its European origins, and certainly from the later nineteenth century, most Australians lived comfortably in large coastal cities, working in service occupations and enjoying a material standard of living largely unequalled elsewhere in the world. The society was isolated, affluent and democratic. By world standards Australia is a fortunate nation. Its residents have long been free from the want, misery and fear that have afflicted others, and its institutions have preserved and reflected an enviable degree of stability and well-being. While significant injustices remain to be corrected, freedom and equality are possessed in greater degree than in almost any other country.

The prosperity and its associated suburbanization did depend heavily on the natural wealth of the continent. Wool, wheat, gold, iron ore and an abundance of other resources have underpinned material affluence. Rich resources in world demand and a small literate population to facilitate the exploitation of resources were for a long time a mostly successful recipe for economic prosperity – though one even more readily associated with a highly paid urban service economy catering to the rural needs and to the 'taking in of each other's washing' than to true industrialization. It is only with the passing of the energy crisis, the closing out of rural markets in Britain, Europe and Japan and with increasing North American rural export subvention, that in recent years this recipe has shown open signs of fundamental failure. The symbol of that failure is the continuing rise in Australia's foreign debt. How Australia responds to this challenge is the key to its economic future.

But for the past and present a high and increasing affluence has been the norm, and for a country to have never had a mass peasantry or an industrial proletariat casts a different light on living and working. For most Australians living and working has been and remains a fortunate experience.

Yet, in this most fortunate nation, the extent of continuing injustice is also a measure of our still limited understanding and sometimes of our distorted spirit. The plight of the continent's original inhabitants, the degradation of the land, the continued existence of poverty, inequality and alienation amongst the later inhabitants themselves, are still major problems. Solutions are never easy, or they would have been adopted, but the increasing recognition of the problems, especially economic and to some extent non-economic, is a cause for cautious optimism.

The intent of this chapter is the depiction of major themes in living and working in Australia. The physical setting – both the built environment and the natural environment – is defined. How Australians work within this environment and the characteristics of Australians as workers is then considered. The pursuit of leisure, pleasure and excellence within these environments becomes the subsequent concern after looking at the business of work. The outcome of this process for real wages, living standards and equality of distribution of income and wealth is then examined and conclusions drawn as to the future of work for Australians. Throughout, an underlying theme is the relationship of Australian myths and legends to the contemporary realities. How much is Australia an Outback society, a society of big government, a masculine land, a British country, a land of the fair go, an outdoors, sporting nation suspicious of matters of mind and culture, a land of easy affluence and material equality? Examining these depictions is the stuff of this chapter.

ENVIRONMENTS BUILT AND NATURAL

Australia's natural riches are not great for a *continent*. But they are great for a country of sixteen million people. Australia ranks sixth among the nations of the world in area, but forty-fifth in population (Table 1.1).

Table 1.1 *Australia and the world's largest nations*

Country	Area ('000 sq. km)	Rank	Country	Population (m.) mid-1987 estimate	Rank
USSR	22,402	1	China	1,062.0	1
Canada	9,976	2	India	800.3	2
China	9,597	3	USSR	284.0	3
USA	9,363	4	USA	243.8	4
Brazil	8,512	5	Indonesia	174.9	5
Australia	7,682	6	Brazil	141.5	6
India	3,288	7	Japan	122.2	7
			Australia	16.1	45

Source: Australia, Department of Immigration, Local Government and Ethnic Affairs 1987. *Australia's Population Trends and Prospects, 1987.* Canberra, AGPS.

It is a dry and arid country. Its rivers are weak and its mountains low. The fertile temperate strip in the southeast between the mountains and the sea holds seven-tenths of the people. Melbourne and Sydney alone have 40 per cent of the population in their greater metropolitan areas, and the eight state and territory capitals account for 65 per cent of the population. Add in the related towns of Newcastle, Wollongong and Geelong, and the concentration is even clearer. Inland of the major arc of settlement there lie only small townships providing basic services to Australia's rural and mining industries. Australians cling to the coast and live in cities. Few have ever been to the interior – which may well explain the grip it has on the minds of the people. But even in the coastal cities the light, the warmth and the vegetation make living a different experience than for those in the countries from which Australians have mostly come. The interpretation of this difference has been an important part of the country's cultural heritage.

Physically, Australia's major cities are of two types.[2] There are the older European-style cities of early settlement: Sydney, Hobart and Brisbane. They have a city centre of congested narrow streets and high-density dwelling. Then there are the cities of the later nineteenth century: Melbourne, Adelaide and Perth. Here the inner cities are well-planned, symmetric and spacious with more medium-density dwelling. And there is Canberra: a modern, antiseptic, unpretentious and meticulously arranged national capital. Of course all the coastal cities, despite their differing form 'down-town', share the twentieth-century sub-urban sprawl that so characterizes Australian living. Living in Australia means modern houses on large allotments near cities: suburban affluence. It was made possible by mechanical public transport in the first instance, and cemented in place by the motor car. The compact urban hubs remained the single centre, while the ever-widening gyre grew. The land, the wealth and the time all came together to provide perhaps the world's most suburban nation. Arthur Koestler wrote of Australia that 'the continent holds two world records: first, in cramming nearly everybody into towns; second, in providing them with such lavish amounts of living space per head that the towns keep bursting at the seams and spilling their contents farther and farther away from the centre into the blue yonder'.[3]

The pattern of settlement has been remarkably stable, though Australians are amongst the world's most mobile people. Each year, 30 per cent of the population change their residence and 20 per cent change their city.[4] Yet in all the years since 1900 the balance of population spread has hardly altered.[5] The exceptions are a small drift to the cities, the rise of a retirement population in southern Queensland and northern NSW and the establishment of Canberra. It is the mobility plus the newness of Australia's European settlement that makes Australia the geographically homogeneous society that it is. Even the broadening migration from new sources in the post-war period has spread across Australia's cities without uniquely concentrating and differentiating. Thus it may be that Victorians enjoy Australian football and Sydney-folk appreciate rugby more. It may be that Brisbane's houses are often timber on stilts and Adelaide's sandstone. Or Melbourne may have a grey stolidity and reserve that contrasts with the sunny hedonism of the Sydney beaches. People in Perth may have barbeques a lot more than those in Hobart. But the trivial nature of the distinctions emphasizes the overwhelming similarities of people, their speech, work, attitudes and lifestyles. Generalizations about people's ways are always simplistic; but less so for Australians than for the occupants of most other countries, let alone continents.

LIVING AND PARTLY LIVING

For many of the world's people the Australian reality of a quarter-acre block and a comfortable house that you choose and buy and cram with consumer goodies is a dream. There is family security, private freedom, one's own garden, domestic convenience,

3

motoring access to bush, sun and sand – a healthy and peaceful life. Yet despite Australian realization of this dream, there is a critic's view that it is only partly living. For those who value diversity there is an awful and awesome monotony to Australia's suburbs, despite the predominance of private housing. For those who value community there is a lack of convenient access to nearby work and a lack of basic urban facilities in many suburbs – the schools, shops, swimming pools, parks and playgrounds, public transport and theatres that are said to make life enjoyable. Associated with this is a pervading inwardness of private life: tall paling fences and large hedges to keep the neighbours at bay. Only for a few are the alternatives of terrace houses, multi-storey apartments and inner-city living an attractive alternative: 'For migrants and misfits' was Robin Boyd's characterization.[6]

Families on low and irregular earnings still can find the cost of adequate housing often beyond their grasp. The substitute policies of government housing assistance, interest rate ceilings, public housing and the like reach some but deny or miss others, leaving gaping gaps in the social safety net. Even the basic amenities of mains water and sewerage, telephone installation, kerbs and gutters sometimes take an eternity to catch up with those who are otherwise well housed. It is here that J. K. Galbraith's notion of private affluence amidst public squalor still has relevance.

Shelter and personal freedom are met, by and large.[7] But enhanced local amenity, lower social costs, reduced travel and less traffic congestion and improved environment would all be welcome. There is little prospect that these will happen. Small-scale autonomous individual decisions are ill-equipped to meet these needs and, outside of the Australian Capital Territory, there is little in the way of effective townplanning that can facilitate a broader view of social amenity. The brief flowering and sudden death of the Whitlam government's urban initiatives is all too indicative. Australian urban life may be more of the same for the foreseeable future. Indeed, and perversely, it was narrow townplanning, in the form of naive doctrinaire building regulations, that effectively ruled out all but the Australian villa neighbourhood even had residents desired some real diversity of living styles. A test of this proposition is whether the pressure for change emerging from the evolving nature of the Australian family leads to greater diversity of housing and community facilities; for it is clear that Australia has moved toward a greater variety of domestic arrangements propelled by the tendency to marry at older ages, to leave home at earlier ages and to have more *de facto* marriages, divorces and step-families.[8]

While effective concern for urban form came and went in a few short years of the 1970s, concern for the natural environment continues to outlive the trendiness of its period of origin. Perhaps it is the enormity of the task and the magnitude of the problem that explains the tenacity of Australian conservationists. It might be thought that a vast continent with so few people, almost all concentrated in a handful of coastal cities, would be less burdened with environmental conscience than most. But the opposite is true. After centuries of coexistence by indigenes with the Australian natural environment, European settlement has brought dramatic change.[9] The fragile arid and semi-arid pasture lands of the inland have been extensively degraded by precarious grazing and by the introduction of exotic animals and plants. Even in the more-favoured soils and moister climates there is immense impact. For instance, in southeastern and central Queensland – the Brigalow Belt – less than one per cent of the former softwood and brigalow communities remain.[10] Further south the early settlement period in the fertile timbered rim east of the Dividing Range, on the well-watered plains just west of the Range and later across in the Australian southwest, saw extensive timber-cutting that eliminated species of trees and cleared much of the original forests. Soil erosion, pasture deterioration, spread of noxious weeds and the silting of streams and rivers have followed.

It took the arrival of the Japanese woodchip industry to draw attention to the issue of forest-resource exploitation, well after much of the most dramatic clearing had actually taken place. The result, however, was a rapid broadening and development of conservation concern, soon also encompassing the rainforests of southwestern Tasmania and northern Queensland, the Great Barrier Reef and the Queensland sand islands. In the latter cases the problem was mining not grazing, and this is also often the concern in areas of the north and west of Australia. This concern includes the issue of uranium mining in Kakadu Park. Tourism, too, now threatens to produce change to the northern environment and, with mining, to confront many of the remaining original inhabitants of the country with the dilemma of preservation or exploitation of their own traditional lands now subject to land rights grants and claims.[11] Other Australians have not had the same type of relationship with the landscape that Aborigines acquired with long habitation. But the burgeoning of conservation concerns does indicate for those others a new kind of attachment to the Australian environment outside the cities that seems set to continue to mute the otherwise transcendent economic imperatives.

WORK AND WORKERS

Just as the relationship of Australians to their built and natural environment has elements of both continuity and change, so too does their working environment.[12] Australia's status as a post-industrial society has not meant the obsolescence of work, only its long-time bias toward tertiary pursuits. Nor does that status mean that all toil is removed from work, which thereby might remain a joy and a pleasure.

In the late 1980s about 40 per cent of the population is in the workforce and immigration contributes significantly to the growth of the labour supply. An unusual and complex system of conciliation and arbitration tribunals sets minimum wages and determines many aspects of working conditions. There is a high degree of unionization. A range of regulatory enactments are in place to prevent unsafe and unhygienic working conditions and to compensate workers for industrial injuries. Individual employee grievances can be pursued via personal complaint, union representation or court proceedings under the law of employment. The acquisition of trade skills is provided mainly through apprenticeship. The workforce is strongly segmented into differing female and male employment concentrations. (Table 1.2 provides a range of data illustrating these points.)

All of these dimensions of labour have, in the broad, characterized working in Australia since early in the century. Such basic continuity of working arrangements must be rare amongst modern nations. For Australia there is nothing so dramatic as wholesale shifts from rural farmers, labourers and artisans to disciplined industrial factory fodder, and thence to service occupations. The manufacturing revolution passed by the mass of the Australian workforce and relatively few were ever employed in small-scale farming (though some had been prior to their emigration). The term 'post-industrial', when applied to Australia, must encompass its having missed a full-blown industrial stage.[13]

But of course there are also changes to be discussed. For the ordinary workers the major changes may have been in the scale of the firm for which they worked, and hence the change in associated social relations, plus improved comfort in the workplace and improved social security in the market place, particularly with the government provision of unemployment benefits after 1945. Further, there were increased real wages and shorter working hours for the employed, though in the 1980s the probability of unemployment was high – typically in the 8–10 per cent range (Table 1.2). Change was also reflected in the increased levels of formal education for the workforce; the massively expanded female labour contribution to paid employment and substantially increased relative earnings for female workers in the market; and a big shift in the source countries of the migrants entering the Australian workforce. Most of these changes occurred after World War II following a prolonged period of structural and institutional stability dating from early in the century through until that war.

More change is in progress. Even some of the more enduring of Australian labour institutions are now under challenge and, indeed, they can perhaps be seen upon closer inspection to have long been under evolution. This is clear, for instance, in that most distinctive area of Australian working life, the conciliation and arbitration system. With minimum awards applying directly to 86 per cent of Australian employees, the influence of the arbitration system is pervasive. Within the system it is the commonwealth arbitral authority that has been pre-eminent. But the nature of that authority has changed considerably. Three broad phases can be distinguished. An early phase when the Conciliation and Arbitration Commission was seen as a major vehicle for social justice, creating a new province of law and order, gave way to a period when the economic constraints on social purpose became recognized and, indeed, so came to dominate that the Commission emerged as a major independent player in economic policy-making. However, with the Fraser government's 1982 wage pause and the Hawke government's Accord with the trade union movement from 1983, the Commission became a component of a more corporatist economic policy system. Indeed, since the limited capacity of the Commission to enforce sanctions on unions in support of its decisions became unmistakable in the 1960s, the Commission has operated via persuasion and voluntary compliance, treading a fine line between rubber-stamping the agreements of unions, employers and government and, from time to time, attempting to lead or impose its own solutions.

Since the mid-1980s the dominant coalition within the arbitration framework has been that between the Labor government and the peak union body, the Australian Council of Trade Unions (ACTU). Operating under the aegis of the 'Accord', agreement was reached which included a commitment by government to provide appropriate tax and welfare measures and economic restructuring in return for a commitment to wage and strike restraint by unions. With such significant influence upon government, and with major strength in a unionized public sector, the position of Australian unions showed fewer of the vulnerabilities evident in the United States or Britain.

No doubt the union leadership is closely aware of the overseas developments and has acted in recent times to limit the excesses that might contribute to enhanced public opposition to union strength. The Australian movement has the advantage of its symbiotic relation with arbitration which provides legitimacy and protection for unions for arbitral purposes. The number of unions and the unionized share of employees has been remarkably stable since the 1950s (Table 1.2). The cost has been the preservation of small craft unions which have limited the ability of the union movement to consolidate into fewer and larger industry-based unions on the northern European model or to transform into company unions on the Japanese or Canadian lines.

Against the relatively monolithic partnership of unions and Labor government, supporting the existing arbitration arrangements, there have emerged considerable articulate

Table 1.2 *Australia's working population, 1901–81*

Census year	Total population ('000)	Foreign born population share (%)	Labour force ('000)	Union share of labour force (%)	Labour force participation			Unemployment rate (%)	Share of employment		Private sector employment share (%)	Female worker segmentation* (%)
					Male youth (%)	Married women (%)	Older males (%)		Agriculture (%)	Manufacturing (%)		
1901	3,774	22.8	1,615	6.0	n.a.	n.a.	n.a.	3.9	25.4	14.7	87.4	84
1911	4,455	17.1	1,990	18.3	90.0	n.a.	87.0	2.8	24.2	18.5	86.2	84
1921	5,436	15.5	2,329	30.2	86.4	n.a.	85.9	5.8	23.8	19.4	80.5	83
1933	6,630	13.6	2,744	26.9	73.0	2.0	37.9	21.0	24.7	20.1	68.6	74
1947	7,579	9.8	3,196	42.7	81.1	3.4	38.2	3.0	15.9	28.5	76.6	78
1954	8,987	14.3	3,702	48.3	79.7	7.0	33.2	2.1	13.5	28.3	77.1	79
1961	10,508	16.9	4,225	44.9	69.6	9.6	26.9	2.3	11.2	27.7	77.7	80
1966	11,550	18.6	4,856	43.7	66.2	14.1	24.9	1.4	9.2	27.6	77.9	80
1971	12,928	20.2	5,563	44.1	55.7	18.0	22.2	1.5	7.9	26.2	78.1	82
1976	13,916	20.4	6,131	45.7	56.0	22.3	16.8	4.7	6.5	22.5	78.6	80
1981	14,927	20.9	6,719	44.6	61.0	22.2	12.3	5.8	6.4	21.0	73.9	81

* The measure of segmentation is the percentage of the female labour force in disproportionately female occupations

Sources: G. Withers, T. Endres and L. Perry 1985. *Australian Historical Statistics: Labour Statistics*, Source Papers in Economic History, No. 7, Australian National University, December; C. Price 1984. *Birthplaces of the Australian Population, 1961-1981*, Working Papers in Demography, No. 13, Australian National University.

sections of the employer organizations and opposition political parties who argue that centralized wage-fixing and industrial relations must give way to a more decentralized and deregulated system if Australian economic performance is to improve significantly. This issue, more than any other, is the feature that distinguished Labor from the Conservative parties in the late 1980s, although there were signs of sympathy with the conservative arguments from within the Labor Cabinet and vice versa.

What is the workforce structure? The service sector orientation has been mentioned. In 1986, agriculture, mining and manufacturing together comprised only a total of 30 per cent of employment. The major growth industries within services were areas such as community services, finance, property and business services, recreation and entertainment and personal services. Occupational structure in turn derives from industry requirements, so that one observes a declining role for rural and mining occupations since the turn of the century and a shift away from manual and trade work to professional and clerical employment. There has been a revival of the share of employer and self-employed workers in the 1980s to almost 10 per cent of the labour force, arresting a previous long-term decline in that share. Recession and tax minimization seem consistent explanations for the turn-around.

Australia has long had the reputation for extensive governmental involvement in the economy. In the nineteenth and earlier twentieth centuries this reputation was well-deserved (Table 1.2). The developmental role played by earlier Australian governments produced large public-sector employment by the standards of the times. And this was significant, since government offered employment on different terms and conditions than much private employment – including enhanced job security, better promotion prospects, better retirement provision and so on. By the 1980s, however, employment characteristics of large private-sector employers approximated those of government and the Australian commitment to growing public employment had moderated so that many other advanced countries had caught up with and exceeded public employment shares in Australia.[14]

The Australian public employment share is almost one-quarter of the workforce – high by US standards but somewhat below the OECD average, thereby complicating local condemnation of 'Big Government' and allegations of its association with poor economic performance. The public sector composition has moved from its historical association with transport and communication and urban facilities to human services such as health, education and welfare.[15] The developmental role of Australian governments has given way to the modern welfare state.

If reliance upon public employment is increasingly a myth in depicting work in Australia compared to other countries, so is the traditional masculine and Anglo-Celtic characterization of Australian workers. The historical measurement of the female component of the workforce is subject to considerable uncertainties – and the depiction of domestic work as not in the labour force is a statistical crudity – but it can clearly be said that the single most significant change in twentieth-century working and living patterns in Australia has been the shift of married women from domestic to market work. As the workforce participation by young persons and older persons has declined, that for married females has risen dramatically – from around 3 per cent in 1947 to almost 25 per cent by the mid-1980s (Table 1.2). When this change is combined with changes in migration an interesting interpretation emerges that deserves some elaboration.

Australia has long been a migrant country. In per capita terms it has maintained the highest migration rates of the advanced countries, along with Israel. But prior to World War II this migration was overwhelmingly British and Irish. Over the 40 post-war years in which migrants and their children contributed almost 60 per cent of labour force growth the sources of migration have moved steadily south and east – from Britain and Northern Europe, through the Southern Mediterranean to the Middle East and then to southeast Asia and New Zealand. A formerly male and British workforce has been progressively transformed into a much more diversified workforce, with a major female and non-British presence.[16] One view of this is that without these sources of labour the Australian workforce and GDP would be puny things indeed. Lacking a rural workforce which can be drawn upon for urbanization, Australia has instead drawn on migration and married women. The expansion of manufacturing in the 1950s and 1960s came from migrant workers, just as the expansion of the tertiary sector has come from women workers. It is these groups who have provided the structural flexibility for the Australian workforce since school-leavers and established workers tend to replicate the existing structures.[17]

How have these groups fared? Many assume that migrants and women are the core of an exploited under-class of worker. Certainly there is some exploitation and discrimination. What is equally evident, though, is the relatively advantaged position of migrants in Australia compared to experience with 'guest worker' migrants in post-war Europe. Controlling for a transition period and allowing for education, training and language differences, we find a broad equity of treatment which belies the view of incurably racist and discriminatory attitudes said by some Australians to be held by many (other?) Australians.[18] The parity of treatment of like characteristics and the record of equal access to social facilities and amenities is particularly clear-cut at the second generation migrant level, where complications of transition and language are small.[19]

The position is not as clear-cut for women workers. The same type of analyses that divine rough parity of treatment for migrants find a gap in treatment of women – a gap that it is tempting to term discrimination.[20] Nevertheless the gap in Australia is smaller than that for the United States.[21] It seems to be strongly related to the more evident occupational segmentation of female workers. In 1911, 75 per cent of the total female workforce was in occupations where over 50 per cent of the workforce was female. In the mid-1980s the figure was exactly the same,[22] a fact reflected in the Segmentation Index in Table 1.2.

But other dramatic changes have occurred. The increase in female wage relativities from 61 per cent of male award wages in 1945 to 96 per cent in 1984 was a major change. This overstates the change in full earnings relativities, but they too change significantly (see Table 1.5). Yet despite this major increase, female employment has increased more than male in most years since the early 1960s. Female unemployment experience has similarly converged toward male levels and in some cases, such as youth, females fare much better.

Feminists rarely acknowledge the advances made in what was held by many to be one of the most chauvinist of societies. And there is still scope for further gains. The path chosen for that advance will be crucial. One option is the 'comparable worth' approach which seeks across-occupation parities.[23] The other is to tackle and break down occupational segmentation directly. Either way the movement toward enhanced and more-equal female work participation seems entrenched. It is to be hoped that, as the workplace battles become resolved, their consequences for family happiness will also be considered. With the two-job nuclear family more flexible work patterns become a necessity, not a convenience. Employers (collaborating with the unions) in the 1980s have been slow to meet the need, except in providing part-time work to women. (Indeed this is the source of much of the married female workforce growth). Shorter work options for males, job-sharing, work-based child-care and the like remain novelties, as does equitable sharing of home duties.[24]

There has been a fear in some quarters that migrants and women crowd other workers out of employment. This assumption has some appeal if a simple fixed employment stock is envisaged. But new workers also expand job opportunities. Statistically it has been shown that immigration actually enhances the job prospects of native workers, even during recession.[25] This finding, widely accepted by economists, has enabled traditional union fear of immigration during recession to be muted and has formed a major basis for the bipartisan return to expanded migration intake levels in the mid-1980s. Labor Prime Minister Gough Whitlam ended the long period of sustained immigration, but a resumption was put in train under the Hawke Labor government.

Statistical analysis also finds that increased married female workforce participation has not increased unemployment overall, but may have increased unemployment rates for young people while reducing them for others.[26]

There has been much concern in the mid-1980s for the position at work of youth and Aborigines. Numerically the latter is a small problem, but its seemingly intractable nature makes it disproportionately important. Aboriginal unemployment rates are exceedingly high, and Aborigines' earned incomes low. Workforce status, therefore, joins other indicators of a fundamental problem, though it is one shared to some extent by other similar countries with small indigenous populations. Whether in Finland, Canada, USA or the South American countries, indigenes are in difficult straits and solutions are hard to find even in the presence of serious policy commitment. For youth there is also a hard-core problem. The difficulty is not so much that youth unemployment is so high, though naturally levels below the prevailing 19 per cent (excluding those in school) would be welcome – and lower youth relative wages and expansion of demand would contribute to this. But this unemployment is not the problem as such, since much of the unemployment is short-term and transitional. The real problem is the small hard-core of long-term unemployed youth for whom the experience is so scarring as to affect adversely their subsequent adult working lives.[27] Some amelioration is obtained by subsidized employment, though such schemes have unjustly attracted a bad reputation, even in the limited area of job creation.[28] Long-term advance, however, requires imagination and a serious social effort to improve the provision of vocational education and on-the-job training – a theme to which this chapter will return.

Overall it remains true in the 1980s that to work in the Australian labour market it is better to be an adult native-born male; although adult male unemployment itself is at 6 per cent, there are constant or declining real wages and, amongst the employed adult males, considerable differences exist. The most striking differences relate to the experiences of the various education groups. In terms of higher wages and lower unemployment it certainly pays to have more years of education.[29] Fortunately one other major change in the post-war labour force in Australia has been the increased investment in secondary and tertiary education. Australia has always been a highly literate society, but it was only after World War II that secondary education was opened up for all and that tertiary education began to cater to more than a mere enclave. Despite these advances education participation rates beyond compulsory schooling in Australia remain low relative to those of most other advanced countries. The US experience with mass tertiary education cautions, however, against simple-minded expansion of post-secondary training. The US pay-off to educational investment, in terms of productivity growth, has been decidedly unimpressive. Particular attention to the *form* of any Australian education expansion is clearly warranted. Related debate, when led by academics, focusses all too readily on 'more of the same'.

There is, and always has been, some truth in the notion of Australia as the 'workers' paradise'. Class relations are muted, wages are high, work hours short and jobs neither too dirty nor too hard. Labour shortages have been common. But periodic unemployment crises occur. Industrial accidents and occupational health problems are not uncommon and are not restricted to manual work: they can as readily encompass repetitive strain injury for keyboard operators or stress for teachers as burns in a steel plant. Alienation in the presence of unstimulating and unfulfilling work can similarly be as great a problem in a service economy as in an industrial society. What Studs Terkel did for the United States with his interviews with workers, Roy Kreigler and Grant Stendal have done for Australia.[30] Interviews with workers show that work is as much a search for daily meaning as it is for daily bread and, if this is not forthcoming, there can be violence as much to the spirit as to the body.

Some reflection of disenchantment is found in absenteeism, industrial disputation and job turnover.[31] All are high in Australia, but Australian strikes are short-lived, even if frequent, and they are occupationally widespread, not being only the prerogative of a few industries. This is a change from Australian pre-war historical patterns. Moreover the decline in industrial disputation under the Accord of the mid-1980s is itself a further change from post-war practice and is much larger than can be explained by similar overseas trends and our own macroeconomic conditions.[32] As regards job turnover, this is high by international standards. The median duration in current jobs is amongst the lowest in the OECD. For those who believe in a narrow view of labour market flexibility this should provide comfort, but it does mean that acquisition of firm-specific skills is being inhibited. The contrast is between an Australian mean job duration of 3.3 years and a Japanese figure of 13.0 years.[33] Nevertheless, within the Australian labour market, much of the turnover comes from a highly mobile segment of the labour force, since most employed people are in jobs which will last a long time.[34]

The overall picture, then, is mixed. Even today the workers' lot in Australia is an advantaged one compared to that in most other countries. But there remain significant problems. Moreover the gap of world advantage may be diminishing. Australia's long-reputed higher levels of real wages for workers may be converging to a closer approximation with other advanced countries. We turn to these issues of real wages, standard of living and income distribution in a later section. But first the interesting question arises of what use is made of the time not spent working, that is, leisure.

LEISURE, PLEASURE AND THE PURSUIT OF EXCELLENCE

It is said that work hours were quite limited even for manual labourers through medieval times until the eighteenth century. Boserup found that medieval peasants usually worked only from sunrise to noon, and then only in the more favourable seasons, and Thirsk estimated that Tudor-era farm labourers devoted no more than 9–10 months of the year to work.[35] Protestantism and the Spirit of Industrial Capitalism served to change all that, so that by the end of the nineteenth century the Australian skilled workers' 40–48 hour week and the unskilled workers' week of up to 70 hours seemed quite benign by European industrial standards. But Australian workers sought to turn their affluence into more leisure and progressively achieved shorter hours, so that 44 hours became the standard by the end of the 1930s. The next great reduction in the standard came in 1947 with widespread adoption of a 40-hour work week. This norm remained until the launching of workers' campaigns for a 35-hour week beginning in the late 1970s. By the mid-1980s the standard for full-time workers, excluding overtime, is a little under 38 hours.[36] The reduced standard hours were supplemented by paid annual leave which was instituted at one week in 1936, extended to two in 1945, to three in 1963 and to four in 1974.

At the same time the increase in part-time work opportunities means that many of those accepting such positions, notably married women, work fewer hours than the market-place norm. Part-time workforce share in Australia is amongst the highest of the advanced countries.

All of these considerations, plus increased longevity and changing labour participation habits, come together to determine total leisure hours. Average leisure hours have increased substantially this century – from increased longevity, reduced working lives and shorter working hours (See Table 1.5). But the increase has been unevenly applied. In particular, a greater benefit has accrued to males, since increased female labour force participation has partly offset the other factors supporting more leisure for women. At the same time, women have only reduced their non-market domestic work a little and men have only increased their domestic contribution a little.[37] Thus a paradox arises. In the midst of generally increased leisure there is a harried class represented by the modern female worker and homemaker. The young, the old, males and full-time homemakers all have more leisure time. But the married female career woman has been much less advantaged. The price of liberation is, therefore, high – at least short of a substantial rearrangement of household duties that has not yet occurred.

Nevertheless the leisure of all has increased. How is it used? The answer is obtainable from surveys and is in conformity with Australia's dominating suburbanism (Table 1.3). Australians take much of their leisure privately at their homes. By far the most popular activities are watching television, reading and listening to music, relaxing around the home, gardening and visiting friends and relatives. Walking is the next most popular pastime and then dining out, but thereafter home-based recreation again comes into its own via arts, crafts and hobbies at home, entertaining at home, exercising and keeping fit at home and playing outdoors with the children. It is only after this long list of activities that a mix of more external, social or cosmopolitan activities make their appearance in terms of popularity. Whereas 20 per cent or more of adult Australians engage in *most* of the home-based activities in any week, fewer than 20 per cent typically involve themselves in *any* of the main external recreations: informal sports, spectator sports, church attendance, movies, theatre, concerts and galleries, and going to parks, libraries, bushwalking or beaches. Thus an image of the healthy outdoor life must be heavily qualified. Australians are not all enthusiastic tennis players, swimmers and runners. Mundane domestic pursuits are the normal stuff of life for the contemporary Australian.

It is notable that in the detailed listing of leisure activities church attendance finds a participation ranking just under that of walking the dog. The modern church attendance rate of around 20 per cent of adults compares unfavourably with a turn-of-the-century church-going habit of over 45 per cent of Australian adults.[38] When this observation is combined with the increased diversity of religious faiths represented in modern Australia, any notion of an orthodox Christian society must be severely qualified. Secular, but tolerant, would seem a more apt designation.

The modern leisure surveys do not seem to pay explicit attention to those vices which may have risen as church attendance has declined. There are categories such as 'indoor entertainment' that are capable of broad interpretation, but little detail is provided. One

Table 1.3 *Australian leisure patterns, 1986*

Activity	Population ('000)	Participation rate (%)
At Home – Indoors		
Watching TV	11,489	94.1
Reading	8,055	66.0
Listening to music	7,660	62.7
Other (8 categories)*	2,514	20.6
At Home – Outdoors		
Gardening for pleasure	4,450	36.4
Informal sport	3,788	31.0
Playing with children	2,790	22.8
Other (2 categories)*	2,223	18.2
Away from Home – Informal		
Visiting friends and relatives	7,846	64.2
Walking for pleasure	3,765	30.8
Dining/eating out	3,673	30.1
Other (14 categories)*	864	7.1
Away from Home – Organized		
Sports participation and spectator	4,797	39.3
Arts participation and spectator	3,382	27.7
Hobbies	1,538	12.6
Other (2 categories)*	1,384	11.3
Total population (aged 14 and over)	12,213	100.0

* The population and participation rate figures given for the 'other' classification are the average for the categories included therein.

Source: Department of Sport, Recreation and Tourism, *Recreation Participation Survey* (February 1986, July 1986), Canberra, mimeo.

should not conclude from declining family size that sex has declined as a pastime. Modern permissive attitudes and the availability of birth control indicate otherwise – at least prior to the AIDS epidemic. Contemporary official inquiries into prostitution have indicated that there may be a quite impressive degree of participation in commercial activity in this arena, supplementing strongly the unrecorded domestic activity.[39]

Better recorded are the quite substantial Australian outlays on alcohol, tobacco and gambling. Butlin has shown that Australian claims to pre-eminence in the consumption of alcohol may be exaggerated.[40] But in gambling, leadership does seem true. For instance the per capita gross outlay in 1986 can be estimated at around $500 per adult.[41] International comparisons of gambling expenditure itself are problematic especially because of illegality. But it is clear from the formal institutionalized facilities available for gambling that Australia is a world leader. The array of (often state-supported) casinos, poker machine clubs, totalizators and lotteries seems unmatched in otherwise comparable nations. Australia remains possibly the only country with a public holiday for a horse race. Perhaps this is one area where the Australian legend represents a widespread reality for the Australian people.

Geoffrey Bolton has written of how Sidney and Beatrice Webb were less than impressed when they visited Australia in 1898. Bolton feels that underlying their negative view of Australians was a:

note of resentment that these descendants of British and Irish working-class migrants should be prospering so unabashedly and enjoying themselves so greatly. The Australians were those fortunate members of the lower orders who had broken loose from British hierarchy and were exercising their own choices about their style of life. It would be difficult for members of Britain's ruling classes and still more for Britain's intellectuals to accept the legitimacy of those choices.[42]

D.H. Lawrence unerringly expressed a similar concern a quarter century later when in *Kangaroo* he wrote of Australia as 'the country where men might live in a sort of harmless Eden', a land where nobody seemed to bother and the 'whole thing went by itself, loose and easy'. But what was there underpinning the freedom, the independence, the lack of affectation? 'Nothing. No inner life, no high command, no interest in anything finally'.[43]

No doubt a similar disdain for suburban preoccupations exists among much of the Australian intelligentsia and associated people of fashion. A different view can be expressed, however. For instance it is arguable that privacy, modesty and indifference provide sparse soil for the delusions of grandeur and the professions of higher purpose that are so often the vehicle of injustice – and for that they are praiseworthy and excellent. For example, while Australians may extol their soldiers, they do not as commonly praise their wars or the causes they ostensibly served.

This interpretation links in well with one view of Australian attitudes to heroes and to excellence. It might seem that a suburban society would eschew its heroes and deprecate its excellence. And it is true that Australia has a tradition of 'cutting down its tall poppies'. But this is a gross over-simplification. There is in the bushman and battlefield legends a worship of heroes, but the heroes are common men and women who display in abundance qualities of bravery, endurance and stoicism. There is also a celebration of great figures in sports, arts and medicine. Despite a past 'cultural cringe' qualification to such celebration, whereby only international recognition conveys legitimacy, it remains true that Australians have taken great pride in their outstanding cricketers and swimmers, painters and novelists, medical scientists and the like. What is distinctive about this is that the same recognition has traditionally been less readily conferred on the senior figures in political and business life. There is a suspicion that political and business success is a matter of luck, machination or exploitation. It is only in the areas of physical or creative excellence that individual achievement can be clearly ascribed to those rare and admirable talents that owe little or nothing to family, fortune or friends, or to the fate of others.

A related consideration is that the suburban lifestyle is actually proving more compatible of late with a richer existence. In particular, there is evident in the last decade or more, a quite spectacular rise in involvement in cultural activities. The interest in television, cinema, reading and arts and craft hobbies has already been noted. Its true cultural content is difficult to define, but the predominance of mass-circulation newspapers, commercial television soap operas and radio pop-music might indicate that the intellectual content is often unstructured and undemanding. At the same time Australian per capita consumption of both fiction and non-fiction books is among the world's highest, and nine out of ten adult Australians do tune to the non-commercial Australian Broadcasting Corporation programmes within any given week. Special telecasts of opera are amongst the highest-rating single programmes screened on television. Moreover in live attendance figures the arts are booming. In 1986 there were over six million attendances at ninety-nine public art galleries and over three million attendances at performances of subsidized professional theatre companies. Arts spectator involvement is about roughly equal to that for professional sports. Moreover, far from being the exclusive preserve of the well-to-do, a lively interest in consuming the arts is as evident across the spectrum of the population as it is for sports. In both cases the more affluent and educated attend more, but in both cases most Australians attend sometime during the year. When media enjoyment of the arts and direct participation in the arts via hobbies and classes is added to attendance, a more complex characterization must emerge. The popular image of the average Australian as a philistine 'ocker' is increasingly inaccurate.[44]

Of course there are people in Australia – just as in other countries – who regard the arts as effete, boring or a waste of time. There is even hostility to the arts, particularly in a monopoly mass media which in its protected entrenched manner has only limited ability or interest to investigate Australian preferences. Equally, television ratings measurement is primitive, and the thought of 'narrow-casting' rather than 'broadcasting' has been an aberration among television executives.

But amongst Australians themselves the indifference or hostility to the arts seems present in only a small minority; the majority are favourably disposed in attitudes and interests to the development of Australian cultural life.[45] Indeed the last decade has seen a major revision in the local acceptability of Australia's own culture so that an Australian film, broadcast, song or book, is an attraction not a deterrent.[46] Even 'cultural cringe' is being conquered. Further, limited as external involvement in sport or arts or the outdoors have been shown to be when compared to domestic activities, they still loom large compared to overseas countries. Australian sporting involvement has long been recognized as such. For instance professional football attendances are a strikingly high proportion of the population.[47] It is less well recognized that the same applies to arts attendance, at least vis-a-vis Britain and North America, if not continental Europe.[48] Perhaps Australians talk about this less, and a certain Australian inarticulateness is a much-asserted characteristic that does seem to have some foundation. Whatever the truth of this explanation, it does seem that the Australian character is more that of Modest Suburban Renaissance than Outback Ocker.

LIVING STANDARDS AND INEQUALITY

Australians have long enjoyed affluence and have taken pride in seeing themselves as members of an egalitarian society. There are, however, important qualifications to these propositions.

It is true that Australia has long been a relatively affluent society. During a significant part of the nineteenth century Australia had perhaps the highest standard of living of any country in the world. This prosperity was based on intelligent exploitation by a small population of the country's highly productive natural endowment. Productivity and hence real wages and real incomes grew at a steady rate for much of the century. From the Depression of the 1890s to World War II, however, there was hardly an increase in real per capita GDP (see Table 1.5). Of course per capita GDP is a flawed measure of standard of living, and there were other important improvements.[49] Leisure hours increased, the range and quality of products improved and health and life expectancy were enhanced. But the basic stagnation of average real income remains, and distinguishes Australia's experience from that of the preceding period and from the experience of many other advanced countries. A substantial increase in real wages and incomes re-occurred in Australia's second 'long boom' from 1947 to 1974. But, despite impressive aggregate growth rates, average productivity growth was behind world standards for developed countries and was falling. Accordingly other countries increasingly approached Australian real wages and real incomes and, in some cases, began to exceed Australian affluence.[50]

For a long period this was not recognized. However alarm began to spread after the end of the long boom and warning sounds became increasingly common. The distinguished economist Helen Hughes warned in her 1985 Boyer Lectures that: 'if present trends continue, in thirty years' time Australia's national income is likely to be only a third that of the ASEAN nations.'[51] Her warning was echoed by others, and the prospect of Australia becoming the 'poor white trash' of Asia began to gain currency in some policy circles.

To some extent this depiction of loss of affluence is misleading. The weaknesses in standard real income measures are not only those of the exclusion of non-priced commodities (leisure, environment, household production, product quality, etc.), though adjustment for these factors via the concept of 'net economic welfare' may reduce the trend growth picture for the post-war period.[52] Equally important are the national accounting convention whereby services are measured at cost and the making of international comparisons by exchange rate conversions. Both of these conventions can mislead considerably. Allowance for them places Australia higher on international per capita income comparisons.[53] But it still shows some other advanced countries overtaking Australia. Of course a high starting point gives others the opportunity to catch up by adoption of unexploited existing technology, but his does not explain cross-over. Australian per capita growth performance may not have been dismal, but it has been mediocre. Pride in Australia's high and rising levels of material prosperity must be muted to this extent.

What of Australia's even greater pride in its egalitarian tradition? The widespread distribution of land and home ownership, the early social experimentation that laid the foundations for the antipodean welfare state and the extensive apparatus of worker protection via arbitration, tariffs and unions create a history that sees Australia as different from other countries in its unyielding commitment to egalitarianism. And to the casual observer this seems easily confirmed. In speech, dress and manner, Australians are not nearly as easily distinguishable from each other as in other countries. Certainly there is an egalitarian style. Lord Bertrand Russell left our shores with more hope for mankind than when he arrived: oral tradition has it that among his formative experiences in Australia in arriving at that conclusion was that of asking for his suitcase to be carried up to his hotel room. The clerk responded: 'What's wrong with you mate? You look healthy enough to me'. Modern travellers to Australia today soon learn to sit in the front of the taxi next to the driver.

But what is the material substance behind the style? There is actually rather limited knowledge here, as data on distribution are not plentiful. It is often claimed that the Australian earnings distribution is more compressed (i.e., more egalitarian) than elsewhere. Historically there may be some strength to this view, but for recent times the evidence is quite ambiguous. In a range of studies that compare inter-industry and inter-occupational pay differences and inter-personal dispersion of earnings, the dominating impression is that of overall similarity across the Anglo-American countries. Where differences do emerge they do show Australia as more egalitarian, but the effect is slight.[54] Both the presence of arbitration and the extent of skilled immigration could account for some greater compression of Australian relativities, but the need to resort to such explanations is evidently small.

Of course it is important to go beyond earnings to income and wealth. High earners have more opportunity to augment their income from capital income, but low earners may have more access to social transfers. The net outcome in moving from earnings to income is thus not clearly predictable. But what the data show is a greater inequality in income than in earnings.[55] They also show, more predictably, a substantially greater inequality in distribution of wealth than in income (Table 1.4).

Table 1.4 *The distribution of income and wealth in Australia*

Measure (Study)	Data year	Percentage share received or held by top x per cent of individual adults		
		10%	20%	50%
Original income (Podder-Kakwani)	1966/7	25.4	40.1	74.7
Disposable income (Podder-Kakwani)	1966/7	22.0	36.5	69.5
Wealth (Gunton)	1969	67.7	83.4	99.6

Sources: The Podder-Kakwani estimates are from R.I. Maddock and N. Olekalns 1984. *The Distribution of Income and Wealth in Australia 1914–80.* Source Papers in Economic History, No.1, Australian National University, May; Gunton estimates from J. Piggott 1984. The Distribution of Wealth in Australia – A Survey. *Economic Record,* 60(170), September.

Two key questions remain to be asked. Has inequality been increasing over time and how does the Australian distribution compare with that of other countries? All the evidence suggests no long-term trend in earnings distribution, but some decline in both income and wealth inequality in Australia over this century (Table 1.5). The increased equality seems to have come more from reducing the shares of the very rich (to the benefit of the middle class) than from raising the relative position of the very poor. Poverty thus remains a continuing problem and one exacerbated by changing household patterns, including the increased prominence of single parents and of young people and old people living apart from their families. The paradox of welfare arrangements to alleviate poverty creating more poverty and dependence, by the incentive effects established, seems to play some role.[56]

Australia has decreased the inequality of its income and wealth distribution. But the outcome is still distinctly non-egalitarian, as is seen in Table 1.4. How does this compare with others? There is limited available evidence compiled on a truly comparable basis. Nevertheless relative to many countries Australia is undoubtedly egalitarian. It does seem that the higher income and wealth groups in Britain also receive or own a greater share of their income and wealth than for Australia. But for the United States, and excepting the very rich, the distributions apparently look quite similar to those for Australia, even historically.[57]

The legend, then, has partial support, but to many it might be surprising that materially Australia is not too divergent from the US pattern. Indeed, if the mid-1980s' Australia media discussion of the very rich, such as the *Business Review Weekly* lists of wealthiest individuals, is any guide (and there is an increasing concentration of ownership in key industries to support it), then even in this area Australia may be approaching US patterns.

Table 1.5 *Australian income and leisure, 1911–81*

Census year	Average weekly wage manufacturing		Gross Domestic Product		Expected life-time hours					
			Per capita	Per employed worker	Market work		Domestic work		Leisure	
	Males ($1967)	Females ($1967)	($1967)	($1967)	Male ('000)	Female ('000)	Male ('000)	Female ('000)	Male ('000)	Female ('000)
1911	29.1	11.2	991	2,622	95	20	37	118	97	108
1921	30.5	12.9	954	2,568	97	20	40	129	109	117
1933	38.0	17.0	845	2,658	98	22	46	137	122	123
1947	35.9	19.6	1,171	2,845	92	24	47	146	137	130
1954	43.9	26.3	1,373	3,422	88	24	48	150	145	134
1961	50.7	28.5	1,594	3,988	86	25	50	153	148	137
1971	70.8	38.8	2,131	5,296	81	33	49	143	155	141
1981	85.2	57.6	2,634	6,390	74	36	54	143	171	155

Sources: G. Withers, T. Endres and L. Perry 1985. *Australian Historical Statistics: Labour Statistics*, Source Papers in Economic History, No.7, Australian National University, December; N.G. Butlin 1986. *Australian Wealth and Progress Since 1788: A Statistical Picture*, Australian National University, manuscript; M. Carter and R. Maddock 1987. Leisure and Australian Wellbeing 1911–1981. *Australian Economic History Review* XXVII(I), March.

Overall, at present, it seems that in Australia the top 1 per cent of adult individuals hold around 25 per cent of private wealth and the top 5 per cent hold 50 per cent of the wealth. This is subject to cyclical variation, such as stock market boom and bust. But the picture is clearly not one that squares at all well with the egalitarian legend. Perhaps the reality is that Australia is more like the United States than is usually admitted. Americans favour equality of opportunity and Australians favour equality of outcome. But, objectively, the resultant distribution of income and wealth are not so disparate. Indeed, in one further dimension of inequality, viz. social mobility, there is evidence of considerable congruence of behaviour. The starker contrast may be with Britain and some European societies.

FUTURE WELL-BEING

Australia has long been an affluent and easy-going country. It has an enviable record of social peace and has provided a rarely paralleled degree of domestic freedom and comfort for its residents. These achievements have been made in the world's first post-industrial and most suburban society. Yet many Australians cling to an older view of their country. Modern suburban Australia with its changing role for women, its embrace of cultural leisure pursuits and its pluralistic immigration seems notably discordant with the Outback legend. The truly distinctive Australia of the late 80s is the Australia of the suburban multicultural society. Even the pleasing informality of lifestyle and classless manner, which does seem more at one with the legend, finds only qualified objective expression in income and wealth distribution. Australia is not dramatically distinguished from the United States, for instance, in matters of distribution. Nor does Australian affluence even serve to distinguish the country as much as it did. There has been a substantial convergence of living standards amongst the advanced and industrializing nations, and Australia has actually fallen behind a little.

If the process of relegation is of concern and is not to continue, what must be done? Short of good luck, the answer is that attitudes must change. The past ability to live well on the natural resources of the country induced far too much complacency. Fortunately there is dramatically increased recognition that there is a problem. In particular the spectacular collapse of the Australian dollar in 1986 brought home to Australians how vulnerable their economy is in the modern world.

A shift toward better use of the nation's human resources is evidently required. This means a change in how Australians work. They do not need to work longer. But they do need to work smarter. This is where Australian achievement has been most lacking. The skill and imagination now needed has not been recognized as necessary in the past and so is missing variously in each of management, unions, education and public administration. Australia's limited investment in training and in applied research and development is part of this neglect. However the ordinary Australian has begun to display a refreshing flexibility in attitude and outlook, as this chapter has argued. The changing role of women and the successful history of integration of non-British migrants are signs of this. There are also signs that appreciation of excellence is beginning to be acceptable beyond sports and into culture. Politics and business affairs are also beginning to be seen as areas where excellence is needed.

How can such flexibility be best directed to further advantage? The great public debate of the 1980s is the challenge between two visions. Both see structural economic change as the key to the way forward. The one view, best espoused by the leadership of the trade union movement, favours a cooperative approach.[58] A natural outgrowth of the unexpectedly successful Accord of the early 1980s, this approach would seek to provide the 'shop-floor' foundation for continuing cooperation. At the core of these proposals is an expanded conception of industrial democracy and a continuing strong, but better directed, role for the government.

The contrasting vision, espoused particularly by some business groups and intellectuals, is the competitive vision. The diagnosis is that too much government involvement in the economic and social affairs of Australians has produced a sluggish economy and a dependent society.[59] A major reduction of and restructuring of government outlays, taxes and regulation, and more reliance upon competitive market processes, is seen as the key to improved performance.

Both visions claim that their reforms would be to mutual advantage. Both imply substantial change. But they are quite different – the cooperative *v.* the competitive is the optimistic way of expressing the difference. Corporatism *v.* conflict is a more pessimistic interpretation. Lively evaluation of the respective merits of these approaches will continue to be the stuff of public discourse of the late 1980s. The way the debate is resolved – consensus, competition or some creative combination[60] – will provide the underpinning for the Australian way of living and working into the foreseeable future.

Notes

[1] The most influential discussion of this is R. Ward 1978. *The Australian Legend* (rev. edn), Melbourne, Oxford University Press.
[2] The distinction is nicely drawn in L. Frost, *The New Urban Frontier*, Melbourne, Cambridge University Press (in press).

AUSTRALIAN SOCIETY

3 A. Koestler 1969. The Faceless Continent. *Sunday Times Magazine*, 25 May 1969.

4 Australia, Bureau of Labour Market Research 1985. *Labour Market Efficiency in Australia*. Canberra, AGPS.

5 D.T. Rowland 1979. *Internal Migration in Australia*. Canberra, Australian Bureau of Statistics.

6 The title of this section, as well as some of its content, draws on I. McKay, R. Boyd, H. Stretton and J. Mant 1971. *Living and Partly Living*. Melbourne, Nelson. The Boyd quotation is from this book, p.36. The basic distillation of Australian urban research is M. Neutze 1977. *Urban Development in Australia*. Sydney, Allen and Unwin.

7 It has been said that personal security has been reducing in Australia with rising crime. This may be true in relation to the security of personal property, since some rise in the rate of petty property crime is evident. But violent crime rates have not increased. Such conclusions are subject to the vagaries inherent in recorded crime data but are supported by S. Mukherjee, E. Jacobsen and J. Walker 1981. *Source Book of Australian Criminal and Social Statistics 1900-1980*. Canberra, Institute of Criminology.

8 Australia, Department of Immigration and Ethnic Affairs 1986. *Australia's Population Trends and Prospects, 1986*. Canberra, AGPS.

9 For an evocative overview the reader is referred to J. Wright, Landscape and Dreaming. In S.R. Graubard (ed.) 1985. *Australia: The Daedalus Symposium*. North Ryde, NSW, Angus & Robertson. Also see *Report of the National Estate*. Canberra, AGPS, 1974.

10 Queensland, National Parks and Wildlife Service 1983. *Eighth Annual Report, 1982-3*. Brisbane, Government Printer, p.28.

11 N. Peterson and M. Langton (eds.) 1983. *Aborigines, Land and Land Rights*. Canberra, Australian Institute of Aboriginal Studies; E.K. Fisk 1985. *The Aboriginal Economy in Town and Country*. Sydney, Allen and Unwin and Australian Institute of Aboriginal Studies.

12 This theme is developed at length in G. Withers, Labour. In R. Maddock and I. McLean (eds.) 1987. *The Australian Economy in the Long-Run*. Melbourne, Cambridge University Press.

13 In the twentieth century, agriculture has not exceeded 26% of employment and manufacturing has not exceeded 30%. Since federation over half of employment has always been outside these two sectors (Table 1.2).

14 D. Aitkin, Where Does Australia Stand? In G. Withers (ed.) 1983. *Bigger or Smaller Government?* Canberra, Academy of the Social Sciences in Australia.

15 N. Butlin, A. Barnard and J. Pincus 1982. *Government and Capitalism*. Sydney, Allen and Unwin.

16 Australia, Secretariat to the Committee to Advise on Australia's Immigration Policies 1987. *Understanding Immigration*. Canberra, AGPS.

17 K. Zagorski 1985. *Social Mobility into Post Industrial Society*. Departmental Monograph No. 5, Sociology Department, Research School of Social Sciences, Australian National University.

18 P. Miller 1982. The Economic Position of Migrants: Facts and Fallacies. *Australian Bulletin of Labour* 8(4); B. Chapman and P. Miller, An Appraisal of Immigrants' Labour Market Performance in Australia. In M.E. Poole, P.R. de Lacey and B.S. Randhawa (eds.) 1985. *Australia in Transition: Culture and Life Possibilities*. Sydney, Harcourt, Brace, Jovanovich; P. Inglis and T. Stromback 1986. Migrants' Unemployment: The Determinants of Employment Success. *Economic Record* 62(178), September.

19 B. Chiswick and P. Miller 1985. Immigrant Generation and Income in Australia. *Economic Record* 61(173), June; M. Evans and J. Kelley 1986. Immigrants' Work: Equality and Discrimination in the Australian Labour Market. *Australia and New Zealand Journal of Sociology*, 22.

20 B. Haig 1982. Sex Discrimination in the Reward for Skills and Experience in the Australian Work Force. *Economic Record* 58(160), March; B. Chapman and C. Mulvey 1986. An Analysis of the Origins of Sex Differences in Australian Earnings. *Journal of Industrial Relations*, December.

21 R. Gregory, A. Daly and V. Ho 1986. A Tale of Two Countries: Equal Pay for Women in Australia and Britain. *Discussion Paper No. 147*, Centre for Economic Policy Research, Australian National University, August.

22 D. Lewis 1983. The Measurement and Interpretation of Segregation of Women in the Workforce. *Journal of Industrial Relations*, September.

23 R. Gregory and V. Ho 1985. Equal Pay and Comparable Worth. *Discussion Paper No. 123*, Centre for Economic Policy Research, Australian National University, July.

24 This theme is also evident in the discussion of leisure (see pp.11-15). The supporting data are in Table 1.5.

25 Committee for Economic Development of Australia 1985. *The Economic Effects of Immigration in Australia*. Melbourne, Committee for Economic Development of Australia (2 vols); G. Withers and D. Pope 1985. Immigration and Unemployment. *Economic Record* 61(173), June; D. Harrison 1984. The Impact of Immigration on a Depressed Labour Market. *Economic Record* 60(168), March.

26 R. Gregory and R. Duncan 1981. Segmented Labour Market Theories and the Australian Experience of Equal Pay for Women. *Journal of Post Keynesian Economics* 3; Australia, Bureau of Labour Market Research 1983. *Youth Wages, Employment and the Labour Force*. Canberra, AGPS.

27 C. Baird, R. Gregory and F. Gruen (eds.) 1981. *Youth Employment, Education and Training*. Canberra, Academy of Social Sciences in Australia.

28 R. Smith 1984. Estimating the Impacts of Job Subsidies on the Distribution of Unemployment: Reshuffling the Queue? *Discussion Paper* No. 95, Centre for Economic Policy Research, Australian National University.

20

[29] P. Miller 1982. The Rate of Return to Education – The Evidence from the 1976 Census. *Australian Economic Review*, 3rd Quarter.

[30] R. Kreigler and G. Stendal 1984. *At Work: Australian Experiences*. Sydney, Allen and Unwin.

[31] P. Kenyon and P. Dawkins 1987. Explaining Labour Absence in Australia. *Working Paper* No. 1, Economics Programme, Murdoch University, August.

[32] M. Zaidi 1986. Do Incomes Policies Restrain Wage Inflation? Some Evidence from Australia, Canada and the United States. *Economic Record* 62(179), December; J. Beggs and B. Chapman 1987. An Empirical Analysis of Australian Strike Activity. *Economic Record* 63(180), March.

[33] OECD, *Employment Outlook*, September, 1984.

[34] R. Gregory and W. Foster 1983. A Preliminary Look at Some Labour Market Dynamics in Australia, Japan and North America. In K. Hancock, Y. Sano, B. Chapman and P. Fayle (eds.), *Japanese and Australian Labour Markets: A Comparative Study*. Australia-Japan Research Centre Monograph, Australian National University.

[35] E. Boserup 1970. *Woman's Role in Economic Development*. London; J. Thirsk 1967. *Agrarian History of England and Wales*. Vol.IV, London.

[36] M. Carter and R. Maddock 1984. Working Hours in Australia: some issues. In R. Blandy and O. Covick (eds.), *Understanding Labour Markets in Australia*. Sydney, Allen and Unwin.

[37] M. Carter and R. Maddock 1987. Leisure and Australian Wellbeing, 1911-1981. *Australian Economic History Review* XXVII(I), March.

[38] H. Mol 1985. *The Faith of Australians*. Sydney, Allen and Unwin.

[39] Victoria, Inquiry into Prostitution, *Options Paper* (2 vols.), 1984; *Final Report*, 1985. Victorian Government Printer.

[40] N. Butlin 1983. Yo, ho, ho and how many bottles of rum? *Australian Economic Review*, 23, March.

[41] B. Haig 1984. Gambling in Australia 1920/21 to 1980/81. In G. Caldwell, M. Dickerson, B.D. Haig and L. Sylvan (eds.), *Gambling in Australia*. London, Croom-Helm; with unpublished updates by the author.

[42] G. Bolton 1984. The Image of Australia in Europe. *Journal of the Royal Society of Arts*, February, p.176.

[43] D.H. Lawrence, *Kangaroo*. New York, Viking Press, 1970 edn, p.16.

[44] The data in this paragraph are drawn from Australia Council, *The Arts: Some Australian Data*, Sydney, 1984.

[45] D. Throsby and G. Withers 1984. *What Price Culture?* Australia Council Occasional paper.

[46] G. Withers 1985. Television Viewing and A.B.C. Program Policy: An Econometric Study. *Australian Journal of Management* 10(2), December.

[47] Pappas, Carter, Evans and Koop Ltd, *Victorian Football League Study*, Melbourne, 1985, mimeograph.

[48] D. Throsby and G. Withers 1979. *Economics of the Performing Arts*. Melbourne, Arnold.

[49] I. McLean and J. Pincus 1983. Did Australian Living Standards Stagnate between 1890 and 1940? *Journal of Economic History*, 43.

[50] I. McLean 1987. Economic Wellbeing: Living Standards and Inequality Since 1900. In R. Maddock and I. McLean (eds.), *op. cit.*

[51] H. Hughes 1985. *Australia in a Developing World*. Sydney, Australian Broadcasting Corporation, p.8.

[52] W. Nordhaus and J. Tobin 1972. Is Growth Obsolete? *Fiftieth Anniversary Colloquium*, V, National Bureau of Economic Research, Columbia University Press; E.F. Gillin 1974. Social Indicators and Economic Welfare. *Economic Papers*, 46; G. Snooks, Household Services and National Income in Australia, 1891-1981. Paper delivered to the Biennial Economic History Conference, Australian National University, 1983.

[53] S. Dowrick and T. Ngyen 1987. Australia's Economic Growth Performance: Measurement and International Comparison. *Discussion Paper* No. 160, Centre for Economic Policy Research, Australian National University.

[54] K. Norris, Market versus Institutional Forces. Paper given at the Australian Wage Determination Conference, University of New South Wales, November 1983. Of course comparisons across a wider spectrum of countries, including the Third World, do show Australia in a more egalitarian light; see World Bank, *World Development Report, 1984*. New York, Oxford University Press, 1984.

[55] R. Maddock, N. Olekalns, J. Ryan and M. Vickers 1984. The Distribution of Income and Wealth in Australia 1914-80: An Introduction and Bibliography. *Source Paper* No. 1, Source Papers in Economic History, Australian National University, May.

[56] The incentive effects are well canvassed in J. Freebairn, M. Porter and C. Walsh (eds.) 1987. *Spending and Taxing*. Sydney, Allen and Unwin. A counter view is given by P. Sheehan and P. Stricker 1984. Welfare Benefits and the Labour Market. In R. Blandy and O. Covick (eds.), *op. cit.* The unsatisfactory state of empirical evidence is made especially clear in Gruen's survey: F.H. Gruen 1982. The Welfare State Debate: Economic Myths of the Left and the Right. *Economic Record*, 58(162), September.

[57] Some indicative work is available, but comparative analysis has been all too neglected in this and other areas in Australia. See J. Piggott 1984. The Distribution of Wealth in Australia: A Survey. *Economic Record* 60(170), September; L. Soltow 1972. The Censuses of Wealth of Man in Australia in 1915 and in the United States in 1860 and 1870. *Australian Economic History Review* XII(2), September.

[58] The most comprehensive and important statement of this view is Australian Council of Trade Unions and Trade Development Council Mission to Western Europe, *Australia Reconstructed*. Canberra, AGPS, 1987.

[59] A representative work in this vein is W. Kasper, J. Freebairn, R. Blandy and R. O'Neill (eds.) 1980. *Australia at the Cross Roads: Our Choices to the Year 2000*. Sydney, Harcourt, Brace, Jovanovich.

[60] A useful presentation of the middle way is given by the ·Brookings Institution's review of the Australian economy: R. Caves and L. Krause (eds.) 1984. *The Australian Economy: A View from the North*. Sydney, Allen and Unwin.

2

*Australian Families: Pictures and Interpretations**

Jacqueline Goodnow, Ailsa Burns
and Graeme Russell

What are Australian families like in the late 1980s? To answer this question we need some single snapshots of contemporary life describing such details as the number of one- or two-parent families, the average age of marriage, the incidence of divorce and the extent to which people share household and child-rearing tasks. Such snapshots are useful and intriguing. Like all snapshots of family gatherings or family members, however, they make little sense unless one asks questions and is given further information. These questions have first of all to do with time-framing: Is this picture any different from earlier ones? How did the change come about? Does the comparison tell us what the future might be? The questions have also to do with the quality of the snapshot: How sharp is the focus? Is everyone present who should be, or is some member of the family mysteriously absent? Is the public surface presented for the photograph truly representative of the way family life proceeds?

The questions one would ask about family photographs are the questions we shall ask also about the statistics that detail family patterns. The statistical material is useful. Its interpretation, however, calls for time-framing, for attention to the quality of the data and for some additional material that gives us a sharper sense of the dynamics of family life. Any picture of the 1980s, in effect, has to consider not only some basic figures but also the current ways in which analysts of the family go about the task of interpreting those figures.

To cope with the double task – some basic information and some essentials of interpretation – we shall concentrate on two of the main types of material presented about families. The first type deals with family structure, the second with divisions of labour and responsibility. These two types of family picture provide the first two sections of the paper. The final section picks up two broad questions that cut across all pictures: What factors give rise to particular family patterns? And is there anything unique about Australian families?

FAMILY STRUCTURE: PATTERNS AND INTERPRETATIONS

Any description of families has to start with a description of some basic features, usually referred to as structure. The features considered (the markers of structure) take several forms. Some markers have to do with the people that families contain: the number of parents or the number of children, for example. Others have to do with an early step in the

*We are indebted to the many colleagues and students with whom we have discussed family patterns past and present. Those discussions have influenced many of the 'family' pieces written by us singly or together. Their time and their insights are warmly appreciated. Appreciated also is the financial support derived from a grant to the first author by the Australian Research Grants Committee.

family life-cycle: the number of people marrying, cohabiting or remaining single; the age of entry into marriage; the extent to which marriage is 'in' or 'out' of the social group to which the family of origin belongs. Later in the cycle attention is given to the occurrence of desertion, separation, divorce, widowhood and remarriage. In between, the markers of structure have to do with features such as conceptions or births before or after marriage; the spacing of children; the ratio of children born to those surviving; the extent to which children, married or unmarried, live with the family of origin.

Increasingly a number of markers have to do with the interweaving of life-cycles. Over the lifespan, people interweave a cycle of marriage and parenting with a cycle of being in or out of the paid workforce. Over the lifespan also, people interweave a general life-cycle with the life-cycle of parenting, with some historical periods marked by having children at home for the whole of a parent's life while others see children leaving home early, sometimes to return after a period, sometimes not.

What do such markers tell us about contemporary families? Let us take one time-frame and see how Australian family structure has changed over the last thirty to forty years. The material will provide not only a picture of the 1980s, but also an indication of how change can occur in relatively short periods of time. We start with a flashback to the period immediately after World War II. This is increasingly referred to as a 'familist' period. It is also the backdrop many people have in mind when they look at current patterns and state that the family is 'no longer stable' or is 'disintegrating'.

The period from World War II to the early 1970s certainly saw the heyday of the suburban nuclear family. Marriage was practically universal; both men and women married young (the average age of first marriage in 1974 was 20.9 for females and 23.4 for males); most couples became parents; and very few children were born out of wedlock. The standard of family living rose steadily. By 1966 almost three-quarters of families owned their own homes, increasingly stocked with domestic appliances and leisure goods aimed at reducing the chores and longueurs of family life. Most of the new homes were in the expanding suburbs of the great cities where government and commerce opened new schools, shops and supermarkets as fast as they could. Mothers of preschoolers mostly stayed home. As their children became older, however, an increasing number of mothers took jobs, usually part-time, in the expanding white-collar sector.[1] The money they earned was spent mostly on household comforts and on keeping the children in school beyond the period of compulsory attendance. The divorce rate remained low – lower than during World War II and the immediate post-war period.[2]

Many things changed in the early 1970s as the 'baby boomers', the children of post-war marriages, became adults. The marriage rate fell; average age at marriage rose; and in 1976 the birthrate dropped below zero population growth, where it has remained. It is estimated that 20 per cent of women now in their thirties will remain childless,[3] and there has been a steady decrease in births to women aged under 25 years (only 31 per cent in 1985). In addition, singlehood has become an important stage of the life-cycle. Between 1969 and 1982 the proportion of 'non-family' units (the Census term) doubled, in large part due to the increasing tendency of young people to leave home early to form their own households, either alone or with one or more friends.[4]

Men and women in the 1980s were not merely more reluctant to enter married life. They were also more ready to leave it. The divorce rate rose steadily after 1971 (from 0.64 per 1000 population in 1960 to 1.77 in 1975) with a special increase (to 4.5 per 1000) following the introduction of the Family Law Act in 1976. Some 40 per cent of marriages contracted in the 1980s are now estimated as likely to end in divorce, although there is a somewhat lower rate among the most recent marriages.[5] As many divorcees re-partner, the incidence of remarriage and the formation of *de jure* and *de facto* stepfamilies has increased. In 1981, for example, over one-third of marriages involved at least one previously married partner. Since then *de facto* partnerships have become more popular among the previously married.[6] Legally married or not, the partners have needed to learn new roles. Conolly[7] has described some of the complexities of modern stepfamily living, with its problematic areas of loyalty and authority relationships.

Such changes do not occur in a vacuum. At the same time as changes occur in marriage, changes are occurring in other areas of involvement, with the most important being those regarded as alternatives to particular family patterns. Take, for example, education and the opportunities for women to be economically independent. Both can present alternatives to marriage or can influence the age of marriage and the number of children. Education has been an area of particular change for women. School participation rates for 16-year-olds increased from 45 per cent in 1967 to over 62 per cent in 1983, and for 17-year-olds from 24 per cent to 34 per cent. Among these 17-year-olds there were, in 1967, 152 boys for every 100 girls. By 1983 the situation had reversed: 96 boys for every 100 girls. The proportion of females in the university population also increased, from 28 per cent in 1967 to 48 per cent in 1984; the picture for the Colleges of Advanced Education was similar. The proportion of women with some form of post-school qualification increased from 10 per cent in 1968 to 33 per cent in 1982.[8]

Longer years of study in itself made for a postponement of marriage, but it also brought changes in attitudes to marriage, parenthood and career plans. Sample surveys conducted in 1971 and 1982 found a striking decrease over this eleven-year period in young people's agreement with statements that defined women's lives in terms of family roles. The decrease was greatest among those with most years of education. For example the percentage of 18- to 34-year-old women who agreed with the statement 'A woman is only really fulfilled when she becomes a mother' declined from 68 per cent in 1971 to 30 per cent in 1982, at which time only 20 per cent of those who had completed secondary school were in agreement.[9] A smaller-scale study of tertiary educated women born in 1957–62[10] found them emphasizing the importance of staying single long enough to establish a career and a clear adult identity.

Involvement in the paid workforce has also undergone changes for both men and women: changes that flow on to family life. For men, better health, fewer pre-retirement deaths and freedom from war and military service have all increased their workforce contribution, although higher unemployment and the move to early retirement have reduced it. For women, changes have been more marked. By 1985 just over half (50.5 per cent) of married women with children were in the paid workforce, compared with 40.7 per cent ten years earlier. The increase has been greatest among the 25- to 44-year-olds, that is, the main child-rearers. These women are, however, much more likely than men to be in part-time and low-status jobs (see Chapter 1, this volume).

Finally, changes have occurred in the extent to which various family members have access to or control over resources. The most dramatic figures have to do with a rapidly growing group: single parents with dependent children. Between 1974 and 1985 the number of female solo parents rose from an estimated 107,900 to 279,000. In 1985, solo parents were responsible for 450,000 children, that is, 11 per cent of all Australian children.[11] A significant minority (30 per cent in 1984) were unmarried. In fact one of the most dramatic of recent statistics is the rise in ex-nuptial births, which tripled between 1956 and 1986 to 16.8 per cent of all births.[12]

As the term 'feminization of poverty' implies, most parents in one-parent households are likely to be female and poor. The great majority (an estimated 85 per cent in 1985, up from 65 per cent in 1974) are reliant on social security benefits, either the Supporting Parents' Benefit (up from 36,000 recipients in 1975 to 158,300 in 1985) or the Class A Widow Pension, which is available to some other groups as well as widows (up from 66,500 in 1975 to 78,100 in 1985). Financially many or most mother-headed families are badly off because of minimal or no maintenance payments by fathers, mothers' poor employment prospects, low government benefits, high accommodation costs and absence of child-care services. An estimated 41 per cent are 'very poor'.[13]

We have provided a thumbnail sketch of some current patterns and of patterns that immediately preceded them. That sketch does not include all the markers of structure but it covers those most commonly used. Not included is material that needs particular comment because of its relevance to current family life. This has to do with the nature of family life for *the upper age-groups in the lifespan*. The general image of 'family' is often one of parents with young children. Increasingly, however, it is being acknowledged that family patterns in later life are essential parts of any picture.

What stands out in late family life in the 1980s? A first striking feature has to do with life without children at home. Australian couples born in the 1860s could not expect *any* time together after the last child had left home: on average, one partner would be deceased by this time. Those born in the 1900s could expect (on average) three years together. With longer life and smaller families, many couples now approaching retirement can expect fifteen years of 'post-parental' life together. In effect, a whole new chapter has been added to marriage: a chapter that coincides with better finances and better health than were enjoyed in earlier periods. These older people are experiencing a situation known to few in earlier generations and the evidence is that this is, in general, a good period of family life.

It is increasingly apparent, however, that the term 'post-parental' is a misnomer for this phase. Leaving home is no longer the once-for-all action that it was when children stayed home until they married. The Australian Family Formation Study found that by 1982 fewer than one-third of sons (31 per cent) and one-half of daughters (45 per cent) first left home to marry; others departed to seek independence for work, study, travel and to escape conflict.[14] A consequence was that half the males and 40 per cent of the females returned home again at least once, and some made multiple re-entries (the 'revolving door'), sometimes with children following dissolution of a relationship. Young concludes that 'since fewer young adults are leaving home for marriage, and since the probability of returning home is greater among those who leave for reasons other than marriage, a likely trend is an increasing incidence of returning home during the transition to independence'.[15]

A second striking feature in the lives of parents with adult children is the pattern of independence. Quite contrary to the stereotype of older parents (60 years plus) as dependent on adult children, the Australian Ageing and the Family Project [16] found that they were more likely to provide various kinds of help to adult children than to receive it. In the case of financial flows across households, the older generation were twice as likely to be the givers (12 per cent) than the recipients (6 per cent), even before the final gift many Australian parents leave to their children: namely, an unencumbered home. The most favoured pattern in Australia is one of emotional ties but material independence – 'intimacy at a distance' in Kendig's words. It is generally only at a late age, and reluctantly, that now-frail parents look to their children (usually daughters) for care. The attitude is well expressed by two over-75-year-olds: 'If you get people doing things for you, you finish up in a rut . . . sort of drop your bundle. If you are doing things for yourself, well, it helps your morale'; and 'I've decided that as long as I can manage here on my own I'll stay here. If I get to the stage where I can't manage for myself, well, that's the end of me, full stop'.[17]

Interpretations: Expanding the time-frame

To make sense of a current snapshot we need to stretch the time-frame, comparing a current picture to more than the past thirty years. Taking this step, with an eye to providing an historical account of Australian families, has become relatively popular in recent times.[18] We take the step now, not because of its popularity, but because of its usefulness as an aid to interpretation. One particular value is the way it allows us to ask whether change occurs in cycles or follows a neat straight line. The neat straight line is the view taken, for instance, by people who look at recent change and argue that 'if we continue to dismantle [the] family at the accelerating pace . . . [occurring since 1965] there will not be a single family left by the year 2008'.[19] Stretching the time-frame also makes it possible to ask: Is the current picture totally new? Have we been here before? It is always tempting to view the current scene as totally new, but reality may present a different picture.

To make the figures fairly concrete, we shall ask about the extent to which women born in the years 1860 to 1951 have not married or not had children (women born in 1951 would, in the late 1980s, now be in their late thirties, and it seems likely that a sizeable proportion of those who are now neither married nor parents will continue with that pattern). The data are shown in Figure 2.1. Marriage and child-bearing rates were at an all-time high among those who were young adults in the 1950s and 1960s, when marriage became so popular that the term 'marriage revolution' was coined to describe the change. Today's figures, however, are similar to those of earlier periods. A similar pattern is found for age of marriage – which averaged around 27 for men and 24 for women until the 1940s, fell to a low of 23.8 for men and 21.4 for women in 1974, but has now climbed back to the earlier figure.

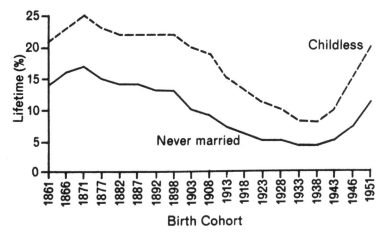

Figure 2.1 Percentages of Australian women who were never married or without children in the generations born 1861–1951. The data are adapted from P.McDonald 1984. *Can the Family Survive?* Melbourne, Institute of Family Studies.

Ex-nuptial birthrates[20] also show that 'permissive' sexual behaviour is nothing new. Ex-nuptial rates climbed to reach a high in the first decade of the twentieth century, then fell steadily to an average of 4 per cent of all live births between 1940 and 1957, after which they rose again. A sharp further rise after 1970 was paralleled by a sudden drop in births within the first seven months of marriage, suggesting that what changed at this time was not premarital sexual behaviour but people's response to premarital pregnancy (that is, they no longer felt that becoming pregnant meant having to get married).

Finally, people attracted to the notion that today's children are unique in the frequency with which they are not cared for by two parents might well review nineteenth-century Australia. That period saw families disrupted by a series of events – migration, the gold rushes, the demands of the pastoral and mining industries and the great depression of the 1890s – that left many children to be reared by single parents and some children without either parent. In the year 1870, for example, family separations were so common that 2498 children passed through the charitable institutions of New South Wales: 0.5 per cent of all persons of all ages in the colony.[21]

Is there then nothing unique about Australian family structure in the 1980s? What may be unique is not so much the structure as the factors that give rise to it. Small families, for instance, have appeared on the scene at various times in Australian history, but the contributing factors have not been constant. A special underlying factor in the 1980s, for instance, is the extent to which women have access to particular kinds of control over their fertility: a control linked to the ready availability of contraceptives (in particular, the availability of 'the pill' from 1968) and the decriminalization of abortion in most Australian states (over the period 1969 to 1971 for the two most populous states, New South Wales and Victoria, but still not extended to Queensland).

Among the factors contributing to current family structures is one that is less obvious than a factor such as control over fertility, but strikes us as especially relevant to contemporary Australia. This is the extent to which family patterns can reflect local conditions, as against needing to follow a national pattern. In the United States the family historian Tamara Hareven[22] has argued that, before modern communications, families lived by local rules and local 'family time' rather than by national rules and time. Depending on economic and social conditions, they developed their own ages and styles of workforce entry, marriage, child-bearing , cross-generational obligations, retirement and the like. One among many Australian examples is Mitchell's and Sherington's[23] portrait of the mining town of Bulli, where 'family life was governed by the state of the coal trade'. Boys were at work in the collieries by the earliest teens, and down the mines by 16 years of age. Women married young and were at risk of being widowed young because of frequent mining accidents. Such local patterns and local traditions are still present. They seem, however, decreasingly likely to occur or to survive.

Interpretations: A closer look at the picture
A closer look at the picture calls for adding three particular kinds of information to the usual reports of total figures. The first concerns 'invisible' people. The second has to do with recognizing that the figures for one social group may not apply to another. The third has to do with considering results by family member, recognizing that the meaning of a current pattern or of a change may be quite different for one family member than for another, and that 'family' statistics may provide no picture of internal dynamics or different realities. Each of these aspects of quality affects our pictures of the 1980s.

Invisible people

Social statistics commonly group people according to legally constituted marital status. Thus we have excellent figures regarding how many people have married each year, at what ages, and in which Australian state, but we have little information regarding those who contracted *de facto* marriages, and how these people differed from the legally married. Similarly we know how many births each year were ex-nuptial, but not how many occurred to stable *de facto* couples and how many to truly 'lone' mothers; and we have only limited knowledge about those couples who separate rather than divorce. A good example of the importance of the invisibles is provided by the finding in 1947 (when the Census for the first time included the category 'married but permanently separated') that for each divorced person in the population there were 2.4 in the married but permanently separated category.[24] In the 1980s sample surveys of *de facto* and ex-nuptial groups have shown that while their membership overlaps with that of the married, it is not quite the same. *De facto* couples, for example, are particularly likely to include two groups: (a), previously married people who see no advantage in formalizing the current relationship, and (b), younger people with less education and less job security than the married.[25]

Differences among social groups

National figures have a way of suggesting a homogeneous country, ignoring the presence of subgroups that differ in religion, ethnicity, class and residence in town or country. In reality any generalization needs to be tempered by looking at particular groups.

Consider some examples. One has to do with the 'large' Australian family of the turn of the century. While rural families in underdeveloped areas continued to raise large families well into the twentieth century (and to be applauded by the authorities for doing so), by 1900 urban families were finding that children had become more of an expense than an economic asset and had found the means to restrict their fertility.[26] A second example has to do with the figures for infantile mortality. The national average has certainly dropped over the last fifty years, to the point where most Australian parents can expect that the children born to them will survive. The infantile mortality figures for Aboriginal children, however, are sharply different. In 1982, for instance, the incidence of infant mortality in Western Australia and Queensland among Aborigines was three times the national average: an improvement from eight times the national average in 1971.[27] We give the figures as an indication only rather than as firm data. It is not always clear who is listed as Aboriginal, and in the other states health authorities do not maintain separate statistics.

A third example has to do with the presence of 'ethnic' groups. After a period of restriction, Australia began in 1945 to encourage immigration. The several waves from different countries have sparked many a discussion of the extent to which the country is now 'multicultural' rather than homogeneously Anglo-Celtic. They have sparked also reminders to the effect that immigration is not a new pattern to Australia. Apart from the Aborigines, the country has been a nation of immigrants since 1788.

Above all, the occurrence of relatively recent immigration has brought an awareness that any national or average picture needs to be supplemented by attention to groups varying in the country of origin. From one 'ethnic' group to another one may readily find variations in the standard markers of family structure: the average number of children, for instance, or the tendency to marry 'in' or 'out' of one's social group. As a contrast to these more orthodox markers we shall choose again a feature of families that is only recently attracting attention but that has particular relevance at a time when the general population is living to more advanced ages. This is the position of ageing parents. The national picture may be one of 'intimacy at a distance, associated with good health, reasonable income, family and social supports and the maintenance of independence'.[28] This picture may not apply at all, however, to a number of immigrants facing their later years. Whereas some 13 per cent of Australian-born women aged 75 and over live with married children, the corresponding figures for northern and eastern Europeans are three times higher. They are four times higher for southern Europeans.[29]

Differences among family members

Discussions about families are often marked by references to 'the family': the state of the family, the good of the family, the declining strength of the family or the family income. Increasingly social scientists interested in families are finding such statements inadequate and are querying pictures presented as if the interests, positions, experiences and viewpoints of all family members are identical or as if what benefits one automatically benefits all others.

In the briefest of terms, the argument starts by noting the frequency with which the state of one family member – the husband or father – has been used as a marker for the entire family. His income, occupation or education, for instance, is often used to define the status of the whole family unit. His political views are assumed to be indicative of the way that the rest of the family will vote. In effect, analysis proceeds as if husband and wife are 'one', but the 'one' is very much male. To this observation is added the point that the experiences and interests of women within families are often very different from those of men. Women, for instance, bear children. They experience economic dependency and violence within marriage more often than men do, and the emotional benefits of marriage may be less. Depression and other emotional disorders are more common in the Western world among unmarried than among married men; the reverse holds for women.[30] Women are also, as Matthews points out in a study of Australian psychiatric records, more likely than men to be regarded as 'emotionally disturbed' if they begin to neglect their family obligations.[31]

The recognition of differential interests helps to sharpen analyses of how particular family structures come into being. The incidence of marriage and divorce, for instance, has come to be seen as reflecting the extent to which each party has alternatives available and the extent to which each party has bargaining or negotiating power.[32] The recognition does more, however, than sharpen the focus for any family picture. It also underlines particular factors that give rise to the current picture and to future change. It is not just 'the family' that initiates change or that responds to legal or technological change. Particular members of families do so and either take other members along with them or leave. It is only when we begin to ask about the expectations and the resources of various family members – males, females, parents, grandparents, children – that we can make either sensible interpretations of a current scene or reasonable predictions of a future one.

DIVISIONS OF LABOUR AND RESPONSIBILITY: PATTERNS AND INTERPRETATIONS

Who is involved, and to what extent, in generating family income, making family decisions, bringing up children and doing work around the house? This type of question is at the core of the second major approach to analysing families. It attracts interest as a way of getting below the surface of family structure. Knowing about structure tells us a great deal about the stage and the characters in any family play, but little about the dynamics or the specific actions. In addition, asking about who-does-what provides a way of linking the way one looks at families with the way one looks at other parts of the general social system. 'The family' is often seen as a section of society quite different from workplaces or markets. In some ways that is true. In other respects, however, the same events occur. In the market there are transfers of goods and services from one person to another, with principles and norms governing what represents a fair exchange. Within families transfers of goods and services also occur, and an equal amount of concern arises about whether particular transfers are proper, inappropriate, rewarding or exploitive.

In recent times work arrangements within families have become a lively topic in the media, with many a family interviewed to describe the way they organize housework, child-care and money management. The interest reflects a number of social changes. One is a trend towards dual employment families with young children, resulting in concern about the equity of women being involved in 'double days' or 'second shifts' and also in the simple practical need to make changes in the way child-care and housework are organized. A second consists of changes in employment patterns for men (e.g., increased levels of unemployment) and perhaps a more questioning attitude by men towards their investment in work and career and a more positive attitude towards investment in family life.[33] A third consists of increased divorce rates. These have led to some second looks at children's contributions when only one parent is resident in the household. Combined with changes in policies and practices, an increase in divorce rates has led also to an increase in disputes between mothers and fathers about maintenance, custody and access, especially since it is no longer taken for granted that men cannot take care of children. The last factor is a general social questioning of the position of women and men in society, sparking a readiness to consider – and perhaps to adopt – new arrangements of family work as well as paid work.

What do we know about current and recent patterns? If we were to choose the briefest of phrases, it could be: somewhat egalitarian in attitudes, less so in practice. To expand on this summary statement we shall quote some figures.

Earning family income

The presence of women in the paid workforce is rightly regarded as a major sign of how family responsibility is divided between parents. It is also known to have effects on other family arrangements. Australian women who are in paid work, for instance, have more say in decisions about money management than do those who are not in the labour force.[34] Married women's labour force participation, however, continues in the majority of cases to be secondary to that of a 'primary' male breadwinner. A 1985 ABS survey, for example, showed that in two-parent families containing dependent children, 90.8 per cent of fathers were employed full-time, 1.8 per cent were employed part-time and 7.4 per cent were not employed; compared with 20.8 per cent of mothers full-time, 27.3 per cent part-time, and 51.9 per cent not employed.[35] Married women also have more periods out of the labour force, work less overtime when employed full-time and leave the workforce earlier than men. In the prime child-rearing age 35–44, married women are twenty times more likely than men to work part-time and the jobs are of lower status and more likely to be dead-end than those of the men.[36] Such figures moderate any expectation that the increased presence of women in the paid workforce will bring about radical changes in the organization of work at home. As Bryson[37] points out, it would be unwise to expect the division of household responsibilities to alter radically while the workforce status of husbands and wives remains so uneven.

Financial management

Earning the money need not coincide with the power to decide how it will be spent or with the task of managing finances (that is, handling the money and making payments). The two aspects of money management are not identical. Edwards' reports bring out the distinction.[38] In her sample of fifty families, for instance, money management (that is, handling money, paying bills) was distributed as follows: mothers (50 per cent), fathers (14 per cent), joint (14 per cent) and 'separate' (each adult managing specific aspects: 22 per cent). Control over finances (that is, influence over decisions about purchases and patterns of spending) showed a different distribution: joint (50 per cent), fathers (40 per cent), mothers (10 per cent).

Child-care and household work

Over the last forty to fifty years, questions have been asked about the relative amounts of time that mothers and fathers give to child-care and to work inside or outside the house.[39] What emerges from these studies? One indication is that attitudes may be changing, with Australians in the 1980s taking less gender-segregated views than were taken in the past. Consider, for example, two Australian studies in which parents were asked for their beliefs about 'women having a maternal instinct and being more sensitive to children' and 'whether fathers have the ability to care for children'. The first study was carried out in 1977–79,[40] the second in 1981–82.[41] The majority of parents in both studies agreed that mothers had a biological advantage over fathers and that they were more sensitive to children, but the size of the majority had changed (78 per cent of fathers in the first study and 58 per cent in the second). The same difference held for the number who believed that fathers had the ability to be competent caregivers *if* the situation demanded it (49 per cent in the first study, 73 per cent in the second). Some recent studies also suggest that there has been a significant shift toward egalitarianism in attitudes about division of household labour in the last ten years.[42]

These 'new' attitudes, however, are less evident in findings for the frequency of actual performance of household tasks.[43] The most frequent pattern is one of relatively traditional divisions in which mothers have the major responsibility for child-care and for work inside the house, while fathers have most responsibility for machinery and for work outside the house (major repairs, outdoor painting, mowing lawns). A similarly segregated view of what parents do is contained within government policies and assumptions about the family, for example, the failure to provide paid paternity leave for federal government employees and the payment of family allowances to mothers (in one area of Sydney in mid-1987 the ratio of maternal to paternal payments was 13,000:1). A picture of segregated responsibilities also appears in general media images and everyday language. Richards, for instance, notes that profoundly different beliefs about what mothers and fathers do are indicated by differences in the everyday language that people use about the two roles. Good mothers are described as spending or giving time to children, good fathers as making or finding time, with the 'implication [that] mothers *have* the time to give, but that father time has to be specially created'.[44]

Optimists may take the view that attitude change is a step towards behaviour change.

Pessimists may see the change as one in words only. The true picture will probably emerge only as we move away from describing current or past patterns in such gross terms as 'who has more responsibility'. Many a move towards shared responsibility may be occurring without there being a shift in the greater overall responsibility of women. If we wish to describe or to understand a current pattern we shall have to accumulate information about specific activities. We already know, for instance, that when fathers become more involved in the day-to-day functioning of households it is more likely to be in the areas of helping to look after children than in 'domestic' work.[45] Their involvement with children is also likely to be most frequent for looking after children at night (for example, settling them into bed), followed by bathing and dressing young children, but lowest for feeding children or changing nappies.[46] Only as we begin to build these more detailed pictures of specific activities will we really be able to tell whether or not, and in what direction, change is occurring.

Interpretations: Adding a time-frame

Divisions of labour and responsibility call for particular care in interpretation. Certainly no other area seems to involve such varied readings of the same figures. Much of the same kinds of material on divisions of labour, for instance, have been interpreted in two opposing ways: as indicating that Australian families are marked by patriarchy (power in the hands of men)[47] and by matriduxy (leadership in the hands of mothers[48]).

Material that provides a time-frame for divisions of labour is not as readily available as material on family structure. The material that is available we shall divide into information about arrangements between adults and arrangements between adults and children.

Between adults

Is there a timeless, apparently 'natural', pattern to divisions of labour, especially divisions based on gender? Or are patterns responsive to changing circumstances – changing technology, perhaps, or the changing costs and benefits of particular arrangements?

Changing technology appears at first sight as necessarily bringing major changes. In fact its impact may be limited. Both in the United States [49] and in Australia,[50] doubt has been cast on the notion that technological change will mean the 'liberation of the housewife'. Labour-saving devices have not resulted in any massive reduction in the number of household hours worked by women. Some forms of work have disappeared, but in their place has come the expectation of houses that are show places, meals that are gourmet productions and children who wear clothes that are 'whiter than white'. The overall result has been 'more work for mother' and an interesting reduction of class differences in the household work that women do.[51]

The changing costs and benefits associated with particular arrangements seem a more promising route to the interpretation of any particular pattern. To sustain a particular lifestyle in the 1980s, two-income families are often necessary. That shift is then followed by a number of changes in cooking and purchasing patterns: eating out, buying frozen or take-away food and preferring recipes that allow quicker preparation by relative novices.[52] This perspective allows for a change in the future: as the costs and benefits alter, some work may move from women to other family members and demarcation lines based on gender may become softened or blurred. A costs-and-benefits perspective may also help make sense even of times when the move has been towards drawing sharp lines between men's work and women's work. The embracing of the notion of women's work was, for instance, especially strong during the 1920s with its rise of classes in 'mothercraft',[53] largely as a reaction against a pattern, especially in rural sectors, of women doing both 'women's work' and a fair share of 'men's work'.

Between adults and children

The usual pictures of household divisions of labour have a way of concentrating on the work that adults do, omitting reference to the contributions of children. In reality Australian children still contribute to household work. In a national survey conducted at the end of the 1970s, only 4 per cent of children described themselves as having 'no special jobs'.[54] The contribution was sometimes small ('I make my bed') and sometimes sizeable: 'I wash the dishes, I clear the table, I clean my room, I sweep the house, and I feed the pigs, feed the chickens, feed the pigeons. And we've got little baby chicks: I feed them and I water the lawn' (contribution from a child in grade 4).[55] The attitude was largely positive, in the sense that 60 per cent of these primary school children described themselves as doing the work in order to help their parents. The children's reservations were not about the work but about its timing ('*every* day') and the lack of choice about the jobs they did.

How does this 1980s picture fit with what occurred earlier and might occur in the future? Adding a time-frame again helps pinpoint what has changed. It also suggests again that the current picture may represent a special time-period and may already be in the process of changing. The most dramatic changes from the past emerge not so much in the amount that children do as in the linking of their work to money. In the earliest days the shortage of labour was such that even children could command good wages.[56] In country, city and mining areas, children continued to make an economic contribution well into the twentieth century. By 1895, however, all the states had committed themselves to the provision of universal schooling, and between 1890 and 1930 legislation was brought in to regulate matters of child labour and protection along with other measures aimed at improving children's quality of life. The Factories and Shops Bill in 1896, for example, decreed that no children under the age of 13 should be employed in a factory, and speakers to the Bill condemned the practice of using children in the tobacco, leather and wool trades and as 'puggers-ups' in the brickyards, 'carrying in their arms masses of wet clay from out of a pit to the table of the maker . . . the average load is 50 lbs, and the quantity thus daily carried by each boy amounts to some 6 or 7 tons'.[57] This and subsequent legislation brought public and parliamentary debate as to what was good and bad for children and – as children were phased out of the paid workforce – led to a rise of interest in the value of some household work as a way of being introduced to the importance of work and 'the dignity of labour'.[58]

For a comment on the future, we have to draw from a US source. Zelizer sees as temporary the current definition of children as 'priceless' but 'useless', with the future bringing a return to greater participation and a greater access to paid work.[59] She speculates that American families may be moving into an era where children will return to being 'useful', partly because of increased need for help to parents (especially in families with only one parent present) and partly because the discussions of children's rights have begun to include comment on the right of children to earn money, the discrimination involved in their current state of exclusion from being able to earn and the social consequences of being shut out from the paid workforce until a relatively late age.

Interpretations: Taking a closer look at the picture

When we considered families in terms of their structure we pointed to two ways of taking a closer look in order to add meaning to any set of tables or figures: considering variations by subgroups and asking about the quality of the picture. We shall now take the same two steps for the picture presented of divisions of labour and responsibility.

Variations among social groups

To be frank, Australian research has been slow to move towards considering families outside the group most available to researchers: namely, the English-speaking groups. Callan's material on the perceived value of children is a beginning.[60] So also is the collection of essays edited by Storer, covering for several social groups both traditions in the country of origin, expressed either in custom or in law, and what is known about the impact of residence in Australia.[61] Such analyses point to major variations in the employment of women outside the home and in the extent to which women exercise control over money or contribute to family decisions. More subtly it seems possible also that variations occur in the style of a mother's and a father's involvement with children, responsibility for them and displays of affection for them.[62] In a Sydney study by Homel and Burns, for instance, Anglo and non-Anglo fathers (61 per cent of the latter were Greek or Cypriots, 20 per cent were either Italian, Maltese or Yugoslavs) were compared for their involvement in various activities related to children.[63] The overall scores for involvement did not differ significantly. Anglo fathers, however, were more involved than non-Anglos in the in-house task of 'seeing children are clean and tidy when necessary'. Non-Anglo were more involved than were Anglos in the more public tasks of 'buying books for children' and 'transporting children to sports activities or functions'. Quantitative similarities can thus be accompanied by qualitative differences which, being harder to measure, are more readily ignored.

One group tends to be near-invisible in the records of 'Australian' patterns: Aborigines. Generalizations about this group are especially problematic because of the diversity in Aboriginal social and family grouping. There is a range from small traditional groups of twenty in Arnhem Land in the Northern Territory to those who live in groups in smaller family units in western-style housing in urban areas. Also there is no uniformity of family patterns within traditional groups: some men have one wife, while others can have up to eight; some men are parents of very young children when in their thirties, others when they are 60. The only in-depth study available is by Hamilton.[64] This points to a strong male/female division of child-care responsibilities. Hamilton's study was of the Gidjingali tribe in North-Central Arnhem Land in 1968–69. A more recent and especially challenging observation has arisen from difficulties experienced by personnel in the Family Law Court when working with Aborigines from the southwest of Western Australia. Aboriginal families did not find it surprising that a father might reappear when a child (a son especially) came close to adolescence. Neither the father's right nor his obligation to exert control at this age was perceived as eroded by years of absence. The court's difficulty lay in overcoming the Anglo conviction that the father had forfeited his rights to influence and in perceiving his reappearance as justifying a change in custody or control.[65]

Are there ways of pulling together the emerging material on these various subcultures? Without some general guiding principles the end result is likely to be a set of isolated pieces, without pattern. One possible principle is offered by Caldwell.[66] It is intended to cover a large number of social groups and describes a general orientation that then gives rise to a number of more specific family arrangements. In Caldwell's view, families may be described in terms of whether income is primarily seen as flowing from children to parents (for example, whatever children earn is handed to parents and managed by them as part of family income) or from parents to children (for example, parents earn in order to provide for children who are expected to be dependent upon them). This general ethos provides a way of describing both differences among cultural groups and shifts in the course of acculturation. A second possibility is even broader, transcending cultural groups or traditions. Brennan urges caution in assuming that the differences seen among immigrant groups always reflect differences in tradition or ethos.[67] In many immigrant families, for instance, both parents are in the paid workforce. The critical factor, however, may be need rather than tradition: the more recent the immigrants, the more likely it is that both parents will be seeking employment.

The quality of the picture for divisions of labour

Perhaps because looking at family activities is a more recent approach than looking at family structure, and perhaps because people are more reticent about family dynamics, questions about the quality of the picture are especially important when one is presented with any account of divisions of labour and responsibility. The 1980s has seen a special rise of such questions. Some of these have to do with what people reveal. Each generation appears to have its silences to break, yielding the impression of sudden increases in the incidence of a particular pattern. The phenomenon is most familiar in the areas of child abuse, domestic violence, incest, infanticide or neglect of ageing parents. It applies also to figures such as the frequency of women being in paid work: possibly higher in the past than was acknowledged, both because of the wish to avoid the impression that a man 'couldn't support a wife' and because some ways of generating income (taking in lodgers, for instance) were not reported. In all instances the incidence may not have changed as much as may first appear. What has altered is the openness of discussion and the extent of reporting.

Some further questions have to do with *what is covered by 'work'*. What does 'labour' actually mean? What is left out of the statistics presented for the past and for the 1980s? How can one gain a better picture? One sharpening of focus has to do with taking note both of the labour and the responsibility. An individual may cease to carry out a particular piece of work but still retain the responsibility to see that the work is remembered and done. In effect to measure only what is actually done may not be an adequate measure of what is happening. Research on families is still struggling towards ways of measuring 'responsibility' as against hours spent or the number of times an activity is actually performed, but at least the need to do so is recognized. A further sharpening has to do with what is counted as 'work'. The usual picture is based on paid work only, treating that as the only contribution to family income. In reality women who are 'at home' and officially 'unemployed' often contribute to family income: minding children, producing food and clothing. The 'informal' or 'domestic' economy escapes the attention of census takers and economists, although economists are certainly now beginning to display a greater interest and to ask whether the models of work and exchange that they apply to the market-place can be applied to households.

The final set of recent challenges has to do with the way our *standard snapshots concentrate on the nuclear or immediate family*, excluding a number of others who contribute labour and responsibility. Who are these others? Some of them are nonresident parents, often written out in the course of describing many families as one-parent families. The nonresident parent has most often not died and still remains a parent, with contributions to child-rearing and house maintenance that are largely unknown. Relatively invisible also is the family of origin. As we have noted, its assistance certainly does not always stop when its offspring become adults or marry, and people have now begun to recognize the extent to which the family of origin makes a difference to men who do not marry[68] and to divorced parents – daughters especially.[69] Most invisible of all are the people who lie outside the kinship framework. Slowly the picture of families is expanding to cover the contributions of babysitters and caregivers in creches or daycare centres[70] and the importance of a network of friends, both as sources of information and as supports during times of stress.[71]

Now coming into recognition is also the importance of gender, neighbourhood, family background and life stage to the nature of networks.[72] As d'Abbs points out, network maintenance is primarily women's work, in Australia as elsewhere, even when the contact to be maintained is with *his* family. Richards goes beyond this to show that the networks vary with children's ages, which determine the nature of many of the crises and needs that the family experiences. Small children, for example, bring the need to keep up good relations with neighbours prepared to mind children at short notice and to pick up items of shopping. Transitions to school-age and to high school bring new demands as well as new resources and opportunities, and the network changes accordingly.

Commenting on the past failure of family studies to acknowledge the importance of networks to family functioning, Richards and Salmon note that their interviewees showed 'far more thoughtful awareness [of network issues] than sociologists in the past have done'.[73] The 1980s might, in fact, be regarded as a time when Australian analysts of families became aware of the multiple connections that family members have to others outside the immediate family and the contributions these others make to divisions of labour and responsibility.

THE FORMATION OF PATTERNS

In the previous sections we have argued that pictures of Australian families require interpretation. We have also considered two ways in which interpretation can proceed: by considering the time-frame and by asking about the quality of the picture. In this final section, we concentrate on interpretation, but in broader terms. The first step consists of outlining a view of families that can be applied in the 1980s, in earlier times and in future times. It can also be used to understand family patterns in any country. The second step narrows down again, asking: Is there anything unique about Australian families?

A general view of family patterns

At several points we have indicated that one way to make sense of a current snapshot is to consider the presence of alternatives. At any time what are the alternatives to entering or leaving marriage, to becoming a parent shortly after becoming sexually active or to motherhood involving being no longer in the paid workforce? We now wish to give a place of its own to the argument that the most important factors at any time consist of the perceptions of the various options and their relative costs and benefits. The factors and processes involved have been elegantly described by Lewis and Spanier in respect of divorce.[74] The evidence points to divorce as being associated with many personal and social characteristics which Lewis and Spanier were able to group into broad clusters comprising the presence of alternatives (to marriage or divorce), the knowledge of alternatives and the perceived balance of various benefits and costs not only in terms of money and housing but also in terms of face, social status, effects on children, companionship, the predictability of what one is used to, the sense that one has failed and the 'moving' costs. The same complex of factors applies to marriage, to being in the paid workforce and to drawing a sharp line between 'men's work' and 'women's work'. The attractiveness of each of these steps to men and women varies with the presence of alternatives and with the personal, social and financial costs and benefits. As a result they cannot always be viewed in any single-minded fashion. Marriage, for instance, is neither intrinsically a step upward nor a trap into an oppressed state. In some groups, and in some historical periods, becoming a supported wife may be an improvement on what is available in the paid workforce. In other cases being a supported wife – excluded from the paid workforce – may be the poorer choice, depriving women of economic independence, the respect often given to family members who visibly bring in money, the company of other women, opportunities for time-out from family life and the pleasure of exercising the skills earned before marriage.[75] In similar fashion, to women who were working an early version of 'the double day', the specialization and segregation offered by the 'basic' or family wage concept was an attractive way to reduce an impossible work load. The specialization may have come to be an albatross for women at a later age, but at the time and for a particular group of women it made sense.

Willingness to undertake parenthood is yet another relevant life choice, one of considerable concern to the many countries that have seen their birthrates steadily decline since the 1970s. It illustrates nicely the distinction between actual costs and opportunity costs (alternative rewards foregone) in decision-making. Caldwell has pointed out that as nations become more and more technological the flow of resources from parents to child grows greater, and the returns from children (other than emotional) get fewer, making parenthood an expensive option.[76] However it is not the poorest people, for whom actual costs are relatively higher, who are most likely to delay and abstain from parenthood, but rather those for whom the 'opportunity' costs (to get ahead in careers, enjoy plenty of spending money, study and travel, be independent and pursue personal interests) are greatest.

We are proposing that family life at any point cannot be considered except in terms of a larger context. Family life is altered by physical conditions (by the distance, for instance, between where one family lives and where the resources of kin, friends, workplace or social agencies are located). Family life is also certainly affected by many other aspects of the community or culture: by economic conditions that offer or deny opportunity to various family members, by legislation that provides or removes various forms of support and by the presence and power of all who feel they have a right or an obligation to thunder and persuade from pulpit, parliament, baby health centre or family magazines. All these factors affect the extent to which any family member, at any time in history, can find alternatives to any action, and will decide for one rather than another in the face of several kinds of cost and benefit.

The same view may be taken not only of families but also of the forms taken by the structures designed to support them. An excellent example is provided in a carefully detailed account by Swain of a refuge for women in Geelong.[77] Kildare opened in 1868 as a refuge for younger 'fallen women' who might be reclaimed from a life of vice by twelve months in an establishment that offered a regular regime of prayer and work, especially in the laundry that was a major source of funds. With fewer takers than expected the institution found itself taking in older women, to the point of becoming 'more like a home for the aged than a house of reform'[78] and developing with the courts a system of a year at the refuge as an alternative, for selected women, to time in gaol. In the search for clientele the refuge turned in the 1890s to the 'single pregnant girl . . . [who] readily accepted shelter however stringent the terms on which it was offered'.[79] The refuge became a lying-in home and, in keeping with a drive to reduce the country's infant mortality rate, mothers were encouraged to stay with their children for the twelve-month period. In the early 1900s even this clientele began to decline, in part because of a partial drop in the stigma of illegitimacy and in part because the baby bonus (£5, introduced in 1912) applied to women married or not. By 1924 the institution 'seldom had more than two inmates. It had lost its major source of income and a lot of public support'.[80] The shift was to a babies' home, where children could stay for long or short periods and, as people became less wary of adopting illegitimate children, be placed for adoption. By the 1950s the home had become more and more an emergency service; a place where a child could be left while a new one was born or parents looked for housing, or where widowed fathers could leave their children until they remarried. Even so, by 1959, the shortage of children 'was so acute that the committee had reluctantly to accept some day boarders, children of single mothers who wished to work during the day but care for their children at night'.[81] That move was short-term, but was returned to again in 1978 when the number of children available for adoption or for long-term stays had again declined to a crisis level. In 1978, a little over 100 years since its first establishment, the refuge that had become a babies' home became a service for Child and Family Support offering 'counselling, preschool, day care, emergency accommodation for children and families, and play groups for young children.[82]

Uniqueness of Australian families

Is there anything unique about Australian families, or are they like all others in the Western industrialized world? We will not attempt to set side by side Australian and non-Australian figures for the many markers of family structure and family divisions of labour. To do so could be tedious. What we shall do is to take a more interpretive stance, asking: What kinds of conditions are thought to give rise to differences, both for the present and the future? We have given this question to a number of people who have analysed Australian family patterns. Some have found the question to have no value. In their view, exploring uniqueness is an exercise in vanity. Australia, like many other countries, is industrialized, capitalist, patriarchal and dominated by the same economic factors that affect many other parts of the world. Others have found the question valid. Their suggestions, along with those of others who have written about the Australian scene, fall into two groups. One group emphasizes Australian structures (legal and financial). The other emphasizes Australia's geography: its size, its distance from other countries and its landscape. Both types of feature affect alternatives and perceived costs and benefits.

Comments on *Australian structures* often note the introduction of a basic wage (designed to cover a man with a dependent wife and children) as a major background to an unusually sharp differentiation of men's and women's roles in Australia. The notion of a 'family wage' that would be paid to the male breadwinner, so that his wife would be free to be at home, was espoused by the union movement and adopted by the new nation in 1907, shortly after Federation. Kingston[83] and Curthoys[84] are among the writers who see support for a wife at home as the result of a strong trade union movement. 'Australia was one of the first societies to see the non-working wife as a desirable goal and a measure of the adequacy and justice of men's wages ... Indeed, the position of the housewife in Australia was ensured and accentuated by the power and relative success of the trade union movement when organized labour was able to insist that more and more men were paid wages adequate for them to keep a wife at home'.[85] Further support was added by later policies. The age and invalid pensions were introduced in 1908, maternity benefit (the 'baby bonus') in 1912, child endowment in 1941, the widow's pension in 1942 and a supporting mother's benefit in 1912. These benefits provided a safety net for families lacking adequate male breadwinners, but along with the structure of the labour force and the taxation system, they also implemented a 'concealed but systematic set of transfers maintaining women primarily as wives and mothers'.[86] In contrast it is only in relatively recent times that women have not been required to leave the public service upon marriage (1966 was the date for the Commonwealth Public Service) and have had the support of legislation for equal opportunity (1984) or affirmative action (1986).

Comments on *Australian geography* are both more colourful and more provocative. One element proposed is the distance from countries of origin. For early immigrants an English visitor – Twopenny – observed in 1883 that they seemed to have suffered a deterioration in their general level of culture, producing a 'homespun' version of English life.[87] For later immigrants the observation is often made that families exhibit 'fossilized' forms of the patterns to be found in the country of origin, turned into stone by nostalgia and by the absence of those 'winds of change' that bring about shifts in the country one has left. Also proposed have been effects from the distance separating families within Australia, at least in rural areas. These distances encourage belief in the value of 'going it alone'. They reduce the possibility of developing social networks. They weaken community controls on the way family life proceeds – and, it has been argued, they cement patriarchal patterns. When there are few alternative openings close by for wives and children (plus a demand on many low-income farms for family labour) they are likely to work under the supervision and control of husbands and fathers.[88]

The final proposal we shall note comes from an expatriate Australian, living in the United States.[89] Returning frequently to Australia, Judith Conway has regularly been impressed – as have been other observers – by the extent to which the lives of men and women in Australia are separated from one another, both in the workplace and within families. She acknowledges the many explanations offered in terms of the early disproportion in the number of men and women, the fossilized holdovers from earlier times, the influence of Irish heritage and the lack of women with status who could act as models to both women and men. To all of these explanations, she argues, should be added the effect of the Australian landscape and Australians' identification with it:

> Historically, what one sees in the natural world and the way one responds to it provide the imagery through which we understand the forces of generation, birth, fruition, and death. For the historian of culture, it matters ... whether native and natural forces stand for growth or sterility ... If we ask what the bush has meant for Australians, it has stood for anti-romantic attitudes towards an unfruitful nature. The continent and the landscape ... have been the setting in which a man or a woman shows that they are not 'soft' Europeans, that they do not give in to nature or to corrupt authority. Their errand ... has been to learn to do without Europe and to see life without the 'illusions' of European culture ... without ... romantic agony.[90]

In such a world, 'nature and nature's forces stand for menace and power ... few romantic stereotypes have meaning'.[91] The result is that 'much Australian fiction explores the relationship to nature and the inevitability of disillusionment ... It seems no accident that Australia's recent great outpouring of achievement in film has reworked the theme of the isolated male hero, and the woman who must reject her sexuality for achievement'.[92] One may disagree with Conway's view, but it is nonetheless a provocative and well-argued reminder that features of the landscape have a powerful effect on the factors we have emphasized throughout as influencing family patterns past or present – the presence and the perception of legal, social and economic alternatives at each step in the family life-cycle.

Notes

[1] Australian Bureau of Statistics (hereafter ABS) 1984. *Social Indicators Australia: No. 4 1984*. ABS Catalogue No. 4101.0. Canberra, ABS.
[2] *ibid.*, and ABS 1984. *Australian Families 1982*. ABS Catalogue No. 4408.0. Canberra, ABS.
[3] P. McDonald 1984. *Can the Family Survive?* Melbourne, Institute of Family Studies.
[4] ABS 1984. *Social Indicators Australia: No. 4 1984*. ABS Catalogue No. 4101.0, and ABS 1984. *Australian Families 1982*. ABS Catalogue No. 4408.0. Canberra, ABS.
[5] See G. Carmichael 1986. Australian divorce rate: Is real decline at hand? In D. Burnard (ed.), *Making Marriage and Family Work*. Melbourne, Marriage Education Institute, and P. McDonald 1984. *op. cit.*
[6] G. Carmichael 1986. *op. cit.*, and S.E. Khoo 1987. A profile of cohabition in Australia. *Journal of Marriage and the Family*. 49, pp.185-92.
[7] J. Conolly 1983. *Stepfamilies*. Sydney, Corgi Books.
[8] See ABS 1984. *Social Indicators Australia: No. 4 1984* and ABS 1986. Women: Social report Victoria. ABS Catalogue No. 4112.2, Canberra, ABS.
[9] H. Gleezer 1984. Changes in marriage and sex-role attitudes among young married women: 1971-1982. *Proceedings of Institute of Family Studies Conference*. Melbourne, Institute of Family Studies, and H. Gleezer 1984. Antecedents and correlates of marriage and family attitudes in young Australian men and women. In *Social Change and Family Policies*. Melbourne, Australian Institute of Family Studies.
[10] A. Burns 1987. Attitudes to marriage among young tertiary educated women. Paper presented to the SAANZ Conference, Sydney, 14-18 July 1987.
[11] B. Cass 1986. *Income Support for Families with Children*. Social Security Review Issues, Paper No. 1. Canberra, Department of Social Security.
[12] ABS 1987. *Births Australia 1986*. ABS Catalogue No. 3301.0. Canberra, ABS.
[13] See E. Ross 1985. *Living in Poverty: Social Need in NSW*. NCOSS Issues Paper No. 3. Sydney, Council of Social Service of New South Wales, and B. Cass 1986. *op. cit.*
[14] See C.M. Young 1984. Leaving home and returning home: A demographic study of young adults in Australia. *Proceedings of the Australian Family Research Conference*. Melbourne, Institute of Family Studies, and C.M. Young 1987. *Young People Leaving Home in Australia*. Canberra, ANU Press.
[15] C.M. Young 1984. *op. cit.* p.73.
[16] H.L. Kendig (ed.) 1985. Contribution of the aged. *Proceedings of the 19th Annual Conference of the Australian Association of Gerontology*. Sydney, and H.L. Kendig (ed.) 1986. *Ageing and Families: A Social Networks Perspective*. Sydney, Allen and Unwin.
[17] A. Day 1984. 'I don't need more help – at the moment': Orientations of the frail aged toward planning for future custodial care. Institute of Family Studies. *Proceedings of the Australian Family Research Conference.* Melbourne, Institute of Family Studies, p.61.
[18] Compare A. Burns and J.J. Goodnow 1985. *Children and Families in Australia*. Sydney, Allen and Unwin; and P. Grimshaw 1983. The Australian family. In A. Burns, G. Bottomley and P. Jools (eds.) *The Family in the Modern World*. Sydney, Allen and Unwin.
[19] A. Etzioni, cited in J. Perrett 1986. The welfare trap and the death of the family. *The Weekend Australian*, 6-7 December 1986, p.23.
[20] See P. McDonald 1984. *op. cit.*
[21] M. Horsburgh 1976. Child care in N.S.W. in 1870. *Australian Social Work* 29, pp.3-24.
[22] T. Hareven 1982. *Family Time and Industrial Time*. Cambridge, Cambridge University Press.
[23] W. Mitchell and G. Sherington 1985. Families and children in 19th century Illawarra. In P. Grimshaw *et al.* (eds.). *Families in Colonial Australia*. Melbourne, Nelson.
[24] A. Burns 1980. *Breaking up: Separation and Divorce in Australia*. Melbourne, Nelson.
[25] S. Sarantakos 1984. *Living Together in Australia*. Melbourne, Longman Cheshire, and S.E. Khoo 1987. *op. cit.*
[26] P. McDonald and P. Quiggin 1985. Lifecourse transitions in Victoria in the 1880s. In P. Grimshaw *et al.* (eds.), *Families in Colonial Australia*.
[27] Department of Aboriginal Affairs 1984. *Aboriginal Social Indicators 1984*. Canberra, AGPS.
[28] H.L. Kendig (ed.), 1986. *op. cit.*
[29] *ibid.*
[30] J. Bernard 1973. *The Future of Marriage*. New York, Bantam.

[31] J. Matthews 1984. *Good and Mad Women*. Sydney, Allen and Unwin.

[32] Compare A. Burns 1986. Why do women continue to marry? In N. Grieve and A. Burns (eds.), *Australian Women: New Feminist Perspectives*. Melbourne, Oxford University Press; and C.N. Degler 1980. *At Odds: Women and the Family From the Revolution to the Present*. New York, Oxford University Press.

[33] Compare L. Bryson 1974. Men's work and women's work: Occupation and family orientation. *Search* 5, pp.295-9; J. Harper 1980. *Fathers at Home*. Melbourne, Penguin; C.F. Grbich 1987. Primary caregiver fathers — A role study: Some preliminary findings. *Aust. Journal of Sex, Marriage & Family* 8, pp.17-26; and G. Russell 1983. *The Changing Role of Fathers?* St Lucia, University of Queensland Press.

[34] See M. Edwards, 1982. Financial arrangements made by husbands and wives: Findings of a survey. *Australian & N.Z. Journal of Sociology* 18, pp.320-38.

[35] ABS 1985. Cited in C. Lever-Tracy and N. Tracy, 1987. Shorter hours – a right to choose. Paper presented to the Fabian Society Conference on Workers and Family Responsibilities, Lorne, Victoria.

[36] C. Lever-Tracy and N. Tracy 1987. *op. cit.*

[37] C. Bryson 1983. Thirty years of research on the division of labour in Australian families. *Aust. Journal of Sex, Marriage and Family* 4, pp.125-32.

[38] See M. Edwards 1982. *op. cit.*, and M. Edwards 1985. Individual equity and social policy. In J.J. Goodnow and C. Pateman (eds.), *Women, Social Science and Public Policy*. Sydney, Allen and Unwin.

[39] See D. Adler 1965. Matriduxy in the Australian family. In A.F. Davies and S. Encel (eds.), *Australian Society: A Sociological Introduction*. Vol 1. Melbourne, Longman Cheshire; Clemenger Network 1986. *Home Truths: How Australian couples are coping with change*. Melbourne, John Clemenger Pty Ltd; H. Fallding 1957. Inside the Australian family. In A.P. Elkin (ed.), *Marriage and the Family in Australia*. Sydney, Angus and Robertson; J. Harper and L. Richards 1979. *Mothers and Working Mothers*. Ringwood, Aust., Penguin Books; G. Russell, 1983. *op. cit.*; O.A. Oeser and S.B. Hammond (eds.) 1954. *Social Structure and Personality in a City*. London, Routledge & Kegan Paul; and B. Wearing 1984. *The Ideology of Motherhood*. Sydney, Allen and Unwin.

[40] G. Russell 1983. *op. cit.*

[41] G. Russell 1984. Unpublished data from a study of mother-child and father-child relationships in middle childhood. Macquarie University.

[42] Compare H. Glezer 1984. Changes in marriage and sex-role attitudes among young married women 1971-1982. *Proceedings of Institute of Family Studies Conference*. Melbourne, Institute of Family Studies.

[43] See H. Glezer 1984. *op. cit.*; J. Harper and L. Richards 1979. *op. cit.*; G. Russell 1983. *op. cit.*; G. Russell and A. Russell 1987. Mother-child and father-child relationships in middle childhood. *Child Development* 58, pp.1573-85; and B. Wearing 1984. *op. cit.*

[44] L. Richards 1987. First catch your ideology! Rethinking and researching traditional family ideology. Paper presented to the SAANZ Conference, Sydney, 14-18 July 1987, p.20.

[45] J. Harper and L. Richards 1979. *op. cit.*; G. Russell 1983. *op. cit.*

[46] G. Russell 1983. *op. cit.*

[47] For example, see L. Bryson 1984. The Australian patriarchal family. In S. Encel *et al.* (eds.), *Australian Society: Introductory Essays* (4th edn). Melbourne, Longman Cheshire.

[48] For example, see D. Adler 1965. *op. cit.*

[49] See R.S. Cowan 1983. *More Work for Mother: The Ironies of Household Technology from the Open Hearth to the Microwave*. New York, Basic Books.

[50] See K. Reiger 1985. *op. cit.*; A. Spearitt 1983. The electrification of the home in New South Wales. Unpublished thesis. University of Sydney.

[51] See R.S. Cowan 1983. *op. cit.*; K. Reiger 1985. *op. cit.*

[52] See Clemenger Network 1986. *op cit.*; J. Robinson and B. Griffiths 1986. *Australian Families: Current Situation* Paper No. 10. Canberra, Department of Social Security.

[53] See M. Lake 1985. Helpmeet, slave, housewife: Women in rural families 1870-1930. In P. Grimshaw *et al.* (eds.), *op. cit.*

[54] See J.J. Goodnow and A. Burns 1985. *Home and School*. Sydney, Allen and Unwin.

[55] *ibid.*, p.59.

[56] See K. MacNab and R. Ward 1962. The nature and nurture of the first generation of native-born Australians. *Historical Studies of Australia and New Zealand* 10, No. 39.

[57] NSW *Parliamentary Debates*, 1896, p.1578.

[58] Compare J.J. Goodnow, in press. The nature and function of children's household tasks. *Psychological Bulletin*.

[59] J. Zelizer 1985. *Pricing the Priceless Child*. New York, Basic Books.

[60] V.J. Callan 1982. Australian, Greek and Italian parents: Differentials in the value and cost of children. *Journal of Cross-Cultural Psychology* 11, pp.482-97.

[61] D. Storer (ed.) 1985. *Ethnic Family Values in Australia*. Sydney, Prentice-Hall.

[62] See G. Bottomley 1979. *After the Odyssey: A Study of Greek Australians*. St Lucia, Queensland University Press.

[63] R. Homel and A. Burns 1985. Through a child's eyes: quality of neighbourhood and quality of life. In I. Burnley

and J. Forrest (eds.), *Living in Cities: Urbanism and Society in Metropolitan Australia*. Sydney, Allen and Unwin.
64 A. Hamilton 1981. *Nature and Nurture: Aboriginal Child-Rearing in North-Central Arnhem Land*. Canberra, Institute of Aboriginal Studies.
65 See E. Ruth 1984. The south-west Aboriginal and family law. *Proceedings of First Australian Family Research Conference*. Melbourne, Institute of Family Studies.
66 J.C. Caldwell 1976. Toward a restatement of demographic transition theory. *Population and Development Review*, 2, pp.3-4.
67 D. Brennan 1983. *Towards a national child care policy*. Melbourne, Institute of Family Studies.
68 See P. Grimshaw 1987. Marriage. In C. Davidson and J. McCartney (eds.), *Australians in 1888*. Sydney, Weldon, Syme & Co.
69 See H. Golder 1985. *Divorce in 19th Century New South Wales*. Sydney, University of NSW Press.
70 See G. Russell 1987. The theory and practice of shared responsibility for parenting. Unpublished ms.
71 P. d'Abbs 1983. *Social Support Networks: A Critical Review of Models and Findings*. Melbourne, Institute of Family Studies; J.J. Goodnow, A. Burns and G.R. Russell 1986. The family context of development. In N. Feather (ed.), *Australian Psychology: Review of Research*. Sydney, Allen and Unwin; S. Mugford and H.L. Kendig 1986. Social relations: Networks and ties. In H.L. Kendig (ed.), *Ageing and Families: A Social Networks Perspective*. Sydney, Allen and Unwin.
72 P. d'Abbs 1983. *op. cit.*; L. Richards and J. Salmon 1984. Family life stage: The neglected divider. *Proceedings of the Australian Family Research Conference*, R. Homel and A. Burns 1985. *op. cit.*
73 *ibid.*, p.125.
74 R.A. Lewis and G.B. Spanier. Theorizing about the quality and stability of marriage. In W.T. Burr *et al.* (eds.), *Contemporary Theories About the Family*. Vol 1. New York, Free Press.
75 See A. Burns 1986. *op. cit.*; C.N. Degler 1980. *op. cit.*
76 J.C. Caldwell 1976. *op. cit.*
77 S. Swain 1985. *A Refuge at Kildare: The History of the Geelong Female Refuge and Bethany Babies' Home*. Geelong, Bethany Child & Family Support.
78 *ibid.*, p.34.
79 *ibid.*, p.43.
80 *ibid.*, p.69.
81 *ibid.*, p.150.
82 *ibid.*, p.170.
83 B. Kingston 1977. *The World Moves Slowly: A Documentary History of Australian Women*. Sydney, Cassell.
84 A. Curthoys 1986. The sexual division of labour: Theoretical arguments. In N. Grieve and A. Burns (eds.), *Australian Women: New Feminist Perspectives*. Oxford, Oxford University Press.
85 See B. Kingston 1977. *op. cit.*, p.140.
86 See S. Shaver 1983. Sex and money in the welfare state. In C. Baldock and B. Cass (eds.), *Women, Social Welfare and the State*. Sydney, Allen and Unwin.
87 See R. Twopenny 1973. *Town Life in Australia*. Melbourne, Penguin Books.
88 M. Lake 1985. *op. cit.*; E. McEwan 1985. Family history in Australia: Some observations on a new field. In P. Grimshaw *et al.* (eds.), *Families in Colonial Australia*.
89 J. Conway 1985. Gender in Australia. *Daedalus* 114, pp.343-68. Special issue of the Proceedings of the American Academy of Arts and Sciences, titled: Australia: Terra Incognita?
90 *ibid.*, pp.363-4.
91 *ibid.*, p.365.
92 *ibid.*, pp.365-6.

3

Social Security and Welfare

R. G. Brown

In Australia, as elsewhere in the Western world, the period during and after World War II saw a considerable increase in public intervention into the workings of the economy and society, producing what is commonly described as 'the welfare state'. The term has no precise meaning. The increased social welfare activity of the post-war years and beyond, to which the term might be thought to refer, was only a small part of wider economic and social changes, some of which continue and have little relevance to social welfare in any defined use of that term. Thus what happened in Australia in the 1940s needs to be seen in the context of a long evolution which in Britain began with the economic, social and political changes that followed the decay of feudalism and the rise of mercantilism and then of modern capitalism. In that sense the social welfare activity of the time was neither the chief cause nor the principal part of what today is loosely called 'the welfare state'.[1]

The term 'welfare state' is a misnomer. It would be hard now, and probably always was, to determine to whose particular welfare the activities of the state are most directed. It is difficult to assess accurately who gains and who loses most from the many public and publicly subsidized corporate benefits, services and subsidies that are part of modern economic, social and political arrangements, only some of which are social welfare benefits by any traditional use of that term. The idea of welfare in modern society has become confused. In one sense all activity is concerned with welfare. The Constitutions of some Australian states, for example, refer to their responsibility for 'welfare and good government'. But if the particular term 'social welfare' is to have a specific meaning – one, that is, that will tell us what activities may be called social welfare, what their particular welfare intentions are, who are their intended beneficiaries, what they will cost and who is to pay – then within the wider general notion of welfare it appears necessary to define, though probably somewhat arbitrarily, what in particular are to be called welfare services.

There is little agreement about the meaning of terms used to discuss welfare – such as social welfare, social services and social policy. In what follows an attempt has been made to maintain a distinction between welfare and social welfare and between social policy and social welfare policy. The term 'welfare' has been used to describe the general intentions of society to achieve individual and social betterment by whatever means: economic, political or social. The term 'social welfare' has been confined to welfare activity in the narrow sense of social welfare benefits, services and programmes designed to enhance the welfare of some identifiable group or collectivity, and publicly acknowledged and accepted as such, and not therefore incidental to some other purpose. In that sense many activities not described as social welfare may enhance welfare, though that is not their primary intention, and some activities described as social welfare may produce diswelfares.[2] The task of distinguishing welfare and social welfare would be made easier if there were some worthwhile measure of general welfare, but none of the present attempts, for example in welfare economics, seem likely to produce a practical measure in the foreseeable future.

The term 'social policy' has been used to describe policies designed with social development intentions, to distinguish them from primarily economic development and physical development policies. Within social policies those that have a specific social welfare intention may be distinguished as social welfare policies. Thus had the demographic projections been realized that were made before the fall in the birthrate in the 1960s, by the end of the century Australia would have had a population of some 25 million about half of whom would have been living in a continuous conurbation along the eastern littoral extending from Geelong to Newcastle. Planning done in anticipation of that growth would have depended upon the production of policies of urban and regional development and would have had physical, economic and social components. Within the many issues of social development which those policies might have addressed, the establishment of a social welfare infrastructure – of housing and community services, of child and family welfare, of health care and special education for the handicapped and so on – would have depended upon production of particular social welfare policies.[3]

In this chapter some of the issues which this raises are considered in the following ways. First, some aspects of the genesis of the so-called welfare state will be discussed with particular emphasis on why it was thought necessary in many Western societies in the 1940s to legislate for social services and to provide social welfare programmes – to establish the assumptions that were made then about what welfare could do, and to show both how these assumptions have expanded under the influence of welfare collectivism and why they may still be valid in the face of objections to them from economic individualism. An achievable path for social welfare policy in the future probably stands somewhere between those two, but inevitably it is one that involves more pragmatism and compromises than would satisfy the ideological commitments of either extreme.

Then follows an account of social welfare provision in Australia in relation to two of the many themes that might have been taken up: (a), the effect of the Australian federal system of government on the provision of social services, and the necessity this poses for an effective form of cooperative federalism if all the auspices of social welfare, governmental and non-governmental, are to collaborate in an adequate system of social provision. And (b), within that, the scope for what are traditionally seen as the social services: income security, health care, education, housing and community services, and personal welfare services, in relation to other initiatives – such as taxation benefits, employment-related services and benefits, and legislated social rights – which may have substantial social welfare effects but are not generally regarded as social services.

The final section returns to questions of the place of social welfare provision in modern society. Some major assumptions are made here which determine substantially the limits to the discussion. It is assumed that Australia will continue to have a mixed-market economy and a pluralist political system in which economic and social objectives are held in uneasy and changing balance subject to the pressures created by, in some cases powerful, interest groups. Within the uncertainties that creates it is assumed that both major political parties will move towards greater economic rationalism modified from time to time by economic and social interventions that appeal mainly to middle-class voters; and that governments at all levels and of all persuasions will seek to minimize their welfare responsibilities. This can be expected to leave identifiable sections of the population disadvantaged, in some cases seriously, because they will not be the beneficiaries of economic development and they lack the political and economic strength to modify the system in their own interests.

Under these conditions what should be the objectives of social welfare policies? To answer that question what is needed is a reconsideration of the basic principles of social welfare provision, a rethinking of the idea of welfare not so much in terms of what fundamentally it is, since that may not be possible beyond a restatement of the differing ideologies which might inform it, but in terms of what pragmatically it can be expected to achieve and how it will be achieved in the kind of economy and society within which it will have to function and over which it may have little influence. This requires a rethinking of the specific intentions of social welfare in modern society which will abstract it from the general intentions of social policy, because it is important that the particular services that social welfare can render to those who need them most should not be lost sight of in the debate about the larger goals of social policy or the struggles between dominant pressure groups to capture public and corporate benefits.

THE IDEA OF WELFARE

The antecedents of the welfare state, at least in the British Commonwealth, go back some five centuries to the public and charitable response to the decay of feudalism which saw the emergence of a property-less, wage-dependent class, free from formal servitude but not free from the vicissitudes of economic and social life – the problem, essentially, of the modern welfare society. We could easily date the beginnings of modern welfare from the work of social reformers of the eighteenth and nineteenth centuries – John Howard with prisons, Elizabeth Fry with asylums, Octavia Hill with housing, and others; or from the mid-nineteenth century factory reforms of Shaftesbury and the urban reforms of Edwin Chadwick; or from the turn of the century Poor Law reforms of the Webbs and the emergence then in many countries of the first public social security provisions. But it is convenient to take the mid-twentieth century proposals of William Beveridge in Britain as a starting point for an examination of the idea of modern welfare. Not merely do his proposals reflect some of the assumptions of the earlier endeavours; more importantly, they were an attempt – the most comprehensive to that time and perhaps since – to make explicit the assumptions on which society might base its social welfare provisions.[4]

The Beveridge proposals for post-war Britain were a logical development of ideas that had begun to emerge at the turn of the century in many countries in Europe and which were strengthened by the almost continuous experience of depression and war. From the idea of 'citizenship' – the notion that those who met their duties as citizens should be guaranteed their social rights as citizens – came the proposal that, in return for service to society in the workforce, people should be guaranteed a minimum adequate level of income security and access to an acceptable standard of social services. Beveridge wrote colourfully of destroying forever the five 'giant evils' of 'Want, Disease, Ignorance, Squalor and Idleness' through income security, health care, education, housing and full employment. And it is interesting in the present economic context to note that he saw the attack on 'idleness' through the maintenance of full employment as the most important of these, believing that if it could be achieved the other aims of post-war reconstruction would be within reach. These proposals, though far-reaching and at the time considered radical, were modest compared with the demands that were later laid upon the state. Beveridge's goal was 'a national minimum – a minimum income for subsistence; a minimum of provision for children; a minimum of health, of housing, of education', with 'room and incentive to individuals to add to it themselves according to their personal capacities and desires'. With respect to income security, for example, he proposed that the state should ensure 'that every citizen, in return for service, has income sufficient for his subsistence and that of his dependents both when he is working and when he cannot work', to provide adequate minimum provision against the common contingencies of life – child-bearing and rearing; unemployment, sickness and disability; old age and widowhood – in return for service in the labour force.[5]

The essential assumption behind these proposals was that the market alone could not be relied upon to maintain an equitable standard of distribution and therefore that it was incumbent on the state, and in the interests of the society and indeed the economy, to guarantee civic minima to all citizens – in contemporary terms, to temper justice in exchange by justice in distribution.[6] The belief was that this would secure both individual and social advance: people would do better for themselves if they were better educated, healthier, better housed and more secure, and the nation as a whole would benefit from that. The emergence of what seemed promising economic and social expertise, notably economic theories of demand-management and to a lesser extent the rise of the social survey movement in sociology and, later, applied social administration, offered the possibility, less optimistically seen today, of benign social engineering available to the state in a new role of honest broker capable of thoughtful intervention in the economy and society. The economic circumstances of the times were more sympathetic to these endeavours than they now are: there was, for the first time in the memory of many, the prospect of a continuing economic surplus some of which could be used to raise the standard of living of the poor without necessarily lowering the absolute standards of the rich. And the maintenance of that surplus depended on an industrial organization which needed, more than it now does, a large, mobile, moderately literate, moderately healthy, semi-skilled labour force which the minimum goals of the new social welfare could help to maintain.

In the aftermath of depression and war what was accepted in Britain in the 1940s, and in essentials in Australia, was the assumption that the state should guarantee an adequate minimum standard of identifiable social services under specified and limited conditions with the dual intentions of providing a minimum income below which no one was expected to fall and access to a range of nominated social services, such as health care and education, in the interests of maintaining civic minima and providing greater equality of opportunity. These intentions were later expanded philosophically, and to some extent in practice, beyond the notion of equality of opportunity to equality of outcome. Then, as contending interests grasped the fact that an expanding public sector could be directed to enhancing their status and standards, pressure mounted to expand public activity, some of it in the traditional welfare services but much of it concerned with activities that extended well beyond them. This led to counter pressures against the continuing expansion of what loosely had come to be called 'the welfare state' – pressures which were strengthened by a recession which saw an end to the economic surplus on which the expansion of public activity had depended. This has raised more forcefully questions about the intentions and achievements of public expenditure and within that of social welfare expenditure; and this in turn has raised questions about what welfare is and is doing.

In these developments, three broad philosophic trends are apparent: a pragmatic approach, which occupies the middle ground and which, in its ebb and flow, probably has been most influential on social welfare provision in Western society; and two polar positions, welfare collectivism and economic individualism, which have formed the boundary assumptions. There was, we might say with hindsight, something utopian in the middle-ground assumptions that a consensual welfare society, based on the notion of 'fair shares', would emerge in the aftermath of depression and war to provide the guiding ethos for an impartial welfare state, seeking equity as a principle of distribution, in which social legislation would bring about gradual change toward a more just social order where extremes of poverty and plenty would vanish. Much that has been done since in social welfare, largely under the influence of this central tradition, has been pragmatic and piecemeal, and has sought limited achievable gains in the short term on the assumption that these could be held and cumulatively would lead to substantial and enduring change in the long term.[7]

There was an excuse for this expediency. The immediate tasks of post-war reconstruction were considerable: gross inequalities in standards and styles of life and serious inequities in service provision revealed by the war provided a sufficient justification for it. It was enough, it seemed then, to establish (for example, through social surveys) that these conditions existed to attract some of the apparently continuing post-war economic surplus to their alleviation and, hopefully, to their ultimate eradication. This approach has been called democratic-welfare-capitalism.[8] It has been criticized by both welfare collectivists and economic individualists, though on substantially different grounds, for its lack of theoretical substance and its practical inutility.

From a position initially not much different from the middle ground, welfare collectivists later moved to a more radical stance which questioned it, through their increasing concern about two related phenomena which in their view weakened the central assumptions of democratic-welfare-capitalism. These were: a growing apprehension that policies of economic and physical development could bring about, and might even depend upon, enduring inequalities in the social order; and an increasing recognition that the influences creating division and inequality in society were too numerous, diverse and powerful for their effects to be more than partially mediated through social welfare legislation alone. By the 1960s evidence in several Western countries, from social surveys and later from official statistics, began to show that, despite the welfare state, there were much higher levels of poverty than had been expected, and particularly high levels among some identifiable groups such as single supporting parents and, in some countries, what was perhaps more unexpected, poverty amongst what came to be called 'the working poor' – families where there was an adult member normally in full employment.[9]

This led collectivists to the view that the social structural differences revealed were so deeply embedded in the economic and social order as to be unamenable to social legislation based on Beveridge principles of gradually rising civic minima and increasing equality of opportunity. They were also convinced from experience of pre-war social service legislation that services directed only to the poor would be stigmatizing and inefficient. Their initial solution was to press for a considerable expansion of social service provision at a high standard to be available to all, topped up by positively discriminating services directed to the most disadvantaged. In the expansionary economic times of the 1950s and 1960s these proposals were moderately influential, and it seemed that there would be a continuing move from selective services, which came into action when the usual institutions of society – the market, neighbourhood networks, the family – broke down, to universal services which took their place as institutions of society in their own right. Initially this institutional emphasis of the collectivists was upon the social services, but the logic of their position decreed that they should advocate an increasingly wider range of interventions into the

48

workings of the economy and society. Their assumption was that, since the influences creating and sustaining inequality were more diverse, powerful and pervasive than could be corrected by the social services acting alone, the more egalitarian social order which they sought would only be achieved if there were policy interventions going well beyond the limits of the social services and modifying substantially the workings of the mixed-market economy. In practice what this might have meant – in terms, for example, of socioeconomic planning – was never made fully explicit, partly because of the supervention in the 1970s of a world-wide economic recession which both increased the problems facing social policy-makers and reduced the surplus available to meet them, and which saw the revival of libertarian opponents of collectivism in whose view the recession, if it had not been caused by collectivist policies, was certainly exacerbated by them.[10]

Opposition to welfare collectivism from economic individualists, always apparent though somewhat muted in the expansionary post-war years, has revived with the onset of the recession of the late 80s, and their views have received more public currency within the larger debate about small government, deregulation and privatization. Their assumption that the exchange market is the most efficient allocator of not only productive but also distributive resources obviously has considerable bearing upon their perception of the role of the social services. With social welfare provision, they appear to be proceeding from two positions – one abstract and one pragmatic. Their abstract position puts them in complete opposition to welfare collectivism; their pragmatic position appears to return them to something like modified Beveridge assumptions.[11]

In its abstract form, economic individualism sees the costs of public social provision as a burden on productivity from which there are few if any gains, and many losses. The public provision of social services on a large scale has helped to create and sustain the economic problems we now face: by overloading the economy through the demand for universal welfare services; by introducing rigidities into its workings through high taxation, regulatory legislation and the growth of large-scale bureaucracies; by undermining individual and corporate initiative; and by the inefficiencies that arise through diverting resources to resolving the problems created by collective public action. Most welfare services are better provided privately so that choice in the market is maximized and market interference minimized. Public provision should be limited to services for the manifestly needy at levels which do not reduce incentives for people to return to the labour market and to seek their own betterment. Reliance on the free market will produce greater economic development, and in turn greater social development, so that much public provision will be rendered unnecessary. Society will not be more egalitarian; inequality may increase, and rightly so if individual initiative is to be maximized, but all will be better off, including the poorest and, perhaps more importantly, there will be more opportunities for betterment. The allocation of social benefits will represent more closely what people want and are prepared to work and pay for. Those really in need of public assistance will be few and readily identifiable, and appropriate strategies for assisting them will be apparent and within the means of society to afford.

Perhaps because they accept that most Western societies have gone so far along the path of public provision as to make unlikely the full implementation of their proposals, individualists appear at times to be moving toward the more pragmatic position that if benefits are to be publicly provided this should be in ways which minimize interference with and maximize choice in the market. In practice this generally means a preference for benefits rather than services, for example cash or cash-like provision such as vouchers, and for public subsidies rather than public services. Income maintenance offers perhaps the best example of a benefit acceptable under these assumptions. By the criteria of conformity to the market most people should make private provision for their income maintenance, for example for their retirement, and the state may offer limited inducements, such as modest taxation concessions, for them to do so. Such public provision as is made should be constrained by economic criteria: it should minimize market distortion; it should be flexibly manageable, for example in relation to fiscal policy; and it should not discourage return to the labour market or reduce incentive for individual betterment. Beyond such modest cash provision, if services are to be provided, they should be subsidiary to the preferred resort to what are seen as the natural institutions of market, neighbourhood and family; and they should be small-scale, devolved to localities and preferably under non-government auspices.

The polar positions of collectivism and individualism appear to move in practice toward a middle ground which places them in political and administrative arenas where economic and social issues are debatable as open questions, the arguments cannot be resolved by reference to first principles and the evidence and information available is partial and limited and the scope for interpretation of it great. In this situation there are unlikely to be any unequivocally 'right' social welfare policies, but only policies which may be more or less useful according to the intentions they are expected to serve and the criteria by which they are assessed. This is the pragmatic middle ground on which much of the social policy of Western society has rested and on which Australia's welfare programmes have developed.[12]

AUSTRALIAN SOCIAL WELFARE

No such comprehensive statement as the Beveridge Report, of what should be the aims of the Australian nation with respect to its welfare services, has been made. Australia's reputation at the turn of the century as a pioneer of social legislation rests on grounds other than innovation in social welfare – for example, on industrial legislation and legislation for adult suffrage. Though there were no Poor Laws as such in colonial Australia, Poor Law thinking often dominated early welfare provision. And much that was done later was largely derived from European practices. There is little, for example, to distinguish early charitable endeavour in the Australian states before Federation from what had been done for half a century or more in Britain. Early forays into income maintenance legislation such as age pensions by some states, and later the commonwealth around the turn of the century, were hardly distinguishable (except for rejection of the contributory 'social insurance' principle) from what was being legislated in several European countries under the influence of the International Congress of Social Insurance. These endeavours largely abated during the inter-war depression. From the outbreak of the Great War until the 1940s, when in Australia as elsewhere interest in post-war reconstruction revived it, there was little new activity in social welfare.[13]

In the years leading up to World War II there were attempts at establishing principles of income security, for example, in national schemes of contributory health and social insurance largely modelled on British experience before Beveridge. These foundered on a complicated set of diverse influences including objections by the medical profession, trade unions and friendly societies, and lack of agreement within the ruling coalition of the United Australia and Country Parties. With the onset of the war those proposals were shelved and never revived. The accession of Labor to office in 1941 saw the introduction of successive instalments of income maintenance on the non-contributory principle and an unsuccessful attempt to establish a scheme of non-contributory health benefits. The latter foundered on opposition from the medical profession and a High Court challenge from the non-Labor government of the State of Victoria.

The early years of the war saw the establishment of what might have been an Australian equivalent of the Beveridge Committee. A Joint Parliamentary Committee on Social Security, with wide terms of reference, was established in 1941 by the non-Labor coalition and continued by Labor until 1946, when it foundered on disagreement between government and opposition about its role, for example, in advocating centralism of powers. It did not produce a final report, but its interim reports covered diverse subjects including reconstruction planning, social security, health care, housing and unemployment. Its deliberations were influenced by the need to establish principles and plans for post-war reconstruction. Its influence was uncertain, but in its proposals for an immediate commitment to post-war reconstruction, and within that a positive role for the social services, it may have both captured the ethos of the times and been influential in creating public attitudes.

The initiative for implementing Labor's plans for a considerably enlarged public role in economic and social planning was taken by the new Department of Post-War Reconstruction, created in 1942 on the recommendation of the Joint Parliamentary Committee. Under the aegis of that department, the principles of Australia's post-war social welfare provision were largely determined within the context of what has been called a wage-earners' welfare state.[14] Emphasis was placed on full employment and the maintenance of wages and working conditions, with income-security provisions funded from consolidated revenue and mainly means-tested on the assumption that this would provide most vertical redistribution, an important but subsidiary element. In essentials the scope and pattern of Australian social welfare activity was determined then. Little has altered in the substance or content of Australian social welfare since – nearly half a century of piecemeal development of social services by governing parties of both political persuasions with little to distinguish them in terms of identifiable goals and principles of provision.

A central fact of Australian social welfare provision – the responsibility of the states for the direct provision of welfare services – was determined under colonial administration when some features perhaps peculiar to Australia – convict settlement and sparse development over long distances, for example – made for reliance on public administration at colony and later the state levels so that local government and private and voluntary activity were less important. At Federation the only clearly social service powers given by the states to the commonwealth were with respect to some nominated forms of income maintenance – mainly pensions. Some powers also were given which might have been construed as having social welfare content, but which it appears were not explicitly seen to be so at the time, such as with respect to marriage and divorce. There is little evidence that the architects of Federation intended the commonwealth to take a major part in social service provision. The Australian form of Federation, which gave nominated powers to the commonwealth and left unspecified powers to the states – unlike the Canadian federation, for example – made it seem likely that the states would be responsible for social welfare. And such might have been the case had not the commonwealth increasingly assumed fiscal power, first by retaining in the early years of federation some of the most flexible source of revenue – customs and excise – and later during World War II by assuming greater powers over direct taxation. The imbalance which this has created between the states and the commonwealth in legal and fiscal powers has been one of the prime forces in determining the form of Australian social welfare provision and the difficulties it has faced in arriving at coherent social welfare policies.[15]

At present levels of public social expenditure the financial supremacy of the commonwealth ensures that it will be the provider of cash social benefits and the financer directly or indirectly of most welfare services irrespective of their level of administration, whether state or local, or of their auspice, whether governmental or non-governmental. In such a system, where fiscal power resides at the centre and the peripheral administrations have the constitutional right to provide and, perhaps more importantly in the present uncertain times, to initiate and innovate, the need for cooperative working relations is considerable. But it cannot be said that Australian experience in social welfare provision since Federation has been notable for this. In the long boom of the 1950s and 1960s the tasks of intergovernmental cooperation in welfare seemed not so obviously onerous as they now do. In the present situation of a smaller economic surplus and greater problems, for example of high unemployment and an aging population, the need for cooperative federalism in welfare policy-making and its implementation is great. It is also likely, even if there were a return to higher levels of economic growth, that resources for welfare provision would not increase correspondingly, since the climate of opinion with respect to that may have changed. If that is so the pressure will be considerable on welfare sectors to devise more cost-efficient and socially effective ways of working, and an essential element of that will be the task of making the federal system work better.

Apart from a peak during the depression of the 1930s, social welfare current expenditures rose slowly between Federation and World War II – from under 2 per cent of gross domestic product in 1900–01 to a little over 5 per cent in 1940–41. With the moves for post-war reconstruction they began to rise more rapidly in the 1950s, and by 1969–70 public authority social expenditures were some 40 per cent of all public expenditures and about 12 per cent of GDP. By 1975–76, at the end of an expansionary period of Labor government, they had risen to some 50 per cent of public expenditure and to nearly 20 per cent of GDP, and they have remained at about those levels. Successive governments of both political persuasions have attempted to contain them since 1975, and the rate of increase in social expenditures has fallen, remaining roughly comparable with the rate of population growth. A small decline in social expenditure relative to GDP was reported in 1985–86, but it is not clear whether this is a trend break, though that seems to be the intention of both major political parties. The broad trends in Australian social expenditures are consistent with those generally in OECD countries where on average, from the mid-1970s, rates of growth in real benefits have kept pace with rates of growth in real domestic product per capita. Within these general trends there have been observable differences in spending and taxing priorities of governments. Recent work on decomposition of social outlays suggests that, while trends in outlays in aggregate may be roughly consistent between countries of similar economic and social development, trends in the individual components of social expenditure are less so.[16]

More careful and detailed analysis of social issues, particularly from a cross-national perspective, should make it possible to develop better policies within the considerable constraints that now rest upon the welfare sectors. While there have been advances in recent years in the social information available, particularly at commonwealth level, the resources committed to this essential task by the federal and state governments have not been adequate (compared, for example, with the level of economic data available). Improvement in the quantity and quality of information also needs to be matched by more sophistication in its use. Greater social intelligence, the careful gathering of evidence and good judgement in its use in developing social policy options, is needed.[17] At present, though there are some important centres committed to social analysis, there is no centre at any level of administration fully capable of providing semi-independent advice on policy development and its implementation. Though the technical competence is there for improving the level of social intelligence available to governments, what appears to be lacking is the public and political will to use it properly. The combination of election-induced welfare provision, the pressure of interest groups, the power of corporate bodies and the readiness of people generally to demand the benefits they want while denigrating welfare benefits for others creates an uncertain milieu within which social intelligence has to be exercised. Nevertheless the task has to be faced of making social welfare policy-making and its implementation more rational within the complex and sometimes turbulent environment of the Australian federal system.

With minor exceptions, the commonwealth government administers cash social benefits; the states provide social services in kind; local authorities have a small but possibly increasing part in the provision of personal and community welfare services; and the non-governmental and private sectors play a part which has never been adequately assessed and which, though considerable, is largely subsidiary to governmental provision. Apart from a referendum in the 1940s, which ratified power to provide cash health and social security benefits already assumed by the commonwealth, and with the exception of two unsuccessful attempts, both by Labor governments – one in the 1940s to centralize powers from the states and the other in the 1970s to devolve responsibility to regions and localities – there have been no substantial moves to change the pattern of social welfare provision. In the current climate of opinion about welfare the demand for services is an embarrassment to governments, and no government of either major political persuasion at any level of administration is likely to seek more responsibility for welfare provision at least until there is some enduring upward movement in the economy. Nevertheless, despite the apparent interest in small government, devolution and privatization, there are few signs that governments will actively divest themselves of their major welfare responsibilities.[18]

Social security

The main element in most Western countries' social welfare programmes is income maintenance, probably the single most important social service provided in economically developed societies and the one on which there appears the most common ground between the differing philosophical positions on welfare. Most appear to accept the need for at least modest income maintenance provision. Nevertheless there are substantial differences, which are not simply technical, about such matters as coverage (for example, the extent to which benefits should be provided only to the most needy), method of financing (principally the extent to which people should contribute directly while in the labour force to their own subsequent income maintenance) and level (mainly the relation of income maintenance benefits to minimum wages). Many other large issues also are raised by a consideration of the place of income security provision within social programmes generally. Examples are: the relation between benefits in cash and services in kind, including the replacement of directly provided services by cash payments or vouchers; the relation between income maintenance provisions, which are regarded as social services, and taxation benefits and employment-related fringe benefits, which are not, and which in aggregate are generally considered less likely to benefit people on low incomes; and the unit for social security – and taxation – purposes, whether the individual or the family – an issue which extends well beyond its significance for welfare.

Responsibility for income security provision rests with the commonwealth, with supplementary provision mainly for emergency relief by some states and non-governmental services. Commonwealth income maintenance outlays are financed from general revenue and are non-contributory. In most cases they are flat-rate benefits for named categories of people, and subject to tests of means which vary with the category of benefit. Social security outlays have risen steadily as a proportion of all public expenditures and of GDP since their introduction. They rose sharply in the years following World War II and are now the largest category of commonwealth social expenditure, comprising over a quarter of all commonwealth government outlays and about two-thirds of commonwealth social expenditure and accounting for about 9 per cent of GDP. The largest category of income maintenance provision over the years has been pensions, including age, disability and widows' pensions, with age pensions the largest single item of income maintenance expenditure, and likely to stay so as the proportion of people of pensionable age is expected to rise from about 16 per cent in 1986 to an estimated 24 per cent at the end of the century. More recently, with the economic recession, outlays on unemployment benefits have risen sharply from a negligible figure in the 1970s to assume second place after pensions in the order of expenditure, with no likelihood – in the medium term at least – of a large reduction in the rate of unemployment or in the proportion of unemployed of long duration. The cost of emergency relief has also risen considerably, but there are no reliable estimates of this because it is distributed through many organizations, mainly non-governmental, for whom there is no regular aggregate reporting. These trends suggest that 'demographic' factors, changes broadly speaking in the beneficiary population rather than welfare policy changes, will maintain the demand for income maintenance benefits at least at current levels for the foreseeable future.[19]

Because of the difficulty of determining the composition of the revenue sources of income maintenance outlays and the differing rules applied to different benefits – for example, the extent to which they are indexed, the liberality of the means tests and the varying supplementary benefits attached to them – it is not possible to say unequivocally in which direction income security benefits as a whole flow. The situation is further confused if other public and publicly subsidized benefits not generally described as social services, such as taxation and employment fringe benefits, are taken into account.

Until recently the major political parties have been committed to expansion of public social security provision. Thus the 1970s saw more liberal provision of many income maintenance benefits including pensions, family allowances and unemployment benefits, and beyond that proposals for expansion of public income security on universal lines, including proposals for national superannuation to provide universal retirement pensions at about 25–30 per cent of average weekly earnings and for a national scheme of compensation for disability and sickness on a no-fault basis. These and other proposals were to have been brought together in 1975 in a comprehensive review of income security with wide terms of reference by an interdepartmental committee monitored by a Cabinet committee. It may have seemed therefore that policies were moving in the direction of the guaranteed minimum income which was recommended by the National Inquiry into Poverty in 1975. But with the onset of the recession these moves were shelved. The issues now seem to be: which income security components will be most contained within the trilogy of proposals to limit the national deficit, reduce taxation and reduce public spending; and to what extent will public provision be replaced by corporate fringe benefits negotiated within the wage structure? These emerging issues raise the question of what is the public responsibility and how will it be discharged for welfare services for those who can exert little pressure on the political processes or through the wage system? The categories of people identified to the recently established Commonwealth Social Security Review as most at risk in this respect are single-parent families, low-income two-parent families with more than three children and low-skill young people.[20]

Health and education

Of the remaining services traditionally described as social services, health care and education have similarities which are not shared so much by the other services in kind, housing and personal welfare services. Health and education have more ambitious intentions: the scale of their operations is greater; they are less clearly directed to the most needy; they are more obviously controlled by strongly organized groups of professionals; and (particularly in the case of health) the influence of a burgeoning and costly technology is important. As more ambitious proposals for their development have been built in to them they have become less selective, more universal, less targeted, more costly and, probably, no longer vertically redistributive. At some stage in that development they have become less obviously social welfare services than something else – merit goods? human capital investments? Many of the philosophical and practical issues surrounding the future of social welfare in society therefore come to focus on health and education as large elements of final consumption services under mainly governmental auspices.

The health services are the most difficult by far to characterize. There has always been uncertainty about what kind and level of health care should be provided as a social service. Beveridge, for example, included 'a minimum of health' within his notion of a guaranteed national minimum, but elsewhere he proposed that 'a comprehensive national health service will ensure that for every citizen there is available whatever medical treatment he requires, in whatever form he requires it'. But it is obvious that he could not possibly have foreseen the manner in which health services would develop in modern society. In their present form they far exceed what might be the goal of a social welfare service with respect to health care – to minimize financial and other barriers to access to basic health care for low-income and other vulnerable groups. The problem of determining what that means in practice is compounded by the difficulty not merely of determining what is a reasonable basic level of care, but also of deciding how it should be provided. For example, the balances between preventive and curative care, between institutional and community care and between personal and public health are issues which divide both the health professionals and the community at large and are not likely to be resolved easily.[21]

It is not possible to describe simply how responsibility is shared between the levels of government and between governmental and non-governmental auspices for the four major components of the health services: hospital and institutional care, community medicine and public health services, personal health and paramedical services and pharmaceutical and technological services. Public sector outlays on health since the 1940s have risen for all levels of government, peaking in the mid-1970s, then declining at commonwealth level, from 4 per cent of GDP in 1975–76 to 2.9 per cent in 1984–85, and remaining relatively stable at state and local government levels, at 3 per cent of GDP. Within that period fluctuations in health expenditures by the commonwealth government are attributable mainly to transfer of funding arrangements, for example, the establishment of Medicare. They now comprise a little under a fifth of all commonwealth social expenditures and about a third of state and local government social expenditures. Despite repeatedly stated intentions to further reduce health service costs, the task has proved difficult. With the rising cost of medical technology the gap between the range of advanced treatments that are medically possible and those which are economically feasible is increasing, and with it the task of determining the basic levels of health care to be provided with public subsidy.

It is reasonable to assume that with the expansion of health provision since the 1940s the poor have benefited, though it is also said that the better-off, the better educated and the more sophisticated have benefited more, and that the major part of public outlays on health now consists of a complex of transfers between different segments of the middle classes. If that is so, it seems unlikely that we can continue to raise the standards of health of poorer people by simply expanding the present system further. The problems of health mainten-ance in society are not simply medical, even on the widest definition of that term: they also have social, economic and political facets. The task facing government in determining health service policies (and within them social welfare policies with respect to health care) is considerable. What level and kind of subsidized health care should be provided for the population at large, and beyond that what level of basic health care should be ensured for the most vulnerable, and how, appear to be questions that will remain unanswered for the foreseeable future. This is so not only because of public uncertainty about what achieving good health means in practice, but even more because of the inability of health professionals to agree on the basic premises on which good health provision should rest.

With education, as with health, it is difficult to separate the welfare component from the general social policy, the welfare service from the merit good. Public outlays on education have followed a similar trend to health outlays, peaking in the mid-1970s, then falling for the commonwealth from 4 per cent of GDP in 1975–76 to 2.2 per cent in 1984–85, and remaining relatively stable for the states at about 5.5 per cent of GDP. They comprise about a fifth of commonwealth social expenditures and a little over a half of state social expenditures. As with health services, it is generally assumed the poor have benefited from the expansion of education since the 1940s but that the non-poor have benefited more, and that much of the public outlay on education involves transfers within the middle class. And as with health services it seems unlikely, therefore, that simply expanding the present system will substantially benefit the poor. Within the services it is possible to identify elements which have a large welfare component, such as community-based pre-school services and early childhood education for Aboriginal children, and special education services for intellectually retarded children. But the current trend towards mainstreaming in education, whatever its merits on philosophical grounds, makes it difficult under the present system of statistical reporting to identify what specifically is being done for the most disadvantaged and what it is achieving.

Housing

In public reporting of social expenditure the term 'housing and community amenities' is sometimes used. Community amenities covers two distinct but related areas of activity – urban development and community development. Urban and regional development policy may have considerable impact on welfare but, in the terms in which social welfare has been described in this chapter, it is not strictly a social welfare service and is more an element of social and economic policy. It has not therefore been considered here, though an extended analysis of housing policy would need to have regard to it. Community and locality development overlaps housing provision and personal service provision and for convenience here has been considered with the personal social services. This discussion of welfare housing has therefore been limited to the provision of shelter and is concerned primarily with its provision for low-income earners as a social welfare function.[22]

Welfare housing, as much and perhaps more than any other social service, illustrates the dilemmas and difficulties of social welfare policy-making and service provision. On the one hand it is markedly affected by non-housing policies, for example, macroeconomic policies, interest rate policies and taxation. On the other hand it appears to offer opportunities for the exercise of cooperative federalism involving cooperation between public and private sectors and between components of the public sector, without the necessary growth of large-scale service bureaucracies and without undue restriction on local choice and local planning. At the same time, it poses the familiar problem of targeting public welfare services to the most needy – in this case preventing the diversion of public subsidies for low-income housing to those for whom they were not intended, for example, land-owners and landlords and middle-income home buyers.

The main instruments of low-income public housing policy in Australia have been the Commonwealth-State Housing Agreements (CSHA), wherein public subsidy has taken the form of commonwealth advances to the states at concessional rates of interest for construction of public housing, loans to home purchasers and rebating public housing rentals. These account for some two-thirds of federal housing outlays. The CSHAs have also been supplemented by programmes for a capital subsidy to first-home buyers and tax concessions on mortgage interest payments and on property rates, which in practice have been primarily of benefit to middle-income home buyers. And there have been various special programmes, the chief among them being for Aboriginal housing, housing the disabled, housing the elderly, emergency accommodation for the homeless and, more recently, special accommodation for non-family groups, the single homeless and women's shelters. Some of these programmes, although intended to be targeted to the most needy, have not always achieved that objective: for example, the Aged Persons Homes scheme, dating from the mid-1950s, is generally considered to have benefited mainly middle-income people. Currently none of these programmes is of significant proportions and it is generally assumed that, in principle, they are capable of being taken up within any general needs-priority system that may be determined within the commonwealth-state agreements, thus avoiding the stigma which sometimes attaches to social welfare provision.

In its original form, as proposed by a Labor government in 1945 (following the Fourth Report of the Joint Parliamentary Committee on Social Security on 'Housing in Australia'), public housing policy was to have been more widely embracing than was implemented in subsequent housing agreements. The original proposal by the commonwealth government for a Commonwealth Housing Commission with responsibility to maintain the quality of housing, regulate land use, protect the environment and provide for rehabilitation and development of the housing stock through state implementation of commonwealth guidelines did not evolve, mainly because of failure of the commonwealth and states to agree on the extent of commonwealth intervention beyond cost sharing and doubts about commonwealth powers under the Constitution. The Housing Agreements which were negotiated were more restricted. They were concerned primarily with the provision of shelter and, within that, most with home-ownership with an emphasis on worker-housing rather than welfare housing – a further instalment, perhaps, of the wage-earners' welfare state. As a consequence they have been less directly targeted to low-income earners than might have been expected in the light of the recommendations on housing of the Joint Parliamentary Committee.

In the forty years since World War II, when public housing programmes effectively began, some 10 per cent of dwellings constructed have been public sector dwellings and about half of these are rented currently as public housing. For many reasons the impact of public housing policies has been less than might have been expected. Housing policies have reflected, as well as their welfare objectives, other objectives which may be in conflict with them, such as the provision of worker housing (sometimes associated with policies of regional economic development) and, more recently, policies of maintaining employment in the building industry. The restraining effect of economic policies at a time of recession, and the competition by mining and industrial sectors for infrastructure funds, have also had their effects. Public housing expenditures peaked in the late 1970s at a little over 2.5 per cent of GDP and have since fallen to just over 2 per cent of GDP mainly because of a fall in commonwealth government housing expenditure. The level of expenditure may continue to fall in the light of current commonwealth-state financial arrangements, particularly if the commonwealth government continues with its stated intention of reducing and ultimately eliminating nominated fund arrangements with the states. Present indications are that most state housing authorities will move into deficit by the end of the decade. Overall the combination of fiscal policies and service policies affecting housing is considered to have favoured middle-class home buyers more than low-income home renters. For home-owners the combination of tax concessions on property rates and mortgage interest, no capital gains tax, no tax on imputed rents and no means tests on capital subsidies for first-home buyers compares favourably with means-tested rental rebates for public tenants and rent relief on a stringent means test for private tenants solely dependent on social security benefits and no tax-deductibility of rents for low-income renters. When to this is added the reduction in public housing stock through the absence of a means test on post-allocation rents for public housing or on the sale of public housing to existing tenants, the welfare impact of public housing policy is weakened even further.

The problem of developing better-targeted welfare housing policies has now become complicated by the effect on lower-middle income earners of rising construction costs, higher land prices and rising mortgage interest rates, putting home ownership, as determined by the traditional relation of mortgage repayment to income, beyond the means of people on average weekly earnings. This can be expected to produce a widening band of lower middle-income earners not eligible for subsidized rental housing and not able to borrow privately for home building, and for whom, as of course for low-income earners, a house may be the only substantial asset and asset-income they can hope to have and the one opportunity they might have to share in capital gains, to hedge against inflation, to obtain security of tenure and to keep housing costs down in times of low income. In the present climate of middle-income pressure group politics, this and the plight of the housing construction industry seem likely to further reduce the impact of housing policies on welfare housing, and to distract effort from responding to those groups in most need: the unemployed; large, low-income families; women, particularly supporting parents; the disabled; the aged with no assets or income other than the pensions; some ethnic groups; and Aborigines. Of these the highest priority groups are likely to be poor people paying market rents for private housing. Recent data from the Department of Housing and Construction, showing applications for public housing and tenancy waiting lists increasing in all states and territories, suggest that the problem is worsening.

Personal welfare services

The personal welfare services or, as they are also called, the social care services, are a varied group which it is difficult to describe in a few words. They are provided under both governmental and non-governmental auspices. Compared with other social services they are a small sector of public outlays; they are generally labour intensive, providing services rather than cash benefits; and their aims are rather more limited in practice than the other social services. They are more obviously directed to the most needy and vulnerable, and they have usually been concerned with providing limited standards of benefit or service directly to individuals and families and to people in neighbourhood groups, mainly through the intervention of an intermediary such as a social worker and generally on a discretionary basis in response to particular assessments of need. They have been directed primarily to people at risk or in need of care or protection, such as neglected or abused children, to people seriously socially disadvantaged, such as the very poor, and to people who suffer substantial disability, such as the frail aged and chronic sick. They have had three main responsibilities: to assist people in trouble who need help to solve acute crises; to sustain people in chronic need and to assist them to maintain the best level of functioning they can in the face of their personal and social disadvantages; and, to a lesser extent, to assist people through re-educative and developmental services to function better in future.[23]

Most industrially developed countries have similar complex networks of personal social services which seem to be related more to their stage of urban and industrial development than to, for example, their economic, political or social systems. The services found in most countries are those supporting people in resolving day-to-day problems, assisting them to re-establish normal functioning after personal crises, providing access to other community benefits and services, assisting handicapped people to get basic care services, arranging substitute care for people who cannot get it through normal institutions such as the family (the social care components); supporting mutual aid and other self-help neighbourhood and community activities (the community development component); and caring for and supervising people who may harm themselves and others (the social defence component). Studies of where people go for help with their personal problems show that, in the first instance at least, they use a variety of informal and formal local arrangements – family, friends, neighbourhood networks, clergy, doctors, the police. The problems which finally get to the professional social care services are mainly those not amenable to easy, informal resolution. They are often serious, long-standing, of multiple causation and intractable. The implications for the role of the personal care services are, first, to strengthen the capacity of local informal sources of help, second, to improve access to and secure better service from the formal services and, third, to strengthen their capacity to deal with the more intractable problems they inherit.

There are no precise accounts of the magnitude of the personal welfare services since they are not usually reported separately in public statistics – in Australia they are aggregated in national social reporting with social security expenditure. From estimates made in countries of similar economic and social development to Australia it appears that typically they amount to between 3 per cent and 5 per cent of public outlays, accounting for about 1 – 2 per cent of GDP. They are not the major social service responsibility of any level of government in Australia, compared for example with social security at commonwealth level, health and education in the states and recreational, cultural and environmental services in local government. They are primarily located in the state governments and in non-governmental services, but there are no accurate estimates of the magnitude of non-governmental operations though they are generally believed to be considerable. In recent years the commonwealth has entered the field of personal welfare service provision, mainly indirectly through grant-aid funding. And there has been advocacy in some quarters for greater local (including non-governmental and private) provision, reflecting the current interest in small government and local devolution.

It is sometimes said that the personal welfare services – which in practice tend to be primarily residual and reactive, responding remedially to people in trouble – should be more preventive and developmental, helping to create the conditions under which crises are less likely to occur and devoting more of their resources to social development and social change strategies. While some social care services are capable of adopting more preventive and developmental approaches, the implications of a greater commitment to that, in terms of funding, organization and expertise, have been little considered. Even in the expansionary times of the post-war era their funding has allowed them to do little more than respond to emergencies and to sustain people in severe chronic need. In the present more stringent times they have had difficulty in maintaining even those basic services. State governments have tended to limit their services to meeting their statutory responsibilities – those mandatory by law, concerned primarily with care and protection, for example, in child welfare and correctional services. Non-governmental services have also been under pressure and they have been able to do little more than respond to emergencies.

The personal welfare services in practice have little control over their work for reasons that go well beyond limitations in their own organization and expertise. Funding apart, the opportunity to pursue more preventive and developmental objectives is rarely open to them. Many complex problems are created in modern urban and industrial societies which are not solved by the major economic and social institutions, the market and the family, or by the more universal and institutional social services such as education and health care. These problems are relegated to the personal welfare services where they are dealt with remedially because their magnitude exceeds the scope of those services to respond to them otherwise. Many of these problems are of multiple and uncertain causation; they are not obviously solvable in the short term, and their ultimate resolution may depend upon economic and social reorganization which it is well beyond the capacity of the personal welfare services to influence. In any society, however well arranged, there will be personal, interpersonal and social problems of some complexity which demand immediate remedial attention. The personal welfare services comprise one of the few institutions able to assume responsibility for that task. Experience suggests, however, that even in the most expansionary times they are unlikely to have adequate resources for even those limited endeavours. Paradoxically, with high general standards of living, the tasks facing the personal welfare services have become more difficult. Changing public attitudes and standards, changing perceptions of the nature of problems and rising expectations of how they should be dealt with have created a more complex environment within which the personal services are expected to work. Neither changes in the social structure nor changes in the structure of the social services, it seems, will necessarily reduce the demand for personal welfare services. Rather, they can only be expected to alter its nature.

It is worthwhile, therefore, to look at the conditions for better operation of the personal welfare services. In their traditional roles they need to be able to respond quickly and effectively to crises, and they need to be flexible and innovative in developing new ways of working to meet changing public expectations. But these requirements are not necessarily consistent. The services need to be more firmly funded, more publicly accountable, more integrated within and between their various auspices, also with a strong input where necessary of professional expertise, and with access to back-up services such as research and information services and other specialist support services which it is beyond the capacity of individual local service units to maintain. These requirements for an adequate basic level of service create pressures for uniformity and centralization which run counter to the need to maintain local initiative and responsiveness, local choice and participation and involvement of indigenous non-professional people. The problem can be seen with respect to provision of services to rural and remote areas. In general people in rural and remote areas have more difficulty in getting an adequate standard of social care services, and the cost to them of getting the services is often greater than for people in metropolises. The problem is only a more extreme form of the manifest inequalities in service provision within metropolises, where studies consistently show that poorer areas have both more problems and less adequate services. It is a difficult task to achieve a workable unity in diversity which will secure a basic equitable standard of social care services while maintaining local initiative and responsiveness.

WELFARE IN CONTEXT

The architects of what came to be called 'the welfare state', began in the belief that legislation for the provision of social services, in a context of relatively full employment, would considerably reduce inequalities, at least of income, and would provide greater opportunities for people to better themselves and in that way might reduce other inequalities, for example, of status and wealth. In this they were optimistic. Much was achieved through social legislation, at least in maintaining civic minima. But what became apparent in the 1960s, before the recession of the 1970s forced an even more painful rethinking, was that too much had been expected of those activities which had been called arbitrarily 'the social services'. Two things became apparent. The first, which has been called analysis of the social division of welfare, was that many flows of benefits and burdens from public and publicly subsidized corporate activity affected distributional justice but were not called social welfare, and in many cases were greater in magnitude, and contrary in direction, to those that were. The second, and a logical extension of the first, was a growing appreciation, for example by welfare collectivists, that social welfare policies were arbitrary and artificial unless they were seen in relation to the larger issues of social policy, and that these in turn had to be considered in a context of the relations between social and economic objectives of society.

Analysis in terms of what has been called the social division of welfare is now commonplace. There are many examples of the expanded notion of welfare which this entails. The two most commonly quoted, and probably the most influential in their effects on distributional justice, are taxation benefits and employment fringe benefits. Were these to be taken into the account of public benefits it is said we would find the received wisdom that 'welfare' benefits unequivocally flow from rich to poor, from producers to consumers, to be incorrect; and would find, for example, that most benefits flow horizontally between the same categories of people at different stages in their lives and some flow from poor to rich.

Could the calculus of the many public and publicly subsidized corporate benefits be properly made, we would have a different view of who ultimately are the beneficiaries of 'the welfare state'.[24]

Other examples of a blurring of the boundaries of welfare can be seen in the emergence of new forms of social action, such as legislation for social rights, and new forms of social provision, such as labour market programmes. These also are not seen necessarily as welfare though they affect the balance of distributional justice. Their continued development can be expected but, because of the pace at which they are emerging, their significance in relation to welfare provision has not been assessed. The burgeoning phenomenon of legislation for social rights is an example of this. The notion of social rights is not clear: it is hard to find a good working definition or even a useful description of them. They may be seen, in part, as a modern extension of the civic and political rights which were secured in Europe and America in the eighteenth and nineteenth centuries, but the parallel is not close, and they may have more affinity with the later idea of human rights as embodied in United Nations charters. They extend well beyond the social welfare notion of the rights of citizens to civic minima in return for service to the state. Recent examples of a general provision of rights include such diverse and extensive provision as legislation for consumer protection and legislation against discrimination in employment. More specifically, in relation to welfare, there are such initiatives as the creation of offices of welfare ombudsman and the establishment of children's interest bureaux, and beyond that the creation of charters of rights for particular disadvantaged groups such as the handicapped. It is clear that some interest groups see the establishment of social rights as a useful tool in achieving what they regard as social justice – more effective in this respect than traditional social services. It seems likely that there will be increasing emphasis on and advocacy for social rights from interest groups, but there are also indications of counter pressures, for example, in recent criticism of the Commonwealth Human Rights Commission. Their expansion shows the difficulty of fitting new developments into a schema of analysis in terms of traditional welfare services and the impossibility of relying on the traditional services to compensate for inequities of market or other distribution and exchange.[25]

The emergence of labour market programmes illustrates not only the shifting boundaries of welfare and the difficulty of determining what is welfare, but also the need to see welfare provision in a broad social and economic context, in particular, to understand the crucial relationship between work and welfare. Like traditional welfare services, labour market programmes have objectives of both equity and efficiency. The relation between the two is probably not a simple trade-off between mutually exclusive alternatives, as is sometimes assumed, but a complex and changing nexus in which in practice they are never clearly separable. The range of objectives of labour market programmes includes such diverse intentions as compensation for disadvantage in labour force participation, improvement in labour market flexibility and job creation. At one end of the range these activities have affinities with traditional welfare services; at the other, with programmes of economic structural adjustment; and in between, the mix of social and economic intentions appears uncertain. The recent commonwealth inquiry into labour market programmes (the Kirby report) concluded that their potential for increasing overall employment was limited, but that they could be important in assisting those who are most disadvantaged by the failure to achieve full employment by increasing their opportunities in the labour market and thereby contributing to labour market flexibility. This emphasizes their affinities with welfare services. And the people identified by the report as most disadvantaged in the labour market

– including early school leavers, women, people with 'disabilities and other disadvantages', older middle-aged people and certain categories of migrants and Aboriginal people – are similar to those identified as most likely to be in need of assistance from traditional welfare services. What perhaps most distinguishes labour market initiatives from traditional welfare is not so much whom they intend to serve but how they will serve them. In their emphasis on community-based rather than individually oriented services they may provide an exemplar for welfare policy-makers who generally have paid less attention to provision of programmes to disadvantaged areas than to disadvantaged people.[26]

Labour market and welfare programmes are similarly limited. There is ample evidence that changes in family composition and in workforce participation so determine changes in family well-being that little else matters; and there is ample ground for assuming that welfare and other remedial and ameliorative public programmes are only partially capable of affecting the major inequalities in primary income which these determine. Family composition apart, the starting point, therefore, for an examination of future welfare policies, is the relation between work and welfare. The greater part of differences in disposable income depends on being or not being in employment, and within that the effect of wage and salary differentials is the most important. The reasons for these differentials are manifold and they cannot be compensated for to any substantial extent by welfare provision alone. What social welfare policies can achieve within the wider context of social policies will be determined primarily, therefore, by the conditions created by the level of minimum wages, the extent of wage and salary differentials, the opportunities people have to engage in employment and to better themselves thereby and, only secondarily, by the extent to which they can be compensated for the lack of these opportunities by welfare and related policies.[27]

The future?

In terms of the distinctions drawn above, social action can be seen to proceed at three levels. The state can develop, in increasing order of inclusiveness, social welfare policies (concerned primarily with the maintenance of civic minima), social services policies (concerned primarily with equalizing opportunity) and social policies (concerned primarily with social development). In practice the differences between them are not always clearly defined. Nor does policy-making at any level necessarily imply direct public intervention. The programmes which implement policies may involve varying mixtures of state, non-governmental and private activity, depending broadly on an appreciation of the quality of the expertise that can be brought to bear and the nature of the ethos or context within which it is to be applied. In that pragmatic sense there are probably no unequivocally 'right' policies but only policies that are good enough for the particular circumstances. Because of uncertainties in understanding what is appropriate expertise, including not only technical but also executive and administrative expertise, and even more because of the turbulence created by the inevitable ebb and flow of ideological differences, policy-making at all levels has tended to be piecemeal and fragmentary. It will probably remain so. Nevertheless a high priority should be given to developing adequate social intelligence so that, allowing for the difficulties and uncertainties, good expertise can be brought to bear with sound judgement.

There obviously are sharp limits to what can be expected of public policy-making and programme implementation in social welfare. What can be done at any level depends upon what is being done at more inclusive levels, and beyond that, to what is happening in the larger economy and polity. At the least inclusive level social welfare policies directed to the most vulnerable are likely to have limited goals, and developed alone may lack the support of the larger society. Perhaps the best that can be expected of these policies by themselves is that they will protect the most needy at modestly adequate levels, and beyond that, possibly may have some capacity for enhancing their equality of opportunity. More could probably be achieved by social welfare policies if it were generally accepted that they should be concerned with positive discrimination on a large scale. But that does not command wide support and, in practice, it is difficult to raise the standards of the very poor without reference to the standards of those better off, particularly those marginally better off – one reason for the collectivist interest in building positively discriminating social welfare services on a wider base of universal social services. At the next level social services policies appear to have at least three intentions: first, to share the risks of life which fall unfairly such as, for example, the risk of being born physically handicapped; second, to increase equality of opportunity so that people may have more equal access to an agreed range of essential services which will improve their ability to advance themselves and the community – for example, by increasing life-chances through access to better education; and, third, to promote investment in human capital – the merit good intention – for example, by maintaining lifetime earning capacity through the maintenance of good health. Social policies, the most inclusive level of social action, are concerned with the relations between social development and economic development. In that sense most policies, whether labelled 'social' or not, have some social policy implications. And the limits to what social policies can achieve, therefore, are probably set ultimately by prevailing assumptions about the relations between economic goals and social goals, in terms of the so-called equity-efficiency trade-off, and the willingness and capacity of society to temper materialist objectives by reference to social objectives. There appears to be little support for this at present, and few signs that this will change.

Recent analysis from OECD countries suggests, on conservative assumptions, that present levels of social services are sustainable over the medium term. On assumptions of a growth in real GDP of about 2 per cent per annum, a slightly unfavourable aggregate demographic experience (an increase in the number of old people almost offset by a fall in the number of young people), and increases in the price of final consumption social services about the same as in the recent past and no increases in the coverage of benefits or services, it has been estimated that most OECD countries should be able to maintain the present real value of services and benefits to 1990. Beyond 1990 demographic pressures can be expected to increase as the products of the post-war baby boom begin to retire and their numbers continue to increase through the first two decades of the next century.[28] It would be realistic also to expect that other pressures will emerge, as has been indicated below, for increases in the scope and coverage of benefits and services. On these assumptions further demands, reflected already in current policies or in emerging needs, will require an increase in the share of GDP for social purposes, or a change in priorities within those purposes, or some reform of existing programmes and their better management to make room for new developments. Present indications are that the first two are unlikely and the third difficult to achieve.

Further demand for welfare benefits and services can be expected. Continuing unemployment amongst young people will increase the demand for labour market services, calling for greater integration of income-support, education and employment-creation policies. Further pressure will be placed on these services from emerging programmes of education for culturally, ethnically and other disadvantaged groups. Changes in the economic and social status of women will both increase the demand for social services, for example, for child-care services, and reduce the supply of those formerly provided free by them, for example, home and community care services for the dependent elderly and others. The demand for an equal place in the workforce for women and the abolition of the labour segmentation of women – key elements in platforms of equality for women – and their demand for equality of treatment from services, such as the social security, taxation and family law systems, pose problems in social policy and social services policy as yet largely undetermined. Continued redundancy and long-term unemployment amongst middle-aged workers will put increased pressure on income-support services. The rise in the proportion of elderly in an ageing population, which will become apparent toward the end of the century and peak within the following two decades, will put further pressure on the income-support system and will increase the demand for both institutional and domiciliary health and social services.

These are examples only of many growing demands, to some extent already predictable at least in their broad trends, which will be added to the backlog of existing un-met needs. These latter also are complex and diverse as to both their causes and the public responses that might be made to them. To take three examples from a very long list, there is the well-documented continuing poverty in clearly identifiable groups such as large low-income families and sole supporting parents, principally women, leading to heavy spatial concentrations of poverty in identifiable urban and rural centres and to heavy concentrations of poverty in young children in identifiable family and social situations. There are the rising rates of crimes of violence against property and people, including child abuse and other abuse within and without the family, partly due to more public awareness of the problems but also apparently due to a rising incidence of them – the contrary to what was expected as standards of living rose and social services became more generally available. There is the growing pressure on families and local communities from policies of maintaining dependent people out of institutions, probably correct in principle so far as that can be said unequivocally about any social policy, but less obviously a cost-saver than was first thought.

In the post-war 'long boom' there was an assumption that rising general standards of living and near universal social services would contain if not eradicate many of the social problems which beset modern society. Although much was achieved those expectations have not been met as well as was hoped: many old problems remain, some are increasing and new problems are emerging. If that were all it might have been possible to continue much as before in the expectation that cumulatively, over the long term, the gains would outweigh the losses. But substantial economic and social changes have put that in question. General standards of living are not rising so rapidly and there is little surplus available for social purposes. Attitudes to 'the welfare state' appear to be changing: if there was a kind of social compact in favour of the public sharing of welfare risks and benefits, that now appears to have given way to the competitive play of pressure groups. In these changing circumstances there is a need to rethink the place of welfare in modern society, to assess realistically what can be done and how, in the uncertain economic and social circumstances within which it must work. If we can assume that neither of the polar positions of right or left – calling for major restructuring of the economy and society – are likely, then we are in much the same situation as we have ever been. That is, we have to devise, with imperfect information and inadequate expertise in a sometimes unsympathetic environment, the best responses we can to the social issues that face us. There are no simple economic solutions to social problems. Economic development directly solves some social problems and indirectly provides the means for solving others through the availability of a surplus for social purposes. But there are problems it cannot solve; and it may create problems. There are no simple social solutions. Some social initiatives, which may or may not involve state intervention, may be reasonably satisfactory for a particular place and time. In such situations the best that can be achieved may be good working compromises which can be re-made and improved as the situation changes or as we understand it better.

This calls for an enlightened pragmatism – sound judgement in the use of the best social intelligence available. The issues raised are complex and the evidence needed to address them thoughtfully is not always readily available. That places the task beyond the means of individual analysts. And it requires a range and level of resources beyond what is currently available to any existing centre of social analysis in Australia. Though excellent work is being done in individual centres, in relation to the whole task that has to be faced it appears fragmentary and lacking in the comprehensiveness and consistency that a continuing review of social policy requires.

At least two things are needed to create an adequate centre for social analysis capable of monitoring the social issues with which we are faced and devising useful responses to them. These are: a sufficient level of expertise and means for making it available to the different levels of government and the other auspices of social action which must be involved if effective social programmes are to be implemented. Such a centre would need to be able to generate and foster the necessary social intelligence and to assimilate that into policy and programme proposals relevant to the different levels of government and to the other auspices. In practice this means a mixture of short-, medium- and long-term options, so that immediately pressing problems are addressed but are not allowed to influence unduly the consideration of longer-term objectives. The centre should have the capacity to keep social policies and programmes under review in a comparative cross-national perspective – probably one of the most useful components of policy analysis today. This requires continuing monitoring of social programmes in terms of standards (how well we are doing what we do); effectiveness (whether what we do is worth doing); and efficiency (whether what we do makes better use of resources than available alternatives). We are used to this approach to economic issues and seem not to begrudge the resources for it, but we are less inclined to see the need for such an approach to social issues.[29]

Such a review of social programmes must pay due regard to the relations between the three levels of action – social policy, social services policy and social welfare policy – not only so that there is as much integration between them as is achievable, but also to ensure that social welfare policies to maintain civic minima are not lost sight of in the development of broader economic and social policies. What is needed is an agenda for social action for the short, medium and long terms which will be sustainable according to the best forecasts that can be made. The expenditures committed to social purposes are considerable and seem likely to remain so. The resources committed to ensuring that those expenditures are well made are modest and are largely uncoordinated. No economically developed society would attempt to manage without an economic agenda. Nor should it be without a social agenda.[30]

Notes

[1] For a discussion of the broader concept of welfare, see Asa Briggs 1961. The welfare state in historical perspective. *European Journal of Sociology* 2, pp. 221-58.

[2] The term 'diswelfare', which has affinities with the concepts of 'disutility' and 'externality', has been used following R.M. Titmuss 1968. Issues of redistribution in social policy. *Commitment to Welfare*. London, Allen and Unwin. See also footnote 10.

[3] See *Population and Australia: Recent Demographic Trends and their Implications*, Supplementary Report of the National Population Inquiry (Australia), (Chairman, W.D. Borrie), Canberra, AGPS 1978.

[4] Of the many histories of the welfare state, one which well discusses its development from feudal antecedents is K. de Schweinitz 1943. *England's Road to Social Security: from the Statute of Laborers in 1349 to the Beveridge Report of 1942*. New York, Barnes.

[5] The Beveridge proposals are contained in his *Social Insurance and Allied Services*, Cmd. 6404, London, HMSO, 1942; and there are useful glosses in other of his works, for example, W.M. Beveridge 1943. *Pillars of Security*. London, Allen and Unwin, and W.H. Beveridge 1944. *Full Employment in a Free Society*. London, Allen and Unwin.

For a discussion of 'citizenship' as a rationale for welfare policies, see T.H. Marshall 1950. *Citizenship and Social Class*. Cambridge, Cambridge University Press. For a critique see R. Mishra 1981. *Society and Social Policy*. London, MacMillan (2nd edn); and for a defence see R. Pinker's Introduction to T.H. Marshall 1981. *The Right to Welfare*. London, Heinemann.

[6] The terms 'justice in exchange' and 'justice in distribution' have been used following I. Manning 1985. *Incomes and Policy*. Sydney, Allen and Unwin.

[7] For an account of the assumptions of what has been called 'the central tradition' in social welfare, and of the extent to which those assumptions have not been realized, see D.V. Donnison 1979. Social policy since Titmuss. *Journal of Social Policy*, 8, pp.145-56.

[8] The term 'democratic-welfare-capitalism' has been used following T.H. Marshall 1981. *The Right to Welfare*. London, Heinemann.

[9] For an exposition of the collectivist position in an Australian context, see P. Allen 1983. Poverty policy issues. In R. Mendelsohn (ed.), *Australian Social Welfare Finance*. Sydney, Allen and Unwin. Allen draws heavily on P. Townsend 1979. *Poverty in the United Kingdom*. London, Lane.

[10] The case for universal plus positively discriminating services in preference to selective services is made by R.M. Titmuss 1968. *Commitment to Welfare*. London, Allen and Unwin. The argument for the existence of collectively imposed social and economic inequalities requiring substantial measures of collective redistribution to redress them is made by Titmuss in the Introduction to R.H. Tawney 1979 *Equality*. London, Allen and Unwin (4th edn).

[11] For an exposition of the individualist position in an Australian context, see W. Kasper 1983. The market approach to social welfare. In R. Mendelsohn (ed.), *Australian Social Welfare Finance*. Sydney, Allen and Unwin.

[12] For a discussion of the problem of large social 'residuals' in economic explanation see J.H. Goldthorpe 1984. The end of convergence. In J.H. Goldthorpe (ed.), *Order and Conflict in Contemporary Capitalism*. Oxford, Oxford University Press.

[13] For an account of cash health and social security benefits see T.H. Kewley 1973. *Social Security in Australia, 1900-1972*. Sydney, Sydney University Press, (2nd edn). A shorter version is given in his *Australian Social Security Today: Major Developments from 1900 to 1978*. Sydney, Sydney University Press, 1980. For an account of charitable services see B.K. Dickey 1980. *No Charity There: A Short History of Social Welfare in Australia*. Melbourne, Nelson. Historical background is also given in R. Mendelsohn 1979. *The Condition of the People: Social Welfare in Australia, 1900-1975*. Sydney, Allen and Unwin.

[14] The term 'wage-earners' welfare state' has been used following F.G. Castles 1985. *The Working Class and Welfare*. Sydney, Allen and Unwin.

[15] See, for example, papers by G. Sawer, R. Groenewegen and R. Wettenhall on, respectively, constitutional, financial and administrative problems of federalism. In A. Patience and J. Scott (eds.) 1983. *Australian Federalism: Future Tense*. Melbourne, Oxford University Press. The issues have also been discussed in various publications of the ANU Centre for Research on Federal Financial Relations (see, for example, R.L. Mathews (ed.) 1976. *Making Federalism Work*. Canberra, ANU, and in reports of the Advisory Council for Inter-Government Relations).

[16] Data on Australian social welfare expenditure are derived from Australian Bureau of Statistics, *Commonwealth Government Finance*, Table 5 and *State and Local Government Finance*, Tables 13 and 15. OECD comparisons are taken from its Manpower and Social Affairs Committee, *Social Expenditure 1960-1990: Problems of Growth and Control*, Paris, 1985, which includes some data on decomposition. Data on decomposition of some Australian welfare expenditures are given also in F.H. Gruen 1985. The Federal budget, ANU Centre for Economic Policy Research, *Discussion Paper No. 120A*, and in Economic Planning Advisory Council (Australia) 1986. Growth in Australian Social Expenditures. *Council Paper No. 17*.

[17] The term 'social intelligence' has been used following T. McKeown, in his discussion of British health care

policies, in *The Role of Medicine*. Nuffield Provincial Hospitals Trust, London, 1976. Useful examples of attempts to improve the empirical base of policy analysis can be found in the work of the Institute for Research on Poverty at the University of Wisconsin, Madison. See, for example, their *I.R.P. Reprint Series*.

[18] For an account of, mainly commonwealth, social welfare legislation since 1970, see the Diary of legislative and administrative changes. In R.B. Scotton and H. Ferber 1978 and 1980. *Public Expenditures and Social Policy in Australia*, Vol.I 1972-75, Vol.II, 1976-78, Melbourne, Longman-Cheshire. The diaries have been continued annually in separate publications for the years 1980-83 as *Diary of Legislation and Policy*, Institute of Applied Economic and Social Research, University of Melbourne.

[19] For an account of the legislative history of social security, see Department of Social Security (Australia), Developments in social security: a compendium of legislative changes since 1908. Development Division, *Research Paper No. 20*, Canberra, AGPS, 1983. The Division has also produced a series of papers on contemporary aspects of social security. A further series of papers is being produced by the current Social Security Review (Consultant-Director, B. Cass) as 'Issues Papers' and 'Background/Discussion Papers' for the Review. A comprehensive bibliography of contemporary Australian sources on income security is given in I. Manning 1985. *Incomes and Policy*. Sydney, Allen and Unwin. Projections of Australian population growth to the year 2001 are given in *Population and Australia: a Demographic Analysis and Projection*. Report of the National Population Inquiry (Australia), (Chairman, W.D. Borrie), Canberra, AGPS, 1975. Trends in unemployment are considered in Economic Planning Advisory Council (Australia). Trends in the labour market. *Council Paper No. 21*, 1986.

[20] Brief summaries of the developments outlined here are given in the diaries of legislation and policy referred to in footnote 18. The Social Security Review was announced by the Minister for Social Security in December 1985. It will continue for two years. The Consultant-Director is Associate-Professor Bettina Cass of the School of Social Work in the University of Sydney. The Review covers three topics: income support for families; social security programmes and workforce participation; and income support for the aged.

[21] For a discussion of these issues, see the *Report* of the Better Health Commission (Australia) (3 vols.), Canberra, AGPS, 1986. See also P. Townsend and N. Davidson 1982. *Inequalities in Health*. Harmondsworth, Penguin: this is an unofficial edition of the Report of the Department of Health and Social Security (UK) Working Group on Inequalities in Health (Chairman, Sir Douglas Black).

[22] A short history of housing policy is given in R. Mendelsohn 1970. *The Condition of the People*. Sydney, Allen and Unwin. For a discussion of housing as welfare, see R.A. Carter 1980. Housing policies in the 1970s. In R.B. Scotton and H. Ferber, *Public Expenditures and Social Policy in Australia*, Vol.II. Melbourne, Longman-Cheshire; and T. Burke, L. Hancock and P. Newton 1984. *A Roof Over Their Heads*. Institute of Family Studies, Melbourne. Urban and regional development is discussed in R.K. Wilson 1978. Urban and regional policy. In R.B. Scotton and H. Ferber, *Public Expenditures and Social Policy in Australia*. Vol.I, Melbourne, Longman-Cheshire.

[23] There is no recent comprehensive account of Australian personal welfare services. An account of state government services is given in Social Welfare Commission (Australia), Family Services Committee, *Families and Social Services in Australia*, Vol, II. Canberra, AGPS, 1978. There are no comprehensive accounts of local government services. Most progress in considering local government responsibility for welfare has been made in Victoria. See, for example, M. Bowman and J. Halligan 1983. *Victorian Local Government's Role in Human Services* (Mimeograph), Department of Politics, University of Melbourne. Estimates of non-governmental provision of personal welfare services are given in V. Milligan, J. Hardwick and A. Graycar 1984. Non-government welfare organisations in Australia. Social Welfare Research Centre, *Reports and Proceedings No. 51*, University of NSW, Sydney.

[24] One of the earliest formulations of analysis in the social division of welfare was made by R.M. Titmuss in the Sixth Eleanor Rathbone Memorial Lecture at the University of Birmingham in 1955. It is reprinted in his *Essays on 'the Welfare State'*. London, Allen and Unwin, 1958. For a later discussion see A. Sinfield 1978. Analysis in the social division of welfare. *Journal of Social Policy* 7, pp.129-56.

[25] There are no general references on 'social rights'. For a recent discussion of citizenship and social rights as bases for social welfare policy see P. Bean, J. Ferris and D. Whynes 1985. *In Defence of Welfare*. London, Tavistock. For an example of recent critical discussion of the Human Rights Commission, see S.A. Ozdowski 1987. Our human rights debate. *Quadrant*, No. 230, pp. 22-9.

[26] See Department of Employment and Industrial Relations (Australia), Committee of Enquiry into Labour Market Programmes (Chairman, P.E.F. Kirby), *Report*, Canberra, AGPS, 1984. Quarterly *Bulletins of Labour Market Research* from the Department of Employment and Industrial Relations (Australia) have included useful bibliographies, some with reference to the welfare implications of labour market programmes.

[27] There has been no comprehensive analysis in an Australian context of the issues raised by a consideration of the relations between work and welfare. For a brief introduction to some of them see S. Marklund 1986. The Swedish model – work and welfare. *A.C.O.S.S. Impact* 16(18) Dec. pp. 9-10.

[28] OECD projections are taken from its *Social Expenditure 1960-1990*. See footnote 16.

[29] Cross-national comparisons are assuming increasing importance as a basis for understanding the scope and limits for social policies and the factors determining that. See, for example. R.L. Walker, R. Lawson and P. Townsend 1984. *Responses to Poverty: Lessons from Europe*. London, Heinemann; and S. Danziger and E.

Smolensk (eds.) 1985. Income transfers and the poor: a cross-national perspective. *Journal of Social Policy* 14 (3) an issue devoted to income transfer policies and their effects on income inequality and work effort. The particular use here of the terms 'standards', 'effectiveness' and 'efficiency' follows T. McKeown. See footnote 17.
[30] The task of determining a suitable auspice for a centre for social analysis is more difficult than that of finding the expertise for it. Several possible modifications of existing arrangements suggest themselves, for example, some cross between the Economic Planning Advisory Council and the Council of Commonwealth and State Ministers of human services probably provides some indication of the auspice needed – a kind of social version of the US President's Council of Economic Advisers.

4

Education in Australia: Conformity and Diversity[1]

Brian Crittenden

THE EDUCATIONAL SCENE A HUNDRED YEARS AGO

Around a hundred years ago the state-controlled systems of 'free, compulsory and secular' schooling were being established in the Australian colonies. The first state to introduce this system was Victoria in 1872; the last, Western Australia in 1892. Although it was some time before the public schools became, in the strict sense, free, compulsory and secular, the pattern of a centralized state system under ministerial control was firmly set. While there have been recent modifications, it remains essentially the same today.

The introduction of the system provoked what has probably been the most intense debate on education in Australia's history. It involved fundamental questions about the place of religion in education, the authority of the state over the conduct of schooling and the neutrality that was fitting for common schools in a pluralist society. The issue of church-state relationships, so significant in the nineteenth century, played a key part in the debate. Most of the opposition to the new system came from the leaders of the Catholic Church. (There was a tendency for the question of the Church's prerogative in education to overshadow that of the parents' right of choice in the schooling of their children.) In an atmosphere of implacable ideological conflict and mutual fear the governments of the colonies decided that, under the new scheme, state aid would be withdrawn from denominational schools. The Catholic Church for its part proceeded to develop its own system of primary and secondary schools. For the next eighty years or so private schools – mostly denominational, of which a large proportion were Catholic – provided education for something like a quarter of Australia's children without support from public funds. The issues of a hundred years ago smouldered away, flaring on occasion. Among Catholics, at least, there was an abiding sense of injustice.

A striking feature of the public system of schools that was taking shape in the 1880s was the small number of secondary schools. The state education departments were preoccupied with elementary schooling. In NSW, for example, there were only five state high schools by the late 1880s. The next was not established until 1906. It was only after 1910 that the system of state high schools in NSW began to grow.

A hundred years ago there were three institutions of higher education: the universities of Sydney, Melbourne and Adelaide. (The total Australian population was around 2.3 million.) Although Sydney and Melbourne had been established for over thirty years, they had made very slow progress. In 1880 there were only seventy-six students enrolled and a staff of six at the University of Sydney. Melbourne was somewhat more vigorous with about 200 undergraduates. On the University of Adelaide, at which teaching began in 1876, an observer of the day commented: 'In five years of existence it has conferred five degrees at a cost of 50,000 pounds, and the professors threatened to outnumber the students'.[2] By 1890 there were about 1400 students enrolled in Australian universities. Institutions of technical education were also in existence by the time of the first centenary, the first being established at Ballarat in 1870.

Several structural features of Australian education that emerged a hundred years ago still exercise a profound influence. What is more striking, of course, is the dramatic change in the relative scale of the enterprise at the levels of secondary and tertiary education. This expansion is even more impressive in that, instead of being a long and steady evolution, much of it has been compressed within the last thirty years. As the rate of increase has in fact been declining over the past few years, the phase of dramatic expansion is located more precisely between the early 1950s and the mid-1970s. The mere fact of the rapid increase in size is, of course, less important than the various social values it reflects and the consequences it has had for educational policy and practice. In the following discussion some aspects of the growth of Australian educational institutions since the early 1950s will be given as a background to identifying significant issues related to the current practice of education in this country. I speak of 'education' only in so far as it refers to the systematic processes of teaching and learning associated with primary and secondary schools, universities and colleges, and institutes of technical and further education. I shall say nothing about the educational role of the family, or the educational influence that can be exerted by the electronic and print media, the arts and many other agencies, or the consequences for education of the recent advances in information technology. The actual influence of families, television and so on can be in conflict with the educational ideals that schools are trying to realize.

THE EXPANSION OF EDUCATIONAL INSTITUTIONS, 1950–75

In 1950 primary school enrolments in Australia were about 1,025,900 with around 33,700 teachers. Twenty years later there were 1,812,000 students and around 64,700 teachers. The relatively higher increase in teachers was directed at improving the general ratio of staff to students and providing staff for a variety of specialized roles. Primary school enrolments grew steadily until 1979 (1.87 million), and have been declining since then because of a lower birthrate. At the end of World War II there were about 181,000 students and 6000 teachers in Australian secondary schools. The increase continued unbroken until 1977, when there were 1,120,000 students and 80,980 teachers. After a few years of decline, secondary enrolments in Australian schools began to increase again and were around 1.25 million in 1984, with nearly 98,000 teachers (full-time or equivalent).

In addition to the rapid increase in the total size of the educational enterprise at the primary and secondary levels there has been a dramatic change in the relative number continuing in the post-compulsory years of secondary schooling.[3] In 1948 the apparent retention rate for the final year (generally the fifth) was about 10 per cent.[4] The rate expanded substantially during the 1960s, and the length of the course was extended by a year. In 1969 the retention rate had reached 27.5 per cent. The scale of the change is well illustrated in the actual final year enrolments in government schools. Between 1950 and 1970 they increased from 6000 to 45,000. The retention rate continued to increase until 1976 (35 per cent), remained static for a few years, but began to increase again in 1981. By the early 1970s a substantial majority were completing Year 10. Between 1973 and 1984 the percentage rose steadily from 82 per cent to 94 per cent. Over the same period the retention rate to the end of Year 11 increased from 48 per cent to 65 per cent.

The proportion of 17-year-olds in secondary school gives another indication of the change that has occurred. In 1955 the percentage was 8.7 (12.5 per cent of males, 5 per cent of females). In 1983 it was 33.5 per cent (32.1 per cent of males, 35.1 per cent of females). The enrolments of 17-year-olds show roughly the same fluctuation from the mid-1970s as the Year 12 retention rate. The temporary decline occurred among males, particularly in government schools. The above figures point to another significant change: the increasing participation rate of females in post-compulsory education. Since 1978 the percentage of 16- to 18-year-old females at school has exceeded that of males.

The growth that occurred over two decades or so in the main sectors of tertiary education (universities, colleges and TAFE) is no less remarkable. Half-way through the second century there were six Australian universities, the last being established in 1911, catering for a very small proportion of the population. There was relatively little development of graduate work, and most staff were preoccupied with teaching. The seventh university was established in 1945. In the next twenty-five years the number of universities more than doubled (to fifteen) and student enrolments increased from about 26,000 to 116,000. By 1978 there were nineteen universities in Australia with an enrolment of 160,000 students. From 1977 to 1982 the annual rate of growth declined substantially from what it had been in the previous decade. While there was a significant increase in part-time and external students and those of mature age (the majority of whom were females), the number of full-time enrolments fell. There was a related decline in the proportion of students coming directly from school.[5] Full-time enrolments and the general rate of growth began to rise again in 1983.

In 1965 the commonwealth government undertook to fund a new institutional form of higher education, the Colleges of Advanced Education (CAEs), in addition to the universities.[6] This sector incorporated existing technical colleges and teachers' colleges which had been developing rapidly during the previous two decades – the latter had expanded in number from seven in 1946 to twenty-eight in 1962. In 1984 there were forty-five colleges of advanced education in Australia with a total enrolment of 175,120 and 9748 equivalent full-time academic staff. They included a mixture of multi-purpose and specialized institutions, offering a wide variety of undergraduate diplomas and degrees and graduate diplomas, along with master's degrees in certain areas. Between 1971 and 1975 total enrolments increased from 70,550 to 125,383; however, the rate of increase declined from 1976 to 1982, although not as much as for universities. By 1980, the CAEs' total enrolments exceeded those of universities. Universities, however, still had a substantially higher proportion of full-time students.

The third major sector of tertiary education in Australia, Technical and Further Education (TAFE), began its phase of remarkable growth relatively late. Following a report on its condition and future direction in 1974, the commonwealth government moved to give TAFE a clear place in the funding and policy-making role such as it had already adopted for other sectors of education.[7] Although TAFE was developing earlier, it is in the past decade or so that the most significant changes have occurred. There are now 215 major TAFE institutions in Australia (together with more than 1300 ancillary centres). In ten years forty new institutions were opened, with several others rebuilt or substantially extended. Courses are offered in six main streams: 1-4, vocational education; 5, preparation for further study; and 6, leisure and personal development. Between 1974 and 1984 enrolments in the last increased from 133,000 to 423,127: in streams 1-5, they almost doubled (458,000 to 831,170). In 1984 TAFE employed a teaching staff of 49,458 (of whom 17,135 were full-time), an increase of 10.5 per cent over two years. TAFE institutions are funded jointly by state and commonwealth governments. The latter provides about 20 per cent of recurrent costs and 70 per cent of capital costs.

In 1983 it was estimated that one-quarter of all Americans were engaged in formal education as their main activity (that is, as students, teachers and administrative staff). Australia has probably not yet become so 'school-based' a society. In the same academic year, however, there were about 2.5 million full-time students in the three main levels of formal education in Australia and around 222,000 equivalent full-time teachers. The enormous expansion in the institutions of education over the past three decades is succinctly reflected in the increasing proportion of public expenditure on education. In 1956–57 it amounted to 2.1 per cent of the gross domestic product. It reached its highest level in 1977–78 at 6.4 per cent. After dropping below 6 per cent for three years it rose to 6 per cent again in 1983.

THE COMMONWEALTH GOVERNMENT AND THE DIRECTION OF EDUCATION[8]

Over recent decades one of the most crucial changes affecting education in Australia at all levels has been the vastly expanded influence of the commonwealth government. Education is not among the activities assigned to the responsibility of the commonwealth in section 51 of the Constitution and so it remains subject primarily to the control of the states. The commonwealth, however, can act in regard to education under other sections of the Constitution (especially section 96, which enables it to make grants to the states on specified conditions). The most important background development was the assumption by the commonwealth in the wartime conditions of 1942 of the exclusive power to levy taxation, a power which it has retained.

Following the Murray report (1957) on universities, the commonwealth government undertook a substantial part of their funding. In 1960 the Australian Universities Commission was established to advise the government on expenditures and on how a balanced development of universities in Australia might be achieved. The Martin report (1964) led to the establishment of Colleges of Advanced Education in 1965 as an alternative to universities at the tertiary level. Many already existing institutions were incorporated in the new arrangement. Again the commonwealth took a large responsibility for funding. Since 1974 it has met the full cost of universities and colleges. The commonwealth also responded to the Kangan report (1974) and substantially increased funding for TAFE colleges, although here the states are still responsible for most of the recurrent cost. The commonwealth government's contribution to tertiary education was substantially increased when it abolished all fees at universities and CAEs in 1974.

Although the states are still responsible for the conduct of primary and secondary schooling, the commonwealth government now plays a significant role at these levels as well. During the 1950s and 60s there were serious strains on state resources to cope with large classes, lack of teachers in certain fields and inadequate buildings and equipment. In the early 1960s the Australian Education Council twice requested the commonwealth to give direct assistance to state schools. Its first response was to provide grants for the effective teaching of science. These funds, along with the introduction of secondary scholarships, were made available to private as well as government schools. (The commonwealth's role in funding private schools will be discussed later.)

The scale of commonwealth involvement in primary and secondary schooling increased dramatically with the election of a Labor government in 1972. An Australian Schools Commission was to be established, and an interim committee, chaired by Professor Peter Karmel, was appointed shortly after the election. Its report in May 1973 set the pattern for commonwealth action that has been followed by successive governments to the present time. The total commonwealth expenditure on schools was $1144 m. in 1974–75, $1314 m. in 1982–83 and $1493 m. in 1985 (all at December 1984 prices). As a percentage of total commonwealth outlays, the amount for schools moved from 1.3 per cent in 1972–73 to 3 per cent in 1974–75 and 2.5 per cent in recent years. In 1983–84 about 38 per cent of the total commonwealth expenditure on education was for schools. In addition to general recurrent and capital grants, the commonwealth is funding a range of specific programmes (disadvantaged schools, basic learning in primary schools, etc.). These amounted to $252 m. in the total expenditure for 1985. In broad terms the commonwealth is now directly responsible for one-fifth of school-level costs and four-fifths of the costs at other levels.[9]

The increased size of the direct commonwealth grants for education is not in itself of special significance. What deserves close attention is the increasing power to shape education policy that the commonwealth has been exercising because of its funding role. Until recently the state systems of education in Australia were egregious examples of highly centralized bureaucratic control. When the population was relatively small and dispersed over a large area, the centralized system had the advantage of curbing serious inequalities in the distribution of human and material resources among the schools. But, in general, such a system is radically inappropriate for a practice such as education. The good in question cannot be produced and distributed like food or electrical power; it requires close attention to a complex range of local and individual variations. Those who are directly supervising the process should have the ability and authority to make significant decisions. Effective schools cannot be set up around the country like a chain of fast-food stores; they need the conditions in which each can develop its distinctive character and style. Whether or not the commonwealth government is exceeding a desirable level in guiding educational policy on a national scale, its role is clearly fraught with danger and deserves to be closely examined. At the very time when state Departments of Education are engaged in some diffusion of authority, a super-centralized government control of education may be building up in Canberra. Those who favour a single national government should not ignore the effects of bureaucratic control on education when raised to this level.

Until fairly recently the national advisory committees (especially the Schools Commission) played a useful role not only in offering the government independent and informed advice on educational policy but also in stimulating debate in the society generally. In its reports over a number of years the Schools Commission elaborated on several themes that have had a central place in the theory and practice of schooling in Australia during the past decade. Probably the most significant are the following: the role of schools in promoting equal opportunity and social equality; the devolution of decision-making in the running of schools; unity and diversity in the provision of education; and the closely related question of a common curriculum (or, at least, a core of common learning). The Universities Commission defended the wider role of universities in extending knowledge and critically evaluating the society, not simply training highly skilled manpower – it argued that how universities responded to what a government perceived as national needs should be a matter for their own judgement.

In the past few years the role of the commissions or their equivalent seems to have changed significantly. Faced with a deteriorating economy, the government itself has been setting broad policy guidelines and asking the commissions to give advice on how, in the light of the guidelines, the total budget it has specified might be distributed. The Participation and Equity programme is a clear example of a particular interpretation of a policy being initiated and promoted in educational institutions at all levels by the commonwealth government. Over the past decade the committees representing each sector of tertiary education have been transformed from independent bodies to advisory sub-committees reporting to a unitary Tertiary Education Commission.[10] The Schools Commission is now much more closely associated with the commonwealth Department of Education. The 1981 report is the last in which the Commission has engaged in broad discussion of educational issues.

Apart from the general difficulties with the bureaucratic administration of education, there are certain widely held values that give cause for special concern over the expanding role of central government in determining educational policy. Those who exercise political power seem to regard the value of education predominantly in instrumental terms. The investment in educational institutions is justified largely because they produce the trained workforce our industrial economy needs and because they are thought to serve politically significant social objectives (such as breaking down class, gender and other barriers that impede entry to positions of privilege). This view is reinforced by the widespread belief in the society generally that the main point of extended education is to qualify for a better kind of job and by the extravagant confidence that many social reformers have in the power of schooling. The vague egalitarianism to which many Australians subscribe, and the impatience with any views that deviate from those of the majority, encourage the development of a single uniform system of formal education. There is also the characteristic Australian expectation that governments should take the major responsibility for the provision of commonly desired services.

In pursuing their proper concern for accountability in the use of public funds, government authorities are inclined to rely on precisely quantified indicators of educational outcomes and of efficiency in achieving them. The educational outcomes regarded as really significant are identified by extrinsic criteria of economic and social benefit. Apart from the fact that the assessment of educational quality requires far more complex procedures than a comparison of neatly measurable inputs and outputs, this approach begs fundamental questions about what is of most educational worth. The logic of this method of central government planning can be seen at its fullest extent in the treatment of tertiary institutions by the present British government. Teaching and research in the physical sciences that directly relate to technological and economic development receive first priority. At the other extreme are most of the humanities, regarded as least useful and so most expendable. The impact of the policy is reflected in a 13 per cent decline in Arts graduates over the past few years. Systematic planning makes for economic efficiency, but it may in the process undermine educational quality. For example, there are some fields of study, such as philosophy, that every university needs on educational grounds, even if it seems more efficient to have a smaller number of larger departmental units in the system as a whole.

The Australian government has not yet adopted anything like the procedure of its British counterpart, but there are some ominous signs; and the kinds of attitude referred to previously, combined with the conditions of a worsening economy, may very well lead it in that direction. There is an urgent need to determine how the commonwealth government can ensure the efficient and responsible use of public funds in education (and make informed decisions on the total allocations) while respecting the distinctive characteristics of the practice on which its quality crucially depends. The issue is only partly about the relationship of commonwealth and state governments in the funding and supervision of education. More fundamentally, it is about the scale of organization for educational institutions at the various levels that is most appropriate for the achievement of their distinctive objectives.

The exercise of government control is related to the more general question of uniformity and diversity in Australian education, which will be referred to in the following comments on the various stages of formal education as they now exist in Australia. Within this chapter a few of the issues that are likely to be of continuing significance will be discussed in detail, although there are many other topics that have at least as much claim to consideration.

THE DEVOLUTION OF AUTHORITY TO SCHOOL LEVEL WITHIN THE STATE SYSTEMS

The highly centralized state systems, so criticized by observers of Australian education, began to be modified in the late 1960s. The devolution of decision-making to the school level was, as we saw, one of the main matters of policy espoused by the Karmel report. The Australian Schools Commission has reiterated the theme in its various reports over the past decade or so, especially that of April 1978. (This is somewhat ironic, given that during the same time the commonwealth government has been engaged in expanding its influence over schools.) In practice, regional administrative units have been set up in all states and the Northern Territory, but scope for decision-making by individual schools is generally still limited. Legislation in South Australia (1972) and Victoria (1975) set the pattern for elected local school councils, enabling parents and others in the neighbourhood of a school to participate in shaping its policies. The range of authority exercised by school councils varies, but has been restricted mainly to questions of curriculum. The crucial exclusion is control over the school's budget (retained by the central authority). If a local body is to be responsible for setting the particular aims and policy of a school and for monitoring how effectively they are achieved, it needs to have substantial authority over the allocation of funds and the appointment of staff.[11] In Victoria, a recent report to the Minister for Education proposed block grants (initially restricted to secondary schools) to be used at the discretion of school councils, subject to general guidelines. Principals would be directly responsible for appointing staff in conformity with policies set by their school council. In its response, the government has decided to make consolidated budget grants to all schools, but to maintain the appointment of teachers as a central responsibility.

There are many practical obstacles to bringing significant educational decision-making to the school level: the entrenched central agencies (whatever may be done to rearrange the boxes in the organizational chart); the teachers' unions, which parallel the state departments of education in their centralized organization and whole-system outlook; some shortage of volunteers to serve on school councils and the need to provide members with training for the task; resistance among teachers to the influence of parents on the school's programme; and the number of teachers who are reluctant for various reasons to take responsibility for the planning of curriculum. Even the efforts to offset some of these problems (e.g., state organizations of parents or school councils) develop features of a centralized bureaucracy. But beyond the practical question, there are fundamental theoretical issues that have not yet been adequately worked out. There is fairly general agreement that most detailed decisions of policy and practice should be made at or near the individual school level. It is equally agreed that the state has a responsibility to protect individual and public interest in the practice of education and to ensure that schools are duly accountable for the use of public funds. Complications arise when there is question of stating more specifically the boundaries of school autonomy and state authority and the role that each of the main groups of participants may justifiably play in the conduct of a school.

On the whole question of a more devolved pattern of decision-making in education there are basic conditions that should guide the evolution of any practical scheme. Governments in Australia must learn to play a more restrained role in determining the content and methods of the cultural transmission in which the schools engage. Public departments of education (or their equivalent) need to be much more independent of government than at present. It would be desirable to experiment with various arrangements in which individual schools made decisions of policy and practice within the context of their membership in a network of several primary and secondary schools.

Exaggerated claims about school-based curriculum planning should be avoided. The effective design of curriculum materials depends on the systematic effort of many agencies and experts. Ideally, as Bruner has emphasized, the society's best scholars should be involved in preparing curriculum content for the education of children. The main responsibility of teachers in schools is to select, supplement and adapt in relation to the best materials available.

For the most part budgets should be allocated as block grants to individual schools or small groups of schools. If policy decisions are to be effectively translated into practice, schools must have some control over the appointment, transfer and promotion of teachers. For this to be possible the general conditions that teachers' unions require for the protection of their members will need to be framed more flexibly. There should be an adequate appeals procedure at state level over the decisions taken by schools on policy and practice, and one not limited to staff appointments and the like. For example, the majority of members on a school council may endorse a programme that upholds the distinctive values of a particular group or way of life in the society and thus violate the neutrality that is expected of public schools in a liberal democratic society. There need to be safeguards against such misuses of local majority power.

DIVERSITY AND CHOICE OF SCHOOLING

If devolution of responsibility is likely to encourage a more reflective, adaptive and varied practice of education in public schools, it does not guarantee everyone a wider range of choice. The direction taken by a local school may satisfy the majority but be unacceptable to a minority of parents or students. The removal or substantial modification of zoning rules would obviously expand the range of choice within the public school system. If larger public schools adopt a somewhat eclectic approach to education rather than endorsing a single interpretation, they can offer students some choice among broad curricular programmes and methods of teaching and learning, not simply among individual subjects.

In the history of Australian education the major issue of choice has been set in terms of public secular or private religious schools. While the general religious, philosophical, moral and other beliefs and values upheld by a school are fundamental grounds of choice, they obscure others that are related more directly to the nature and practice of education. There are significant differences of emphasis in the curriculum as a whole (e.g., in relation to liberal and vocational studies, content and skills, intellectual development and personality adjustment, the objectives of social adaptation and transformation); in pedagogical procedures (for example, how individual differences in ability and interest are accommodated); in the kind of discipline that characterizes the school; and in the broad pattern of authority that determines a school's policies. There is also radical disagreement on how broadly the educational role of the school should be interpreted and what else it might do as a social institution. The differences outlined, and others, give reasons for choice in education that are independent of the choice between a common school and one that reflects a particular way of life.

The exercise of choice in education is obviously linked with the question of government funds for private schools. Any child who attends a government school receives education free of charge regardless of family income. Should all children who attend schools that satisfy the basic conditions on which the state may reasonably insist be entitled to the same contribution from public funds? Here the answer should be in the affirmative, if we assume that there should be substantial freedom of choice in the society on contested values, that parents have a primary authority over the upbringing of their children and that formal education should be an integral part of the whole process by which children are inducted into adult life.

Because most of the non-government schools in Australia have been associated with religious denominations (of which the Catholic Church has been the major agent), the issue of educational choice without financial penalty was complicated until very recently by the undercurrents of the nineteenth-century debate over the relationship of church and state and by anti-Catholic bigotry. Public funding for private schools was reintroduced in Australia during the 1960s. The pressure of rapidly increasing enrolments had seriously affected all schools, with Catholic schools particularly affected. Between 1946 and 1960 their enrolments increased by 98 per cent. The cost of new buildings and the growing proportion of lay teachers was becoming impossible. By the late 1960s the commonwealth was making per capita grants to private schools and the 'state aid' issue had re-emerged as among the most important in domestic politics. Electoral chances depended on a favourable attitude. In 1974 the Labor government adopted the recommendation of the Karmel report that there be a scale of funding based on criteria of need – this involved a substantial increase in the general level of commonwealth grants for private schools. Since then the level has been maintained although the details of allocation have varied.

Despite the relative ease with which the dramatic change of policy occurred,[12] there has been some opposition. However the old anti-Catholic sectarianism that resurfaced in the mid-1960s has virtually disappeared in the past few years. This change has been encouraged by a growing tolerance of religious groups for one another, and a growing apathy about religion generally. Since the Second Vatican Council (1963–65), the Catholic Church has adopted a more ecumenical outlook and as a result is regarded more tolerantly by other religious groups. The emphasis on multiculturalism has also encouraged religious toleration. In recent decades, the Catholic population has become ethnically more diverse; and the political allegiance of Catholics is no longer predictable. There is still antagonism from those who regard any religiously-based education as undesirable, but the main critics now are those who see 'state aid' as a threat to public schools. At the time commonwealth grants to private schools began, their proportion of the total enrolment was declining. Since the late 1970s, however, the trend has reversed itself. In 1984, 25.2 per cent were enrolled in non-government schools (above the previous high level of 24 per cent in 1955).[13] In addition to the changing balance of enrolments, many critics seem to be convinced that funds allocated to private schools reduce what would otherwise be spent on public schools.

The question of public support for educational choice has also been complicated by the existence of expensive private schools whose students gain a disproportionately high number of places in universities, especially in courses leading to the more prestigious occupations. It is this outcome rather than the charging of high fees that causes discontent. We need to remember that in the present pattern of private schooling in Australia, only a small proportion are attending expensive schools. In 1981 about 80 per cent were in schools regarded as being in the most needy category for commonwealth grants. In relation to average recurrent resources, Catholic schools in 1981 (with nearly 80 per cent of the private-school enrolment) were still well below the resource targets adopted in 1974 for all schools. Other private schools, and government schools in most states, were substantially above them.[14] Even at the senior secondary level, the most sensitive for the policy of equal opportunity, probably not more than a third of students outside the public system are in expensive schools.

The contribution from public revenue of a standard amount for the education of children in any approved school (whether it is run by a public or private agency) should not be confused with the government's role in promoting fairness in the opportunity for education and the other goods that are conditional on education. There are many ways in which the state can act for this end without discouraging choice of schooling. These include: a taxation system that contributes to a fairer distribution of commonly desired goods; the provision of supplementary grants to offset disadvantage in both private and public schools; and adequate opportunity for all students in public schools (not simply those in the more affluent areas) to take a rigorous, carefully sequenced programme of academically related studies, if that is what they wish. The state is perhaps justified in setting an upper limit on the fees that may be charged before it reduces or withdraws the standard grant. It is well to remember, however, that well-to-do parents who send their children to a public school are not controlled in the uses they make of their income to improve their children's education (for example, hiring a tutor).

For the most part choice within and between public and private schools relates to a fairly limited range of the significant dimensions on which the practice of schooling might differ. In Australian educational practice generally, there needs to be more diversity and choice on grounds directly related to educational theory and principles. While this can and should occur in public and private systemic schools, it would be very desirable for many more non-systemic private schools of this kind to be established.[15] During the 1970s, about 100 small non-government schools, outside the category of traditional private schools, were established in Australia. They are controlled, in various combinations, by parents, teachers and social groups (particularly, ethnic and religious). Although the majority reflect various approaches to schooling associated with Christian religious values, some are based on distinctive pedagogical principles (such as those of Montessori or Steiner). If a sufficient number of schools reflecting diverse interpretations of education is to be encouraged, and if choice is not to be constrained by family income, public funding for non-government schools will need to approximate the per capita cost of public schooling.

Diversity and choice in schooling are not, of course, simply to be encouraged for their own sake. They are defensible because (a), they are closely linked to the freedom of the members of a liberal democratic society to hold, and live by, fundamentally different beliefs and values, and (b), they encourage initiative and can lead to the improvement of educational practice. Some, perhaps many, of the approaches to schooling allowed by this freedom may be defective. But, like beliefs and practices generally, the appropriate means of change are reasoned persuasion and experience. It must also be remembered that there is no single right content or way of teaching and learning for the development of an educated person – even when the characteristics of such a person are agreed on.

As indicated earlier there is no question of the state allowing, much less providing financial support for, unqualified diversity in schooling. The state must protect the right of children to the conditions commonly regarded as necessary for worthwhile education. It should also expect all schools to provide an effective induction into the beliefs, values and attitudes on which the legal and political institutions are based and those on which the cohesion of a pluralist society depends.

The question of a compulsory common curriculum relates to both of these matters and also to the objective of protecting equality of opportunity. The Curriculum Development Centre, in its first existence as an independent commonwealth body, issued in 1980 a proposal for a common core curriculum across Australia.[16] This contained a broad framework for constructing the details of the entire curriculum. It has influenced more recent state programmes. Such an approach either goes too far in prescribing what should be taught in all schools or fails to distinguish with any precision what the core of essential common learning should be. A reasonably precise core of this kind can and should be identified in terms of (a), essential knowledge and intellectual skills, (b), the indispensable moral values for a pluralist society, and (c), the most significant features of the social institutions and evolving culture in which all Australians participate.[17] But the emphasis must be on what can clearly be supported as essential.

A theme that has recurred in policy discussion by the Schools Commission is the need to defend the 'strength and representativeness' of the public school system.[18] The 1981 report reviewed various measures to serve this objective, some of which limit choice outside the system (such as setting an annual quota on the new places in private schools that would receive public funding). However a protectionist policy for public schools is not desirable (or necessary). A common school in which students from diverse ways of life mix has distinct educational and social merits that will appeal to many people. If anything needs to be done to defend the public schools, it is to ensure that there is an adequate range of choice and level of quality in their educational programmes. Arrangements in which public and private schools share facilities or enter into more ambitious forms of collaboration may well deserve to be encouraged. They should be regarded, however, not as a common blueprint but as among the options that users of the schools are free to choose.

In summary, while there are substantial constraints to which diversity and choice in education should be subject, governments in Australia must resist the strong traditional inclination to exert too much control. On issues such as the criteria for school registration, or the common learning all schools are to encourage or procedures for accountability in the use of public funds, what is strictly necessary for the good of individuals and society in the provision of education must be carefully distinguished from what governments and their advisors believe would be desirable for everyone.

*   *   *

SECONDARY EDUCATION IN THE POST-COMPULSORY YEARS

Perhaps the most urgent question regarding the role of schools is that of the educational programme and institutional form appropriate for the senior secondary school. The significant increase in the relative number of adolescents staying at school for years 10-12 (for most students, Year 10 is beyond the point of compulsory schooling) was referred to earlier. The vast majority now complete Year 10, about two-thirds complete Year 11 and the proportion staying to Year 12 is approaching one-half of those who begin secondary school.[19] Participation by virtually everyone in six years of full-time secondary schooling has now been accepted as a central objective of government policy. Despite the volume of criticism (especially in the United States) of prolonged secondary schooling, the policy has been widely accepted in Australia with almost the status of a self-evident truth.[20] The Blackburn report (1985), for example, simply assumes that keeping everyone at school to the end of Year 12 is desirable.[21] The target proposed by this report for Victoria is that 70 per cent of each age cohort be completing Year 12 by 1995 (with places for half of these in institutions of higher education).

The expanding proportion of young people staying on at school, and the enthusiastic support for this trend, reflect a variety of influences. Among the most important are these: the pervasive belief in schooling as a key instrument of individual economic advancement and general prosperity; the credentialling process, by which occupations artificially raise the formal education hurdle in order to select from an increasing number of applicants or to gain prestige and justify a higher place on the scale of incomes; characteristics of the Australian economy which have led to a sharp and increasing decline since 1975 in employment opportunities for 15- to 19-year-olds; the effects of scientific technology on the nature of work and the substantial relative growth of occupations in the service sector; the example of what is done in other advanced industrial societies; and the movement, sponsored by commonwealth and state governments, to achieve equal average outcomes (or proportional representation) for designated groups in schooling, higher education and the occupations to which education directly leads.

The model of social equality through schooling now commonly advocated is one in which all groups regarded as significant are to be proportionately represented among those who enter and graduate from institutions of higher education. The principle is also to be applied to each of the more prestigious faculties and related professions. (See, for example, *Commonwealth Tertiary Education Commission Guidelines for the 1985–87 Triennium* issued by the Minister for Education and Youth Affairs, July 1984.) In this model, the membership of social classes is shaken up each generation as individuals move up and down the scale. It tries to ignore the powerful influence of family background on educational achievement (as well as other relevant factors that vary among groups) and does nothing of itself to change any actual injustices in the system of rewards in our society. There has also been strong support for the 'full participation' policy on the less altruistic ground that it provides a way of coping with the embarrassing social and political problems of the high unemployment rate among 15- to 19-year-olds.[22]

The main positive argument for the policy seems to rest on the claim that the nature of work in advanced technological societies requires everyone to have a more advanced educational background – one that emphasizes the general intellectual skills on which adaptability and effective retraining depend. Whatever the strength of this kind of argument, the direct conclusion usually drawn refers to the number of years everyone needs to spend in secondary school. What is lacking is any detailed account of the level and range of formal education that everyone should have in order to enter effectively into the adult world of our society. (This should, of course, take account of all the main aspects of human life and not simply that of being an agent of the economy.) If this were done, an informed judgement might then be made on how many years of full-time schooling would usually be required.

There have been several undesirable consequences of the increasing participation rate in the later years of secondary schooling. To some extent they are felt in the years before the minimum leaving age, but they are exacerbated as more and more adolescents stay longer at school. In particular there is confusion on what educational role the senior secondary school should play. The junior secondary school has moved away from a preoccupation with the sequential acquisition of discipline-based knowledge and intellectual skills towards a smorgasbord of optional studies related to all kinds of practical activities in the society. The school has increasingly been assigned the role of an omnipurpose institution in the life of adolescents. With the growing pressure of diverse interests – including lack of interest in a rigorous study of the systematic modes of knowledge and inquiry – the same confusion has spread to the later years as well. It is not unlikely that the pattern of the first four years will simply be continued for a further two. We may end up with more time spent by everyone at school but with less education.

The obvious accompaniment of this confusion is uncertainty about the role of teachers and the kind of preparation that might fit them for their task. For most of them the main experience in life has been formal education: they spend sixteen or so years as students, and then re-enter the school as teachers. They have usually acquired some grasp of a few academic disciplines and various techniques for teaching subjects at the secondary level that are linked with two of these disciplines. What they are called on to do as teachers (even within the formal curriculum) is often quite remote from their background of knowledge and skills.

An ironical aspect of the trend towards a curriculum that tries to be relevant to all interests and useful to all manner of practical activities is that it undermines what seems to be the main argument in support of full participation to Year 12 – that our social and economic conditions now require everyone to have a more thorough general or liberal education.

A more fundamental problem with this trend is that for certain kinds of learning it overestimates the need for schooling, while for other kinds it overestimates the capacity of schooling to contribute. Although schools, like other social institutions, always stand in need of some reform, they can be suitable places for acquiring the skills of literacy and numeracy and for gaining an introduction to the main areas of systematic knowledge and inquiry as the intellectual perspectives that enable us to interpret and understand the human and physical world. But schools cannot have more than a limited capacity to train students to apply theoretical knowledge in the resolution of complex social problems or to acquire competence in vocational and other practical activities. For those adolescents who have no stomach for sustained full-time theoretical studies,[23] there is no point in trying to attract them to stay on at school by offering an intellectually trivial programme of pre-vocational, 'life adjustment', current interest, recreational and similar courses, or by pushing the school into activities that are beyond its scope and that can be better engaged in elsewhere.[24]

As a first move in trying to disperse the confusion, we need to face questions about the distinctive educational role of the later years of secondary schooling before deciding on a policy of participation. What kinds of learning come within the competence and responsibility of schools? How is the educational role of Years 11 and 12 distinctive in relation both to the earlier stages of schooling and to tertiary institutions in so far as they engage in the same kinds of learning? Elsewhere we have argued that the first question should be answered in terms of a general or liberal education and that it should be possible for everyone to achieve the minimum desirable level by the end of Year 10.[25] (There would need to be a substantial reform of what schools actually do in the name of liberal education.) While there are fundamental continuities between the earlier stages and the programme in Years 11 and 12, the latter should include more specialized work and give attention to 'second order' questions about the way in which particular kinds of knowledge are tested and developed. Years 11 and 12 deepen the intellectual skills and broad introductory knowledge of the humanities, arts and sciences acquired by the end of Year 10. If this is done well, it should provide a more thorough general education for anyone who completes Year 12 and at the same time lay an adequate foundation for the work of higher education.

The main consequence of the position just outlined is that, after Year 10, further secondary schooling should be only one of several constructive options open to young people.[26] Other options would include: full-time vocational education (with some component of related liberal studies); part-time employment and part-time study (whether in liberal or vocational education); and opportunities through community service or normal employment for breaks from full-time schooling. To provide a number of these choices our society needs more flexible conditions for the employment of young people. In relation to educational programmes, we need to encourage a diversity of educational forms: Years 11 and 12 as part of a secondary school; separate institutions at this level; those that emphasize vocational studies; and others that offer a comprehensive range of liberal and vocational studies and are open to students of all ages. With appropriate adjustments to its programmes, TAFE can contribute significantly to the desirable variety of educational options.[27]

Following the Blackburn report (1985), the Victorian government is busily engaged in implementing a policy that works in the opposite direction to the one stated. The objective is to have all older adolescents in the same kind of institution (the senior secondary school) engaged in a programme of general education subject to a common curriculum framework and other conditions on which the award of a common certificate depends. No attention is being given to alternatives other than staying in full-time schooling, and the choice between general and vocational education is being actively discouraged. There even seems to be an unwillingness among the designers of the new programme to recognize the diversity of abilities and interests that at present exists among students in Years 11 and 12 and this will be greatly magnified if the policy of full participation succeeds. It is curious that at a time when universities and colleges acknowledge that their expectations should not apply to everyone at school in Years 11 and 12, the policy being implemented is in favour of one kind of programme for everyone.

The drive for conformity is encouraged by many advocates of the ideal of equal group outcomes. Their objective is furthered if, as in the case of a subject designated as a common course, differences in the kind and level of work done are blurred. There is a paternalistic reluctance to allow 16- and 17-year-olds to choose different types of educational pro- grammes because of the inevitable consequences such choice has for later opportunities. What fairness requires is that everyone who wishes to pursue systematic discipline-based studies in Years 11 and 12 should have adequate opportunity to do so. Apart from the direct educational benefits, such studies form the background for entry to higher education. Our society also needs to provide adequate opportunities for adults who wish to take different educational paths from those which they followed after Year 10.

ENTRY TO HIGHER EDUCATION: SELECTION AND CURRICULAR ISSUES

A large proportion of students in universities and colleges enrol directly from secondary school. Most of those admitted in other categories have completed some work at Year 12 or equivalent. To maintain a good standard in higher education, these institutions depend on an adequate introduction to systematic knowledge and intellectual skills being achieved by the end of Year 12. Various subjects (such as mathematics, physical sciences and languages) build directly on earlier work. Universities and colleges have an immediate interest, therefore, in the kind and quality of educational programmes undertaken by those senior secondary students who aspire to higher education. Scholars in the various disciplines also have a professional concern for the quality of what is taught in the name of academic subjects, regardless of the links with further study. There should be no question of universities and colleges determining the whole curriculum of the senior secondary school, but the recent tendency to treat them as intruders or, at best, simply another interest group, radically misunderstands the overlap of educational purposes between the institutions at the two levels. It seems that universities and colleges (and tertiary institutions more generally) will need to set out their expectations much more clearly – not only for those areas in which there is direct continuity, but also in relation to the common background of historical knowledge of social and cultural movements that is assumed, general skills of literacy and numeracy, abilities in the reading and writing of expository prose and the skills and attitudes needed for independent study. Perhaps the best balance between the needs of higher education and the freedom of secondary schools is for relevant subjects to be designed with a detailed core of common studies and a broadly outlined range of electives.

The selection of applicants for higher education raises even more serious problems than the question of appropriate content at Years 11 and 12.[28] It is not simply that there are too few places in total for the number of qualified applicants. Even if this were not the case, there would still be intense competition. Most applicants have an order of preference among institutions and courses. In most universities and colleges there are at least some courses, usually leading to the highly regarded occupations, where the demand far exceeds the places available. The level of need in a society for the latter, and the cost of training, constrain the number admitted to these courses. At present most students who qualify for the Higher School Certificate (or equivalent) apply for entry to a university or college. With the rising retention rate the proportion of those applying may decline, but the actual number will increase. According to one recent prediction, enrolments in higher education in 1992 are likely to be 25 per cent above the 1982 level.[29] Apart from the other problems which this increasing enrolment may engender, the issue of selection will become even more acute.

The main criteria for a satisfactory process of selection are that it should make a fair comparison among applicants in relation to their expressed preferences, that it should be based primarily on evidence of knowledge and skills relevant to work in higher education, that it should not unnecessarily constrain the practice of education in secondary schools, that it should be reasonably economical in cost and time and that it should be as uncomplicated as possible. In addition to questions about how adequately various methods of selection meet these criteria, there are two other aspects of selection that are being raised with increasing insistence. There is resentment over the restriction that external assessment places on curricular design in the secondary school and on the freedom of teachers in the process of assessment. Supporters of the policy of proportional representation for designated groups in higher education challenge selection based simply on individual performance and want procedures (such as group quotas) that offset what they see as systematic disadvantage. In addition to academic achievement, characteristics of personal suitability are no doubt relevant for the practice of various professions (such as medicine, teaching, counselling) to which degree programmes lead. However, as a basis for excluding applicants from entering a programme, they should be applied only in clear-cut cases.

It is clear that universities and colleges will need to review their selection procedures and be prepared to justify publicly what they do. In relation to such a review the following general points should be considered:

(a) There are various ways in which common tests can be combined with internal assessment to provide reasonably comparable results across a large number of schools.

(b) For applicants whose academic performance places them near the threshold for selection, it would be desirable to use several indicators of ability and aptitude for the final selection.

(c) Sub-quotas for qualified applicants from certain groups may be justified.

(d) For highly competitive courses it would be desirable, where possible, to base selection on work done during the first year or two of a more general course at university or college level.

(e) Within each state the institutions of higher education should agree on the selection procedures that directly affect the senior secondary school and adopt prerequisites that are consistent for the same kinds of courses.

Another important aspect of the selection process is the decision students make on their preferences for courses and institutions. In regard to courses that are directly related to an occupation, a number of the factors that influence choice – such as conditions of work, income, social prestige – are outside the control of educational agencies. However there needs to be a much more systematic and concerted effort by schools, tertiary institutions and vocational associations to help secondary students from early in Year 10 to make informed and realistic choices about further studies.

For various reasons, of which methods of selection are only one, there have been significant changes over the past two decades or so in the educational characteristics of students entering universities and colleges. In part these are the consequence of changes in the secondary school curriculum, such as less sustained sequential work (clearly detrimental for subjects such as mathematics, languages and sciences) and the decline in the study of history and literature. In part they are due to the increasing proportion of each age group engaging in higher education and to the relative number being admitted on special grounds (such as mature age and social disadvantage). While the comparison of standards over time is difficult to make, very few experienced academics would doubt that in certain areas there has been a clear decline among first-year students as a group. It is probably most obvious in the skills of written English.

There is an urgent need for universities (and perhaps colleges) to review thoroughly the content and teaching methods of first-year courses. It has recently been suggested that, as in the United States, our general bachelor programmes should extend over four rather than three years. This may eventually become necessary. But it would be preferable to work at improving the quality of secondary education and to provide a preliminary year at university for students who satisfy the general conditions for selection but are deficient in subjects that are crucial for the programmes they wish to follow. If the programme were expanded to four years, the first could be a general preliminary year which appropriately qualified students would not be required to take. At the same time universities should ensure that they are offering an adequate advanced or honours programme for students seriously interested in scholarly work, and not simply in a general or vocational degree. It would be desirable for such programmes to begin in the first year.

A more complex question – one that has not been very intently addressed by Australian universities – is how to develop an appropriate level of common intellectual culture among their students.[30] The ideal is now more remote with the proliferation of optional subjects, narrowly specialized studies and a slackening of the structure of degree programmes. There are fundamental and unresolved problems about bringing the sciences and humanities together in a common liberal education and about the place of liberal studies in professional degrees. In at least the first year of higher education there is need for a number of structured common courses that enable students to study significant developments in the humanities, arts and sciences within an historical context and in relation to several major contemporary themes. In each main area of liberal education there should be appropriate courses for non-specialists. In many cases these could be integrated with studies in professional programmes.

Although the balance may be somewhat different, the place that liberal studies have in the professional or vocational programmes of colleges and TAFE also needs to be more closely examined. Every field of specialized study (from English to computer programming) should be related to a broader context of human values and experience. This is particularly important when the main object of study is a set of technical skills. Students should gain at least some awareness of the history of the practices in which the skills have developed, the aspects of the cultural and social context most closely related to the exercise of the skills and the kinds of moral issues that practitioners may have to face. In conditions of rapidly advancing technology, there is a more pressing need to acquire knowledge for interpreting and evaluating the uses to which the technical skills are put.

THE BINARY SYSTEM OF HIGHER EDUCATION

As we saw earlier, the commonwealth government formally established a clearly defined binary system of higher education in 1965. The related recommendation of the Martin report was not strictly followed. It envisaged, in addition to universities, both technological colleges and teachers' colleges. On the curriculum for colleges, it stressed the need for technical training to be related to appropriate liberal studies. It emphasized, however, that colleges should not try to replicate the methods and programmes of universities as this would defeat the basic objective of introducing greater diversity into Australian higher education. The report said little on the distinctive nature and role of colleges in relation to universities. Apart from suggesting that colleges should be concerned mainly with diploma courses, it saw the major difference as 'the greater emphasis on the practical and applied aspects of the subjects of technical colleges as opposed to the more general and analytical treatment developed at the university'.[31]

In the course of their development the distinctiveness of colleges in relation to universities has become more blurred than in 1965. For example, the educational characteristics and aspirations of students in each sector are not remarkably different, and colleges now offer a wide variety of degree programmes, including master's level programmes. Still there are important differences. University staff, unlike their college counterparts, are expected to conduct research as a normal part of their duties,[32] the formal academic qualifications of university staff are generally higher and the conduct of PhD degrees is still the preserve of universities.

At present the kinds of research appropriate to universities and other institutions, and their funding, are under close scrutiny. The case is being made for colleges to have a greater part in research and its funding and to run PhD programmes. We are also entering a period where the demand for places in higher education is likely to increase substantially. Despite the difficulties and frustrations of the task, it would therefore be opportune to review the kind of basic diversity we need in higher education.

Although the issue is by no means straightforward, there are several important characteristics that give a sound basis for a distinction between universities and other institutions of higher education. These have to do with comprehensiveness in the range of disciplines and fields of study; the relative emphases given to systematic theoretical knowledge, applied theory and practical training; the extent to which the academic role requires both teaching and research; and the degree of responsiveness to local needs that is expected. Although the characteristics admit of varying degrees and combinations they point to two broadly different types of institution. But they also suggest important variations that might be encouraged within each type, such as independent professional schools in relation to universities and specialized research institutes associated with either universities or colleges. Rather than seeking to dismantle the binary system, we need to ensure that it is interpreted more flexibly.

THE INDEPENDENCE OF UNIVERSITIES

If academics are to realize the intellectual values that are the basic point of a university's existence they need substantial independence in their work, individually and collectively. To many academics, and others, it seems that a new threat to this independence is now taking shape. It is loosely called 'privatization', a process that extends from the charging of fees in public institutions to the setting up of private universities and colleges.[33] Although privatization is attacked on various grounds, one basic criticism of all its forms is that the proper independence and detachment of institutions and academics are seriously threatened. In the case of the proposed Bond University, staff associations and the commonwealth Department of Education were united in their instant disapproval.

The reaction against what goes by the name of privatization is too sweeping and uncritical. It seems that some opponents simply take it as a self-evident truth that there should be no engagement in education not wholly supported by public funds.[34] No doubt the desire to maintain a roughly equal and uniform system exerts a strong influence, although the prospect of different salary scales may bring the principle of envy rather than fairness into play. Some of the grounds on which the enthusiasm for privatization is based are clearly dubious, particularly the claimed benefits of submitting higher education to market forces.

(Judged on educational criteria, their operation within the public system has not been encouraging.) But there is nothing in the nature of fee paying, private funding for research, selling educational services to overseas students or private ownership of institutions that necessarily debases standards or undermines the independence and integrity of academics. Without proper safeguards and vigilance any of the forms of privatization may, of course, have these and other undesirable effects. State and commonwealth governments should ensure that appropriate general conditions are established and observed. In regard to details, the academics directly involved should examine each proposal on its merits and see to it that the independence necessary for their work is adequately protected.

The source of an institution's funding is irrelevant to the question of its intellectual quality. What counts are the standing of its staff in the disciplines they profess, the conditions required for the award of degrees and the reputation of its graduates.

The encouragement, with appropriate safeguards, of private funding and initiatives, far from hindering the well-being of higher education in Australia, seems to have clear advantages. The most obvious of these is the additional resources that would be provided. Over the past ten years government funding in real terms per student has declined by 8 per cent in higher education. (For the same period there has been a 50 per cent increase per school student.)[35] The present shortage of places and the rising retention rate to Year 12 make it fairly clear that an adequate expansion of higher education in Australia will need private as well as public funding. But there could also be advantages in the way of educational innovation and challenge that might shake up the complacent sameness of the present system.

While the varieties of privatization hold dangers for academic independence if implemented uncritically, there are other developments that are, or could be, greater dangers. In the intense reaction to the proposals for privatization these should not be overlooked. Here attention will be drawn briefly to three of them.

The present public system, with all funding and related policy-making concentrated in the commonwealth government, itself unduly limits the independence of universities and colleges. For efficiency and accountability in the use of public funds some regulation and coordination of the work of universities (and colleges) is obviously necessary. But there are serious limits on how far this can go before it begins to defeat the distinctive purposes for which universities exist. At the extreme, individual universities lose any distinctive character and become like clones, or else diverse parts of a single entity. As the central bureaucratic structure that controls the whole system increases, the administrative bureaucracy within each university becomes larger and more powerful. The consequence is a decline in the collegial role that academics should play in shaping the policies of their field and the institution of which it is (or should be) an integral part.

Staff associations have been vehement opponents of privatization as a threat to academic independence. Yet, ironically, the Federation of Australian University Staff Associations is eagerly pursuing the 'industrialization' of universities, an outcome that also threatens academic independence. A body sponsored by the Federation has sought and gained federal registration as a union; and a body representing universities has secured registration as an industrial association of employers. There may eventually be several professional associations representing sections of academic staff before the Conciliation and Arbitration Commission.

An obvious consequence of these 'moves' is the strengthening of centralized decision-making in which universities are treated as part of a single entity. Employment conditions, whether of tutors or professors, cannot be neatly separated from questions about the conduct of teaching and research and how a university should fulfil its distinctive role. Because of this, and the artificial division it sets up between employers and employees in a university, industrialization strikes another blow at the ideal of collegial control of a university. To the extent that corporate decision-making in a university is deficient on matters affecting conditions of employment, it needs to be strengthened. It is not a satisfactory solution to refer such matters to an external body before whom academics appear in the industrial categories of employers and employees.[36]

A more subtle threat to academic independence comes from those within the universities who espouse various forms of radical epistemological relativism. If what we call knowledge is largely a reflection and instrument of group interests (class, ethnicity, gender etc.) in the struggle to hold or gain political and economic power, there is no significant common ground of intellectual values against which the proper neutrality and commitment of the university can be assessed.

CONCLUSION

A theme that has recurred in our discussion of the contemporary practice of education in Australia is the extent of uniformity in its control and content. There are, of course, aspects of educational practice in which uniformity is desirable and others in which it is at least unavoidable (such as the common conditions that must be set for the responsible use of public funds). Nor, as stressed earlier, is diversity in education a good simply for its own sake. But the nature of education is such that we must do more at virtually all levels to shift the locus of detailed decisions on its content and organization from the systemic level to that of individual institutions. Although state and commonwealth governments need to set general objectives and guidelines for the sake of the public good and the protection of individuals, high-quality education can be achieved in institutions of varying size, with quite different patterns of curriculum and administrative control, established through public or private initiative, and so on. In our attitude to the provision of education we will have to overcome what seems to be a bias to conformity in our cultural tradition and a simplistic confidence in the efficacy of central government planning.

There is another aspect of narrowness in our thinking about education – one that we share with other industrial societies. We have tended to confuse schooling with the whole of education, and we have an immense faith in the power of the school to deliver solutions to our social and economic problems. As consequences of this faith most young people spend an increasing number of years in the traditional pattern of full-time schooling and the range of educational and other activities in which schools are expected to engage continually expands. Writing about America in the early 1960s, Paul Goodman commented: 'it is simply a superstition, an official superstition and a mass superstition, that the way to educate the majority of the young is to pen them up in schools during their adolescence and early adulthood'.[37] As he acknowledged, however, the credentialling process has fed on the superstition and has artificially produced a connection between longer schooling and access to many occupations. This is one reason why the releasing of educational institutions from the unrealistic burden they have come to bear is now an immensely difficult task.

Next to the valuing of formal education as an instrument of national economic affluence, most weight has been placed on its supposed power to produce true equality of opportunity. As already noted, this ideal, mixed in with the quite different one of a more equal society, has been a basic educational policy of commonwealth governments since the early 1970s. At several points in this chapter, we have referred to the present form that the policy of equal opportunity and outcomes takes: the proportional representation of designated groups at the various levels of education, occupation, political power, and so on. Consistent with the other values that are at stake, we should certainly do all that is possible to guarantee all members of our society a fair opportunity to satisfy their needs and interests in formal education and to acquire the other goods to which education gives access. There has, however, been a strong tendency in Australia (and elsewhere) to exaggerate the capacity of educational institutions to promote ideals of equality. This fixation on schooling has distracted attention from the need for a more sustained direct attack on the gross forms of economic inequality and the social conditions that systematically deny particular groups equal opportunities for commonly desired goods. It also leads to the distortion of educational values by the desperate measures that are sometimes adopted (such as certain uses of admission quotas, treatment of all student interests as of equal educational worth and assessment that blurs the difference between personal effort and intellectual achievement). In addition to encouraging an exaggerated view of the school, and straining its capacities, the quest for equality in and through education has been another powerful source of opposition to diversity in educational practice. Inequality seems to be more manageable when everyone attends the same kind of school (and university) in a single, centrally controlled system.

The expansion of education in Australia over the past few decades has been a significant achievement. To enhance its quality and attain other social objectives more adequately we must be more imaginative about both the possibilities and the limitations of schooling. On the first, there is need for tolerance and encouragement of diversity in the ways of organizing and engaging in formal education; on the second, there is need for a concerted effort to find more appropriate means for dealing with the personal and social problems of the young and to develop worthwhile forms of work for adolescents and young adults as alternatives to an extended engagement in schooling. These are fundamental themes for reflection as our nation reaches its second century.

Notes

[1] The statistics have been drawn, for the most part, from public reports and inquiries, mainly those of the Commonwealth Schools Commission and Tertiary Education Commission. I note, in particular, Commonwealth Schools Commission, 1984. *Australian Schools Statistics*. Canberra Publishing and Printing Co.

I am also indebted to the following: Australian Council for Educational Research, 1964. *Review of Education in Australia 1955-62*. Hawthorn, Vic., ACER; Australian Council for Educational Research, 1953. *The Non-Government Schools of Australia: A Descriptive and Statistical Account*, compiled by W.C. Radford, Melbourne, Melbourne University Press; A. Barcan, 1980. *A History of Australian Education*. Melbourne, Oxford University Press; D. Clark, Fortress Australia at the Crossroads. *Financial Review*, five part series, 4-8 August 1986; R.M. McDonnell, W.C. Radford and P.M. Staurenghi, 1956. *Review of Education in Australia 1948-1954*. Melbourne, ACER; *Official Yearbook of the Commonwealth of Australia*, Canberra, AGPS. (*Yearbook Australia* since 1977.); P.H. Partridge, 1968. *Society, Schools and Progress*. Oxford, Pergamon Press. Barcan and Partridge offer very useful comments on the development of Australian educational institutions and the guiding ideas. Several topics I have mentioned in this chapter are discussed more fully in *Changing Ideas in Australian Education*, Hawthorn, Vic., ACER, 1981.

[2] R. Twopenny, 1973 (1883). *Town Life in Australia*. Ringwood, Vic., Penguin Books (first published London, Elliot Stock), p.145.

[3] In 1943 the minimum leaving age was set at 16 in Tasmania and 15 in New South Wales. In the mid-1960s all other states adopted 15 as the minimum age.

4   The apparent retention rate is an estimate of how many of those who begin secondary school at the same time continue to the senior years (10-12). In 1962, a further (sixth) year was added to the secondary school in NSW. It had existed in some states for students who wished to matriculate. All states now have a preparatory grade plus 12 years of primary–secondary schooling, although there are some variations over the year at which secondary schooling begins.

5   From the mid-70s the Australian economy reflected a general slackening of growth in Western economies. The unemployment rate rose sharply in 1975. It was most severe among the younger age groups, especially the 15- to 19-year-olds. In this group the rate rose from 4.2 per cent in 1974 to 10.1 per cent in 1975 and 17 per cent in 1980. The labour market and other economic factors no doubt affected the participation rate of young people in higher education. For discussion, see Commonwealth Tertiary Education Commission, 1982. *Learning and Earning.* Canberra, AGPS, Vol.2, Appendix B, pp.79-165 (by M. Hayden).

6   The recommendation for an alternative form of higher education was made in the report of the Committee on the Future of Tertiary Education in Australia (Chairman, L.H. Martin), 1964. *Tertiary Education in Australia,* Melbourne, Government Printer, Vol.1, chs. 5 and 6. The commonwealth's role in relation to universities had been shaped by the Committee on Australian Universities (Chairman, K.A.H. Murray), 1957. *Report.* Canberra, Government Printer.

7   Australian Committee on Technical and Further Education (Chairman, M. Kangan), 1974. *TAFE in Australia.* Canberra, AGPS. A recent inquiry has made further important recommendations on TAFE programmes: *Report of the Committee of Inquiry into Labour Market Programs* (Chairman, P.E. Kirby). Canberra, AGPS, 1985. See also *Education and Technology*, Report of Australian Education Council Taskforce on Education and Technology. Melbourne, AEC, 1985.

8   Since this chapter was prepared, the commonwealth government has taken significant steps towards greater central control and uniformity, especially in higher education. After the return of the Labor government in the 1987 federal election, a super-ministry of Employment, Education and Training was established under a new Minister, Mr J.S. Dawkins. In October, Mr Dawkins announced that the Schools Commission and the Tertiary Education Commission would be abolished and replaced by an inclusive body with strong representation from business and industry, The National Board of Employment, Education and Training. One consequence of this change is that the processes on which the development of policy for education depends will in future be located mainly within the government department.

In December 1987 the Minister issued a Green Paper on higher education. Its basic plan is to establish a 'unified national system' in which each institution is funded on the basis of a negotiation process with the government. The level of funding is to depend on the extent to which an institution is prepared to undertake teaching and research (and adopt admission, credit transfer and other procedures) that accord with government priorities. Funding levels are to be reviewed in the light of an institution's performance in meeting agreed objectives. Despite the differences of political ideology, this 'contracting' procedure and the economic instrumentalism on which priorities are based are very similar to what is embodied in the Conservative government's Bill on education at present before the British Parliament.

9   Quality of Education Review Committee (Chairman, P. Karmel) 1985. *Quality of Education in Australia.* Canberra, AGPS, p.187. For more details on commonwealth funding, see ch.2 of this report.

10   The Universities Commission was established in 1959. In 1977 the Tertiary Education Commission came into existence as the coordinating body for the three components of the tertiary sector (universities, colleges and TAFE).

11   See Ministry of Education, Victoria, 1986. *Taking Schools into the 1990s.* Melbourne, Government Printer; 1986. *The Government Decision on the Report of the Ministry Structure Project Team*, Melbourne, Government Printer.

12   G.V. Portus, writing a few decades earlier, thought there was practically no chance of a revival of state support for private schools. 'In my judgement it will take nothing short of a religious revolution to alter the minds of Australians on this question'. *Free, Compulsory and Secular*, Oxford University Press, 1937, p.26. For a brief account of the argument over the reintroduction of state funding, see M. Hogan, 1984. *Public versus Private Schools.* Ringwood, Vic., Penguin Books. This book gives details on the funding arrangements.

13   In 1984, the percentage of total enrolment in non-government schools for each major sector of schooling was: 22.9 (primary), 27 (junior secondary), 32.8 (Years 11 and 12). The comparable figures for 1982 were: 21.3, 26.2, 33.9, with 23.8 per cent of the total enrolment being in non-government schools.

14 Total recurrent expenditure per student (at December 1984 cost levels) is as follows:

	Government schools	Catholic schools	Non-Catholic schools
Primary	$2002	$1493	$2053
Secondary	$3124	$2401	$3087

See *Quality of Education in Australia*, paras. 2.12-13.

15   For many, smallness of scale is a matter of deliberate policy. See M. Norman 1980. *Small Schools Study.* A Report prepared for the Australian Schools Commission, October 1980.

[16] The Curriculum Development Centre was established as an independent body by the commonwealth government in 1975. Its status and budget were substantially reduced in 1982. For a time it operated as part of the commonwealth Department of Education. In 1984 it was placed under the Curriculum Development Council within the structure of the Schools Commission. It is now a unit within the commonwealth Department of Employment, Education and Training.

[17] I have discussed the content of a common core curriculum in *Cultural Pluralism and Common Curriculum*. Melbourne, Melbourne University Press, 1982, ch.5.

[18] Interim Committee for the Australian Schools Commission (Chairman, P. Karmel) 1973. *Schools in Australia*. Canberra, AGPS, para.2.13. The theme recurs in Schools Commission 1981. *Report for the Triennium 1982-84*. Canberra, Union Offset, paras.3.26-3.34.

[19] As noted earlier, male retention rates, particularly for government schools, declined somewhat during the middle 1970s. For females, the rate has been rising steadily and now exceeds that of males in each of the three senior years of the secondary school. There are sharp differences among the main types of school in retention to Year 12. For some time it has been around 90 per cent in non-Catholic private schools; Catholic schools increased their rate from 37.7 per cent in 1973 to 51.3 per cent in 1983; and in the same decade the rate in public schools rose from 27.9 to 33.77 per cent.

[20] I have referred to recent government policy in Secondary Education – Reshaping the Pattern. *Current Affairs Bulletin* 69(9), 1984, pp.26-30 and in Education after Year 10: The Role of the Secondary School. In Imelda Palmer (ed.) 1986. *Melbourne Studies in Education 1986*. Melbourne, Melbourne University Press, pp.116-19. Criticisms of extended schooling are discussed in The Identity Crisis in Secondary Education. *Australian Journal of Education* 25(2), 1981, pp.146-57.

[21] *Ministerial Review of Postcompulsory Schooling* (Chairperson, J. Blackburn) 1985 (2 vols.). Melbourne, Government Printer.

[22] G. Lehmann, in *The New Academy*, comments on such a use of schooling:

> How will we keep the unemployed employed?
> With instruction, not games,
> with books, not blood, I say.
> Like aqueducts the new academies will stand
> piping knowledge into our slums
> and will never end.

From P. Neilson (ed.) 1986. *The Penguin Book of Australian Satirical Verse*. Ringwood Vic. Penguin p.252.

[23] This is not simply, or even primarily, because they lack ability. For many it is a matter of having interests and abilities that are better served by doing something else. There is also restlessness to enter the adult world.

[24] In the United States, where the retention rate to the end of high school has been stable at around 70 per cent since the mid-1960s, three curriculum 'tracks' have developed in response to student choice. They are the academic (about 35 per cent of students), the vocational (about 25 per cent) and the general track (about 40 per cent). The last includes credit for work experience and for personal development courses such as training for marriage. Each track is itself a smorgasbord of electives. On the curriculum in American high schools and related matters, see D. Ravitch 1984. The Continuing Crisis: Fashions in Education. *The American Scholar*, Spring 1984, pp.183-93.

Despite the long experience of a high retention rate in high schools, the United States still has a high level of unemployment and gross disparities of income. The proportion entering college is impressive, but the pass rate is much less so. Even with 'grade inflation', at state universities it may be less than 50 per cent after five years.

[25] B. Crittenden 1986. Education after Year 10: The Role of the Secondary School. *op.cit.*, pp.126-40.

[26] Although the Schools Commission and the Blackburn report advocate full participation to the end of secondary schooling, both support some diversity of institutional form for Years 11 and 12. The former comments: 'To meet these needs [of a much more varied group of students] a much greater diversity of institutions is required, including some that would be experimental in the early stages'. *Report for the Triennium 1982-84*, para.5.35. The Blackburn report (para. 8.10) suggests three ways of modifying the present organization of the senior secondary years: complexes of existing schools, separate senior secondary colleges and all-age community colleges. These are clearly worth consideration, but they do not offer young people an alternative to continuing in full-time secondary schooling.

[27] There need to be the kinds of revision to TAFE programmes that are suggested in the Kirby report. Special attention should be given to the provision of appropriate liberal (or general) studies as part of a vocational education.

[28] In Victoria, for example, the Victorian Tertiary Admissions Centre received 43,539 applicants for 1986, of whom 21,857 took up places in universities and colleges. The applicants include 27,955 who had completed Year 12 in 1985. (Around 90 per cent of those who satisfied conditions for the HSC applied for entry to a university or college.) Around 5000 qualified applicants failed to gain a place.

While the majority of entrants have successfully completed Year 12 of secondary school, a substantial proportion are admitted in various other categories (including mature age). In some universities, these other categories account for over 40 per cent of enrolments. It should be noted that universities and colleges already use a variety of selection procedures in addition to Year 12 examination results – for example, interviews, aptitude tests, supplementary essays, folios of work in art etc. and teachers' reports.

[29] In *Quality of Education in Australia*, it is suggested that enrolments in higher education will increase by 25 per cent by 1992.

[30] I have discussed the question of liberal studies and universities in *Liberal Education and the Advancement of Common Learning: Some Lessons from America on the Role of Universities*. Occasional Paper No.4, Centre for Study of Curriculum and Teacher Education, School of Education, La Trobe University, 1983.

[31] Martin report, para.5.136. See also para.6.75.

[32] Over 95 per cent of public funding for research has been going to universities.

[33] For a balanced discussion of privatization and higher education, see D. Smart 1986. The Financial Crisis in Australian Higher Education and the Inexorable Push Towards Privatization. *The Australian Universities' Review* 29(2), pp.16-21.

[34] On the question of fee paying, it is now often assumed that the reintroduction of any system of fees would violate a basic moral right. Although there are public benefits to be calculated, those who attend universities and colleges do gain considerable personal advantages: a substantial public subsidy for what they choose to do, generally improved opportunities for employment and higher income and the cultural benefits of a higher education – all this, with no account taken of socioeconomic background or actual income or whether a student is undertaking a first or a further degree. A general policy of free higher education can perhaps be justified in our society, but the case should certainly not be regarded as self-evident or as a matter of inviolable right.

[35] The statistics are set out in D. Smart 1986. *op. cit.*, p.21.

[36] For a recent discussion of some of the issues in the industrialization of universities, see the articles by I. Palmer and J.F. Scott in *The Australian Universities' Review* 29(2), 1986. The Australian Association of University Staff gained registration as an organization of employees in November 1986.

[37] P. Goodman 1964. *Compulsory Mis-education and The Community of Scholars*. New York, Vintage Books, p.140.

5

*Changing Attitudes and Values in Post-war Australia**

F.L. Jones

This chapter was begun with the initial ambition to trace historically general patterns of the ways in which the values and attitudes of ordinary Australians have changed since the end of World War II. This period is one during which there have been major changes in Australian society – its ethnic composition, economic fortunes, political complexion and family life have changed substantially. So have attitudes towards many social and moral issues such as abortion, censorship, divorce and capital punishment, to mention only a few.

However the information needed to document such changes do not exist in a form comprehensive enough to describe the detail of changing values and attitudes across a range of social issues over the last four decades. Let me give just one example. The social psychologist, Norman Feather, pioneered a programme of systematic research into the value systems espoused by contemporary Australians. In a series of studies he compared parental values with those of their children, women with men and native-born Australians with persons born in different countries.[1] Valuable as his work is, it covers only a few years of the period with which this chapter is concerned. Impressionistic accounts, such as those contained in works by Pringle,[2] Horne,[3] McGregor,[4] Conway[5] and others provide an even less certain basis for inferring general trends, although they offer insights into changing views about the Australian character.

The only source of *continuous* information on the behaviour, opinions and values of ordinary Australians from all walks of life is the series of Australian public opinion (Gallup) polls conducted from 1941 onwards, first by the Roy Morgan Research Centre and more recently by the McNair-Anderson market research company. Despite gaps in the record, in terms of both the data that have survived to the present day and their subject-matter, these surveys are a mine of information. They record how the Australian public viewed different issues that confronted them in their daily lives as private individuals and as citizens (the early surveys included electors only). There are, however, at least two problems in using these polls for trend analysis.

The first problem is that not all the polls were archived. Although there were commercial surveys at regular intervals from 1941 onwards, only a fraction of the original data survives for re-analysis today. There is, however, a comprehensive set of such holdings in Australia,

*I hereby acknowledge with gratitude the assistance of the Social Science Data Archives at the Australian National University in providing the data sets on which the analyses have been based. The original studies were conducted by the Roy Morgan Research Centre; McNair Anderson Associates; and the Australian Values Steering Committee. The original investigators bear no responsibility for further analysis of these data. The studies actually used were: SSDA Studies Nos. 78, 79, 85, 86, 98, 99, 100, 161, 395 and 375.

those held by the Social Science Data Archives (SSDA) at the Australian National University. These holdings comprise at present 224 polls from 1943 to 1983 (SSDA Bulletin, No. 11, August 1987). Their coverage is more complete for later than for earlier years.

The second limitation of these surveys for trend analysis is that they were mainly designed to monitor public reaction to highly topical issues confronting government, business and community leaders at the time. There is, therefore, little continuity in the questions asked, with the notable exception of voting behaviour and voting intention – the central focus of Gallup Polls the world over.[6] We therefore cannot ask of these data: What exactly did the Australian people think about, say, the existence of God in the late 1940s compared with the 1960s and the 1980s?, because such a question was not asked at regular intervals. Moreover opinions on some topical issues are bound to be volatile and susceptible to change as a result of media attention and public debate. The evidence for voting intention presented below, however, suggests that volatility affects absolute levels of support for, or against, particular issues, rather than the underlying structure of association of differences between groups.

One way to minimize these problems is to proceed more descriptively – by looking for cleavages of opinions across groups that may have weakened or strengthened over time. For the sake of economy in presenting the results three historical 'slices' have been taken, beginning with the late 1940s and ending in the early 1980s, with an intermediate cut in the mid-1960s. This timespan has the advantage of beginning and ending with comparative studies of public opinion conducted in several countries, the results of which are available in book form. Regrettably the original records for the first survey, Buchanan's and Cantril's *How Nations See Each Other*,[7] have not survived. Thus it is not possible to rework their data. However we can extend their findings, at least for Australia, with some opinion polls taken around the same time. After discussing the main contours of public opinion in the late 1940s, the surveys from the mid-1960s will be discussed before coming finally to the Values Study of 1983 – a survey carried out in almost thirty countries in the early 1980s.[8]

For reasons already mentioned exact comparisons cannot be made over the years. But comparisons are possible for specific social, moral and political issues for each period in terms of the major structural cleavages that characterized Australian society at the time. Such cleavages include region (the urban/rural divide), religion (largely Protestant *v* Roman Catholic, especially at the beginning of the period), generation or cohort, gender, social class (defined in terms of occupation and two indicators of economic position, phone and car ownership) and voting behaviour. Data on these characteristics were routinely collected in the Gallup Polls over this period.

AUSTRALIAN PUBLIC OPINION, 1948–49

Buchanan and Cantril, writing of the results of the 1948 comparative surveys, reported that, of all the nine national groups represented in their sample, Australians expressed the highest degree of economic security (other nationalities surveyed were the British, French, West Germans, Italians, Mexicans, Dutch, Norwegians and Americans). Australians also rated high on Buchanan's and Cantril's index of national satisfaction. Only the Americans scored a higher rating. They also judged that Australia had a loose class structure compared with most of the European countries, but not as loose as Norway or the United States.[9] When Australians were asked which foreign people they felt most friendly towards, three out of five (somewhat surprisingly) nominated the Americans. But this was probably because the pollsters told Australians that, in answering this question, they should not think of the British as foreigners. Australians' emotional ties to Britain weakened later as defence needs, trade exchanges and even immigration flows focussed increasingly on southeast Asia and the nations of the Pacific rim. Nonetheless memories of vital American support in the Pacific during World War II must have been fresh in many Australians' minds.

Although Australians rated high in terms of national satisfaction, they placed their federal government farthest to the 'Left' of any of the nations surveyed: over half (54 per cent) thought their government was too far to the 'Left'. This level of implied disapproval far exceeded that in any other country, including those where many thought their government too far to the 'Right' (as in Italy, for example). Most Australians saw themselves and their compatriots as peace-loving, generous, brave and intelligent, a stereotype shared with most other nations. Compared with Australians, however, all the other nationals (except the Norwegians) rated themselves collectively as more hard-working. The French and Italians rated themselves highest on intelligence, while the Germans and Italians rated themselves as less peace-loving. The Americans had the most positive self-image of any of the nations surveyed.[10]

These descriptive findings say little about what divided the citizens of each nation. For evidence about that it is more instructive to look at other opinion polls addressed specifically to local issues, focussing on a selection of items taken from three polls conducted in Australia in 1948 and 1949. Details of each survey can be found in the relevant SSDA Catalogue.[11] For reasons of space all the results cannot be presented but mainly indicative figures are provided, together with some illustrative material. Items selected deal with social and moral issues and with the degree of government involvement in the economy. Two prominent trends of the post-war period relate to the liberalization of codes of personal behaviour and increasing government intervention in the economy.

Australia in the late 80s is officially a multicultural society. It was not so in 1948, when the native-born majority expected 'New Australians' to assimilate rapidly to the dominant British-Australian culture. The change in self-perception from a culturally uniform to a culturally diverse society resulted from immigration policies initiated immediately after World War II by the Australian Labor Party (ALP). Early in the post-war period the ALP government adopted a policy of large-scale immigration that went beyond traditional dependence on Britain to include, in time, bilateral agreements with European countries which before the war had contributed only small numbers of new settlers. In 1947 the federal government also concluded an agreement with the International Refugee Organization under which many thousands of displaced persons arrived from war-torn Europe. As a result, in 1949, the year in which the ALP lost federal office and began a spell of almost a quarter of a century on the opposition benches, 170,000 permanent new settlers arrived in Australia, half of them refugees from parts of Europe that had not previously been major sources of migration to Australia.

Given the bias in Australian policy in favour of British settlers and the strong antipathy towards non-European migration (the 'White Australia' policy), we may be surprised that the 'new' immigration policy commanded early and widespread community support. Of course the Labor government was well aware of the need to 'condition the Australian public' to a large influx of non-British settlers, and in the second half of 1946 it launched a public relations programme.[12] Three years later, in December 1949, the Gallup Poll asked Australians this question: 'As you know, many thousands of non-British immigrants, mostly displaced persons, have come to Australia from the continent of Europe since the

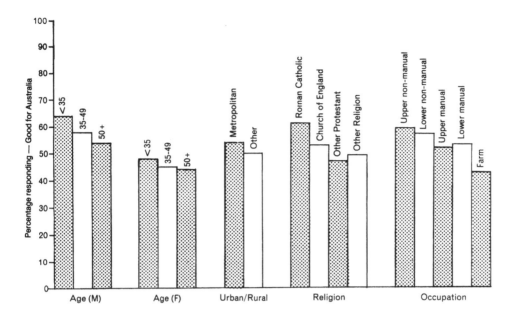

Figure 5.1 Attitudes to immigration of non-British settlers. (In the long run, do you think their coming here will be good, or bad, for Australia?) Poll taken 2 December 1949.

war. In the long run, do you think their coming here will be good, or bad, for Australia?' The findings are given in Figure 5.1, for different categories of respondents.

In the sample as a whole, a small majority (52 per cent) believed that non-British immigration from Europe would benefit Australia. Women were not so positive as men, nor were older Australians compared with young adults. For example only about two in five women over 50 years of age thought this policy would benefit Australia in the long run, compared with three out of four men under 35. Women and older people were more conservative.

As for rural/urban differences, people living in large cities were slightly more likely to favour non-British immigration than persons in smaller centres, with farmers being more conservative still. The organized labour movement tended to distrust large-scale immigration as a threat to working conditions, so manual workers did not favour non-British immigration as much as non-manual workers even though it was part of Labor policy. Religious differentials show Roman Catholics most in favour of the 'new' migration – reflecting Catholic anti-establishment tendencies and pro-Labor sympathies,[13] the humanitarian commitment of the Catholic hierarchy to refugee resettlement and their view that European immigration would strengthen Catholic elements in Australia.[14]

This level of community tolerance of non-British immigration did not of course extend to persons of non-European racial origins, and press reports criticised the deportation of the Asian spouses of Australians who had served, and married, while on overseas war service. The self-styled 'National Australian Newspaper', *The Bulletin*, proudly carried on its masthead the racist slogan, 'Australia for the White Man', a motto that persisted until the end of 1960 – when it was quietly dropped.[15] Nonetheless in the late 1940s even *The Bulletin* was capable of castigating the Labor immigration minister, Arthur Calwell, for inciting racial hatred through his insensitive application of the White Australia policy to partners of racially mixed marriages.[16] Needless to add, the plight of Australia's indigenous Aboriginal population was hardly yet on the political agenda.

Support for non-British immigration generally remained strong during the post-war period in the community at large and on both sides of politics. But one institution that did weaken over the period was formal religion both as an influence on personal behaviour and as a divisive force in Australian social and political life. It is difficult to imagine, for example, that anyone would now want to convene a symposium on 'Catholics and the Free Society', although it seemed eminently sensible to do so as recently as the early 1960s.[17] In the late 1940s sectarian sentiment was even stronger and the influence of religious belief on behaviour more pervasive. The opinion polls reflect these facts.

In December 1949 the Gallup Poll asked: 'Which do you think has had the greater influence on your own life – religion or politics?' Almost three out of five Australians said that religion had been a greater influence on their lives than politics. Religion was more important for women than for men, and for older people than the young. Almost three in every four women aged 50 or older rated religion a more important influence on their own lives than politics, compared with only one in every two men aged under 35. A similarly low ratio occurs among adherents of the Anglican church, due presumably to a high degree of nominalism. The middle classes were more likely than the working classes to choose religion as the stronger influence, as were those who lived outside the large cities.

The same survey included another question about how important religion and politics were as 'influences on the community in general'. The answers show that Australians believed religion was less important for others than it was for themselves. For every person who thought religion had a greater influence on the community in general, there was another who thought politics equally important (some, of course, answered 'neither' or 'both', and do not appear in these comparisons). This ratio of one to one contrasts sharply with the ratio of almost three to one who said that religion had been more important in their own lives. There seems to be a tendency for people to magnify the secular trend in the society at large, compared with their own experience. Perhaps, however, respondents were contrasting the past influence of religion in their own lives with the present influence of religion in the community at large.

Even though the Australian state school system is nominally secular, nine out of ten Australians in the late 1940s believed that children in state schools should be taught about 'God, Christ and the Bible' (question asked in May 1948). But opinion was split evenly between those that thought children should be taught separately by a visiting Minister of their own denomination and those who wanted children to be taught together by a specially trained teacher. There were age and religious differences as well. Older people were generally more in favour of separate instruction than younger people, and Roman Catholics were strongly in favour of separate instruction – even though most Catholic children went to separate parish schools anyway. Differences between occupational groups were, however, minimal.

Community attitudes to literary censorship also were less liberal then than now. In May 1948 the Gallup Poll asked: 'If the authorities consider a book to be obscene and unsuitable for adults, do you think it should, or should not, be banned?' Three out of every five persons endorsed the right of the authorities (state governments for books published locally, the

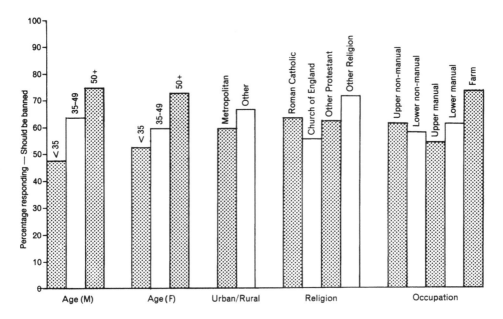

Figure 5.2 Attitudes to book censorship in Australia. (If the authorities consider a book to be obscene, do you think it should, or should not, be banned?) Poll taken 22 May 1948.

federal government for imported ones) to ban a book if they thought it obscene. While there was little difference between the attitudes of men and women, older persons were more likely to be censorious than persons under 35, who were more evenly divided in their opinions (see Figure 5.2).

Those who lived outside large cities and those who worked in farming were also more conservative on this issue, while nominal Anglicans were the most liberal of four religious groupings identified in these data. Even such an apparently innocuous question as being able to go to a picture theatre on a Sunday evening (question asked in December 1949) drew a largely negative response, with only two in five agreeing that 'picture theatres in the district should be open . . . on Sunday evenings'. In this regard women were more conservative than men. However the age gradient is more prominent, with older people more traditional than the young. Roman Catholics, having done their duty by the church earlier in the day, were more permissive than non-conforming Protestants, the reservoir of 'wowser' feeling about Sunday observance. Blue-collar workers were less opposed to Sunday night entertainment at the picture theatre than farmers, white-collar workers or residents of small towns.

So far the focus has been on issues where there seemed to be significant divisions of opinion. Now to an issue on which broad consensus existed: equal pay for women. For most of this century women in Australia received a specified fraction of the wage that a man received for doing similar work. In 1939 the ratio of a woman's basic wage award to a man's was 54 per cent. During the war many women were drawn into areas of work that had been the preserve of men. The government temporarily established a special wages tribunal, the Women's Employment Board, to recommend on the wages such women should receive.

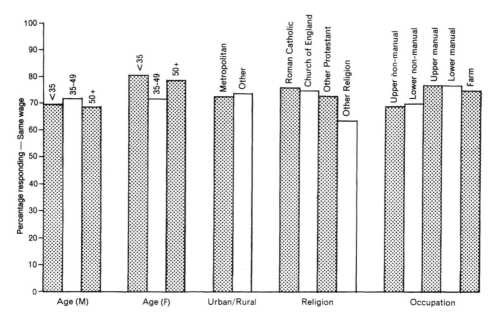

Figure 5.3 Attitudes to equal pay for women. (If a woman is doing the same kind of work as a man, and doing it as well, do you think she should be paid the same wage as a man – or less?) Poll taken 2 December 1949.

For women doing 'men's' work, the relativity became 90 per cent, and for women doing 'women's' work, 75 per cent. This second figure was ratified by the federal arbitration authorities in 1950 following an inquiry into the basic wage.[18] The weight of public opinion, however, was heavily in favour of full equality, as Figure 5.3 shows.

Three out of four Australians agreed with the proposition put to them in December 1949 that 'if a woman is doing the same kind of work as a man, and doing it as well . . . she should be paid the same wage'. While more women than men supported equal pay, support was general across all sociodemographic groups. It fell below two out of three only among adherents of 'other religions', who made up only 6 per cent of the population. However it took another three decades before the Arbitration Commission adopted the principle of equal pay. Public action lagged well behind public opinion because none of the government, employers or the trade union movement fully supported equal pay. The metal trades unions, whose wage claims instigated the inquiry by the Court, supported equal pay to eliminate existing discrimination.[19] However the Court believed not only that equal pay would put an intolerable strain on the economy but also that there were powerful social reasons why a (married) male worker should get a higher basic wage than an (unmarried) woman. In a majority decision the Court ruled against the employers' support of the pre-war relativity and legally sanctioned the 'going rate' of 75 per cent as socially and economically acceptable.[20]

Just one week after Australians offered these opinions to the Gallup Poll they voted the Labor government out of office. Among the reasons for Labor's defeat was its programme of national planning which attempted to go beyond the provision of social services to include the nationalization of key industries, especially banking.[21] The state of public opinion a week before the election can be gauged from answers to the question: 'If Labor wins the election, do you think the Federal Parliament should, or should not, go ahead with Labor's plan of nationalising some industries?' (poll of 2 December 1949). Only one in three Australians supported the nationalization plans of the Labor government. Support was weak across all age groups, and was especially weak among women. As we shall see later, women were less likely to support the ALP than men. Support was lower in the country than in the city, stronger among Catholics than among the adherents of other religions and closely related to occupational class. Manual workers, the electoral base of the ALP, were the strongest supporters of nationalization, but not even a majority of them were in favour of carrying out that part of ALP policy.

There was such mistrust of nationalization that it coloured opinions on free medical provision and prices and rent control, issues canvassed eighteen months earlier in May 1948. A bare majority favoured 'the Government's plan to provide free medicine, to be paid for from Social Service Contributions' (poll conducted on 22 May 1948), with opinion dividing along much the same lines as over nationalization and prices and rent controls (see Figure 5.4). These proposed controls were not particularly popular – especially among older persons, country residents, non-Catholics and the middle classes. A referendum on this issue the following weekend was, predictably, lost. Only two in every five voters supported the proposal, and it failed to gain a majority in any state of the commonwealth.

These opinion poll data reveal cleavages of opinion that are sharpest when they follow the contours of political debate at the time. Issues such as immigration and equal pay commanded more general community support than proposed government intervention aimed at restructuring the national economy and society. One way to highlight these

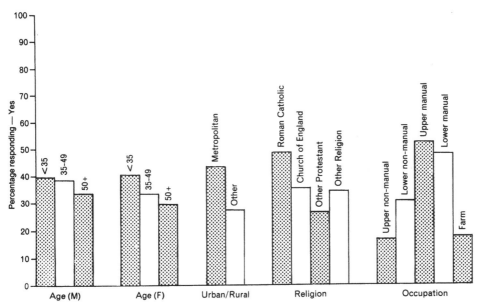

Figure 5.4 Attitudes to government prices and rent controls. (. . . are you likely to vote yes in favour or no against next Saturday's referendum giving Federal Parliament permanent power over Prices and Rents?) Poll taken 22 May 1948.

structural cleavages is to look at voting patterns in the late 1940s and at how they differed by age, sex, region, religion and social class.

Because this analysis is more complex than other analyses reported here, readers interested in technical detail should consult the more extended account.[22] Here we give only the broad results.

Assume that we sampled a thousand persons at random from the Australian electorate in the late 1940s, and that we knew nothing about them save that they had voted in the 1946 election and were eligible to vote in the December 1949 election. The best we could do to predict their voting preferences would be to say that they would lean marginally towards the ALP. Because 51 per cent of the electorate had voted ALP in 1946, or intended to vote ALP in 1949, our 'best guess' would be that any voter chosen at random would favour the ALP. Using this logic, we would be wrong almost as many times as we were right. On 511 occasions we would correctly identify a Labor supporter, but on the other 489 occasions we would be wrong.

By using survey data on the age, sex, occupation, religion and other characteristics of Australian voters we can improve substantially on this crude estimate. For example, between 1946 and 1949, overall support for the ALP declined by 10 percentage points. Both in 1946 and 1949, voters under 35 were more likely to be Labor supporters than older voters. Men were also more pro-Labor than women, as were urban dwellers compared with those who lived outside large cities. Labor support was strong among those who entered the electorate during the Depression and the Second World War, and weak among women and rural residents because it directed its appeal predominantly to the unionized labour force. There was, as well, a strong religious division, with Roman Catholics more likely to support Labor than Protestants. To the extent that Irish-Catholics perceived the conservative party as supporting Imperial ties and pro-establishment, the Labor party was their natural home.[23]

This religious division was quite independent of occupational class and economic differences, which further divide the electorate into opposing camps: the urban proletariat versus the middle and farming classes (the pro-Labor effect for those in farming is not significantly different from upper white-collar workers). Economic possessions also distinguished one class of voters from the other. Class and religious cleavages were strong. To give an extreme example, an unskilled Catholic man under 35, who lived in the inner-suburbs of Sydney or Melbourne and owned neither a phone nor a car, was virtually certain to vote ALP. The odds of such a man voting Labor were about 19 to 1. At the other extreme, an older non-conformist woman, married to the local doctor or bank manager in a country town, was very unlikely to vote Labor. The odds of her voting for the LCP were 50 to 1 in 1946 and 200 to 1 in 1949. Of course these extremes are illustrative only, and they represent small groups of voters. Nonetheless Australians that were alike in all respects except their nominal religious affiliation differed by 30 percentage points in their propensity to vote ALP rather than LCP, a difference matched by the division between blue-collar and white-collar workers. Competing class interests strongly divided the electorate, and so did religious loyalties.

PUBLIC OPINION AND CLASS VOTING IN THE MID-1960s

By the mid-1960s the Australian political scene had become more complicated than it was in the late 1940s. Following a major split in the ALP in 1955 (over Communist influence in the trade unions) a new Catholic-oriented, anti-Communist labour party (Democratic Labor Party, or DLP) emerged and attracted significant numbers of former ALP voters.[24] The ALP leader, H.V. Evatt, who had been associated publicly with Communist influence in the party through his role in the Petrov affair and his winking at unity tickets in trade union elections, was appointed Chief Justice of New South Wales early in 1960. His former deputy, Arthur Calwell, assumed the ALP leadership and almost led his party to victory in 1961. Five years later, however, the ALP suffered its worst defeat in the post-war period, polling only 40 per cent of the primary vote.[25] Calwell resigned his leadership and in 1967 his former deputy, Gough Whitlam, succeeded him. The Vietnam War was then taking its toll, domestically and overseas, with Australian regulars and conscripts supporting the American involvement. At this stage, however, public support for keeping Australian forces in Vietnam was widespread. According to the Gallup Poll, for every two persons in favour of bringing Australian forces home, there were five who favoured keeping them there. The tide of public opinion was soon to change.

In 1956 Australians saw the launching of a new medium, television. The world a year later witnessed the Russian launching of Sputnik and with it the inauguration of the space race. The first technical innovation consolidated trends towards mass culture and centralization, while the second produced in Australia and the West generally a drive to improve the quality and quantity of science education. In 1956 the Menzies government, already conscious of Australia's technological lag, had commissioned the Murray inquiry into higher education – an inquiry whose findings took on a special urgency after the Russian rocket launch a few weeks after its publication in September 1957. The Murray report 'was to have far-reaching significance for the Commonwealth not only in university but also ultimately in secondary, primary, and other tertiary education'.[26] Federal intervention in higher education is but one example of increasing central control in the economy and society.

One unanticipated consequence of the push for improved science education was that it served to revive the 'state aid' issue, an issue that had lain dormant since the turn of the century. Increased financial demands for science equipment, together with the pressure of providing new places for children born during the post-war baby boom, revived old claims from church (especially Catholic) schools for government money. Soon after its ideological split in the mid-1950s the ALP had abandoned its earlier policy of direct support for private schools in favour of one of indirect aid to students.[27] Not surprisingly when Calwell, a staunch Roman Catholic, succeeded Evatt to the ALP leadership in 1960, he was promptly criticized by the Catholic hierarchy for both the ALP's tenderness towards Communists and its failure to offer state aid to church schools.[28]

The 'religious issue', or sectarianism in Australian politics, once more became a regular feature of political commentaries in the Australian media. It reached crisis point in July 1962, when Catholic schools in Goulburn in southern New South Wales went on 'strike' and 1350 Catholic school children applied for entry to local state schools. The next year the NSW State Conference of the ALP resolved to ask the state government to provide science laboratories in all schools, a policy rejected later by the Federal Conference just as it was by the state government itself.[29] In stark contrast, the Menzies LCP government went to the polls with a promise of limited state aid for science laboratories and science teaching, a promise that helped it win the next election. It was only after Whitlam succeeded Calwell as ALP leader that the ALP abandoned its opposition to state aid. That policy shift largely defused the religious issue in Australian politics.

On the race relations front, the worldwide trend towards decolonization brought the White Australia policy under increasing attack. Public concern was also growing about the plight of Australia's indigenous 'colony', the Australian Aborigines. In 1961 the federal government established the Australian Institute of Aboriginal Studies largely, it must be said, to record the remnants of what was thought to be a dying culture. Two years later the Social Science Research Council, now the Academy of the Social Sciences in Australia, launched an ambitious project on Aborigines in Australian society under the direction of the late Charles Rowley.[30] In the same year the University of Sydney enrolled its first two students of Aboriginal descent, Charles Perkins led the 'Freedom Rides' through outback New South Wales and *The Bulletin* of 28 December 1963 hailed 1963 as the 'Year of the Breakthrough' for Aboriginal people. In 1967 the Australian people voted overwhelmingly in support of a referendum to remove the constitutional restriction on the federal government from making laws affecting the welfare of the Aboriginal people in any state and to repeal section 127 of the Constitution so that the census could count Aborigines among the Australian citizenry.[31]

How did the Australian people divide in terms of these and other issues in the mid-1960s? The Gallup polls around this time are mostly silent about race relations.[32] But whatever public opinion was then – or now – racial violence is far from gone. Interracial violence, on the streets and in public institutions, is still frontpage news. In 1987 the federal government announced a Royal Commission into the deaths of Aborigines held in custody in Australian prisons since 1980.[33] Calls for a treaty that recognizes Aborigines' historical land rights under the constitution have so far gone unheeded. The 'compact of understanding' proposed by the Prime Minister falls well short of Aboriginal demands.[34]

We will turn now to other aspects of government intervention, namely the economy. Findings come from three opinion polls conducted in February, July and September 1966. According to the data in Figure 5.4, in the late 1940s only a minority (a little over one-third) of the Australian population favoured federal control over prices and rents. By the mid-1960s Australians were much more tolerant of central intervention. In September 1966 the Gallup Poll asked: 'If a referendum were held to give the Federal Government power to control prices and interest rates, do you think you would probably vote Yes or No?' Close to two-thirds (63 per cent) answered 'Yes' to this question, and all major groupings in the community supported government intervention. The lowest level of support (53 per cent) came from traditionally conservative segments of the population such as upper white-collar workers. Most support (70 per cent) came from older men, skilled manual workers and the members of minor denominations. Other groupings ranged somewhere between these limits.

Because the Gallup Poll asked a similar question about price control in both periods it is interesting to compare the extent of convergence in opinion between social classes. In 1948 only one in six upper white-collar workers supported central control over prices and rents compared with about one in two blue-collar workers. By 1966 this gap had narrowed considerably (Figure 5.5). About one in two upper white-collar workers favoured central control over prices and interest rates, as did around two out of three blue-collar workers. Not only had public opinion as a whole shifted in favour of greater central intervention in the economy, but the division between classes had narrowed as well.

Similarly, on the question of state aid to church schools, the population by now expected a significant contribution from government. In February 1966, less than three years after the Menzies government had announced financial aid for science laboratories and science

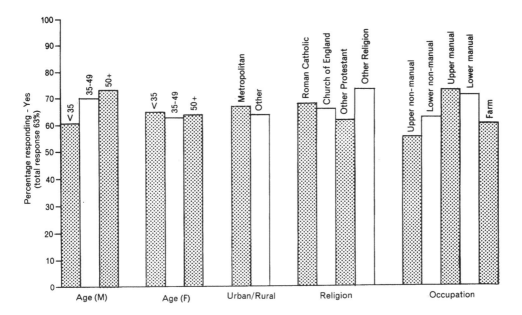

Figure 5.5 Attitudes to prices and interest rates control. (If a referendum were held to give the Federal Government power to control prices and interest rates, do you think you would probably vote Yes or No?) Poll taken 17 September 1966.

teaching, the Gallup Poll asked respondents if they were for, or against, government aid to church schools. A majority of 61 per cent was in favour. Among Catholics there was almost universal support (88 per cent), but fewer than half non-conformist Protestants (46 per cent) favoured federal aid. There were only minor differences by occupational class, age, sex or region of residence.

The residue of anti-Communist feeling from the 1950s was still apparent in attitudes to the admission of mainland China into the United Nations and to Australian military support in South Vietnam. In July 1966 the Gallup Poll asked whether Australians favoured China's admission to the United Nations or not. About two in five Australians were still opposed. Women were more opposed than men, especially those aged 35 or older. There was also more opposition among people living outside the capital cities, among Catholics and among the middle classes. Conservative voters were more opposed than Labor (but not DLP) voters. Even so in none of these groupings did a majority express opposition. The perceived Communist threat to Australia's foreign and domestic interests, while tangible, was not dominant. In terms of Vietnam, however, public opinion was more 'hawkish'.

In November 1964 the Menzies government announced a decision to draft by lottery a proportion of 20-year-old men to serve a period of two years compulsory military training.[35] In 1966 it decided these national servicemen should also serve in Vietnam. In both July and November of that year, the Gallup Poll tested public opinion by asking if they should have been kept in Australia (Figure 5.6).

A bare majority (52 per cent) believed that they should have been kept at home. This opinion was strongest among middle-aged women (the women most likely to have 20-year-

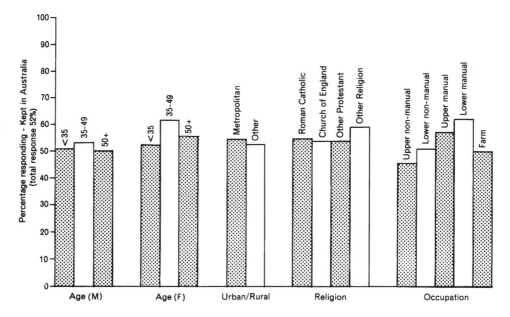

Figure 5.6 Attitudes towards sending national servicemen to Vietnam. (Do you think national servicemen should have been sent to Vietnam, or kept in Australia?) Poll taken 16 July and 18 November 1966.

old sons) and blue-collar workers (the ALP opposed both conscription and military involvement in Vietnam). But there was little in the way of other systematic differences in public opinion. It took another two to three years for Australians to swing strongly against the Vietnam War. In this respect Australian public opinion first lagged behind, and then followed, the growing opposition to the war in the United States itself.

In terms of other social issues a double standard applied to expectations about the social behaviour of young women and men, as answers to a question about the legal age of drinking at hotels show. A large minority (37 per cent) favoured giving this 'right' to young men at the age of 18, but many fewer (23 per cent) believed that it was proper for women to drink at the same age. Those who did not nominate 18 as the most appropriate age commonly nominated 21. Women were less likely than men to favour 18 as the appropriate age for legal drinking for young men, and there was a strong age gradient as well. Older people favoured older ages than younger respondents. Anglicans were more permissive than the members of other denominations (especially non-conformist Protestants). Class differences reflect not so much a difference between white-collar and blue-collar workers as a difference within each broad class: upper white-collar workers were more likely than lower white-collar workers to favour 18 as the legal drinking age, and so were upper blue-collar workers compared with lower blue-collar workers. Wowser sentiment was stronger among older persons, women, non-conformists, the lower middle class and the lower working class. It also constrained women's rights more than men's.

A similar pattern appears in relation to attitudes towards Sunday observance and gambling. In the mid-1960s most Australians thought it should be illegal even to bake bread for sale on Sundays (Gallup Poll, September 1966). Many more opposed Sunday betting on horse races, as Figure 5.7 shows. Women were marginally more opposed to Sunday horse racing than men, as were older persons generally. Protestants, especially non-conformists, opposed the provision of gambling opportunities on the Sabbath. As for class differences, there was stronger opposition in the lower segments or the non-manual and manual classes, but no strong class division otherwise. Australian society in the mid-1960s was still conservative in its social behaviour, but tolerated a greater degree of governmental control in economic life than it had in the aftermath of wartime controls. There was still some political mileage in anti-Communism. How did these changes translate into electoral cleavages?

Before we can compare voting patterns with the late 1940s we have to decide how to treat those who supported parties other than the ALP or the LCP. In the political science literature[36] it is customary to exclude DLP supporters from analysis and to focus only on differences between Liberal and Labor voters. Since the second preferences of DLP voters went overwhelmingly to the LCP a case could be made for grouping them with LCP voters. To anticipate a little, grouping LCP and DLP voters together has the effect of heavily diluting the apparent effects of religion on voting, because the DLP attracted a dispro-portionate share of Catholic voters. The analysis reported below excludes DLP voters. However similar analyses were carried out with DLP and LCP supporters grouped together. The only difference in findings is the one already mentioned: the religious cleavage is even weaker.

For the voting analysis three opinion polls for the first half of 1966 (February, April and

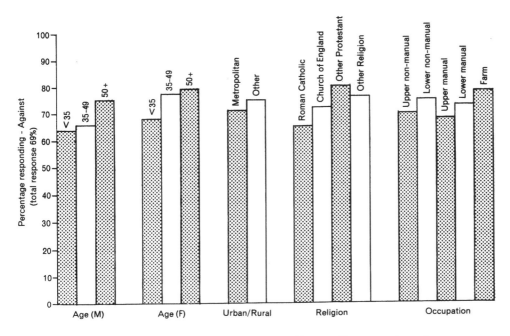

Figure 5.7 Attitudes to betting on Sunday horse races. (Are you for – or against – horse races on Sunday, with entrance charges, and betting like Saturdays?) Poll taken 18 November 1966.

July) were used, relating to how people said they voted in 1963 or intended to vote in the federal election later that year. As already stated, the analysis includes only voters preferring either the ALP or the LCP. Again, only general findings are given here.[37]

The overall level of support for the ALP between 1963 and 1966 was low compared to the late 1940s. Only about two in every five voters favoured it, and ALP support declined between 1963 and 1966 by a couple of percentage points. In the mid-1960s, the youngest cohort was the most conservative. This cohort, which included many voters who entered the electorate after the 1955 split in the ALP, gave Labor its lowest level of support among any new cohort of voters in the post-war period. The middle-aged cohort roughly corresponds to the youngest cohort in the late 1940s, which was then strongly pro-Labor. This cohort effect persisted over the intervening period. Women were still more conservative than men, but there was now no additional effect of residence. Because support for Labor was so low, there was little residual anti-Labor sentiment to be tapped outside the capital cities.

The effects of religion, however, were much weaker. Although we have no data on religiosity, only nominal affiliation, the DLP seems to have attracted the more devout members of the Catholic denomination away from the ALP. Increasing numbers of European Catholics in the electorate also muted the religious divide, because they were more anti-Labor (or, rather, more anti-Communist) than Catholics of Irish extraction. As Mistilis[38] shows for the late 1970s, and it was presumably true a decade earlier as well, Catholics from non-English-speaking countries were marginally anti-Labor, whereas English-speaking Catholics were pro-Labor. But whatever the source of these differences, the importance of the Catholic/Protestant division almost halved between 1949 and 1966 in its effect on the major political divide.

Occupational class, however, was equally important at both times, as was phone ownership. But car ownership no longer discriminated between voters. In 1966 only one in four households did not own a car, compared with almost two in three in 1949. These patterns of effects on voting behaviour are remarkably stable over time. By using an appropriate statistical model we find that most effects are similarly strong in both periods. Only a minor part represents changes in relationships. Religion, cohort (age), car ownership and place of residence have different (weaker or stronger) effects over time, with religion showing the greatest change. Age, or cohort, effects are the next most important difference.

However there is no evidence of any decline in the importance of occupational class, a result that contradicts the earlier conclusions of both Alford[39] and Kemp,[40] who argued that the effect of class on party declined between the end of the Second World War and the early 1960s. Aitkin[41] found no consistent evidence of trend over this period either, a finding consistent with our analysis.

Most of the difference in voting patterns over these two decades is the result of a weaker religious divide between the two major parties, rather than weakening class effects. However, according to Kemp,[42] the decline in class voting that began after the Second World War became more marked after 1960, and in the next section evidence to support that claim will be given. To anticipate the argument, Whitlam's accession to the ALP leadership in 1967 helped it broaden its appeal to white-collar workers, although other changes also helped moderate the traditional white-collar/blue-collar divide in politics. For example more white-collar workers, including women, joined unions and became politically active.

PUBLIC OPINION AND CLASS VOTING IN THE EARLY 1980s

In 1980 Donald Horne published a book in which he singled out the years between 1966 and 1972 as a 'Time of Hope'.[43] Over this brief period the federal ascendancy of the LCP disintegrated, and a procession of Liberal leaders (Holt, Gorton and McMahon) gave way to Whitlam and the Labor Party in December 1972. By then the 'permissive society' had already been installed. Censorship had been liberalized under the guiding hand of Don Chipp, who became Minister for Customs towards the end of 1969 and later introduced Australians to the R-certificate for sexually explicit films. Protest movements had burst onto the scene spanning issues such as anti-imperialism, Vietnam, environmental pollution, the counter-culture, sexual liberation, the women's movement, Aboriginal land rights, gay rights and participatory democracy in the streets, on the shop-floor and in the universities. Australian artistic talent flowered in theatre, film, literature and television.

All these changes had begun before Whitlam led the ALP to power and they symbolize the climate of change that contributed to Labor's victory. Trends such as these were scarcely the product of conscious design but were diffuse consequences of the affluent society and the rise of post-materialist values: a concern for the rights of future generations (the zero population growth movement) and for the environment generally; a rejection of consumerism, especially among the young; and a demand for rights of individual expression. Many protest fashions were imported from the United States where traditional constraints on forms of personal behaviour had also diminished.[44] New political parties came and went, including the Liberal Reform Group, the Australian Party and the Workers Party. Even the DLP lost its reason for existence once the ALP dropped its resistance to state aid. Its demise came swiftly after a senior DLP Senator (Senator Gair) accepted Labor's offer to become Australia's next Ambassador to Eire.

The 1970s were also a time of social and political turmoil. The body politic was scarified by the 1975 constitutional crisis when, on 11 November, the Governor-General dismissed the Labor government because it could not secure supply from an obstructive Senate. The wounds caused by that divisive decision began to heal only with the accession of the Hawke government to power in 1983, the retirement of Fraser from federal politics and the promotion of consensus politics.

Among the major social and economic changes that occurred were the increased participation of married women in the paid labour force; equal pay for women; the passage of the Family Law Act in 1975; the declining importance of the manufacturing sector as a source of employment; high inflation spurred by Labor's decision in 1974 to use the public service as a 'pace-setter' for wages and conditions, as well as by the 1973–74 explosion in oil prices provoked by the Organisation of Oil Producing Countries;[45] and high rates of unemployment, especially among young school-leavers.

A few indicative statistics tell the story. At the end of the 1960s about two in five married women with a dependent child worked for pay for a week or more during the year. By the end of the 1970s over half did. In 1969, the year in which the first of two 'equal pay' decisions were taken by the federal arbitration authorities, minimum awards for women averaged only 72 per cent of the men's award. Ten years later the relativity was over 90 per cent. In the 1960s only three to four in every 1000 married women were involved in a divorce, compared with eleven to twelve in the early 1980s (the divorce rate peaked at almost twenty in 1976, the first full year of operation of the new Family Law Act). On the employment front, between 1967 and 1983 Australia's manufacturing industries shed over

125,000 jobs, although the labour force as a whole increased by 1.3 millions; the unemployment rate rose from 2 to 10 per cent of the labour force; the average spell of unemployment worsened from three to forty-two weeks; and between one in four and one in five of teenagers could not find work.[46] As for inflation, prices had doubled between 1947 and 1953 as a result of the Korean War and the boom in wool prices. But over the next decade prices were fairly stable, rising one-quarter above their 1953 level. Even between 1963 and 1973 prices rose by only around half. But between 1973 and 1983 they almost trebled.[47] The pace of social change was rapid on many different fronts.

Before turning to a description of public opinion in the 1980s we will compare how far traditional class and religious cleavages in voting persisted over these years of rapid change. The analyses of voting in the 1980s differ slightly from those discussed earlier because in 1973 the McNair/Anderson polling agency took over the Australian Gallup Poll from the Roy Morgan Research Centre. Their background questions differed. For example they used a different occupational classification and did not ask about religious affiliation in every survey. In addition the Roy Morgan Research Centre has not deposited primary data with the Social Science Data Archives since 1973. However the Australian Values Study, which Morgan conducted for a consortium of researchers in 1983, is publicly available, and to augment its small sample size (around 1000 persons 21 years or older) it is combined with a McNair/Anderson poll from the same year that did include religion. The combined sample size is still smaller than for the earlier periods, but it is large enough to make reliable comparisons. As in the previous analyses of voting, what follows draws on the detailed results of Jones and McAllister.[48]

In 1983 the youngest cohort was less conservative than the middle cohort, which in turn was more conservative than persons over 50 (we have excluded persons aged 18 to 20 years, since they were not eligible to vote in the earlier periods). Women were only marginally anti-Labor, and in the electorate as a whole the ALP enjoyed a comfortable advantage over its opposition. But it was very unpopular among farmers. The composition of the farming community changed considerably over the post-war period, and now has many fewer farm employees. By 1983 farm workers were mostly proprietors and their families.

The effects of religion were much as they had been in the mid-1960s; phone ownership discriminated less between voters; and car ownership was so widespread that the polling agencies no longer bothered to ask about it. As for the effects of occupational class, the non-manual/manual cleavage had weakened.

For example the correlation between vote and occupational class was only 0.24 in 1983, compared with 0.41 in the 1960s. This decline is significant but not as dramatic as others, such as Kemp, have suggested. If, for example, we extend his trend line from 1975 to 1983,[49] the implied correlation would be a paltry 0.01, or near enough to nothing. But our analysis shows that occupational class remained an important influence on voting in federal elections, even if its effect was weaker than it had been a generation or two ago.

Throughout the post-war period the percentage of new voters that had manual jobs and supported the ALP averaged around 70 per cent, except in the 1950s. Then, because of the disastrous Labor split, it hit a low of just over half. Among non-manual workers the trend was more uneven, with fewer than half in each cohort of new voters supporting the ALP until the end of the 1960s. Since then the ALP has improved its share of their support. One factor in this change has been a deliberate attempt by the ALP to win white-collar support. Even before he became leader of the ALP, Whitlam had stressed the need for the party to attract more support from intellectuals, professionals and white-collar workers.[50]

110

Despite reduced support among manual workers in the 1950s because of conflict over Communist influence in the unions and the party, the working-class vote for the ALP was as high in the 1980s as it had been in the late 1940s. But technological change and the decline in manufacturing as a source of jobs meant that the working class was smaller. On the other hand, the ALP had become more acceptable to white-collar workers and to women. These gains reflect not only the changing electoral appeal of the ALP and its attempt to win over the middle ground of politics, but also the changing nature of white-collar work itself, including greater unionization. In other words, the decline in the traditional class cleavage resulted not so much from any loss of support among manual workers as from increased support among non-manuals.

As for the religious cleavage, in the early years of the century religion was even more important politically than occupation. A Catholic manual worker was much more likely to vote Labor than his non-manual peer (a difference of over 30 percentage points). Even at the beginning of the 1950s the differential was large (25 percentage points), but the ALP/DLP split in 1955 dissolved this electoral advantage, at least among new voters. Since the mid-1970s there has been some drift back to the ALP of Catholic voters, but the religious cleavage is now only a pale shadow of what it was half a century ago.

Religion, however, is still an important element in Australian social life, even if organized religion does not hold as central a place in the general order of things as it did a generation or two ago. Bouma and Dixon[51] have recently disputed the view that Australian society is essentially secular and irreligious by pointing to the widespread support accorded by the public to religious beliefs and even practice. Table 5.1 provides some relevant evidence from the 1983 Values Study for Australia, four European countries, and averages for ten European countries.[52] Denmark is included as a representative of the more secular Scandinavian countries, Great Britain because of its historical importance as a source of population and institutions, West Germany as representative of a more mixed religious Western European country and Italy as a predominantly Catholic country in southern Europe. Table 5.1 summarizes answers to seven questions about traditional Christian beliefs. Australians are more conventional in their religious beliefs than any of these European countries. Marginally more Italians believe in God, but as the second panel of the table shows they believe in a different kind of God than do most Australians. In terms of the general pattern of responses Australians were most like the British and Italians, and least like the Danes, who were the most secular. Most Australians believed in God, the existence of a soul, sin and heaven, and large minorities also believed in a life after death, the devil and hell. Australians and the British were unusual in that slightly more believed in heaven than in a life after death. This discrepancy is not so much an inconsistency as an indication that their heaven caters for more than just the spiritually pure.

Although the data are not given in full here, it is of some interest to illustrate the diversity of religious belief within the Australian population in the early 1980s. Take, for example, belief in life after death. About three in five Australians endorsed this belief, but it was more frequently endorsed by women over 50 (three out of four) than by men under 35 (one in two). A similar differential existed between Catholics and Anglicans, with other Protestants in between; and about two-thirds of farmers, lower white-collar workers and conservative voters shared this belief. In terms of these comparisons, more Australians endorsed a traditional belief system and were far less secular in their orientation than the Danes. However these beliefs do not imply widespread religious observance. Only one in two Australians attended a religious service more than once a year (apart from weddings,

Table 5.1 *Endorsement of traditional beliefs in Australia and selected European countries (c. 1983)*

Belief	Australia	Denmark	Great Britain	West Germany	Italy	Ten countries
Per cent believing in						
God	85	58	76	72	84	75
A soul	73	33	59	61	63	58
Sin	69	29	69	59	63	57
Life after death	59	26	45	39	47	43
Heaven	64	17	57	31	41	40
The devil	42	12	30	18	30	25
Hell	40	8	27	14	31	23
Beliefs about higher power						
A personal God	42	24	31	28	26	32
Some sort of spirit or life force	38	24	39	40	50	36
Don't really know what to think	14	22	19	17	11	16
Don't think there is any sort of spirit, God, or life force	7	21	9	13	6	11

Source: S. Harding and D. Phillips 1986. *Contrasting Values in Western Europe*, pp.46–7, and the Australian Values Study.

funerals or baptisms), and regular church attenders were more likely to be Catholic than Protestant.

The Values Study also asked respondents about a range of morally debatable actions. People in each country were asked whether the action concerned could always be justified, never be justified, or was somewhere in between. A score of one represents 'never justified' and a score of ten 'always justified'. Thus an average rating near one means that almost everyone said the behaviour was never justified; a score near ten means that most people thought it could always be justified; and a score around the middle of the scale means many respondents either held polar views, thought it depended on circumstances, or both. As the results in Table 5.2 show, most of the behaviours were judged negatively. Only a few were seen as justifiable under some circumstances. For example one in six Australians thought divorce could never be justified; one in sixteen thought it was always justifiable; but the most common response implied that it depended on circumstances (one-third gave a scale score of five).

In all countries discussed here one of the least justifiable behaviours is taking and driving away a car belonging to someone else (joyriding). The overwhelming majority of Europeans and Australians (nine out of ten) say such an act is never justified, and see it as marginally more reprehensible than political assassination. This level of disapproval reflects both the importance of private property in capitalist societies but also the fact that joyriding is basically anarchic. It strikes at individual rights randomly and without motive. A political assassin might, by contrast, be acting out of high purpose – for example, an attempt on the

Table 5.2 *Justifiability of morally debatable behaviour in Australia and selected European countries (c. 1983)*

Behaviour	Australia	Denmark	Great Britain	West Germany	Italy	Ten countries
Killing in self-defence	6.5	5.4	5.3	4.4	5.5	5.4
Divorce	5.0	6.9	5.0	5.0	5.0	5.0
Abortion	4.3	6.4	4.0	3.8	4.3	4.1
Euthanasia	5.2	6.1	4.4	4.3	3.0	4.0
Homosexuality	3.7	5.2	3.4	3.5	2.5	3.3
Prostitution	3.9	4.1	3.0	3.4	2.1	2.9
Married person having an affair	2.8	2.6	2.5	2.6	2.8	2.8
Lying in own interest	2.7	2.0	2.7	3.2	2.0	2.8
Keeping lost money	3.0	2.0	2.4	2.8	2.8	2.8
Under-age sex	2.2	1.5	1.8	2.6	2.7	2.7
Suicide	3.1	3.4	2.7	2.8	1.8	2.6
Cheating on tax	3.0	2.4	2.7	2.5	1.8	2.6
Avoiding a fare	2.2	1.6	2.0	2.2	1.7	2.1
Not reporting damage to parked car	2.6	1.4	2.3	1.8	2.0	2.1
Fighting with police	2.4	1.6	1.7	2.1	1.8	2.0
Claiming unentitled state benefits	1.7	1.3	2.7	1.9	1.4	2.0
Accepting a bribe	1.6	1.2	1.6	1.9	2.0	1.9
Buying stolen goods	1.7	1.2	1.9	1.5	1.4	1.8
Threatening workers who won't strike	1.9	1.7	1.7	1.7	1.7	1.7
Taking marijuana	2.8	1.9	1.7	1.4	1.4	1.7
Political assassination	2.0	1.3	1.8	1.4	1.3	1.5
Joyriding	1.3	1.1	1.2	1.2	1.4	1.4
Average score	3.0	2.8	2.6	2.6	2.4	2.7

Source: S. Harding and D. Phillips 1986. *Contrasting Values in Western Europe*, pp.8–9, and the Australian Values Study. Ratings are on a scale of 1 (never justified) to 10 (always justified).

life of a dictator. It is important to bear in mind that respondents were not asked to say which behaviour was the worst, only if it could be justified.

In other respects what is striking about these results is their consistency across countries. The greatest dissimilarity is between Denmark and Italy while, not surprisingly, Australia and Great Britain have the most similar rankings (the correlations between ratings are 0.80 and 0.94 respectively). The Danes are particularly severe on offences against public order and more lenient in terms of personal freedoms. They are more tolerant of divorce, abortion, euthanasia and homosexuality. Australians are near the norm for Western Europe as a whole, except for the first item in the table. More Australians think it is justified to kill someone in self-defence.

As for differences of opinion within Australian society – take just one item as an example, the justifiability of divorce. This item rates near the middle of the scale (sometimes justified, sometimes not). In the sample as a whole, one in six persons said divorce was never justified.

Older people were more disapproving than the young (one in four of those 50 or older, compared with one in eight under that age). A similar differential set Catholics apart from Protestants, but only about one in twenty of those with 'no religion' thought divorce unjustified under any circumstances. White-collar workers were also more liberal in their views about the justifiability of divorce. Conservative voters were less liberal than Labor voters (19 versus 14 per cent stating that divorce was never justified).

In view of recent social changes and the dissolution of traditional bonds it might be reasonable to suppose that feelings of social alienation are on the increase. While we do not have trend data, Table 5.3 gives some comparative information. These data suggest a trade-off between individual freedom and a sense of belonging. The Italians and the Danes are polar types: Italians are more likely to feel lonely than the Danes, who in turn are less likely to think that they have much freedom of choice over their lives. The Australians, British and West Germans lie somewhere between these extremes, except that marginally more Australians than Italians agree that they have considerable personal freedom. Only small minorities admit to the use, actual or potential, of personal violence in political demonstrations, and Australians have the highest level of trust in their fellow-citizens, followed by the Danes and the British.

We can gain some further insight into this pattern of responses by examining a range of political values shown in Table 5.4. Italians display a low interest in politics and have little confidence in their political institutions. They also show a high implied level of dissatisfaction with existing economic arrangements. Respondents were asked how they thought business and industry should be managed. The four choices given to them were: (a), the owners should run their businesses and appoint the managers; (b), the owners and the employees (workers) should participate in the selection of the managers; (c), the government should be the owner of businesses and appoint the managers; or (d), the employees (workers) should own the businesses and should elect the managers. Table 5.4 shows that in

Table 5.3 *Cross-national differences in indicators of alienation in Australia and selected Western European countries (c. 1983)*

Indicator	Australia	Denmark	Great Britain	West Germany	Italy	Ten countries
Per cent who:						
Never or seldom feel lonely	68	80	66	68	43	62
Rarely or never feel life is meaningless	76	77	73	70	64	67
Have a great deal of freedom of choice over their life	51	36	43	41	48	36
Have engaged, or might engage, in violent political acts	6	1	4	3	3	5
Believe most people can be trusted	48	46	43	26	25	30

Source: S. Harding and D. Phillips 1986. *Contrasting Values in Western Europe*, pp.204–5, and the Australian Values Study.

Table 5.4 *Political values in Australia and selected European countries (c. 1983)*

Political value	Australia	Denmark	Great Britain	West Germany	Italy	Ten countries
Per cent who are:						
Interested in politics	47	44	39	50	27	41
Confident in parliament	58	36	40	53	31	43
Believe that:						
(a) Owners should run their businesses	55	41	50	47	29	35
(b) Owners and employees should participate jointly	34	41	37	37	47	41
Believe social change should occur through:						
(a) Revolutionary change	4	3	4	2	6	5
(b) Gradual reform	73	60	66	53	70	65
(c) Society must be defended against subversive forces	22	24	22	38	18	22

Source: S. Harding and D. Phillips 1986. *Contrasting Values in Western Europe*, pp.78–9, and the Australian Values Study.

most countries one of the first two arrangements was favoured, (b) was preferred in Italy and (a) in Australia. But in all the countries included in this analysis a majority, and usually a large majority, believed that social reform should be gradual. Only in West Germany was there extensive concern that subversive forces needed to be held in check.

So far as the pattern of economic management is concerned, joint participation was favoured by one in three Australians. There was not much variation in this level of support across age groups or by gender, except that there was marginally more support among men under 35. There were no differences across religious denominations either, except that those with no stated religion favoured joint management (the figure was 10 percentage points higher than in the sample as a whole). Somewhat surprisingly only a few percentage points separated upper white-collar workers and lower blue-collar workers on this issue. Only farmers stood out in having a low level of support for joint management (one in five). However opinions split rather more decisively along party lines, with two out of three conservative voters favouring owner-control compared with fewer than one in two Labor supporters.

Finally we come to some measures of well-being in which respondents used a 10-point scale to rank their satisfaction with various aspects of their lives. The results are given in Table 5.5. The Danes emerge as marginally more satisfied than any of the other countries. They are more satisfied with their home lives, household finances, jobs and their lives as a whole. In all four countries, and in the ten European countries taken as a whole, most people are less satisfied with their household finances than with their home life. Italians are the

Table 5.5 *Indicators of subjective well-being in Australia and selected European countries (c. 1983)*

Indicator	Australia	Denmark	Great Britain	West Germany	Italy	Ten countries
Satisfaction rating with:						
Life as a whole	7.6	8.2	7.7	7.2	6.6	7.1
Home life	8.4	8.7	8.4	7.6	7.3	7.8
Household finances	6.7	7.4	6.8	6.9	6.3	6.6
Job	7.7	8.2	8.2	7.5	7.1	7.3
Per cent 'very happy, all things together'	34	30	38	10	10	21
Per cent 'very proud' of nationality	70	30	55	21	41	38

Source: S. Harding and D. Phillips 1986. *Contrasting Values in Western Europe*, pp.184–5, and the Australian Values Study. Ratings are on a 10-point scale. The higher the rating, the higher the degree of satisfaction expressed by the respondent.

least satisfied, and their rankings are around 10 per cent lower than those for the Danes. The British and the Australians are the next most satisfied, although both these countries outrank even Denmark in the percentages reporting that they are 'very happy, all things together'. National pride is far more marked among the Australians, followed by the British. West Germans are less likely to endorse nationalistic sentiments.

Among Australians about one in five ranked their life satisfaction at the top of the scale. But fewer young people, especially young men, expressed that degree of satisfaction compared with those 50 or older. Since young people were not particularly dissatisfied with their job or with their home lives, it seems simply that older people are more likely to have come to terms with their life situation. There were remarkably few differences in satisfaction levels by class, religion or political preference. As for pride in being Australian, national sentiment was stronger among the old than the young: three out of four Australians 50 or older were 'very proud' of their nationality, compared with only two out of three persons under 35. There were few religious differences – except for a low degree of national pride among those with 'no religion' (only one out of two replied 'very proud'); upper white-collar workers were only a little more nationalistic, as were Labor voters.

The dominant impression to emerge from these descriptive figures and the more rigorous analysis of cleavages in voting patterns is that the traditional divisions that characterized Australian society a generation or two ago have been heavily diluted by processes of social change. Class, religion and region still affect people's views about the world around them and the way those views are translated into political action. But Australia in the 1980s is a much more pluralistic and culturally diverse society than it was even twenty years ago. The groupings that can be mobilized by a simple appeal to class interest, religious divisions or ethnic origin have diminished in size but increased in number. Australians are now better educated. They have access to mass media that provide a larger window on their world. Voters are more aware of political affairs,[53] and politicians are more aware of the needs and aspirations of different interest groups in the society. The political successes of the Australian Labor Party in the 1980s have been partly due to its more successful appeal to 'issue-oriented' groups such as environmentalists.[54] For better or worse, opinion polls are now becoming a sensitive tool for tracking and targeting issues that help identify potential coalitions in the electorate.[55] Admittedly opinions are less stable than the underlying values that they reflect, and people's actions and values do not always coincide. There is, however, a growing body of academic surveys that attempt to identify this deeper structure and to map its contours over time. They, together with the commercial opinion polls that are now a central feature of our social and political life, should ease the task of some future chronicler of Australian mores.

Notes

[1] See N.T. Feather 1975. *Values in Education and Society*. New York, Free Press.

[2] J.D. Pringle 1965. *Australian Accent*. London, Chatto and Windus.

[3] D. Horne 1964. *The Lucky Country: Australia in the Sixties*. Ringwood, Penguin Books.

[4] C. McGregor 1966. *Profile of Australia*. London, Hodder and Stoughton.

[5] R. Conway 1972. *The Great Australian Stupor*. Melbourne, Sun Books.

[6] See S. Mills 1986. *The New Machine Men: Polls and Persuasion in Australian Politics*. Ringwood, Penguin Books, pp. 67-77.

[7] W. Buchanan and H. Cantril 1953. *How Nations See Each Other: A Study in Public Opinion*. Urbana, University of Illinois Press.

[8] G.D. Bouma and B.R. Dixon 1986. *The Religious Factor in Australian Life*. Melbourne, MARC Australia.

[9] W. Buchanan and H. Cantril 1953. *op.cit*., p. 68.

[10] *ibid*., pp. 46-7.

[11] For details see Social Science Data Archives (SSDA), Bulletin No. 11, August 1987.

[12] A. Markus 1984. Labour and immigration 1946-9: the Displaced Persons Program. *Labour History* (Nov.), pp. 84-5.

[13] H. Mayer (ed.) 1961. *Catholics and the Free Society: An Australian Symposium*. Melbourne, F.W. Cheshire.

[14] T.C. Truman 1958. Church and State: The teaching of the Catholic Church on intervention in politics. *The Australian Quarterly*, 30 (Dec.), pp. 42-3.

[15] P. Rolfe 1979. *The Journalistic Javelin: An Illustrated History of the Bulletin*. Sydney, Wildcat Press.

[16] *The Bulletin*, 1 June 1949.

[17] H. Mayer (ed.) 1961. *op.cit*.

[18] See F.L. Jones 1984. Income inequality. In D.H. Broom (ed.) *Unfinished Business: Social Justice for Women in Australia*. Sydney, Allen and Unwin, pp. 104-6; B.O. Pettman (ed.) 1977. *Equal Pay for Women: Progress and Problems in Seven Countries*. Washington, Hemisphere Publishing Co., pp. 76-7.

[19] Department of Labour and National Service 1968 (3rd edn), *Equal Pay: Some Aspects of Australian and Overseas Practice*. Melbourne, pp. 18-19.

[20] *Commonwealth Arbitration Reports*, Vol. 68, pp. 698-846. See especially pp. 815-19; for a dissenting opinion see pp. 782-6.

[21] See F. Alexander 1967. *Australia since Federation: A Narrative and Critical Analysis*. Melbourne, Thomas Nelson, pp. 162-9.

[22] See F.L. Jones and I. McAllister 1989. The Changing Structural Base of Australian Politics since 1946. *Politics* (forthcoming).

[23] D. Aitkin 1982. *Stability and Change in Australian Politics* (2nd edn). Canberra, ANU Press, pp. 162-6.

[24] For DLP figures see P. Reynolds 1974. *The Democratic Labor Party*. Brisbane, Jacaranda Press.

[25] See D. Aitkin 1982. *op.cit*., p. 5.

[26] D. Smart 1978. *Federal Aid to Australian Schools*. Brisbane, University of Queensland Press, p. 31.

[27] *ibid*., p. 54.

[28] *The Australian Quarterly*, June 1960, p. 103.

[29] *The Australian Quarterly*, December 1963, p. 91.

[30] C.D. Rowley 1971. *Outcasts in White Australia: Aboriginal Policy and Practice, Vol.II*. Canberra, ANU Press. See pp. v-vi.

[31] *Year Book of Australia*, 1967, p. 1293.

[32] See T.W. Beed *et al*. 1978. *Australian Public Opinion Polls 1941-1977*. Sydney, Hale & Iremonger and the University of Sydney Sample Survey Centre, pp. 93-4.

[33] *Canberra Times*, 18 August 1987.

[34] *Canberra Times*, 3 September 1965.

[35] *The Australian Quarterly*, March 1965, p. 83.
[36] See, for example, R. Alford 1963. *Party and Society: The Anglo-American Democracies*. Chicago, Rand McNally & Co.
[37] For detailed results see F.L. Jones and I. McAllister 1989. *op.cit.*
[38] N. Mistilis 1984. Explaining partisan patterns amongst immigrant electors. In J. Jupp (ed.), *Ethnic Politics in Australia*. Sydney, Allen and Unwin, p. 83.
[39] R. Alford 1963. *op.cit.*
[40] D.A. Kemp 1978. *Society and Electoral Behaviour in Australia: A Study of Three Decades*. St Lucia, University of Queensland Press.
[41] D. Aitkin 1982. *op.cit.*, pp. 152-4.
[42] D. Kemp 1978. *op.cit.*, pp. 66-8.
[43] D. Horne 1980. *Time of Hope: Australia 1966-72*. London, Angus & Robertson.
[44] *ibid.*, p. 57; *New York Review of Books*, 12 February 1987, p. 33.
[45] See F.H. Gruen 1978-9. *Surveys of Australian Economics* (2 vols.). Sydney, Allen and Unwin; and I. Seymour 1980. *OPEC: Instrument of Change*. London, Macmillan.
[46] Australian Bureau of Statistics, *Social Indicators No. 4.1984*. Canberra, ABS.
[47] *Yearbook of Australia*, 1985. p. 107.
[48] F.L. Jones and I. McAllister 1989. *op.cit.*
[49] D. Kemp 1978. *op.cit.*, pp. 65, 67.
[50] *The Australian Quarterly*, December 1965, p. 103.
[51] See G.D. Bouma and B.R. Dixon 1986. *op.cit.*
[52] S. Harding *et al.* 1986. *Contrasting Values in Western Europe*. London, Macmillan.
[53] D. Aitkin 1985. Australia. In I. Crewe and D. Denver (eds.), *Electoral Change in Western Democracies: Patterns and Sources of Electoral Volatility*. Sydney, Croom Helm, p. 89.
[54] See *The Bulletin*, 4 August 1987.
[55] See S. Mills 1986. *op.cit.*, pp. 12-14.

6

The Population

W.D. Borrie

ORIGINS

At the census date of June 1986 the Australian resident population was 16.02 million. All but a very small minority of these people were of European origin, either immigrants or the scions of former settlers who had chosen to leave Europe's shores as part of the greatest migration in human history – the European settlement of the 'New World'. Australia and New Zealand were the last major land areas to be colonized by European settlers. In Australia's case this colonization began because the imperial government wished to find a new and suitably remote place for the surplus felons who were piling up in the penitentiaries and hulks around Britain, particularly after the American War of Independence had closed off the American colonies as suitable repositories. As with other countries settled in this age of European expansion, the white settlers overwhelmed the indigenous people who, in Australia's case, had been in the country for many thousands of years. Exactly how many of these Aboriginal people there were in Australia in 1788 is still a matter of conjecture – possibly between about 300,000 and 500,000.[1] As the European population grew, the number of Aborigines decreased to 70,000 or perhaps fewer in the late nineteenth century. The twentieth century saw a revival to about 170,000 people in 1981.[2]

For the first thirty-five or so years of European settlement after 1788, the transportation of convicts was the prime motive for the retention of eastern Australia as a British colony. Apart from the free settlers derived from the military and civil establishment of the convict system, there were few non-convict settlers until after 1830: the main non-convict element in New South Wales and Van Diemen's Land by that time was the expanding number of colonial-born.[3] When the convict system ended in New South Wales in 1840, almost 80,000 convicts (about two-thirds from Great Britain and one-third from Ireland) had arrived in the colony. Thereafter, until 1853, Tasmania bore the brunt of the system, and in all a further 68,000 convicts were despatched from Great Britain to Tasmania. With the 9600 also sent to Western Australia between 1852 and 1868 and approximately 5000 despatched to Norfolk Island and Moreton Bay, the total convict arrivals in Australia from 1788 until 1868 was of the order of 163,000.

Given the technology of transport at the time and the fact that the total population of the British Isles around 1830 was only about 11 million, we may identify convictism as a quite massive system of emigration. Nor was it all bad in terms of colonial development. The British government stood the major cost of transport and of victualling the population. The convicts may not have been ideal labour, but they were assigned to landowners and provided the labour force for major programmes of public works. After serving their sentences, the majority stayed in the colonies, often to become themselves employers of labour and landholders. As early as 1821, emancipists in New South Wales had 29,000 acres in cultivation, held 212,000 acres in pasture and owned 43,000 horned cattle and 174,000 sheep. In all these fields they exceeded the properties of the free settlers.

It is questionable whether this level of economic development would have been achieved in thirty-five years of settlement under any other system. There was little interest in Britain in the colonization of faraway Australia until after the Napoleonic Wars, when deteriorating economic conditions and relatively rapid population growth in Britain encouraged the acceptance of the theories of overpopulation of Thomas Malthus and other contemporary political economists. The main outlet for 'surplus' population (primarily the poor) was seen as North America: eastern Australia was still seen as a necessary extension of the penal system. But ideas in Britain were changing. There were new theories about colonization by 'free' settlers, with the cost of settlement being financed, not by the imperial government, but by colonial revenues raised by selling instead of granting land – a system first introduced in New South Wales in 1831 – and by bounties levied on prospective employers to pay the passage costs of labourers. By the 1830s this form of assisted immigration had taken root. Passage assistance, not only for the worker but for his family as well, became the cornerstone of immigration policies for 150 years in the Australian colonies, and after 1901 in the Federation. Assistance was the price Australia (and New Zealand) paid to overcome the tyranny of distance in competition with the drawing-power and proximity of North America.

THE RISE OF THE FREE SETTLEMENTS

In the Census of 1828, only 4121 persons were recorded as having arrived free in New South Wales. Free immigration expanded rapidly from this point and this element, together with the colonial-born, soon became the major component of the population.[4] Moreover the emphasis upon *family* migration – and the introduction of some shipments of single female immigrants – established a better sex ratio and laid the basis for permanent natural increase. The establishment of the company colony in South Australia, with an emphasis from the beginning upon family settlement, further assisted the trend to demographic normality.[5] Amongst the convicts the male-female sex ratio had been of the order of 5:1; by 1850 the sex ratio had been reduced to 1.4:1 in an estimated total Australian population of 405,000. By this stage the future shape and direction of Australia's population had been firmly established, with peripheral settlements clustered around growing cities in Western Australia, South Australia, Victoria, New South Wales and Tasmania and in the growing numbers in the areas dependent upon the Port of Brisbane, which was to be recognized as a separate colony in 1859. By this stage, too, the imperial government was committed (in collaboration with the Colonial authorities) to the continued emigration of people from Great Britain and Ireland.

By 1850 all but a fraction of Australia's 405,000 people were in the southeastern sector of the continent. South Australia with about 64,000 had progressed steadily since the first settlers arrived in 1836; but Western Australia, with barely 6000 people, was struggling to remain viable. Then came the goldrushes, which boosted Australia's population above the million mark by 1858.[6] The biggest rise occurred in Victoria, which had been established as a separate colony in 1851. The capital generated by gold set Australia on the course it was to follow for a century – the export of primary commodities – a course which was for a time to give Australia probably the highest living standard in the world. In terms of human resources, the major benefit arising from the goldrushes was the creation of a mobile workforce which was redistributed widely across the continent as the goldfields were worked out. The main beneficiaries in this redistribution were New South Wales and (after 1891) Western Australia.

The rush to the goldfields generated labour shortages elsewhere in the colonies, in both rural and urban areas. By this time all colonies had established assisted passage schemes and these were used to boost the flow of new settlers. In an estimated gain of 178,000 immigrants up to 1850, 114,000 were assisted; in the next ten years 230,000 immigrants were assisted in a total inflow to all the Australian colonies of 671,000; and over the next forty years, 1861–1900, there were 388,000 assisted immigrants in a total net gain of 766,000 new settlers. The Australian colonies, through the policy of assisted immigration, had captured a substantial place in the emigration from Europe to the New World; but that assistance was almost totally restricted to settlers from the British Isles, and immigrants, whether assisted or not, had to be white.[7]

The input of predominantly male gold-seekers in the 1850s offset to some extent the endeavour to achieve a more balanced sex ratio, which remained about 140 males per 100 females until the 1870s. Despite the imbalance, the level of fertility was sufficient for natural increase to add more to population growth by 1860 than net immigration. The combination of natural increase and immigration gave Australia one of the highest growth rates in the world from 1860 almost until the end of the century. Total growth rates averaged well above 3 per cent a year until 1890, with about two-thirds derived from natural increase and a third from net immigration. An Australian population of 2 million was reached in 1877, just eighty-nine years after the first European settlement. The third million was added by 1889 in the short span of twelve years; and sixteen years later the 4 million population mark was passed.

FEDERAL AUSTRALIA: A DEMOGRAPHIC PROFILE

What was the nature of this population at the time of Federation? The best profile is that presented in the Statistician's Report of the first Australian Commonwealth Census in April, 1911, when the recorded population was 4.4 million.

The sex imbalance had been largely overcome, with an excess of only 3.8 males in every 100 of population. The population was young, with a median age of only 24 years; 31 per cent were under the age of 14 years, 65 per cent were of 'working age' (defined as aged 14–64) and only 4 per cent were aged 65 years and over. This was a population set for high demographic growth rates for some time ahead although, as will be shown later, there was clear evidence that the transition to a much smaller family size had already set in. The latter trend and a period of net *emigration* had brought about a sharp decrease in births between 1898 and 1903, with the result that the number of children aged 5–13 who were at school actually declined in the first eleven years of this century. Hope for rectification of this trend lay in the statistics that described 49 per cent of women as 'reproductive' (aged 15–44) and only 18 per cent as 'sterile' (aged 45 and over). The rest (aged 0–14) were 'immature'.

In terms of place of residence, the development of primate cities in each state was clearly apparent. Concentration in the southeastern sector had continued, although growth had been rapid in the newer colonies of South and Western Australia, and particularly in Queensland. Over all Australia, the state capitals harboured 38 per cent of the population. Almost half of the population of South Australia already resided in Adelaide. Sydney, with

38 per cent of those residing in New South Wales, was already a city of 630,000 people. Melbourne had 589,000 residents and 45 per cent of Victoria's population. In rank order by States, the situation was:

	Population	Capital City	Per Cent in Capital City
NSW	1,638,083	629,503	38
Victoria	1,310,746	588,971	45
Queensland	601,045	139,480	23
South Australia	405,819	189,646	46
Western Australia	275,098	106,792	39
Tasmania	190,635	39,937	21
Northern and Federal Territories	4,843		
	4,426,269	1,694,329	38

Australia was peopled primarily by the Australian-born, the products of the high fertility of the colonial families; almost 84 per cent of the population was in this category. Of the remaining 16 per cent, almost all were European-born; and all but a fraction of these were born in Great Britain and Ireland (Figure 6.1). Multiculturalism in Australia at this time had more to do with Irish Catholicism and Protestantism than with ethnic origin, particularly within the field of education. In terms of religious affiliation, the population divided into approximately 21 per cent Catholic, 77 per cent other-Christian and 2 per cent 'others'.

Such were some of the demographic and sociological features of White Australia 123 years after the first European settlers arrived. Altogether, given the distance from the United Kingdom, the source country of almost all new settlers, the alien nature of much of the environment and the problems of remaining competitive with the high costs of transport, we must regard these achievements by Federation as impressive. But the post-gold era of expansion had come to a stop in the eastern colonies which had temporarily abandoned their policies of assisted immigration. Only Western Australia, with the opening of new goldfields, continued to attract new settlers after 1890, but many of these poured in from the other Australian colonies rather than from overseas. Whereas Western Australia's net immigrant gain from all sources was 50,000 between 1901 and 1905, Victoria had a net *emigration* of 50,000, Queensland a *loss* of almost 2000 and South Australia a *loss* of 20,000. Altogether Australia experienced a net *emigration* in this period of 17,000 people. Immigration assistance policies were not revived until after 1906.

AUSTRALIA AND THE DEMOGRAPHIC TRANSITION

Whereas immigration had added over 740,000 people to the colonies in thirty years after 1861, the net gain over the next thirty years to 1920 was only 283,000 – almost all of it from a new burst of activity in the decade preceding the outbreak of World War I. Increasingly population growth was becoming dependent upon natural increase, which had itself

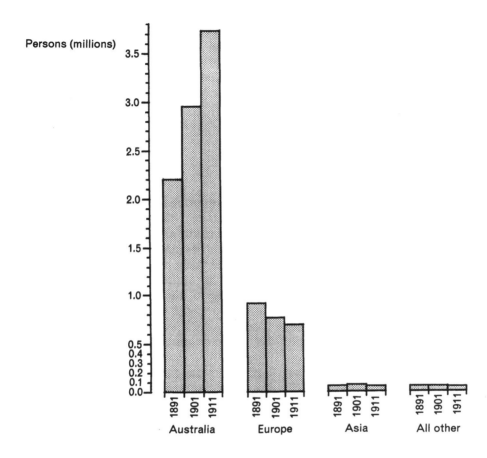

Figure 6.1 Birthplaces of Australian population 1891–1911. *Source:* Statistician's *Report*, 1917, Census of the Commonwealth of Australia, 3 April 1911, Vol. 1, p. 117.

declined from around 2 per cent of the population before 1890 to 1.4 per cent in the year of Federation. Compared with the levels of today, this was still a high rate – sufficient to double a population in about fifty years – but low enough to stimulate the establishment of a Royal Commission in 1903 by the Legislative Assembly of New South Wales to inquire into the causes and implications of the decline of the birthrate – the first such inquiry in the English-speaking world.[8] With immigration also in a slump, total growth rates had slipped from their earlier 3 and even 4 per cent to around 1.5 per cent. They were never to return to the higher levels, and a major reason was the demographic transition which was then occurring in many of those parts of the world with which Australia was closely associated – Western Europe, the British Isles and North America.

These events were associated with major changes in economic structure and organization and associated changes in standards of living, residential patterns, literacy, transportation, health standards, the control of infectious diseases and moral attitudes towards contraceptive practices. Phasing and timing of the demographic transition associated with these changes varied in different countries, but the situation with regard to marriage and fertility was much the same, as have been the patterns that have evolved by the mid-1980s.[9]

In colonial Australia, a relatively high proportion of the female population was married, as was to be expected from the sex ratios and the policies of 'family' immigration. Data from Colonial Censuses, analysed and presented in the 1911 Commonwealth Census, record the following percentages of women who were married in the stated age-groups:

	1881	1891	1901	1911
20–24	44	38	31	33
25–29	71	65	55	58
30–34	82	78	72	70

The figures indicate two things: the relatively low proportions (compared with the last two to three decades in Australia, which will be discussed later) who were married before age 30, particularly from 1891 onwards; and the clear indication of marriage postponement during the years of economic recession in the 1890s. But the pattern that had evolved by 1911 was to be remarkably constant right through to the 'baby-boom' years of the 1960s. Postponed marriage was a significant factor in lowering birthrates from 35 per 1000 of the population in the 1880s to about 26 in the first decade of this century. But more than postponed marriages were involved in this downward trend: a further factor was the beginning of the secular trend towards small families which, with the contrary but mild hiccup of the 'baby boom' of the 1950s and 1960s, has been consolidating in Australia over the past century.

Early colonial families appear to have been large by any standard, with an average of 6.7 children for women born in 1841–46 who lived to the end of their fecund years around the 1880s. Twenty years later the average had dropped to 5.3 children, and so on downwards to about 2.4 for women born 1904–09 and thus completing their child-bearing around the later 1940s (Figure 6.2). The 'two-child family' had emerged and has been consolidating and extending its hold ever since, as will be illustrated later.

Australia was never in danger of imminent population decline, even in the depression years of the 1930s, because it was well stocked until the 1950s with young persons born during the era of the large family. Nevertheless as the birthrates dropped from the mid-20s of the early years of this century to 16 and 15 per 1000 of population in the depressed years of the 1930s, grave concern was expressed about the future population-building capacity of Australia. In addition, the relatively smooth flow of new settlers from the British Isles had been broken by a series of international events. First, just when immigration turned sharply upwards (with a net gain of 184,000 new settlers in the years 1906–15), war not only cut off the flow for four years but also cut into the cohorts of young and fit Australian men (with 58,000 deaths on the battlefields). This was followed by another upsurge of immigration based on ambitious plans devised by Winston Churchill and others for a grand redistribution of the *white* population of the British Commonwealth of Nations, to be implemented under the UK's Empire Settlement Act of 1922. Australia was the main Dominion partner with Britain in this scheme; and while it did not achieve its grandiose objective, its result was substantial, though costly. From 1921 to 1930 the net gain from immigration, almost all of it from the British Isles, was over 300,000, with over 200,000 assisted immigrants amongst them. The whole scheme was terminated with the onset in 1929 of the Great Depression, and for another decade immigration was of no importance in population growth.

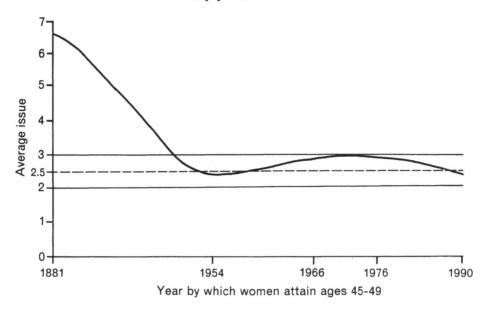

Figure 6.2 Australia's evolution of the small family system. *Source:* Based on figures in National Population Inquiry, *Supplementary Report, Population and Australia* 1978, fig. 1.3, p. 10. Canberra, AGPS.

With a birthrate below the 'intrinsic' level required to sustain long-term population growth and migration going into reverse, a state of gloom prevailed amongst policy-makers. The Census of 1933 recorded 6.6 million people – an addition of almost 2.2 million in the twenty-two years since the first Commonwealth Census of 1911. This was quite an impressive performance, but many believed that a faster growth rate could be generated again. But how and from where? The British government had become coy again about embarking on major migration and development schemes, having in mind the failure of the '£34 million Agreement' which had been negotiated with the Australian government with the aim of assisting emigrants to settle in their thousands on farms carved out of newly prepared land, particularly in Victoria. Also, Britain's own Oversea Settlement Board, alarmed by the prediction of population decline in its own country, had warned the Dominions in its final *Report* in 1938 that while the Dominions might reasonably expect some British immigrants, they must be increasingly careful not to start 'emptying the tank'.[10]

POPULATION BUILDING AFTER 1945[11]

The World War of 1939–45, like the First World War, had a traumatic impact upon attitudes and policies relating to population. After 1914–18, the emphasis was on boosting immigration through an extension of 'Empire Settlement'. After 1939–45, it was recognized that the Mother Country was not an inexhaustible reservoir; and that while rapid population growth through planned immigration was desirable, the field of recruitment would have to be extended to non-British – but strictly 'white' – countries. Chifley's Labor government, with the vigorous prompting of its Minister of Immigration, Arthur Calwell, agreed to target immigration at 70,000 a year. This, with a similar level of natural increase, was calculated to sustain population growth at 2 per cent a year, thus doubling the 1947 population of 7.6 million in about thirty-five years.[12] After considerable delays arising from shortages of shipping and the need to establish an adequate infrastructure for selection and recruitment, a new era burst upon Australia with the arrival of about 180,000 European displaced persons in three years from July 1948. But there was also a backlog of some 200,000 British intending-emigrants. As more adequate transport became available they all began to flow freely into Australia, most of them as nominated and assisted immigrants.

Thus began the greatest era of population-building through immigration in Australia's history. In twenty-five years from 1947, 3.1 million persons came to Australia with the declared intention of settling. About a fifth of these subsequently left the country – about a normal level of loss – giving a net gain in the years 1947–73 of about 2.3 million. The greatest single source was the British Isles (40 per cent). Refugees (38,000) made up 12 per cent of arrivals and were constituted from many birthplace groups. Sizeable minorities of non-refugees also came from Italy (11 per cent) and Greece and Cyprus (7 per cent). This was the flow that established the base of 'multicultural Australia', although the concept was not really articulated until after the arrival of the Vietnamese and other refugees from Southeast Asia. They were also the groups who provided the supplement to the declining workforce resulting from the decrease in births during the 1930s and, to some degree, war deaths of 33,800 young men. Immigrants were the backbone of post-war reconstruction in Australia and an important element in the economic boom of the 1960s. They accounted for about 43 per cent of population increase in the intercensal period 1947–71 and, if the children born to them in Australia are added, their contribution is raised to over 53 per cent (Table 6.1).

Table 6.1 *Settler arrivals and loss and proportions assisted, 1947–73*

Birthplace	Settlers arriving		Settler loss	Percentage lost	Percentage arriving assisted
	Numbers	Percentage			
British Isles	1,234,400	39.9	260,340	21.1	86.8
Germany	120,840	3.9	37,410	31.0	75.3
Netherlands	143,390	4.6	35,760	24.9	56.5
Italy	354,050	11.4	81,530	23.0	16.8
Greece, Cyprus	219,580	7.1	49,140	22.4	33.6
Malta	72,160	2.3	11,240	15.6	61.7
Yugoslavia	159,610	5.2	20,260	12.7	61.4
Other East Europe	216,770	7.0	14,060	6.5	73.3
Others	574,770	18.6	109,360	19.0	45.6
Total	3,095,570	100.0	619,100	20.0	63.5
Refugees	382,000	12.3	26,000	6.8	68.0

Source: C.A. Price 1975. Australian Immigration. Commissioned Paper No.6, p.15. Printed in National Population Inquiry, *Population and Australia*, Vol.1, p.124.

The target, established after the war, of a population growth from immigration of 1 per cent a year was not sustained throughout the period, although as an average annual input it did considerably exceed Calwell's 70,000. But the high net inflow of new settlers occurred while another remarkable demographic phenomenon was taking place – the post-war 'baby boom'. This doubled the growth generated by net immigration, with the result that the *total* annual average population increase was sustained around the 2 per cent level envisaged by the post-war planners. The pattern of annual average increases per cent for the period 1946–70 was:

	Natural Increase*	Net Immigration*	Total*
1946–50	1.36	0.91	2.26
1951–55	1.38	0.95	2.32
1956–60	1.40	0.83	2.22
1961–65	1.24	0.74	1.98
1966–70	1.11	0.91	2.02

* As per cent of total population

Australia's population did in fact double its size, from 7.6 million in 1947 to 15.2 million in 1982, which implied an exponential growth rate averaging just on 2 per cent a year.

The 'baby boom' was an extremely complicated amalgam of changing variables.[13] A discussion of these variable factors is essential for an understanding of current demographic trends, because demographic events have essentially long-run, generation effects rather than only short, transitory ones. The one thing that the baby boom was *not* was a permanent reversal of the trend towards the small family, averaging about 2.5 children, which had become so apparent by the late 1930s. The average number of children born to women aged 45–49 at the Census of 1954 (i.e., the birth cohort of 1904–09) was only about 2.5 children. This family size was not sufficient to bring the intrinsic rate of growth to a replacement level, that is, where the present generation will be replaced by at least equal numbers in the next generation (see Figure 6.1). It is apparent from the performance of women who reached age 45–49 at the time of later censuses, up to 1981, that there was some increase in completed fertility, but it never exceeded an average of 3.1 children and has quite clearly dropped away again to below replacement level. For over a decade now, the net reproduction rate in Australia has been below replacement level and has remained between 0.8 and 0.9. This is the rate that applied in the early 1930s. Completed family sizes of one and two children, with a small proportion of three-child families, now seem to be the 'norm'.

If family size rose so little during the 1950s and 1960s, why was there such a boom in new babies, from 111,300 in 1935 to 160,500 in 1945, and again to 207,700 in 1955, with a final peak of 276,400 in 1971? The answer is complex. First, many births occurring around 1945–46 were those that had to be postponed while husbands were serving in the armed forces. Second, many marriages and births had been 'postponed' during the severe economic recession of the 1930s, and many 'postponements' were 'made up' during the next decade. But far more significant through the 1950s and 1960s was the marked fall – of more than three years – that occurred in the average age of brides and grooms at first marriage and the tendency to have births quickly after marriage. In addition there was a marked rise in the proportion who married: in the 1920s and indeed right back to 1891, as already illustrated, the proportion of young women who were recorded in the censuses as married by age 20–24 years was about one-third; by the 1960s the proportion was approaching two-thirds. These changes in marriage patterns and in the phasing of births, rather than changes in completed family size, were the basic causes of the baby boom.

The boom suddenly burst, and the number of births fell from 276,400 in 1971 to 245,200 in 1974: the slump continued with an annual average of only 224,000 births per year in the period 1976–80.[14] Marriage age also began to rise again and the proportions marrying to fall. At the same time the gain through new settlers had also slumped: settler arrivals were down to an annual average of 73,000 in 1976–80 compared with 160,800 in the boom years of 1966–70. Nevertheless the role of immigration had been and continued to be of great importance. Even through the baby-boom period new settlers and their children had still accounted for over half the nation's growth, as indicated earlier; and as the slump in natural increase continued into the 1980s, net settler gain rose once more, to an average of 103,000 in each of the fiscal years 1980–81 and 1981–82, matching the natural growth rate of 0.83 so as to yield a total national growth of 1.66 per cent. Australia probably still had the fastest growth in the 'developed' world (Figure 6.3).

The demographic events of this great post-war era of growth changed the face of Australia: it almost doubled the population; it turned declining numbers in the younger sector of the workforce (because of the decrease in births in the 1930s) into a substantial increase; together with rising participation rates, it accelerated the growth in secondary and tertiary education – a growth which led to an increase in the number of universities from 7 to 19 and the creation of over 50 Colleges of Advanced Education; it gave a great boost to

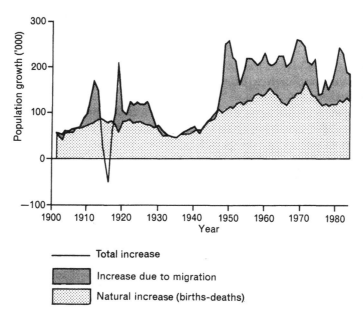

Figure 6.3 Components of population growth, Australia 1901–1984. *Source: Demography Bulletin* Ref. No. 4.9 for various years, and *Australian Demographic Statistics* Cat. No. 3101.0 for various quarters. ABS.

major city growth, since about four of every five immigrants settled in the state capitals; and it created the concept of multicultural Australia.

Not all of these factors were considered to be desirable in themselves. The burst of immigration to record levels in 1969 and 1970 led to a widely supported call for lower annual immigration targets. Considerable support also emerged for 'zero population growth', with a family size of two children and no immigration. Ecologists were gaining support for the view that continuing population growth would lead to deterioration of the natural environment and pressure upon limited natural resources. The falling away of net immigration through the 1970s was not, however, evidence of government acceptance of such radical concepts as zero growth: it was due rather to an economic downturn. Nevertheless there was a widely-held view that some of these problems had been exacerbated by pressing immigration too hard. Considerable attention was also given to an aspect that had dominated immigration policy formation for many years: the 'numbers game', with fixed targets on an annual or triennial basis, with special privileges for settlers of British origin. Increased emphasis was being placed upon human rights and their application in the area of immigration, leading to the principle of no discrimination on the ground of race.

Australia's experience with the massive Displaced Persons immigration had much to do with this change of attitude: their settlement proved that non-British immigrants could contribute both economically and culturally to the country. From as early as 1956, non-Europeans residing in Australia had been able to attain permanent residence, to be naturalized and to bring in wives, children and aged parents. The dictation test, the traditional cudgel of 'White Australia', was abolished in 1958. From 1966, highly qualified Asians with professional and technical skills could be admitted as immigrants, with the right to have their families accompany them. But the final leap to the abolition of racial discrimination came when the Whitlam Labor government decreed in 1973 that future immigration policy would be based on the 'avoidance of discrimination on any ground of race or colour of skin or nationality'. This did *not* mean an open door policy, because firm control of the inflow of immigrants, in terms of the assessed capacity of the *economy* to absorb them, was retained; and on these *economic* grounds the Labor government drastically reduced the immigration intake. The reduction was achieved primarily by restricting worker immigration to those who could be assured of jobs, but if that test were passed the immigrants could have their families join them. Refugees were exempt from this employment restriction. The overall intake target was reduced from 140,000, which the Liberal-National government had prescribed for 1971–72, to 80,000 for 1974–75, and again to 50,000 in 1975–76. Settler arrivals during these years (to which reference was made earlier) were close to these target figures. The Fraser Liberal-National government, which came to office in September 1975, began to raise the immigration targets again, though retaining quite rigid economic controls. It also moved quickly to accept Asian refugees and to strengthen the emphasis on family reunion. Both unions and employers had firmly rejected the 'guest worker' type of migration that had played such a significant role in manpower policies of North and Western European countries through the 1960s and early 70s: such a scheme was against Australia's long tradition of family migration. The categories to be admitted under 'family reunion' were also extended beyond dependent children and aged parents to include siblings, provided that for persons in this latter category there was a guarantee of employment. Simultaneously the government opened the way for refugees by raising the approved intake in 1978 from 9000 to 14,000 a year.

The outcome of these major changes was that intakes of new settlers became more diversified.[15] Refugees played an important role: between 1975 and 1984, Australia resettled about 90,000 Indochinese, who have since been granted full immigrant status with the right to seek entry for their families in the same way as non-refugee settlers – a right that they use very efficiently. In addition about a further 100,000 non-European immigrants have come from Asian and Pacific countries. Over the whole post-war period 1947–85, the non-European-born segment has increased from about 0.5 to 2.5 per cent of the Australian population. 'Asians' settling in Australia have represented many ethnic backgrounds. Ethnic Chinese have been the largest group, but these have come to Australia from many sources such as Singapore, Hong Kong, Malaysia and Vietnam. Other significant sources of non-European settlers have been India, Pakistan, Lebanon and the Pacific Islands. Refugees generated from armed conflicts and political revolutions in Southeast Asia have been major ingredients of recent immigrant inflows.

These major changes in policy over the last twenty years or so have been associated with the concept of 'multicultural Australia'. Just what does this mean in demographic terms? Naturally the continuous though fluctuating inflow of new settlers from 1947 to 1985 (yielding a net settler gain of about 3.1 million in a total population increase of 8.1 million) reduced the proportion of Australian-born in the total population from 90 to 80 per cent. Over the same period there developed a great diversity of people in terms of birthplace groups. An intercensal comparison of the situation in 1947, 1981 and 1986 is summarized in Table 6.2. This table illustrates the basis of multicultural Australia. Birthplace figures oversimplify the position, because many Australian-born will be the product of 'mixed' marriages, and some Australian-born may still feel themselves to be of non-Australian background. A basic aspect of Australia's multiculturalism is the great variety of relatively small birthplace groups – over 100 of them – many of which are no longer being replenished by any significant inflow of new settlers. That is basically true of the birthplaces of the Displaced Person settlers of 1948–49 and of the Italians, Greeks, Turks and Lebanese. Non-British immigration to Australia has been largely made up of 'period' migration. This has planted 'seed' immigrants, who have then been followed by families and relatives for a generation or so before stabilizing or even declining. The result has been the spread of

Table 6.2 *Percentage distribution of the Australian population by major birthplace regions, censuses of 1974, 1981 and 1986*

Birthplace region	1947	1981	1986
Australia	90.1	79.4	78.7
UK and Ireland	7.1	7.8	7.4
Europe	1.5	7.5	7.5
Middle East	0.1	1.0	0.9
Asia	0.3	1.8	2.6
Oceania	0.6	1.5	1.6
Other (Africa and America)	0.3	1.1	1.3
Total	100.0	100.0	100.0

Sources: Based on figures supplied by Dr C.A. Price, Department of Demography, Australian National University; and, for 1986, *Australian Population Trends and Prospects 1987*, Department of Immigration, Local Government and Ethnic Affairs, p.68.

birthplace groups rather than the dominance of any one of them. Of the non-British (that is, outside UK and Eire), the only birthplace groups comprising more than 1 per cent of the population of Australia in 1981 were the Italians (283,000; 1.9 per cent), New Zealanders (185,000; 1.2 per cent), Yugoslavs (154,000; 1.1 per cent) and Greeks (151,000; 1.0 per cent). The high level of trans-Tasman migration after 1981 increased the share of the New Zealand-born in the total Australian population to 212,000 (1.4 per cent) by 1986, but all the other birthplace groups were reduced because mortality was greater than new immigration in this intercensal period. In 1986 the only other group to remain above the 1 per cent level was that of the Italians (262,000 or 1.7 per cent). It is this great diversity of small groups which renders so difficult many aspects of current multicultural policy, such as language instruction, in a population which is still almost 90 per cent English-speaking in terms of 'native' tongue. But what is certain is the cultural impact of this great wave of new settlers arriving since 1947. On the whole the interaction of new and old Australians has been achieved with a minimum of conflict – integration has worked. Unfortunately the story is less happy in the case of Australia's own Aborigines.

THE ABORIGINES

The population of Australia before European settlers arrived in 1788 is a matter of some controversy. For many years the accepted figure, based on anthropological evidence relating to the estimated number of Aboriginal tribes, was about 300,000. More recent research using epidemiological and archaeological evidence has tended to raise this to 500,000 and even above the million mark. But there is little hard evidence. What is quite certain is that contact with Europeans had disastrous results in Australia, as did similar contacts elsewhere associated with the expansion of European empires in the late eighteenth and early nineteenth centuries. European settlement occurred early enough in Australia to bring with it the scourge of smallpox – the biggest killer in eighteenth-century Europe – which had a severe impact upon the Aborigines in an outbreak in 1789, followed by a less-devastating recurrence in 1829. Other diseases brought with Europeans were those that formed a normal part of European colonization: venereal diseases, measles, influenza, whooping cough and tuberculosis. All killed disastrously on first contact, not only in Australia, but in the Pacific Islands, New Zealand and wherever the tentacles of empire spread. Wars and killings in the processes of settlement were other factors all too common.

In Australia the Aborigines were excluded from the colonial census counts. Estimates made almost certainly undercounted the true numbers. The occurrence of a massive decline after contact with Europeans is no longer disputed. After a century of white settlement, the number of Aborigines appears to have been about 130,000. The decline continued for another fifty years to a low point of around 67,000 in 1933. The reasons for the decline appear to have been relatively low fertility, very high infant mortality (probably 150 or more deaths per 1000 live births) and high adult mortality from early middle age. Overall the Aboriginal life expectancy probably did not exceed 35 years, while that of the European population was rising to about 60 years.

From about 1930 the situation began to change for the better and between 1933 and 1981 the enumerated Aboriginal population had grown from an estimated 67,100 to 171,100. Growth came from a rise in fertility, yielding birthrates of about 35–40 per 1000 and a marked decrease in infant mortality (about 25 per 1000 live births in 1981). There was an extension of life expectancy to about 54 years. Growth rates appear to have exceeded 2 per cent a year by the 1970s and the Aborigines, with 40 per cent of their population aged 0–14, show considerable potential for relatively rapid growth for the rest of the century, although fertility levels have been almost halved in the last twenty years or so. The estimated total fertility rate for Aborigines indicates a decrease from approximately 6.6 births in 1961–66 to 3.3 in 1976–81. This decline is probably associated with increasing urbanization (over 60 per cent of Aborigines now live in towns and cities) and increased exposure to European lifestyles and values. While all these demographic statistics suggest a marked improvement in many aspects of Aboriginal lives, *relatively* they still lag far behind the rest of Australia's people. 'White' Australia has infant mortality rates less than half those of the Aborigines; and Aboriginal expectations of life are still at least twenty years below those of non-Aboriginal Australia. Much progress has been made – a point that is often overlooked – but much more is necessary before the term 'disadvantaged' can be discarded as a description of the position of Aborigines compared with that of non-Aborigines.[16]

While there is little doubt that Aboriginal growth rates are still higher and that life expectancies are still much lower than amongst the non-Aboriginal population, precise measurements of such differences remain very difficult because of the lack of a clearly defined denominator in the case of the Aborigines. Since 1971, censuses have asked Aborigines (and Torres Strait Islanders) to identify themselves as such if they consider themselves to be of Aboriginal background. This 'self-identification' approach reflects the prevailing community attitudes rather than any constant factor such as degree of Aboriginality through parentage or caste, which had been the basis of earlier enumerations. While the 'self-identification' principle avoids classification on the grounds of race, it has resulted in wide variations of numbers which appear to reflect the prevailing community attitudes at the date of each census. Consequently the recorded numbers of Aborigines and Torres Strait Islanders have fluctuated widely since 1971 rather than showing any consistent demographic trend. The figures recorded at each census since 1971 have been:

1971	1976	1981	1986
115,900	160,900	159,900	227,600

The figures for 1971 and 1976 seem reasonable when analysed in the light of other annual demographic data. The figure for 1981 seems clearly deficient: there appears to have been an unaccountable flight at that time from the concept of 'Aboriginality'. The 1986 figure suggests strongly, however, that many more persons with some degree of Aboriginal ancestry wished to be identified in the census as Aborigine. As already indicated in the introduction to this chapter, the recorded intercensal increase in the Aboriginal population between 1981 and 1986 is far above what could have been achieved by natural increase.

CONTEMPORARY TRENDS AND ATTITUDES

What are the prospects of natural increase in Australia? In terms of the demographic revolution that has been an important part of the transformation of European societies, where does Australia stand and what are its prospects? Earlier, the course of demographic transition from about 1880 was outlined. This transition saw the reduction of average family size from 6+ children to about 2.5. It was also accompanied by a transformation of life expectancies from less than 40 years to about 60 years early this century, rising to well over 70 years today. The beginnings of these changes were almost simultaneous, but mortality fell more quickly than fertility, so that in the early stages of the transition natural growth rates began to rise. The colonies were healthy – and wealthy – places, and their rates of *natural* growth were amongst the highest in the world – over 2 per cent a year until about 1875; then around 2 per cent through 1895, around 1.5 to 1.7 per cent right through until almost 1925, slumping to below 1 per cent through the Great Depression of the 1930s, then rising again to as high as 1.4 per cent by 1957–58, but falling away again after 1971 to about 0.8 per cent. While many of the developed countries showed similar *trends*, few sustained such high levels, a major reason being that Australia was supplementing its cohorts in the child-bearing age groups with periodic waves of young immigrants whose age-composition was favourable to procreation.

Australia had become a member of a segment of the world that was unique in human experience. No major agglomerations of people had before achieved such low levels of mortality (with expectations of life creeping up to 75 years for males and 80 years for females) or such widespread voluntary control over fertility. With about 90 per cent of females now living from birth to the end of their fecund years, clearly some modification of their fecundity was essential if astronomical rates of growth were to be avoided. In terms of growth, what an average of 4.5 children did when life expectations were about 35 years (only 150 years ago), 2.5 children will provide today. It is apt to describe this unique situation as one in which the forces of fecundity and mortality are no longer in equilibrium, for human fecundity (i.e., reproductive potential) is geared to a life expectation of about half of the expectations now existing in 'developed' countries.

This phenomenon may be the most compelling rationale for the universality of the two-child family in modern Australia and in other highly 'developed' countries in Europe and North America.

There are those in Australia who say that 16 million people are enough; and a few who say that this is already too many. Arguments to support these views are the threats to wilderness areas and estuaries, the pressure on land resources, the destruction of soil fertility through leaching resulting from irrigation, and the overcrowding of the states' capital cities wherein almost two-thirds of Australia's population already live and work. These views first appeared with any strength in about the mid-1960s and perhaps reflected at first a degree of stereotyping of views held in much more crowded countries such as Britain, Germany and the United States. But while such views are almost certainly held by a relatively small minority in Australia, their arguments have been given shape and form in a number of scholarly publications.[17]

It might be argued that the strongest support for these slow (or even zero) growth concepts is the rising generation of young Australians of reproductive ages, for they have been marrying later and divorcing more than their forebears did; they have also been postponing births and having fewer births through their fecund years than did any previous generation in Australia's history. Recent trends towards higher marriage age and a longer interval between marriage and first birth are in marked contrast to the events of the baby-boom years of the 1950s and 1960s, which were described earlier. The problem is to decide which period is normal. Which has attributes that are likely to continue?

The 1950s and 1960s were clearly 'abnormal' in the sense that they broke with the traditional patterns with regard to the lowering of marriage ages for both men and women, the rapidity with which they had their children after marriage and the high proportion of

133

pre-nuptial conceptions and births. Despite the pill, marketed first in 1961, the young unmarried women were not good contraceptors. By contrast the post-1971 young people of Australia have been returning to patterns which have more affinity with tradition. Their higher marriage age and lower proportion marrying and their pattern of postponing first births and of spacing births are redolent of the 1940s rather than the 1960s. But they are probably the most efficient contraceptors of all time and seem to be both meeting their two-children targets with great efficiency and reducing the number of pre-nuptial conceptions. Like the generation of the 1960s, they are still divorcing in large numbers (about one in four marriages), but there is evidence that the divorce rate may have peaked and be turning down.

These demographic patterns, together with social and economic changes with respect to leisure and work for women, have changed and given new dimensions to 'the family' in Australia, even to the point of suggesting that the family is 'under threat'. There have been increases in one-parent households, 'blended' families and *de facto* living arrangements. There is clearly increasing variety in what constitutes a 'family'. Most of these new arrangements are now accepted by Australian society; but the inference that the traditional nuclear family of *married* parents and their children is on the way out is not warranted by the evidence so far available. The high proportions of young women recorded as married in 1971 (Table 6.3) was a unique phenomenon in Australia's marriage history and the levels prevailing in 1981 (which exclude 'separated' and 'divorced' so as to avoid bias introduced by the high incidence of these phenomena at this time) were still much above levels that had applied before the baby boom. By 1986 the proportions *legally* married were back to about the traditional levels of 1921 and earlier years. These 1986 figures, however, exclude those living in *de facto* but socially accepted relationships, which are now a significant and perhaps permanent factor in the 'marriage' scene of Australia, as of many other countries.

Table 6.3 *Percentage of women in each age group married at Census dates*

Age group	1921	1947	1971	1981*	1986*
20–24	33.2	48.0	63.7	46.4	33.6
25–29	61.8	77.0	86.8	74.5	64.1
30–34	73.3	83.3	91.1	83.1	75.6
35–39	76.7	83.5	91.5	85.1	79.1

*   Excluding 'separated' and 'divorced'
Source: Derived from data on conjugal status, Australian censuses.

In other words, Australia is still a nation with a high proportion of cohabiting couples. If surveys taken in the 1970s are any guide, all but a very small fraction of those couples marry in order to have children.[18] Many couples, in fact, are likely to be disappointed because of physiological impairments which affect some 10 per cent of marriages. The surveys taken in 1976 and 1979 showed that only 3 per cent of younger married women (aged 20–24) expected to remain childless, but that few wanted large families: there was an overwhelming attraction to the two-child family. Many people were prepared to postpone having children until the time was economically propitious, but the preference was then to have children fairly quickly. Thus attaining the ideal of two children requires only about three or four years of married life out of a total *fertile* married lifespan averaging 20–25 years.

All this makes sense in terms of women's desire to be gainfully employed; and the evolution of this family pattern is interrelated, as to both cause and effect, with the revolutionary change since the mid-1960s in the proportion of married women in the nation's workforce. From 1966 to 1971, the increase of married women in the workforce exceeded the increase of all males; and the upward trend has continued, though more slowly, since then. A physiological fact to be noted is that a family requires only two births to have a 90 per cent chance that parents will be replaced by their children – that is, that the two children will survive and grow to the ages their parents were when the children were born.

As already emphasized, it is this disharmony between the fecundity potential and mortality that makes modern Western societies unique in human experience and makes positive interference to prevent procreation through most of a women's fertile years a necessity if explosive growth rates are to be avoided.

In this regard, as in so many others, Australia is a typical product of the mortality transition. In the late nineteenth century, Australia may well have had the highest expectation of life in the world: it had a booming economy, at least to the end of the 1880s, with high incomes and national standards of life in a healthy environment which was vastly different from that of the industrial cities of Europe. But the expectation of life at birth was still only about 50 years at the turn of the century, when infant mortality was also about ten times higher than it is today. For another sixty years, the major advance in life expectation came in the elimination of infectious diseases affecting particularly young children but also adults in what today would be termed early middle age. The degenerative diseases (cancer, heart failure, etc.) continued to take their toll of those who did survive the 'middle-age' killers of tuberculosis, pulmonary afflictions and other infectious diseases. When expectations of life from birth attained levels of about 65 years for men and 70 years for women, around the 1960s and 1970s, expectations of persons above those ages had virtually been halted. The striking phenomenon since then has been improvements at these higher ages.[19] In other words, the attack on infectious diseases had achieved its major objective by the 1960s, and since then the main thrust to increased longevity has been in the attacks upon degenerative diseases. Expectations of life at birth in 1971 of 68 years for men and 75 years for women, had been pushed upwards by 1983 to 72 and almost 79 years respectively. Australia is no longer at the top of the life-expectation table, but still ranks within the first half dozen or so (Figure 6.4).

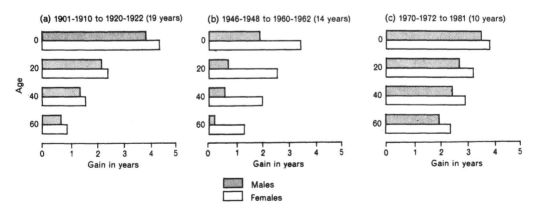

Figure 6.4 Gain in years of expectation of life at selected ages 1901–10 to 1981. *Sources:* Based on official life tables, ABS.

AUSTRALIAN SOCIETY

ACHIEVEMENTS AND PROSPECTS

What is the demographic product of the first two hundred years of European settlement and endeavour? Some major features are:

a population of a little above 16 million – the product of relatively high natural increase and the absorption of great waves of immigrants digested, as one commentator put it in the 1920s, on the boa-constrictor principle of alternative spasms of gluttony and somnolent digestion;

a population still predominantly of British origin, but also of great ethnic diversity;

a population which is (and always has been) highly urbanized. In 1981, 86 per cent of Australia's population lived in urban areas and 63 per cent in the capital cities of states and territories: this may be compared with the situation in 1921 when the corresponding proportions were 62 and 43 per cent – both remarkably high for their time;

a population which appears to have completed at last (after major temporary interruptions on the way, such as the slump of births during the Great Depression of the 1930s and the boom in births in the 1950s and 1960s) the transition from high to low fertility – that is, from completed family sizes averaging 6 children to family sizes averaging just over 2 children. As this change has occurred, differentials in family size by residential area, religion, ethnicity and occupation have become smaller. The most conspicuous difference in the 1980s is that between Aborigines and the rest of the population, but even this difference is being reduced as Aboriginal fertility falls, particularly in urban areas;

a population enjoying great longevity, with expectation of life at birth approaching 80 years for women and 76 years for men – and apparently still improving;

a population still well stocked with young people, the products of the baby boom, and thus with good potential for an innovative and flexible labour input in a period of structural change in the economy, and for sustaining the number of births until the end of the century as an 'echo effect' of the past baby boom;

a population which has therefore a great potential for growth until the end of the century and beyond;

a population, however, wherein the level of fertility is intrinsically below replacement level, has been so for a decade, and looks like remaining so for at least some time ahead.

What are the demographic prospects? There are two aspects to be considered: natural increase or decrease arising from the current relationship between births and deaths; and international migration.

Births will exceed deaths for the rest of this century. This relation arises from the favourable age composition mentioned above. But the current level of reproduction will not sustain that position for more than another generation. If fertility remained just below replacement level, with a total fertility rate of 1.93 – a reasonably optimistic assumption, given the pattern of recent years – and there were a continued slow increase in life expectancy, Australia's population would grow through natural increase alone from its 1986 level of 16.02 million to about 17.6 million by the year 2001. But growth would then be slowing down to about 0.5 per cent (compared with 0.8 per cent in 1985) and reducing further year by year; and by about the year 2021 growth would have come to a halt with a population around 18.6 million, whereafter slow decline would occur. This scenario is valid only for the assumptions given, and it is to be emphasized that few projections so long range as that given above turn out to be correct. Population projections, like other projections which try to anticipate social and economic behaviour, have a fairly dismal record in terms of their ultimate accuracy.

Choosing an assumption about immigration is also fraught with difficulties. A reasonably safe supposition may be that Australia will continue to be an attraction for immigrants. In addition current government policy favours immigration at an annual rate of 100,000 or more a year. This will yield a net gain of, say, 75,000–80,000 a year. The government's positive approach is supported by a major inquiry into the costs and benefits of immigration, which found that immigration was a benefit to economic growth.[20] Some economists and most ecologists and conservationists would disagree; but the commitment of the present Labor government to immigration, the known wish of the Liberal-National coalition to raise immigration levels, the commitment of all parties to continuing at least the acceptance of refugees and the encouragement of family reunion arrangements all seem to imply, for the foreseeable future, a minimum net immigration intake of 50,000 or 60,000 a year. Furthermore the government is apparently confident that Australia has the capacity to attract new settlers and terminated the policy of government assistance to intending settlers (except for refugees) in 1985. This ended a policy that had played a significant role in the peopling of Australia since 1831. Its role was still significant, though of declining importance, in the post-war years. From 1959 to 1982, over half the settler arrivals were in the assisted categories. This proportion had declined to a quarter in 1980–82. Present government policy appears to include the continual recruitment of workers with economic skills known to be in short supply, so that an assumption of an average net gain of 75,000 immigrants a year is reasonable. Such an intake would raise the levels of population to about 19 million by 2001 and to 22 million in 2021.

The following, therefore, is perhaps a minimum scenario for Australia's population over the next thirty-five years or so:

	Population in millions		
	1986	*2001*	*2021*
Without immigration	16.0	17.5	18.6
With immigration averaging 75,000 net a year	16.0	18.9	22.0

Whether the population will be above or below these figures will be less important, in terms of economic and social policy, than the structure of the population that is evolving under the impact of current and expected levels of fertility and mortality. It seems certain that Australians want, expect and will pay for further gains in longevity. It also appears unlikely that there will be a return to the desire for large families: a hundred years of history, current surveys and the analysis of available fertility data all go against such an occurrence, although there may be short-run variations in the levels of natural increase, as there have been in the past, through changes in marriage patterns and in the phasing and timing of births. If these hypotheses hold good, Australia will move towards a population structure where there will be relatively little difference in the size of age groups from age 0 to about age 50, with an increasing decrement through deaths thereafter. Australia will have achieved a stable age-sex structure which is vastly different from that of the 1980s. This is illustrated in Figure 6.5.

The *stable* population sector of Figure 6.5 illustrates the age and sex structure that would finally emerge, and thereafter remain constant, if assumed levels of fertility and mortality remain unchanged. For the purposes of this illustration, the assumptions are that Australian fertility will settle at replacement level, that life expectancies will also remain constant at present levels of about 75 years for men and 79 years for women, and that there will be no immigration or emigration. The shape of this *stable* profile, which would emerge in about sixty years' time, is clearly very different from the present position with its 'bulge' of young people arising from the baby boom and its 'deficit' of older people when compared with the stable profile. As the 'bulge' passes into the older age groups there will obviously be an increase in the average age of the population, and eventually the 'bulge' will swell the ranks of the 'deficit' aged 65 years and over. At the same time, however, those in the 'juvenile' group, aged 0–14 years, will decrease by an almost equal amount. This in turn means that the *proportion* of the total population of 'working age', 15–64 years, will remain fairly constant, but the mean age of this segment will increase.

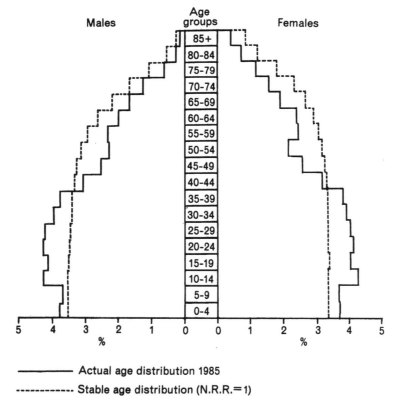

Figure 6.5 Stable age distribution(N.R.R.= 1) and actual age distribution *Source: Australian Demographic Statistics*, December quarter, Cat. No.3101.0 (Preliminary estimate), ABS.

The actual age structure in 1985 and that of the stable population are as follows:

Percentage population distribution by age group

Age group	1985 actual	Stable and stationary population
0–14	24	21
15–64	66	65
65 and over	10	14
All ages	100	100

This is the demographic basis of the 'problem' of ageing about which social and economic planners seem so worried. The social and economic aspects of the 'problem' are seen as the greater financial and social service burden that this increasing number of aged will impose upon those who earn income. This burden on the worker will be relieved to some degree by the decreased proportion of juveniles; but each aged person gained will cost more to maintain than is saved from each juvenile lost. Thus an increased total dependency burden is anticipated in the transition to the stable situation. There are significant implications for social welfare policies, such as the provision of appropriate domiciliary and medical services for the frail aged; but the most important matter is probably the need for the present generation of workers to prepare for their own old age through adequately funded superannuation schemes.

Earlier reference was made to the emergence of that unique person, the resident of the developed world of the twentieth century, with an expectation of life exceeding 70 years and the capacity to ensure generation replacement with an average family size of just over 2 children per family. Australians are part of that scene. As already noted, *predictions* of future demographic events are hazardous; but the one demographic prediction that seems to be absolutely safe is that the search for longevity will continue, whatever the cost; and therefore that the 'burden' of the aged *will* increase, as an inevitable consequence. It is sometimes suggested that more immigrants (who are usually heavily concentrated at the time of their movement between the ages of 20 and 39) will ease the ageing 'problem'. But immigrants grow old too and, should the flow of new settlers cease for any reason, the end result will be an exacerbation, not alleviation of, the ageing process. The situation portrayed in the model of the stable population will not be greatly changed, whether or not immigration is used to push up the size of Australia's population by a further 2 or 3 million in the next fifty years or so.

Thus important concerns which emerge from the demographic evolution of the last century or so include:

the changing role of women in a society wherein reproductive participation is reduced to about a tenth of their fecund years;

the increasing average age of the labour force (not its *decrease* as a proportion of total population);

the provision of meaningful activities for fit persons in the upper age brackets;

the need for contributory superannuation to ease the burden of public support for aged persons after they retire; and

the availability of support systems (housing, hospital and medical services) for the frail aged.

These few examples illustrate the dimension of policy changes that must be faced for the rest of this century and presumably through the next. The fact that solving these new problems will require major revisions in the distribution of the national income, new approaches in the field of education and a revision of the whole social welfare system is no excuse for inaction. The basic demographic structure of the population over the next half century or so is definable now and bears very little relation to the structure that existed as late as only fifty years ago – the structure which motivated the building of the welfare services as they exist today.

The demographic factors of longevity and small families had no place in Australia's first 150 years of European settlement. The only fact likely to be common to both past and future is immigration: but from where and in what quantities? There are forces in Australia, for example, the 'Greenies', who will press for low targets or indeed no immigration at all; but as already indicated, present and likely future policy seems to be and seems likely to remain against them. Any government is likely to hold firm, within the overall principle of no racial discrimination, to administrative controls governing such factors as levels of skill, employability, refugee status and eligibility under family reunion, to which potential immigrants are subjected. Where suitable immigrants will spring from is difficult to forecast. Population pressure in Asia is by itself a poor basis for forecasting. Also, while it may be argued that impending and actual population decline in the traditional immigrant sources in Europe makes these nations unlikely to continue to be sources of immigrants in the long term, there is evidence that many thousands of people in the United Kingdom and elsewhere still look upon Australia as a desirable country for resettlement. It is therefore difficult to project the form of future pressures for immigration. The biggest movements of recent years have been refugees and illegal immigrants, particularly in the American continent, but also in Europe. It is proving increasingly difficult, in face of the growing international mobility of people, to control land frontiers or to deport 'illegal' entrants. Australia has had the protection of sea-frontiers, but this aid to the implementation of planned policy may become weaker in the near future than it has been in the past. The arrival of 'boat people' over the past decade is already evidence of this, as also is the increasing difficulty of catching up with those who enter the country on temporary visas and 'overstay' to seek permanent status.

On the immigration front, as well as on the vital front of births, deaths and natural growth rates, new challenges and new problems for the next century are clearly emerging. If Australians and their governments want their people to continue to grow in the next 100 years or so, as they have done almost continuously for the past 200 years, increasing reliance will have to be placed on immigration, as was the situation at the beginning of our history, to achieve this objective. Should fertility and mortality remain at present levels, immigration will be the only factor sustaining growth within a generation from now. Whether or not this proves to be the case will in turn depend almost wholly upon the decisions of future Australian parents about the number of children they will have. Mortality decline, which was a signicifant factor generating growth in the past, has no longer any significant demographic growth potential, for 90 per cent of deaths occur now to those above child-bearing age. The only impact of further longevity will be to accentuate the ageing process of the population.

As Graeme Hugo concluded in his admirable study based on the 1981 Census:

> The directions that Australia takes in the remainder of this century are dependent upon a myriad of interacting political, social and economic forces, the accurate anticipation of which is extremely difficult, if not impossible ... Yet looking forward and attempting to anticipate the future and to prepare for it with insight and flexibility is essential for the welfare of society and an important responsibility of the social scientists ... we are too often surprised by demographic changes which are readily identifiable and predictable.[21]

Notes

1   For a discussion of estimates of the pre-1788 population of Aborigines, see J.P. White and D.J. Mulvaney (eds.), 1987. *Australians to 1788*. Sydney, Fairfax Syme and Weldon Associates, Chapter 5.

2   This figure, which is the assessment of A. Gray and L.R. Smith 1983. *Australian Aboriginal Studies* 1, pp.2-9, is about 11,000 above the 1981 Census enumeration of 159,897. The suggestion that the 1981 Census seriously 'underestimates' the Aboriginal population is further supported by the tentative total of 227,600 Aborigines enumerated at the Census of June 30, 1986. This implies a growth rate of over 7 per cent p.a., 1981-86, which is almost three times the rate as assessed from vital data. The controversies about 'how many Aborigines' seem set to continue with respect to both pre-1788 and post-1988 figures.

3   The two major studies of convict settlement in Australia are A.G.L. Shaw 1966. *Convicts and the Colonies*, London, Faber & Faber: and L.L. Robson 1965. *Convict Settlers in Australia*. Melbourne, Melbourne University Press. For an interpretation of the society produced by the convict system, see J.B. Hirst 1983. *Convict Society and its Enemies. A History of Early New South Wales*. Sydney, Allen and Unwin.

4   For the history of free immigration to Australia to 1851, see R.B. Madgwick 1937. *Immigration into Eastern Australia, 1788-1851*. London, Longman Green & Co. (reprinted, Sydney University Press, 1969).

5   See A. Grenfell Price 1924. *The Foundation and Settlement of South Australia 1829-1845*. Adelaide, F.W. Preece.

6   For an account of the gold rushes and their longer-term social and economic effects see G. Serle 1963. *The Golden Age*. Melbourne, Melbourne University Press.

7   Short accounts of immigration policies and flows to the Australian colonies from 1860 to 1919 are given in F.K. Crowley 1945. The British Contribution to the Australian Population 1860-1919. *University Studies in History and Economics* 2 (2), pp.55-83, University of Western Australia. See also W.D. Borrie 1980. British Immigration to Australia, pp.101-116. In A.F. Madden and W.H. Morris-Jones (eds.), *Australia and Britain*, Sydney, Sydney University Press.

8   Royal Commission on the Decline of the Birth Rate and on the Mortality of Infants in New South Wales: Vol. I, *Report and Statistics*. New South Wales Government Printer, Sydney, 1904. A second volume of *Other Evidence, Exhibits, etc.*, was printed but withdrawn from publication, basically because of its illustrations of contraceptive instruments and contrivances which seem to have rendered the volume 'improper' for public circulation. T.A. Coglan was closely associated with the work of this commission: the statistical presentations clearly bear his stamp. For a study of the social and political environment in which this remarkable inquiry was conducted see Neville Hicks 1978. *This Sin and Scandal: Australia's Population Debate 1871-1911*. Canberra, ANU Press.

9   For accounts of the demographic transition in Australia, see E.F. Jones 1971. Fertility Decline in Australia and New Zealand, 1861-1936. *Population Index* 37(4), pp.301-38: L.T. Ruzicka and J.C. Caldwell 1977. *The End of Demographic Transition in Australia*. Australian Family Formation Project, Monograph No. 5, Department of Demography, ANU; and The National Population Inquiry, *Population and Australia*, Vol.1 (1975), ch.2, and *Supplementary Report* (1978), ch.2. Canberra, AGPS.

10   W.D. Borrie 1949. *Immigration, Australia's Problems and Prospects*. Sydney, Angus and Robertson. ch.III. There was also a growing scepticism in Australia about the population-carrying capacity of Australia's 'vast open spaces': see W.D. Forsyth 1942. *The Myth of Open Spaces*. Melbourne, Melbourne University Press.

11   For major studies of the growth and structure of Australia's population, with particular reference to the period since 1945, see U.N. Economic Commission for Asia and the Pacific, Country Monograph Series, No.9, *Population of Australia* (2 vols.), New York, 1982; and Graeme Hugo 1986. *Australia's Changing Population, Trends and Implications*. Melbourne, Oxford University Press. A valuable official analysis of recent trends (with excellent graphs and diagrams) is: Australian Bureau of Statistics, *Australian Demographic Trends*, Canberra, 1986.

[12]   The basis of post-war immigration policy was laid down by the Hon. A.A. Calwell in a statement to the House of Representatives on 2 August 1945: *Immigration – Government Policy*. His ideas were more fully developed in A.A. Calwell 1945. *How Many Australians Tomorrow?* Melbourne, Reed and Harris. Menzies virtually endorsed the Labor policy on immigration in a speech to the Australian Citizenship Convention in January, 1950. While annual targets and actual annual intakes have varied considerably since then, immigration has continued to be accepted as an important factor in Australian economic and social development.

[13]   For a study of the causes and nature of the 'baby boom', see L.T. Ruzicka and J.C. Caldwell 1977, *op.cit.*, ch.4; and The National Population Inquiry, *op.cit.*, Vol.1, ch.2 and *Supplementary Report*, ch.2.

[14]   The factors involved in the 'baby bust' phase after 1971 have been analysed by L.T. Ruzicka and C.Y. Choi 1981. Recent Decline in Australian Fertility. *Yearbook of Australia*. No. 65, Canberra. See also Department of Immigration and Ethnic Affairs, National Population Council, What's Happening to the Australian Family? *Population Report 8*, Canberra 1987.

[15]   The ethnic composition of the Australian population has been analysed comprehensively by Dr C.A. Price, e.g., U.N. Economic and Social Commission for Asia and the Pacific, *op.cit.*, Vol.1, ch.III. Also in Department of Demography, ANU, Working Papers in Demography, No.13, 1984. *Birthplaces of the Australian Population 1861-1981*.

[16]   Demographic statistics relating to Aborigines are still very inadequate. The three main sources used for this section of the chapter are: The National Population Inquiry, *op.cit.*, Vol.II, chs.XI-XIV; Graeme Hugo 1986. *op.cit.*, ch.8; and U.N. Economic and Social Commission for Asia and the Pacific, *op.cit.*, Vol.I, ch.VI.

[17]   For example, R. Birrell, D. Hill and J. Nevile (eds.) 1984. *Populate and Perish. The Stresses of Population Growth in Australia*, Sydney, Fontana.

[18]   Australian Bureau of Statistics, *Birth Expectations of Married Women*, Canberra, 1976 and 1979.

[19]   Graeme Hugo 1986. *op.cit.*, chs.2 and 6. See also Christobel Young, 1986. *Selection and Survival, Immigrant Mortality in Australia*. Department of Immigration and Ethnic Affairs, Studies in Migrant Education, Canberra, AGPS.

[20]   N.R. Norman and K.F. Meikle 1985. *The Economic Effects of Immigration on Australia*. Vol.I, Melbourne, Committee for Economic Development of Australia.

[21]   Graeme Hugo 1986. *op.cit.*, p.317.

7

*An Economy in Distress?**

J.W. Nevile

By the middle of the 1980s there was a widespread perception in Australia that the economy was performing far less well than previously, that our economic institutions were out-moded, our captains of industry were unenterprising and that the attitudes of many Australians towards work and self-reliance had changed for the worse. In short, many felt that Australia was in danger of becoming a 'banana republic' and the 'sick man', not of Europe, but of the western rim of the Pacific.[1] In part this perception was based on an observable deterioration in economic performance as shown by the traditional measures: growth in output, rates of inflation and levels of unemployment. In part it was based on new indicators, some factual and some less so, such as the fear that successive large government budget deficits were leading to a spiralling and unmanageable public debt, and that excessive foreign borrowing showed that Australia was living beyond its means and could no longer afford the standard of living to which it had become accustomed.

This chapter will both examine the extent to which the Australian economy did perform less well overall in the 80s than in earlier periods and the degree to which this deterioration in performance was atypical of Western economies. Almost all Western economies suffered a marked break in their fortunes around 1974 – with higher inflation, higher unemployment and lower growth being widespread since then compared with the previous twenty-five years. It is easy to document a positive answer to the question: 'Did this also happen in Australia?' An equally important question is whether the Australian economy performed worse than that of most other comparable economies. On the one hand if a deterioration in Australian economic performance is similar to that in the rest of the Western world, then it is probably due to world-wide trends which we have little ability to influence. Improvement may still be possible and should be sought; but it will probably require an exceptional effort on the part of Australia. On the other hand if Australian economic performance is distinctly worse than typical overseas experience, this may be due to features of the Australian economy itself, making improvement somewhat easier to achieve.

The next five sections will examine the performance of the Australian economy in the key areas of output growth, unemployment, productivity, inflation and debt. The final section will draw the threads together, assess the overall performance, and discuss the types of policies necessary to improve the performance of the economy.

* The author's thanks are due to Penny Neal for research assistance.

Figure 7.1 Rates of growth of constant price GDP and constant price GDP per head. *Note:* Due to a break in the population series it is not possible to calculate the rate of growth per head in 1971–72. *Source:* Calculated from figures in ABS, *Australian National Accounts, National Income and Expenditure* (Cat. no. 5204.0), various issues; *Australian Demographic Statistics* (Cat. no. 3101.0), various issues.

OUTPUT GROWTH

The most basic function of any economy is to produce goods and services. Figure 7.1 shows the rate of growth of total output, or gross domestic product (GDP) in constant prices each year since 1964–65. While GDP is the best indicator of the size of the economy and its growth rate is important in many contexts, growth in GDP per head is more relevant to growth in living standards, and is also shown in Figure 7.1. There is no doubt that economic growth slackened in the second half of the 70s and, despite the three good years of 1983–84 to 1985–86, has remained low since then. The story is much the same whether one focusses on GDP or GDP per head and, to save repetition, we only examine the latter. It is the slow rate of growth of living standards that underlies most people's concern about poor economic performance.

In looking at growth rates it is important to compare years which are at the same stage of the business cycle. Any country can show a good growth rate if the first year is at the trough of a slump and the last at the height of a boom. The years 1964–65 and 1973–74 are comparable, as are 1974–75 and 1986–87. Figure 7.1 shows a clear break at the end of 1973–74. Despite the good years from 1983–84 to 1985–86, the average rate of growth in GDP per head was 1.5 per cent in the period 1974–75 to 1986–87, and exactly twice that in the period from 1964–65 to 1973–74. The decade ending in 1973–74 was a particularly good one for economic growth in Australia, but over the whole period from 1950–51 to 1973–74, growth in GDP per head averaged 2.2 per cent.

How important is this decline in economic growth? In the heady days of the late 60s and early 70s, when the economy was growing rapidly, there was a movement decrying growth. Once a country became as rich as most Western countries were in the 60s was there any point in becoming richer? In part the posing of this question was a reaction against the excessive materialism of the consumer society.[2] As such it was not really an argument against economic growth but the particular form the fruits of economic growth were taking. There is no reason why the extra output that economic growth makes possible should be more and bigger cars, boats and other consumer durables. It can equally well be in the form of better public health and more symphony concerts – or better sporting facilities and more rock concerts if that is what people want. In any case, once economic growth was greatly reduced, doubts about its value were also reduced. Today the emphasis is squarely back on the benefits of growth, both from those on the right who emphasize the desirability of individual initiative and accumulation of wealth, and also from those on the left who believe that the public sector also needs to grow (in absolute terms even if not relative to the private sector) and hanker after universal sewerage in Australia to go with universal suffrage. If one takes as appropriate criteria for judgement both the desires of the overwhelming mass of the population and the views of intellectuals there is no doubt that the decline in the rate of economic growth is an indication of poor performance by the Australian economy.

However almost all Western economies have grown slowly since 1974 compared to the previous twenty-five years. Has Australia's growth in GDP per head been unusually low? Table 7.1 shows the annual rate of growth of output per head in the largest Western economies, a number of smaller ones and also for the OECD countries as a whole.[3] Since it is easier to grow from a low base they are ranked in the table by the size of output per head in 1974 and the size of output per head is also given for 1985 (the last year for which statistics are available). Thus those who wish can see how far Australia has slipped and which countries have passed us.

It is clear from Table 7.1 that Australia was not a high performer in the output stakes. But neither were we a very low performer. In fact although the growth in output per head in Australia was somewhat lower than that for the OECD as a whole, and our growth rate ranked twelfth out of twenty countries, if one excludes the three countries where there were particularly unusual circumstances – Japan, Norway and New Zealand – Australia is almost the middle country in growth rates. Excluding again the special cases of Japan, Norway and New Zealand, we were passed by one country, West Germany, and ourselves passed one country, the Netherlands. Australian performance can be summed up as typical of OECD countries. Moreover this was a distinct improvement on earlier post-World War II experience. Such accurate statistics as those in Table 7.1 are not available for the earlier period, but it is clear that Australia performed relatively worse. Our growth rate of GDP per head then was less than half that of many OECD countries and well below the average for the OECD as a whole.

Nevertheless a less kind way of making the point that since 1974 Australian performance has been typical of the OECD as a whole, could be to say that Australian performance has been mediocre, leaving plenty of room for improvement even by the not very demanding standards of international comparisons of growth rates since 1974. It is useful, therefore, to examine more closely Australia's relatively low rate of growth in GDP per head over the last decade or so.

A low rate of growth in GDP per head could be because of a decline in the number of hours worked (on average) by each person in the country, because of a decline in the rate of productivity growth or because of both of these things. There was a substantial decline in the number of hours worked per head in the period since 1974, largely, though not entirely,

Table 7.1 *Gross domestic product per head (various countries in 1985 constant price $US)*

	1974	1985	Annual growth rate (%)
USA	14,070	16,494	1.4
Canada	12,558	15,223	1.8
Sweden	11,091	12,639	1.2
Netherlands	10,545	11,269	0.6
Denmark	10,151	12,254	1.7
Australia	10,136	11,738	1.3
New Zealand	10,010	10,037	0.0
West Germany	9,965	12,179	1.8
France	9,936	11,445	1.3
Norway	9,678	13,897	3.4
United Kingdom	9,545	10,915	1.2
Belgium	9,419	10,680	1.1
Italy	9,151	10,841	1.5
Finland	9,101	11,442	2.1
Austria	8,591	10,729	2.1
Japan	8,411	11,803	3.1
Spain	7,178	7,595	0.5
Ireland	5,448	6,704	1.9
Portugal	4,965	5,526	1.0
Greece	4,880	6,001	1.9
Total OECD	10,287	12,297	1.6

Source: Calculated from figures in Australian Bureau of Statistics, *Gross Domestic Product at Purchasing Power Parity in OECD Countries, 1985*, Catalogue no. 5226.0.

because of the dramatic rise in the unemployment rate. This will be examined in the next section, before productivity growth is analysed in the following one.

UNEMPLOYMENT AND HOURS WORKED

Unemployment is, of course, a social evil in its own right as well as an economic failure that reduces the level of output per head of population. The point was put succinctly and well many years ago by a report of a US Senate Committee.

> Whether measured by economic and material loss or by human suffering and wasted skills the cost of unemployment is high. Unused natural resources remain to be used in the future. But work, the creative activity of man, once wasted can never be recovered; what might have been produced is lost. The damage to individuals and to society from unemployment often cannot be repaired.[4]

The percentage of the workforce recorded as unemployed is shown in Figure 7.2. The increasing failure since 1973–74 of the Australian economy to provide employment for

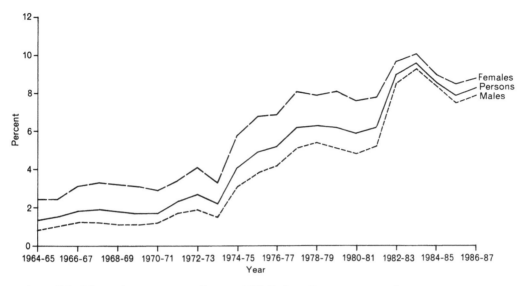

Figure 7.2 Unemployment rates. *Source:* ABS, *Labour Statistics, Australia* (Cat. no. 6101.0), various issues.

those wishing to work is clear. Over the business cycle from 1970–71 to 1973–74 the unemployment rate averaged 2.2 per cent. In the cycle from 1981–82 to 1985–86, despite a strong boom, it averaged 8.3 per cent. There had already been a persistent but very small upward trend in unemployment rates before 1974. For example, in the boom year 1964–65, the first year in Figure 7.2, the unemployment rate was 1.3 per cent. A decade earlier, in the boom of 1954–55, it was 0.8 per cent. If this trend had continued unchanged the unemployment rate would have been 3.6 per cent in the boom year 1985–86. Instead it was 7.9 per cent.

The economic costs of this rise in unemployment are epitomized by the fall in our growth rate. Other things being equal, the growth rate of output per head would have risen, not fallen, in the period since 1974 if only the previous trend rate rise in unemployment had continued. Moreover, not only would the growth in output have been greater, but we would now have a larger stock of capital goods including equipment, residential and non-residential buildings and also a larger stock of the intangible capital represented by human skills.

However the social costs of the big rise in unemployment are more important than the economic costs. The impact of the social costs can be better understood if one looks at the composition of unemployment and the average duration of a spell of unemployment. Table 7.2 shows unemployment rates by age and sex in August 1974 and 1986. Unemployment has increased the least for middle-aged women, and in every age group unemployment has increased more for males than females. As is well known, teenage unemployment is disgracefully high, but Table 7.2 reveals what is less well-known: the large increases in unemployment among what might be called prime-age males, that is, men between the ages of 20 and 34.

147

Table 7.2 *Percentage unemployment rates by age and sex, Australia, 1974 and 1986*

August	15–19	20–24	25–34	35–44	45–54	> 55
			Males			
1974	5.0	2.9	1.3	1.3	1.2	*
1986	18.7	12.3	6.8	4.6	5.5	5.5
1986/1974	3.7	4.2	5.2	3.5	4.6	
			Females			
1974	6.7	3.6	3.5	3.4	1.9	*
1986	19.5	9.9	7.6	6.0	4.5	3.0
1986/1974	2.9	2.8	2.2	1.8	2.4	

* numbers too small for reliable estimates
Source: Australian Bureau of Statistics, *The Labour Force, Australia*, catalogue no. 6203.0.

Even 10 per cent unemployment would not have such bad social consequences if it meant only an involuntary and poorly-paid holiday of one month a year for most of the population. But, of course, unemployment is not like that. Even more distressing than the rise in the unemployment rate is the increase in the length of the average spell of unemployment. In the early 70s, less than 25 per cent of the unemployed had been unemployed for more than two months. By August 1986, more than 25 per cent of those unemployed had already been unemployed for more than a year, and 20 per cent of males and 11 per cent of females unemployed had been unemployed for more than two years. In this respect teenagers did better than their elders. There is a tendency, especially among males, for the length of the spell of unemployment to be longer the older the person. Table 7.3 gives the median length of time people unemployed had already been unemployed by age and sex. These are, of course, uncompleted spells of unemployment since only those still unemployed are included in the figures. Hence the median length of spells of completed unemployment must be greater than the figures shown in Table 7.3. It is clear both that the Australian economy has performed badly as far as unemployment is concerned and that the social consequences of unemployment are not confined to teenagers.

A marked increase in unemployment was common in OECD countries after 1974. Has Australian experience been particularly bad compared with the records of other countries? Table 7.4 shows the unemployment rate in 1974 and 1985 for a number of Western countries.[5] The size of the increase in the unemployment rate in Australia is typical of that in OECD countries. In fact we improved our ranking slightly from having the ninth lowest unemployment rate in 1974 to the eighth lowest in 1985.

Table 7.4 suggests an interesting regularity. For the majority of countries their ranking in the rate of growth of output per head corresponds closely to their success in holding down the rise in the unemployment rate.[6] Of the two factors determining the rate of growth of output per head, productivity growth and change in the numbers of hours worked per head, the latter, which is dominated by the extent of the rise in unemployment, seems to be the

Table 7.3 *Median duration of current period of unemployment in weeks, Australia, August 1986*

Age	Males	Females
15–19	15	15
20–24	19	17
25–34	26	13
35–44	26	23
45–54	52	26
55–59	55	*
Total (including 60 and over)	26	16

* numbers too small for reliable estimates

Source: Australian Bureau of Statistics, *The Labour Force, Australia*, catalogue no. 6203.0.

Table 7.4 *Unemployment rates, various countries*

	1974 (%)	1985 (%)	1985 – 1974 (percentage points)
United States	5.5	7.2	1.7
Canada	5.3	10.5	5.2
Sweden	2.0	2.8	0.8
Netherlands	3.0	15.7	12.7
Denmark	3.5	9.3	5.8
Australia	2.3	8.2	5.9
New Zealand	0.1	3.9	3.8
West Germany	2.1	9.3	7.2
France	2.8	10.2	7.4
Norway	1.5	2.5	1.0
United Kingdom	2.1	11.3	9.2
Belgium	2.4	13.5	11.1
Italy	5.3	10.6	5.3
Finland	1.7	6.3	4.6
Austria	1.3	4.8	3.5
Japan	1.4	2.6	1.2
Spain	3.1	21.9	18.8
Ireland	5.3	17.8	12.5

Source: OECD *Labour Force Statistics, 1964–1984* and *Main Economic Indicators*, September 1986.

most important. However it is possible that the causation could run from growth in output per head to changes in the unemployment rate.

Although the most important factor in recent years, unemployment is only one of the factors influencing the average number of hours worked. Another is the participation rate, or the proportion of the relevant age group which is in the labour force. In the decade ending in 1988 there has been hidden unemployment, as people who despair of finding jobs cease looking and hence are no longer recorded as unemployed, but drop out of the labour force with a consequent decline in the participation rate. In August 1974 the participation rate for the civilian population was 61.4 per cent in Australia, having shown an upward trend for the previous quarter century. This upward trend was largely due to the increasing participation of women in the labour force. The upward trend continued until it peaked at 61.8 per cent in 1977, and then fell slightly to a trough of 59.7 per cent in 1983. By 1986 it had risen again to be virtually at the 1974 level. Participation rates generally fall during recessions as high levels of unemployment discourage job seeking, and it was no coincidence that the trough occurred in 1983 when the unemployment rate was at its highest level since the 1930s.

While over the period since 1974 there has been no trend in the participation rate, this overall stability is the result of offsetting trends among males and females. While the female participation rate continued to rise, that for males showed a downward trend both for married and unmarried men. This fall in the male participation rate is most marked the older the age group. For example, in the age group 60–64, the rate for married males fell from 77.4 per cent in August 1974 to 44.1 per cent in August 1985, and that for non-married males fell from 60.5 per cent to 36.3 per cent over the same period. To some extent this was due to voluntary early retirement, and the increased leisure chosen by these retirees should be considered just as valuable as the output foregone because of their retirement. But to some extent the fall in the participation rate was due to the fact that older men who become unemployed find it very hard to obtain another job and tend to drop out of the labour force. To the extent that this is the case, the decline in the male participation rate reflects an increase in hidden unemployment and a decline in Australian economic performance.

The overall stability of the participation rate hides another important trend: the increasing importance of part-time work. Even among males, the proportion working full-time fell from 96.5 per cent in August 1974 to 93.5 per cent in August 1985. Among females the proportion working full-time fell from 70.6 per cent to 62.7 per cent over the same period. Again, to some extent, this increase in part-time work was because of a desire on the part of the workers concerned to work less than full-time. But it is also because of an inability of those looking for full-time work to find it, and the extent to which this is so marks a deterioration in economic performance.

A final reason for a decline in the average number of hours worked, and hence in the growth of output per head, could be a decline of the proportion of the population of working age. Demographic changes, however, have played no part in Australia's relatively poor growth performance. From 1950 to 1974 there was a slight downward trend in the proportion of the population in the age group 15–64; but from June 1974 to June 1986 this age group actually increased from 63.5 per cent to 64.1 per cent of the total population. While there was a slight increase in the proportion of the population over 64, this was more than offset by a decline in the proportion under 15.

Was the decline in hours worked in Australia greater or less than that which occurred in other countries? It is hard to get up-to-date statistics on hours worked in all the countries in Table 7.1. However in a recent article Maddison[7] gives figures on hours worked for the period from 1973 to 1984 for the biggest five OECD economies, the so-called G5, or Group of 5, countries. From these one can calculate the annual growth rate, or rather decline, in hours worked per person for each of these countries, and the resulting figures are given in Table 7.5 along with comparable figures for Australia. If the period were to be extended one year to 1985, Australia would probably perform slightly better relative to the average performance in these five countries because the boom in 1985 was stronger in Australia than was typical in the OECD. Nevertheless any changes in relative performance resulting from extending the period would be small. The decline in hours worked has been substantially greater in Australia than in the major OECD countries; whereas, as Table 7.5 shows, there has been only a relatively small difference between the increase in the recorded unemployment rate in Australia and that for the G5 countries as a whole.[8] Hidden unemployment appears to have increased more in Australia than in these countries. Thus not only has the decline in hours worked per person been an important element in the low economic growth rate in Australia since 1974, but also this decline has been larger in Australia than it has been on average in the major economies of the Western world. One reason for our mediocre economic growth performance has been identified.

PRODUCTIVITY GROWTH

The other factor determining the growth in output per head is the rate of productivity growth. Commentators have blamed Australia's poor performance on low productivity growth due to such factors as our penchant for protection, our industrial relations system and our taxation system.[9] While some, but not all, of the factors identified by commentators undoubtedly have been responsible for holding back the rate of productivity growth in Australia, it does not follow that overall our productivity performance has been low compared to other countries. While at first sight productivity growth has been low in Australia, more detailed analysis shows that, not only has Australia's productivity performance improved relative to that of other countries in recent years, but also, correctly interpreted, the figures show that the true level of productivity growth is probably better than the average in the major Western economies.

From 1950–51 to 1973–74 output per person employed grew by 2.2 per cent a year in Australia. From 1974–75 to 1986–87 it grew by only 1.5 per cent a year. However, in the second period, there was an increasing trend to part-time employment, so that output per hour worked grew at 2.1 per cent a year. Figures on total hours worked are not available for the earlier period, but one major reason for the decline in hours worked in the last decade or so – the increase in part-time work among those who could not find full-time employment – would not have been significant in the earlier period, and it is very unlikely that there would have been anything like the same gap between growth in output per person employed and growth in output per hour. Thus the rate of growth of labour productivity has declined only modestly in Australia since 1974 compared with the previous twenty-three years. This is in marked contrast with the United States, Japan and most European countries where, generally speaking, the rate of growth of labour productivity declined by about 50 per cent. In fact in recent years the rate of growth in output per hour worked has been higher in Australia than the average for the G5 countries where it averaged under 2 per cent. Australia did better than the average for the Group of 5 because of the very poor performance of one country, the United States. In each of the other four countries output per hour worked grew

Table 7.5 *Changes in the labour market, various countries, 1973 to 1984*

	Annual decline in hours worked per head of population (%)	Increase in unemployment (percentage points)
France	1.7	7.6
West Germany	1.2	8.3
Japan	0.3	1.3
United Kingdom	1.4	9.1
USA	(0.3)*	2.4
Weighted average of the above 5 countries	0.3	4.1
Australia	0.9	6.4

* growth not decline

Sources: Calculated from figures in the Reserve Bank of Australia, Occasional Paper No. 8A and A. Maddison, Growth and Slowdown in Advanced Capitalist Economies. *Journal of Economic Literature*, June, 1987.

faster than in Australia. Nevertheless the fact remains that since 1973 the labour productivity growth rate in Australia has been much closer to the rate in these four countries than it was in the previous twenty-five years.

Labour is only one of the factors of production. At the very least one ought also to consider capital. In the 1950s and 60s capital productivity was not high in Australia compared to the major OECD countries,[10] and in the period since 1974 our rate of growth of capital productivity has actually been negative. That is, the stock of capital has grown faster than output and the capital-output ratio has increased. There is nothing inherently wrong with this. Indeed increasing the capital-output ratio is one way of improving labour productivity and living standards.

An increase in the capital-output ratio has been common in Western economies in recent years. In many countries it has been larger than in Australia. In other words capital productivity has not declined as much in Australia as in many countries. For example for the G5 countries it declined on average by 1.8 per cent a year compared to a decline of 1.2 per cent in Australia. Thus increases in the capital-output ratio helped more (on average) to increase labour productivity in those countries than in Australia but, nevertheless, the increase in labour productivity was higher in Australia than in the Group of 5.

It is probably more helpful to look at the increase in output per head and to estimate how much of this growth was due to the increase in capital per head, how much to changes in the average number of hours worked per head and how much to other factors. This is done in Table 7.6 and one additional factor, structural change, has been identified. Again the period 1973 to 1984 has been chosen so as to make use of data in Maddison,[11] and again Australia's

Table 7.6 *Sources of growth in output per head of population, various countries, 1973 to 1984*

	% Growth in GDP per head	Due to				
		Change in hours worked per head	Increase in residential capital per head	Increase in non-residential capital per head	Structural change	Residual productivity growth
France	1.5	-1.2	0.1	0.9	-0.1	1.8
West Germany	1.6	-0.8	0.2	0.8	0.1	1.3
Japan	2.7	-0.2	0.4	1.5	0.2	0.8
United Kingdom	0.9	-1.0	0.2	0.6	-0.3	1.4
USA	1.1	0.2	0.1	0.4	-0.1	0.5
Average of above 5 countries	1.5	-0.2	0.2	0.7	0.0	0.8
Australia	1.1	-0.6	0.3	0.4	0.1	0.9

Source: Calculated from figures in Reserve Bank of Australia, Occasional Paper No. 8A, Australian Bureau of Statistics publications catalogue nos. 5204, 5221, 5226 and 6204, and A. Maddison, Growth and Slowdown in Advanced Capitalist Economies. *Journal of Economic Literature*, June, 1987.

relative performance would probably appear slightly better if the period were to be extended by one year.

Table 7.6 separates out residential from non-residential capital. This is necessary because figures for the stock of capital do not necessarily give a good indication of the contribution of capital to production, or the flow of capital services. Generally the shorter the life of a capital asset the larger the flow of capital services compared to the value of the asset. Consider the cost of renting a car compared to its purchase price as against that of renting a house compared to its purchase price. This lack of correspondence between the value of different types of capital goods and the annual flow of capital services obtained from using the goods would not matter if the stock of the different types of capital goods grew at roughly the same rate. There have, however, been marked discrepancies between the rate of growth of the residential and the non-residential capital stocks. Hence it is desirable to consider these two types of capital separately.

Economic growth has always been associated with structural change. If productivity were at the same level in all sectors this would be of no significance in analysing productivity growth. But, of course, it is not. Historically one of the major sources of productivity growth world-wide has been the transference of labour from a low productivity agricultural sector to higher productivity secondary industry. Agricultural productivity grew rapidly in many countries in the twentieth century, with a corresponding decline in agricultural employment. Once this modernization of agriculture is complete, or nearly complete, the scope for productivity gain by shifting workers from agriculture to secondary industry largely disappears. The modernization of agriculture was an important factor in productivity growth in France and West Germany in the twenty-five years ending in 1973. It was a minor but positive influence in the United Kingdom and the United States. In all four countries it has been of little significance since 1973. In Japan, however, the shift of employment out of agriculture was not only very important in the period before 1973, but continued to be significant, though of much less importance, after that date. Because Australian agriculture was already highly productive by 1950, Australia has had little benefit from this source of productivity growth either from 1950 to 1973 or since 1974. We have, however, benefited from the increasing importance of a highly productive mining sector.

In recent years structural change has had another effect on productivity growth. There has been increasing employment in the service sector. In parts of this sector, including public administration, the conventional measures used to measure output arbitrarily assume productivity growth to be zero. In the service sector as a whole, the level of productivity tends to be lower than in secondary industry, so that the shift to employment in services has been a drag on productivity growth. This drag has been a little greater in Australia than in America and Europe.

If one is prepared to make the conventional assumptions about the relative importance of capital and labour in the productive process[12] it is possible to dissect the increase in output per head of population into that due to changes in hours worked per head, to changes in the capital stock per head, to structural change and to everything else. This final factor can be called residual productivity growth. It reflects things such as changes in the education and skill levels of the labour force, the degree of entrepreneurship in the community and the speed at which new technologies are adopted and diffused throughout industry – in short, all those things which people have in mind when they complain about the low level of productivity growth in Australia. Because it is a residual, however, it also reflects errors made anywhere else in the analysis, and no significance should be placed on small differences.

Table 7.6 dissects the increase in output per head in this way, both for Australia and for the G5 countries. It is striking, to say the least, that residual productivity growth is higher in Australia than in Japan, though the difference is not large enough to be significant. Similarly no weight should be put on the fact that the Australian figures for residual productivity growth is higher than the average figure for the G5 countries. Nevertheless it is clear that Australia has performed as well as Japan and better than the United States – the two countries with which our economic institutions and attitudes are most often compared to our disadvantage – but we have not performed as well as the three largest European economies. So much for Eurosclerosis!

Perhaps even more important is the fact that Australian performance since 1973 has been so much better, relative to the Group of 5 countries, than it was in the previous quarter century. From 1950 to 1973 residual productivity growth averaged 2.7 per cent a year in the G5 countries. Japan had very rapid growth in this period, but even excluding Japan the average was 2.3 per cent a year. Data for Australia are much more sketchy for the earlier period, but all estimates imply a residual productivity growth of only 1.5 per cent a year or less.[13] At best, this is little over half the average of G5 countries.

If we return to Table 7.6 as a whole, several important generalizations can be made. First, Japan had the highest rate of growth in output per head because of the much greater rate of capital accumulation in that country than in any other. France and West Germany also had both high rates of capital accumulation and high rates of growth in output per head. The lesson is clear: a high rate of capital accumulation leads to rapid growth. However all the figures in Table 7.6 are per head of population. Australia had a faster rate of population growth than any of the other countries, and also had a greater rate of capital accumulation (or savings and investment) than any other country except Japan. It is harder to increase capital per head when the number of heads is growing rapidly. This is not to say that the migration programme has necessarily depressed living standards in Australia. Migrants bring with them intangible, or human, capital in the form of skills and training acquired overseas. Also migrants tend to have a higher propensity to save than native born Australians. Nevertheless a large migration programme does require a large savings effort if it is not to reduce the rate of growth of output per head.

The second generalization stems from the strong inverse correlation between the rate of residual productivity growth and the decline in the number of hours worked per head of population.[14] An important factor in residual productivity growth seems to be a ruthlessness in labour-shedding in the form of putting workers off and working shorter hours than normal. This may be good for productivity, but it does nothing for the increase in output per head of population or for living standards. Australia seems to be in a middle situation with respect to labour-shedding, and there is no obvious reason why we should wish to increase residual productivity growth by being more ruthless.

Finally, it is clear that if we can increase the demand for labour, and reduce unemployment without reducing labour productivity, we will increase output per head and living standards more than we will by chasing productivity growth. However, productivity growth may be important in reducing unemployment. This will be argued in the final section of this chapter.

INFLATION

Figure 7.3 shows the rate of growth of the consumer price index each year from 1964–65 to 1986–87. Inflation started to accelerate in Australia early in the 1970s. This was typical of OECD countries. By 1973 only Sweden and Norway had rates of inflation lower than those prevailing at the end of the 1960s.

In 1974 the rate of inflation started to rise rapidly in Australia. After peaking in 1974–75, it fell substantially over the next four years but then drifted upwards until brought down, first by the recession of 1982–83 and then by the policy of wage restraint facilitated by the Accord. In 1985 inflation was still higher in Australia than in the majority of OECD countries. Table 7.7 gives, for the usual group of countries, the rates of inflation in 1974 and 1985 and the annual rate over the whole period. While Australia was the median country for the whole period as far as inflation was concerned, by 1985 it had slipped to thirteenth place in the inflation ranking, and the rate of inflation in Australia continued to rise after that until it reached 9 per cent in 1986–87. The rise after 1985 was largely due to a fall of one-third in the value of the Australian dollar on the foreign exchange market, which occurred in 1985 and the first half of 1986. Part of this devaluation was because of the decline in Australia's terms of trade, that is, the prices received for exports compared to the prices paid for

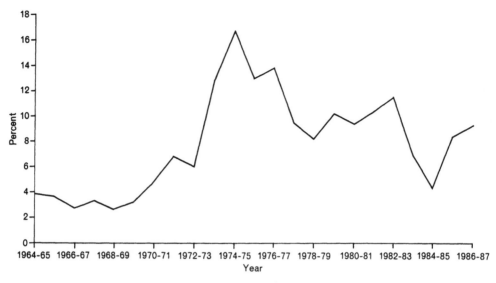

Figure 7.3 Rate of growth of the Consumer Price Index. *Source:* ABS, *Consumer Price Index* (Cat. no. 6401.0), various issues.

Table 7.7 *Annual rate of growth of the Consumer Price Index, various countries, 1974 to 1985*

	1974 (%)	1985 (%)	1974 to 1985 (%)
USA	11.0	3.6	7.43
Canada	10.9	4.0	8.28
Sweden	9.9	7.4	9.81
Netherlands	9.6	2.2	5.59
Denmark	15.2	4.7	9.07
Australia	15.1	6.7	9.81
New Zealand	11.2	15.4	13.43
West Germany	7.0	2.2	4.13
France	13.7	5.8	10.16
Norway	9.4	5.7	9.07
United Kingdom	15.9	6.1	11.77
Belgium	12.7	4.9	7.43
Italy	19.1	9.2	15.11
Finland	16.7	5.9	10.16
Austria	9.5	3.2	5.38
Japan	23.2	2.0	6.50
Spain	15.7	8.8	15.33
Ireland	17.0	5.4	13.94
Portugal	28.0	19.6	22.33
Greece	26.9	19.3	18.04

Source: IMF, *International Financial Statistics Supplement on Price Statistics* 1986.

imports. But part of the devaluation was due to factors over which Australia had more control. Overall Australia's record on inflation must be judged as being poor.

How important is this failure to reduce inflation either to the level of the 1960s or to that in the countries with which Australia trades or competes internationally? Four arguments against inflation can be found in the economics literature: first, that it has adverse effects on the personal distribution of income and wealth; second, that it is a hidden tax; third, that it reduces the efficiency of the economy; and finally, that people do not like it.

In the case of Australia there is no evidence that inflation has any significant effect on the distribution of income. Nevile and Warren[15] showed that the years of high inflation in the mid-1970s had virtually no effect on the income distribution of families in Australia. The share of the lowest 20 per cent of families did decline by 0.7 per cent to 6.5 per cent, but the next three quintiles all increased their share slightly, largely at the expense of the highest quintile, and the Gini coefficient remained constant. This result arises because, in Australia at least, the position of groups most likely to be harmed by inflation – pensioners, public servants and non-unionized labour – has been protected by public policy. One also has to compare the effects of inflation on income distribution with the effects of anti-inflationary policy on income distribution. Nevile, Podder, Tran-Nam and Warren[16] show that the Fraser government's years of fighting inflation first also did not have a large effect on the pattern of income distribution, though the small changes that occurred were in the direction of greater inequality, with the highest quintile of households gaining at the expense of all other households and the Gini coefficient increasing slightly. This relatively small effect of anti-inflationary policy was recorded only because of social welfare policy. If it were not for social welfare payments there would have been a disastrous fall in the share of the bottom 20 per cent of households from 4 per cent of private income to only 1 per cent of private income. In general, in Australia, the effects of inflation on income distribution are both small and better than the also small effects of anti-inflationary policy.

There is no hard evidence on the effects of inflation on wealth distribution in Australia, but it seems unlikely that overall these effects have been large. The form of wealth most adversely affected by inflation is financial assets with fixed nominal values. In the 1970s this was the case with anticipated as well as unanticipated inflation due to interest rate controls. About 20 per cent of all net household assets in Australia are in the form of financial assets. The significant thing is that, except for the very rich, those owning (or paying off) their homes have far more financial assets than renters. This is most pronounced at the lowest income levels where owner-occupiers have four times the level of financial assets of renters. Since home ownership is the form of wealth most affected favourably by inflation (because of interest rate controls and also because the price of homes rises faster than the general price level), the effects of inflation on wealth distribution cancel out to some extent.

Those renters who have a significant amount of financial assets compared to their income are, in general, the rich. There is no evidence that, as far as direct personal ownership of financial assets is concerned, inflation has had an adverse effect on the pattern of wealth distribution. The gainers have been home owners and the losers those who lent to them. Apart from cooperative building societies the main lenders have been savings banks, which are wholly owned by general trading banks. Bank profits have not suffered with inflation, but there has undoubtedly been some cross-subsidization from large corporations to home buyers. Before the deregulation of interest rates on deposits savings bank depositors fared badly, but these were largely either people using the savings bank as a convenient store of value for relatively small amounts of money or people establishing themselves as good bank customers in order to get savings bank loans to build houses. There is little evidence that inflation has had major adverse effects on wealth distribution and it certainly has not affected the distribution of wealth enough to influence, in turn, the distribution of income.

In the mid-1970s, when the rate of inflation was higher than the rate of interest, inflation was, in effect, a tax on those who held government bonds. This hidden, or not so hidden, tax has largely disappeared now that interest rates have become sensitive to the rate of inflation and have risen enough, or more than enough, to compensate holders of financial assets for the diminution of the value of their assets through inflation.[17]

Inflation affects the efficiency of the economy in a number of ways. It reduces the share of profits in income[18] which reduces investment. It increases uncertainty, both about relative prices and about how long any particular rate of inflation will last. If Australia continues for long to inflate faster than countries with which it trades or competes, there will have to be further devaluations of the Australian dollar which will have relatively small, but undoubtedly adverse, effects in the short run on the cost of servicing the foreign debt.

The biggest reductions in efficiency due to inflation are almost certainly through the interaction of inflation and the tax system, particularly the taxation of business enterprises. First, in the case of most but not all business, the failure to adjust nominal magnitudes for inflation when calculating business income for tax purposes results in an over-statement of profits, and hence a higher level of tax than is appropriate, reducing after-tax profits. To the extent that this is the case it reduces investment and hence economic growth. For many businesses, especially small businesses, the conventional historical cost accounting used for tax purposes has caused severe cash flow problems, which also reduce the level of investment. A more important point is that historical cost accounting has very uneven effects, with a bias against capital-intensive industries and methods of production. This distorts the allocation process and reduces economic efficiency. Finally, the fact of inflation and its interaction with the tax system leads to considerable resources, which might have been used more productively, being spent on discovering and implementing ways to minimize tax liabilities. In principle, the answer to the problems due to the interaction of inflation and the tax system is to reform the tax system and to replace historical cost accounting with a more appropriate system. The practical and political difficulties of doing this are large, but perhaps no greater than the practical and political difficulties of reducing the rate of inflation to, say, 2 or 3 per cent.

The final argument against inflation is that people do not like it. While this is true, it is hard to measure its importance; and it is also true that people do not like the costs of reducing inflation.

According to the foregoing discussion the principal argument against inflation is that it reduces economic efficiency, and hence output and economic growth. The section on productivity growth suggests that these effects have not been too important in Australia. The effects of inflation on efficiency rise more than proportionally as the rate of inflation rises; hence it would be prudent, to say the least, to keep in place policies that maintain downward pressure on the inflation rate, and certainly the authorities should never be complacent about rises in that rate. But the relatively poor performance of the Australian economy with respect to inflation is less important than the rise in unemployment.

DEBT ISSUES

By the second half of the 1980s there was a widespread belief in Australia that government deficits had led to an unmanageably large public debt and that governmental overseas borrowing had led to a crippling overseas debt. The reality was quite different. Australia had a low public debt, both by historical standards and compared to other countries; and governments had not borrowed excessively on overseas markets. Private citizens, however, had borrowed very large amounts overseas and the overseas debt, if not crippling, was an important problem constraining economic policy.

There are two concepts of public debt: gross debt and debt net of financial assets owned by government. The net debt concept is the one most directly related to the sum of past budget deficits and is the most relevant in assessing the debt situation of governments. However the international statistics on gross debt are better, and that is the one almost always used in international comparisons. In the case of Australia, gross debt and net debt have tended to move together, so that one reaches similar conclusions when making historical comparisons whichever concept is used.

It is also useful to distinguish between the debt of general government and the debt of public business enterprises such as Australian Airlines or Telecom. While a strong case can be made for excluding the debt of public enterprises, it is included below when making historical comparisons for Australia. This is done to show that, even taking the worst case where all possible debts are included in the public debt, that debt is not unduly high and is lower than it was twenty years ago.

The net public sector debt was 47 per cent of annual GDP at the end of 1965–66. The percentage steadily declined until 1974–75 when it was 21 per cent. It was still 21 per cent in 1977–78, but then showed an upward trend till it reached 34 per cent in 1984–85, the last year for which reliable precise figures are available. In the next two years the ratio of public debt to GDP continued to rise, reaching about 36 per cent in 1986–87, but the rate of increase of this ratio slowed markedly after 1984–85. If the annual amount of public sector borrowing is kept at the 1986–87 ratio or less, and given fairly conservative estimates for the growth of nominal GDP, the ratio of public debt to GDP will peak in the early 1990s at a figure below that for 1965–66. Such a forecast, like all forecasts, is based on a number of assumptions which may or may not prove to be correct; but the historical record is factual, and by historical standards the level of public debt in Australia is reasonably low at present.

By international standards, too, the level of public debt is very low in Australia today. In making international comparisons it is meaningless to include the debt of public enterprises because what is included in the public sector varies so widely from country to country. To give a single example – in Australia, Telecom is a public enterprise; in America, telephone services are provided by private firms; and in the United Kingdom a few years ago they were provided by a public enterprise but now are in the private sector. Hence all international comparisons are for the general government sector, that is, excluding public enterprises.

Some figures which enable international comparisons are given in Table 7.8 and, for purposes of comparison, figures are given for 1973 as well as 1983, the last year for which data are available for all the countries included. Unlike the case in most countries, public debt in Australia fell as a proportion of GDP between 1973 and 1983. In 1983 the ratio of public debt to GDP was lower than in any of the Group of 5 countries. In the Western world only Finland had a lower ratio, and the Australian ratio was less than half the average level. Australia is not a country where the level of public debt is of pressing concern.

Unfortunately the opposite is true with respect to the level of foreign debt. Although Australian governments have not borrowed unduly large amounts in foreign countries in

Table 7.8 *Gross public debt as a percentage of GDP, various countries, 1973 and 1983*

	1973 (%)	1983 (%)
France	25.1	29.8
West Germany	18.6	41.0
Japan	17.0	66.9
United Kingdom	69.7	54.1
USA	40.9	43.5
Average of above 5 countries	35.4	47.4
Australia	31.8	24.5
Average for 20 countries*	36.0	49.7

* the six listed in the table plus Austria, Belgium, Canada, Denmark, Finland, Greece, Ireland, Italy, Netherlands, Norway, Portugal, Spain, Sweden and Switzerland.
Source: OECD Department of Economics and Statistics Working Paper, No. 30.

recent years, this is not true of the private sector. Table 7.9 shows the very marked rise in the 1980s in the ratio of foreign debt to GDP. In some ways this ratio may be a misleading indicator. Year-to-year movements are often dominated by exchange rate changes and may be irrelevant, except for the pyschological effects which they may have on overseas lenders. A more important figure is the ratio of interest paid overseas to exports, and figures for this are also given in Table 7.9. This ratio also rose rapidly in the 1980s and by the middle of the decade was high by international standards, but still nowhere near as high as that in heavily indebted Latin American countries. In 1985–86 gross interest payments were 18 per cent of exports. This compares with 33 per cent for Mexico, 40 per cent for Brazil and 50 per cent for Argentina.

The rapid rise in the ratio of debt to GDP in 1984–85 and 1985–86 was due far more to the fall in the value of the Australian dollar than to the incurring of new debt. Since most Australian foreign debt is denominated in overseas currencies, its ratio to Australian GDP (which is measured in Australian dollars) always goes up when there is a substantial fall in the value of the Australian dollar on the foreign exchange market. The effect on the ratio of interest paid to exports is very much less. If export prices were determined solely in purely competitive world markets, with Australian exports a very small part of that market – so that prices received for our exports in foreign currencies were not affected at all by what happened in Australia – devaluation would not affect the ratio of interest paid to exports. In fact world markets are not purely competitive, and for many commodities Australian supplies make up a substantial part of supplies coming onto the international market. Devaluation may be expected to have a small adverse effect on our terms of trade in the short to medium run. Perhaps more important is the likelihood that after a devaluation both export and import prices are cut in foreign currency terms. This does not affect our terms of

Table 7.9 *Foreign debt and interest paid overseas, Australia, 1974–75 to 1985–86*

	Gross foreign debt % of GDP	Net foreign debt % of GDP	Interest on gross foreign debt % of exports
1974–75	9.36	3.36	3.75
1975–76	7.95	3.14	3.92
1976–77	8.98	4.47	3.59
1977–78	10.71	6.51	4.09
1978–79	11.81	7.40	5.03
1979–80	11.20	5.67	4.96
1980–81	11.11	6.18	5.26
1981–82	15.70	10.57	7.89
1982–83	21.03	13.59	11.52
1983–84	22.92	15.36	13.36
1984–85	31.91	23.84	15.58
1985–86	38.37	30.39	18.24

Sources: Reserve Bank of Australia, *Bulletin*, and Australian Bureau of Statistics, *Australian National Accounts National Income and Expenditure*, catalogue no. 5204.0.

trade, but since interest payments (in overseas currencies) are unchanged it does raise the ratio of interest payments overseas to exports.

In short, the Australian overseas debt is a major problem. While still nowhere near as bad as in countries such as Brazil and Argentina, it should not be allowed to continue to grow indefinitely compared to our export income. If it does, sooner or later overseas creditors will refuse to continue lending to Australia – forcing a sharp and very painful re-adjustment. Every time there is a current account deficit on the balance of payments the overseas debt increases. Small current account deficits are normal in a country still developing its resources and its economy, but small in this context means averaging around 10 to 12 per cent of exports. Australia's current account deficit peaked at 38 per cent of exports in 1985–86. While it has fallen in 1986–87, it is still far too high. As is shown in the next section this is the major constraint on increasing economic growth and reducing unemployment in Australia.

CONCLUSION

In the fifteen years from the first oil shock to 1988, Australian productivity growth has been typical of OECD countries. The main reason why output per head of population has grown more slowly is the increasing unemployment both recorded and hidden. A fall in investment has also played a part, but this was largely the result of the low rate of economic growth, reflected in rising unemployment, rather than a causal factor in its own right. On the side of inflation the performance of the Australian economy can only be described as mediocre. While it is important to prevent the rate of inflation moving upward into the double digit range and an accelerating inflation rate would be disastrous, the consequences of a stable inflation rate in the range 6 to 9 per cent are nowhere near as bad as those of a level of unemployment in the same range. Despite widespread belief to the contrary, the level of the public debt is low in Australia and is not a problem. However the high and worrying level of foreign debt is the major constraint on policies to reduce the level of unemployment.

Unemployment is a serious problem in its own right, and this chapter has argued that the rise in unemployment, along with the associated effects of the relatively low rate of economic growth on investment, has been the major cause of the low rate of growth of output per head in Australia since the mid-1970s. The experience of the first three years of the Hawke government showed that it is possible to reduce unemployment for a while, but unless there are changes in our economy the consequent mounting level of foreign debt will lead to a reversal of the policies that give rapid economic growth and falling unemployment. The seasonally adjusted unemployment rate fell from 10.3% in September 1983 to 7.8% in December 1985. Over the next two years unemployment fluctuated mildly and averaged 8.1%.

Relatively expansionary budgets gave Australia rapid economic growth from mid-1983 to mid-1985 with, after a slight lag, a consequent reduction in unemployment. While expansionary budgets can produce economic growth, if a country grows much faster than its trading partners, as Australia did in 1984 and 1985, eventually it will import more than it exports and have a balance of payments problem and rising foreign debt. In the case of Australia this balance of payments problem became a crisis because of the decline in our terms of trade.

An important point is that, although in 1985 and 1986 the decline in the terms of trade was particularly severe, this was not an isolated event, likely to be quickly reversed, but the culmination of a long-standing trend. The prices of Australia's traditional exports have shown a downward trend relative to prices paid for imports since the Korean War. Over the last thirty years it has taken, on average, 2 per cent more exports each year to pay for the same volume of imports. Since 1970 things have become even worse, so that it has required 3 per cent more exports each year to pay for the same volume of imports. There is no reason to think that this trend in the terms of trade will change in the next few years or even in the 1990s. The balance of payments problem may ease, but it is not going to disappear permanently without vigorous new exporting and import-competing industries. The alternative to establishing these industries is a policy of restricting imports through more or less permanent recession.

A policy to restore and maintain a high rate of economic growth in Australia is only possible if Australian import-competing industries remain competitive internationally and new export industries are developed. This will require a high rate of productivity growth, not only in export and import-competing industries, but in all sectors of the economy. The level of productivity in industries whose products do not enter into international trade affects costs throughout the economy, and hence in export and import-competing industries. In short, while the record of productivity growth in the Australian economy has been relatively good since 1974, every effort must be made to improve it. Otherwise the Australian economy will continue to have a high level of unemployment and a low rate of economic growth as the permanent recession option is, perforce, adopted.

While there may be little argument that international competitiveness is essential for Australian economic growth, at first sight the claim that international competitiveness must be based on productivity growth sounds implausible. In two years in the mid-1980s the trade-weighted index of the value of the Australian dollar declined by one-third. Future productivity growth may be of the order of 4 or 5 per cent a year, if we are lucky. How can productivity gains compare with the massive effects of substantial devaluation? Nevertheless devaluation is not the answer to a lack of international competitiveness. At the best, all it can do is buy time to make the changes necessary to have internationally competitive export and import-replacement industries of the size that will support vigorous economic growth.

There are at least three flaws in the argument that devaluation alone can produce international competitiveness as a condition for economic growth in Australia. First, devaluation only works if accompanied by measures that reduce its inflationary impact, such as the tight monetary and fiscal policy in Australia in 1986–87. Measures such as these normally reduce demand, increase unemployment and act against the economic growth the devaluation is supposed to facilitate. Second, in the case of Australia, many of its exports, and to a lesser extent of its imports, are such that the changes in the relative prices caused by the devaluation will have relatively small effects on the amounts exported or imported. Finally, devaluation itself may worsen our terms of trade and certainly increase, in the short run, the burden of interest payments on the foreign debt.

Import controls have been suggested by some as the solution, but experience has shown that they lead to inefficiencies that reduce productivity and economic growth, not least because in Australia they lead to the development of import-replacement industries which are too small to be efficient. Australia does need import-replacement industries, but efficient ones with growth in output based on productivity growth; not industries that can only survive through protection, at considerable cost to the consumer and hence (through wage costs) to all other industries.

There are no quick fixes or easy solutions. The achievement of sustained economic growth and a return to something that can be described as full employment depends on a major improvement in the rate of productivity growth in Australia. There are signs of hope that this will occur. One could list dozens, if not hundreds, of changes in any society that would increase the rate of growth of productivity. In Australia two are particularly important. They are both concerned with attitudes as much as with objective laws, customs or procedures; and there are indications that the relevant attitudes are changing.

The first is attitudes towards protection, particularly, but not only, within the manufacturing sector. In the past too many firms looked to protection to guarantee profitability. Manufacturing industries in Australia expanded rapidly after World War II behind tariff barriers. While these barriers may have been necessary to produce the rapid expansion of manufacturing, the emphasis on import replacement allowed Australian firms to restrict their horizons to the Australian market and reduced further the level of competition in a small market already enjoying significant levels of natural protection. Thus many firms have, in the past, been sheltered from the need to seek out all sources of productivity gain or even to resist practices which greatly reduced productivity. The sure road to maintain profits seemed to be to lobby for higher tariffs, not to make every effort to increase productivity. There are encouraging signs that these attitudes are changing and that more and more Australian firms are realizing that they cannot rely on protection to ensure their long-run survival.

The second change required is even more important. In many industries and firms in Australia we desperately need a change in the attitudes of management towards unions and unions towards management. It is no secret that the industrial relations climate has been a critical element in determining the rate of productivity growth in Australia. The quality of industrial relations in the workplace can affect the receptiveness of workers to new practices and process technologies and determine the extent to which potential productivity gains are realized or are offset by manning rules, job classification and demarcation arrangements and so on.

Trade union attitudes to technological change are greatly influenced by management attitudes towards trade unions. Where management gives high priority to ongoing consultation and information sharing and is sensitive to job security issues and those issues relating to the impact of technical change on work-skills and job satisfaction, unions generally are much more cooperative. While there are notable exceptions, to a large extent Australian management deserves the unions it gets.

Australia will never overcome its present economic problems while a large section of management and unions focus on the shortcomings of each other, and not on how they can work together to the benefit of both. Whatever one thinks of the details of the so-called Swedish model, one feature that would greatly improve conditions in Australia is the widespread cooperative atmosphere that exists between management and unions, particularly in the private sector, in Sweden. In the fifty years following World War I, Sweden transformed itself from one of the poorer countries in Europe to one of the richest countries in the world. There were a number of factors contributing to this success story but, to quote the Business Council of Australia: 'An important ingredient was undoubtedly a productive workforce and a long tradition of harmonious relations between employer and employee which contributed to a willingness to accept change and to strong productivity growth.'[19]

Yet for the first twenty years after World War I Swedish unions and management fought each other bitterly until both sides realized how unproductive this was. A similar widespread revolution in attitudes in Australia would do wonders for our rate of productivity growth and enable the Australian economy in the 1990s to once again be one which provided full employment and rising living standards.

Notes

[1] See, for example, J.A. Scutt (ed.) 1985. *Poor Nation of the Pacific? Australia's Future.* Sydney, Allen and Unwin.

[2] This was only one, if the most widespread, of arguments against economic growth. For a discussion of the arguments for and against see J.W. Nevile 1979. *The Root of All Evil: Essays on Economics Ethics and Capitalism,* Australian Council of Churches, Sydney.

[3] The Organization for Economic Cooperation and Development is an association of almost all the Western countries, including Japan.

[4] Report of the Senate Special Committee on Unemployment Problems (86th Congress, 2nd Session, Report no. 1206) p.15, US Government Printer, Washington.

[5] Portugal and Greece are omitted from those countries which were included in Table 1 because of the difficulty of obtaining reliable data about their unemployment rates in 1974.

[6] The exceptions are Sweden, the United States and New Zealand, which did better than their growth rates would suggest in containing the rise in unemployment, and Denmark, West Germany and Ireland which did worse.

[7] See A. Maddison 1987. Growth and Slowdown in Advanced Capitalist Economies. *Journal of Economic Literature.* June.

[8] It is true that the averages for the G5 countries are dominated by the relatively good performances of the United States and Japan, which produce about two-thirds of all the output of G5 countries. But the United States and Japan also have a big influence on the rate of growth of output in the OECD as a whole, and both had higher rates of growth in output per head than did Australia.

[9] See, for example, H. Hughes 1985. Australia and the World Environment – the Dynamics of International Competition and Wealth Creation. In J.A. Scott, *op.cit.*

[10] See, for example, J.W. Nevile 1967. How Productive is Australian Capital? *Economic Record,* September.

[11] A. Maddison 1987. *op.cit.*

[12] The most important and controversial is that factors of production (labour and capital) are paid their marginal

products (or the value of the extra output produced as a result of employing one more unit of the factor of production). This implies both constant returns to scale and a competitive economy.

[13] See, for example, A.J. Kaspura and G. Weldon 1980. Productivity Trends in the Australian Economy 1900–1901 to 1978–79. Department of Productivity Research Branch Working Paper 9, Canberra.

[14] The correlation coefficient is -0.95.

[15] See J.W. Nevile and N.A. Warren 1984. Inflation and Personal Income Distribution in Australia. *Australian Economic Review*, 4th Quarter.

[16] See J.W. Nevile, N. Podder, B. Tran-Nam and N.A. Warren 1988. Inflation, Anti-Inflationary Policy and the Distribution of Income in Australia. *Centre for Applied Economic Research, Working Paper*. University of New South Wales, Kensington, April.

[17] It is still the case that the whole of interest is subject to income tax, whereas part of it is not strictly income in an economic sense but compensation for the decline in real value of the principal sum on which the interest is paid.

[18] See J.W. Nevile 1975. Inflation, Company Profits and Investment. *Australian Economic Review*. 4th Quarter.

[19] *Business Council Bulletin*, Oct. 1986, p.6.

8

Industrial Relations: Stability and Turmoil

Keith Hancock and Don Rawson

Unless the portents observable late in 1987 are greatly misleading, industrial relations will be high on the agenda of political and public debate in the late 1980s. Soon after the centenary, the first of a series of steps was taken which have much influenced the formal structure of industrial relations and, arguably, affected profoundly the informal context. The most conspicuous feature of the formal system is the institutions of conciliation and arbitration established under laws of both the commonwealth and the states. These laws can be changed, of course, and recurrent controversies have surrounded actual and projected alterations. In 1987, the dispute seemed especially bitter. It focussed not only on the tribunals of conciliation and arbitration – though these were very much under scrutiny – but on related issues, too. Foremost among the latter was the power exercised by trade unions. Another cognate issue was the quality of industrial relations at the workplace.

The Labor government in 1983 established a Committee of Review of Industrial Relations Law and Systems (the Hancock Committee).[1] That Committee in 1985 supported the continuation of a federal conciliation and arbitration system and submitted recommendations intended to enhance its performance. The government accepted many of these recommendations and, in May 1987, introduced an Industrial Relations Bill to give effect to them. Aspects of the Bill were strenuously criticized by representatives of employers and other commentators. Shortly before the dissolution of the Parliament in June 1987, the government deferred the Bill; and it subsequently announced that the Bill would be modified so as to allay some concerns of the objectors. Nevertheless the re-elected government maintained its commitment to a centralized conciliation and arbitration system. The Opposition, on the other hand, had published an industrial relations policy which implied a reduced role for conciliation and arbitration.[2] Leading members of the Opposition were critical of the Hancock report and indicated sympathy for 'deregulating' the labour market. The division of opinion about industrial relations played a lesser part in the election campaign than might have been expected. Moreover, in November 1987, the Opposition Shadow Minister for Industrial Relations (Senator Chaney) introduced a Private Member's Bill which would have enhanced the capacity of the Australian Conciliation and Arbitration Commission to enforce its decisions; and the dismantling of the system was represented as a long-term rather than a short-term or medium-term goal. Despite this apparent change of emphasis, the system and conduct of industrial relations are likely to be a major focus of political debate in the next few years and perhaps for much longer.

THE UNIONS

A century ago, Australian unionism was large and lively. Catastrophic defeats in the strikes of the 1890s were a severe setback; but the recovery was rapid and by 1910 Australia was well on the way to becoming the world's most unionized nation. It was clearly so by 1920 and it retained that position for some fifteen years. Since 1920, Australian unions have, more or less, covered about half the total number of employees.

The conciliation and arbitration systems of the commonwealth and the states contributed to the growth of unionism. They did so, first, because they obliged employers to recognize and deal with unions and, second, through their capacity to grant preference in employment to unionists over non-unionists (though in practice preference was not widely granted). It is easy, however, to exaggerate the role of conciliation and arbitration in the growth of union membership. Membership grew just as rapidly in some other countries, such as Britain and Germany, where there were no comparable industrial relations systems. Conciliation and arbitration also influenced the structure, organization and activities of the Australian union movement. It is *partly* because of arbitration that we have a great many small unions; that the way in which they divide up Australia's unionists has little to do with the present structure of the economy; that unions are on the whole run cheaply; and that they have some claim to be regarded as the most democratic in the world, if this is measured by the proportion of members who vote in union elections.[3] But again it is easy to exaggerate the influence of the arbitration systems. Australian unions have many resemblances – too many, most would say – to British unions. Many things about Australian unions are due much more to their being unions than to their being Australian.

The most obvious of these widely shared characteristics is a perception of belonging to 'the labour movement'. Members of such a movement believe, rightly or wrongly, that they are working to produce a better society. Further, they usually participate in some kind of confederation. Although union federations were formed in the various Australian colonies well before the end of the nineteenth century, a national union federation, now the Australian Council of Trade Unions (ACTU), was not formed until 1927. We shall shortly consider its recent development. For the moment it is enough to say that almost all important Australian unions now belong to the ACTU. In that sense the claim of Australian trade unionism to constitute a 'movement' has been strengthened. The term 'labour movement', however, also draws attention to a different, though perhaps compatible, set of possibilities. About a century ago unions in some countries, including Australia, gave dramatic expression to their wish to change not merely working conditions but society at large by forming political parties to which the unions actually belonged, through the process of affiliation. The link between unionism and the Australian Labor Party (ALP) remains a vital factor in Australian industrial relations – perhaps more vital than ever before. But it is not as simple as it might appear. Unionists are now less likely to belong to ALP-affiliated unions. About one-third of them belong to unions which are affiliated with the ACTU but not with the ALP.

This briefest of historical sketches and generalizations has a place in a consideration of Australian industrial relations in the late 1980s, because it provides some background against which we can see what has been happening to Australian unions in recent years and consider the possible outcomes which face them. Their future is less certain than for many years, depending as it does upon their powers of adaptation to rapidly changing conditions.

167

Size and shape

During the past ten years the proportion of the Australian workforce which belongs to unions has probably been shrinking. We say 'probably', because two sets of union membership figures now published by the Australian Bureau of Statistics (ABS) suggest rather different conclusions. Every year since 1913 the ABS has collected and published figures based on returns submitted by the unions themselves. According to these figures, the proportion of workers who belonged to unions – what has been called union density – varied little between 1976 and 1986, neither falling below 54 per cent nor rising above 57 per cent. This seemed in contrast to marked declines in union density in Britain, the United States and elsewhere. In 1977, however, the ABS began to publish statistics derived from samples of the labour force. This series gives a significantly different picture. For mid-1976, union density, as measured by the sample data, was 51 per cent, whereas the trade union returns indicated a density of 56 per cent. The sample data suggest that union density has declined to 46 per cent in 1986.

The labour force sample surveys demonstrated the extent to which union membership is concentrated in the public sector. Only 34 per cent of private employees belong to unions, compared to 71 per cent of public employees. As the ACTU Secretary, Bill Kelty, told the ACTU Congress in September 1987, unionism in the private sector is 'very weak' – at least by the standards which have usually been applied to Australian unionism. Because union membership is stronger in the public sector, it also includes a much higher proportion of non-manual workers than tradition might suggest. Forty per cent of Australian unionists are classified by the ABS as managers and administrators, professionals, para-professionals and clerks. These make up 61 per cent of public-sector unionists but only 21 per cent of private-sector unionists. Women employees are less likely to belong to unions than males. Union density in 1986 was 50 per cent for men and, for women, 39 per cent. This was only partly due to women being more likely to work part-time than men, the corresponding percentages for full-time workers being 49 and 43 respectively. It was also due to many women working in industries where unionism was weak among both genders – notably some sectors of manufacturing and also finance and business services. This was partly compensated by high proportions of women in highly-unionized sectors such as teaching and nursing in the public sector. In 1986, 35 per cent of Australian unionists were women.[4]

One of the most common, and least disputed, comments on Australian industrial relations is that there are 'too many unions'. We depend here upon the data supplied by the unions. According to these, there were 326 separate trade unions in June 1986.[5] Most of these are small and of no significance except perhaps to their own members. Almost half (155) contain fewer than 3 per cent of unionists; and over 60 per cent of the unionists belong to the twenty-six unions with more than 40,000 members. It may seem strange that there should be so many unions in a country wherein industrial relations is so subject to regulation through the conciliation and arbitration systems. In fact these systems have never made any serious attempt to control the number of unions or to regulate their membership according to any rational plan. Commonwealth and state laws provide that a new union cannot normally be registered if there is a union already registered to which the workers concerned might 'conveniently belong'. But, once registered, a union may be protected by such provisions even though the former reasons for its boundaries, and even for its very existence, have ceased to be relevant to modern industry. It is not surprising that, after eighty years of this process, the structure of unionism is both untidy and outdated.

What can be done about this is not so simple. There have been some changes for the better. Recent High Court judgements have enabled the federal arbitration tribunal to cover additional areas of employment and this tends to favour larger unions. The Hancock report (and the aborted Industrial Relations Bill of 1987) sought to prevent the registration of new unions under the federal arbitration system if they had fewer than 1000 members, and to encourage the formation of unions covering wide ranges of workers within particular industries. But action at the federal level alone cannot resolve the problem of the very small unions, most of which operate within single states. More importantly, these very small unions are *not* the main structural problem of Australian unionism. The outdated or arbitrary character of the boundaries between many of the larger unions, including some of the largest, is a more serious handicap to the unions themselves and to the industries in which they operate. Whatever role there may be for changes in the law, the principal initiative must come from the unions themselves. There are now signs of progress in this direction and, like most of the recent important changes in Australian unionism, they involve the greater activity and reforming zeal of the ACTU.

The rise of the ACTU

In the 1970s and early 1980s the composition of the ACTU was virtually transformed, because this was the time when the growing segments of unionism, principally non-manual workers in the public sector, joined the ACTU. These workers were not newcomers to unionism, most of their unions having been founded by the 1920s, but until the 1970s they had kept themselves distinct from the main body of unionism. By three successive mergers between 1979 and 1985 the ACTU absorbed the alternative federations, increasing its size by 25 per cent. Every Australian union with more than 10,000 members, except for the Association of Professional Engineers, Australia, now belongs to the ACTU. It is not hard to find good reasons why the previously separate unions joined the ACTU. Well before the election of the federal Labor government in 1983, governments of all parties treated the ACTU as the representative of unionism. Similarly, as the determination of wages and salaries became a more centralized process dominated by the Australian Conciliation and Arbitration Commission, the ACTU emerged as the most effective representative of unionism in this respect also. The ACTU, after the mid-1970s, enhanced its appeal to 'white-collar' unionism by compromises with respect to egalitarianism in wage policy.

The ACTU's current leaders are well aware of the possibility that unionism faces a decline. The response which seems to be most immediately available is to reform the structure of unionism. The ACTU has 162 affiliates. Of these, forty-one have fewer than 1000 members, and ninety-six have fewer than 5000. But even the larger affiliates do not fit well into industry categories, although 'industrial unionism' has been a stated objective of the ACTU since its foundation. The ACTU leadership has urged union amalgamations in seventeen 'broad industry categories', including a residual 'large conglomeration – general unions' category.[6] Some preliminary steps in this direction, such as the establishment of further 'federations' of unions within industries, have already occurred. How much further they will proceed remains to be seen; but if unions are to have an important input in influencing the development of particular industries, the rationalizing of unionism itself on industry lines is a necessary prerequisite.

The ACTU has made dramatic growth not only in affiliated membership but also in professional competence and expertise during the last decade, although it remains a small and under-resourced organization by the standards of many other national union feder-

169

ations. It now faces the task of spreading this improvement in cohesion and competence over the disorderly structure of Australian trade unionism. In doing so it faces many difficulties but has at least two great and interrelated advantages. One is the virtual disappearance of conventional 'radical' or quasi-revolutionary unionism. The other is its close and successful relations with the Labor government of recent years. Such developments are obviously part of the changing political position of unions.

Unions and politics

Factional groups within the ACTU and individual unions have long since ceased to reflect any consistent disagreement as to the goals of unionism and rarely indicate any fundamental differences as to tactics. This was one of the necessary conditions for the establishment of the 'Accord' – to give its full title, the 'Statement of Accord by the Australian Labor Party and the Australian Council of Trade Unions Regarding Economic Policy' – published in February 1983, just before the election of the Labor government. That document has since been much analysed and its significance has changed as the policies set forth in it have variously been achieved, been modified or dropped out of sight. What remains essential is the assumption that there is a community of interest between the Party and the unions; and that while unions can and must continue to operate under non-Labor governments, they have a major interest in seeking the success of the ALP. The ACTU statement 'Future Strategies for the Trade Union Movement' in May 1987 argued that 'the unions need to maintain, and consolidate, their links with the ALP'. Thus, although unionists are now more likely to be well-off than in the past, and although their unions are less likely to be affiliated with the ALP, the connection between the ACTU and the ALP remains; and in some respects it is closer than before.

One part of an explanation for this is the high proportion of unionists who work in the public sector. After growing rapidly during the later 1970s and early 1980s, public sector employment is under threat, in Australia as in most capitalist countries. 'Privatization' of publicly owned industry has become a popular programme. Indeed, as the ACTU 'Future Strategies' document noted with some dismay, 'it has even proved attractive to sections of the ALP'. Privatization may well be a threat to the conditions of many public employees. Beyond doubt, it is a threat to their unions. Not surprisingly the one aspect of the Hawke government which was unanimously condemned at the 1987 ACTU Congress was its willingness to open a debate on the possibilities of privatization. 'Left' and 'Right' and public- and private-sector unions were united in making it clear that this – and not the government's taxation or social security policies or even falling real wages – was wholly unacceptable.

One reason why unions may be even more favourably disposed to Labor governments than in the past is that the non-Labor parties have become more sharply anti-union. This is not because the unions have changed – they are in fact less of a handicap to employers than in the past – but because public opinion has become less favourable towards them. This phenomenon is not purely Australian: as the ACTU's 'Future Strategies' paper puts it, 'the union movement throughout the world is very much on the defensive' and this is related to 'the generally poor public image of the union movement'. The ACTU leaders appreciate that, with declining union density, out-dated union boundaries and inadequate contact with their own members, Australian unions would be vulnerable to the hostile actions of future non-Labor governments. The actions of the National Party government of Queensland during the years 1984–87 have illustrated some of what the unions may have to fear.

In some respects the unions see themselves as very much on the defensive. In other respects they are presenting themselves as seeking positive change in the organization of Australian industry and the Australian economy, although seeking to do so in collaboration with employers and for the ultimate benefit of all classes.

THE EMPLOYERS' ASSOCIATIONS

Employers' organizations in Australia have received far less than their due attention.[7] This, while regrettable, is capable of explanation. Employers' associations are not only less distinctive than trade unions but, in most respects, less important and less powerful. This does not mean, of course, that *employers* are less powerful than unions: the reverse is more likely to be the case. But associations of employers are another matter. In fact they sometimes fail to secure the membership of powerful and important employers.

Australian legislation often purports to treat unions and employers' associations as similar. The British Trade Union Act of 1871 called both employers' and employees' organizations 'trade unions', and in New South Wales a Trade Union Act on the British model still exists. The Commonwealth Conciliation and Arbitration Act applies to both the common term 'organization' and in most respects presumes that they can be made subject to the same provisions. In fact they are different types of bodies. Most obviously a trade union is composed of individual men and women; whereas an employers' association may comprise other collective bodies. The members of a trade union, as individuals, are usually in a weak bargaining position; they form or join a union so that they may share in its collective strength. The constituents of an employers' association may be strong or weak; but they are not *necessarily* weak. They need their associations to carry out tasks which are required by the industrial relations system. They do not need them to give them a place in society.

There are other differences, some related to this essential difference. There is a case for arguing that employers' associations have been reactive, responding to the existence and the perceived threat presented by trade unions.[8] The creation in 1977 of the most important central employers' body, the Confederation of Australian Industry (CAI), arguably owed much to the development of the ACTU under the presidency of Bob Hawke. One very obvious difference between unions and employer associations concerns the public sector. With few exceptions, public employing authorities have no formal contact with organizations of private employers. Another difference is that the employers' association lacks the range of interests which characterizes the trade union. If the employers' association expresses a view about education or foreign policy or Aborigines, which is not likely, it will be based on the particular interests of its members, not on a perception of itself as a body seeking the general betterment of society. However, employers' associations do have multiple purposes and activities, and this is one of their great problems. They will be concerned with the conditions under which their employees work and in this respect have common interests in opposition to those of unions. But they are likely to have other interests, relating to trade policy, which divide manufacturers from farmers and importers from exporters. Australian employers and their organizations have grappled with the problems arising from this mixture of shared and opposed interests throughout this century, with mixed success.

The period since the establishment of the CAI has been one not of further consolidation but of continuing differences and divisions. During this period the unions have been united in supporting what has so far been the winning side in several senses, of which the ALP is only one. They are nearly unanimous in their support of the conciliation and arbitration systems, whereas opposition among employer organizations has grown, weakening the position of the CAI whose essential function has been to organize employer representation before the Australian Conciliation and Arbitration Commission. The CAI has also faced the difficulty of trying to combine this industrial function with other roles.

The CAI consists of eleven 'Foundation Members' – principally comprehensive state and territory employers' federations; twenty-five 'Ordinary Members' – representing employers in particular industries; and four similar bodies called 'Affiliated Associations'. It includes industrial, trade and manufacturing secretariats – the first based in Melbourne, and dealing with industrial relations questions, and the other two, based in Canberra, dealing with government policy relevant to trade and manufacturing. Its list of affiliates is impressive, but it does not include the Master Builders' Federation of Australia (MBFA) and it no longer includes the National Farmers' Federation (NFF). The Metal Trades Industry Association (MTIA) gave notice of leaving the CAI at the end of 1987. The CAI faces a dilemma. It is very much the 'official' representative of employers in the eyes of the federal government and the Australian Conciliation and Arbitration Commission. Together with ACTU and government representatives, it sits on the National Labour Consultative Council (NLCC) and the Economic Planning Advisory Council (EPAC). But its integration in the machinery of conciliation and arbitration and in tripartite organizations with government and the ACTU gives rise to hostility among rival organizations which are unenthusiastic or hostile towards the arbitration system and to collaboration with the ACTU and with government. Such attitudes had some part in causing the departure of the NFF from the CAI. The MTIA, however, left the CAI not because of its industrial relations policies but because of its unwillingness to devote itself entirely to industrial relations.

Some of the largest companies played a minor part, or no part at all, in the work of the CAI and other employer associations, and this helped give rise in 1983 to the Business Council of Australia (BCA), a body made up of about eighty chief executives – most from major companies, but a few also from public corporations (the Australian Telecommunications Commission; the Commonwealth Banking Corporation) and a government-owned company (Qantas Airways). The BCA has been treated respectfully by the Hawke government. It made a submission in its own right to the Australian Conciliation and Arbitration Commission in the National Wage Case of 1987, though it has adopted a somewhat equivocal attitude towards the arbitration system (see also p.173).

Radical views of the possibilities for change have been expressed by a number of other employer organizations, which have sometimes backed up their words with actions. For example, the NFF provided support for Mudginberri Station Pty Ltd in an important case wherein the Trade Practices Act was invoked against the Australasian Meat Employees Union in 1985–86, leading to damages of $1,760,000 being awarded against the union.[9] And in December 1985 the Melbourne Chamber of Commerce (whose president, Andrew Hay, is president of the national body, the Australian Chamber of Commerce) provided support for a small manufacturer, Dollar Sweets Pty Ltd, which successfully sought relief under the common law against union picketing.[10] Such action was seen by these organizations as an alternative to conciliation and arbitration. Mr Hay said at the time of the Dollar Sweets judgement: 'We will be advising our members to bypass the [Conciliation and Arbitration] Commission and go to court. We think, as far as small business is concerned, that the Commission is injurious; therefore its role ought to be greatly restricted'.

The employer associations mentioned here represent but a few of the thousands that exist across the country, very often as constituents of the major federations. It is probably true, as Andrew Hay implied in the passage just quoted, that the more radical proposals and actions tend to come from the smaller employers; but the attitude of the BCA implies that even the largest employers might welcome radical change, including the restriction or abolition of the conciliation and arbitration systems and a related marked decline in the importance of unionism, should circumstances seem favourable.

THE TRIBUNALS

A network of awards, determinations and registered agreements (subsequently described simply as 'awards') regulates employment – displacing terms of engagement that might otherwise be established by contract. These awards arise from the operations of industrial tribunals; and in 1983, 86.0 per cent of all employees worked under them. The field is divided between commonwealth and state tribunals, the respective coverages in 1983 being 34.7 per cent and 50.7 per cent. Over the post-war period the trend has been toward an increase in the coverage of state relative to commonwealth awards. This trend has been due to shifts in the composition of employment rather than transferences of areas from commonwealth to state control. Recent legal developments noted below imply a probable reversal of the trend. The coverage of females in 1983 (89.7 per cent) exceeded the coverage of males (83.6 per cent). Among male employees, coverage by federal awards (42.0 per cent) slightly exceeded state award coverage (40.9 per cent); but 65.4 per cent of females worked under state awards, compared with only 23.7 per cent under federal awards.[11]

The capacity of the commonwealth tribunals to make awards is derived, in the main, from the Conciliation and Arbitration Act (in force, but subject to many amendments, since 1904). This Act, in turn, is an exercise of the power conferred on the federal Parliament by the Constitution to make laws dealing with conciliation and arbitration 'for the prevention and settlement of industrial disputes extending beyond the limits of any one State'. Three important aspects of this constitutional authority are:

it does not authorize direct prescription by Parliament of the terms of employment. Parliament may establish mechanisms of conciliation and arbitration; it may prescribe their methods of operation; and it may specify criteria to be taken into account. But it must stop well short of determining the outcomes;

the exercise of the functions of conciliation and arbitration is linked to industrial disputes; and

the industrial disputes must be interstate in character.

The legal issues generated by these requirements cannot be analysed thoroughly within the scope of this chapter. It is important to note, however, that commonwealth tribunals cannot make 'common rules' binding automatically all employers and workers within defined industries or occupations. Rather, those bound must be parties to disputes. The restrictiveness of this requirement – as of the criterion of 'interstateness' – has been much diminished by the High Court's definition of a 'dispute'. Nevertheless the lack of authority to make 'common rules' is a restriction on the scope of commonwealth awards.[12]

State tribunals operate under laws of the respective Parliaments, which are subject to none of the restraints set out in the previous paragraph. State Parliaments can and do legislate directly about the terms of employment; they can and do prescribe some of the contents of the awards made by state tribunals; and they can and do authorize the making of common rules. These facts partially explain the extent of state coverage.

The states, nevertheless, are vulnerable to displacement by commonwealth award-making. Awards of the commonwealth tribunals have the force of federal law; and, by virtue of Section 109 of the Constitution, they prevail over state laws on the same subjects. The survival of active state jurisdictions is due, first, to some limitations on the commonwealth's constitutional authority and, second, to the preferences of unions and employers. A significant recent change pertains to the former. For many years, the High Court construed the term 'industrial' as limiting the kinds of employment which might be subject to awards. That is, some kinds of work were held not to be 'industrial' and therefore incapable of giving rise to 'industrial disputes'. The criteria for differentiating between industrial and non-industrial employment excluded from the former work which was neither manual nor related closely to commercial pursuits. For example, school teachers, many kinds of hospital employees, fire-fighters and social workers could not be covered by commonwealth awards. The High Court in 1983 reversed the line of decisions which had enforced this distinction.[13] Henceforth 'industrial dispute' would bear the meaning accorded the term by popular usage and would encompass all disputes about the terms of employment between employers and employees (or their representative associations). The processes whereby the consequences of this decision (especially the registration of associations not previously within the federal system) are worked out will be protracted; but there are definite possibilities of federal award-making moving into new areas.

Inevitably the commonwealth-state division of authority causes anomalies and difficulties. It is not uncommon for areas of work to be regulated by federal awards in some states and by state awards in others. Indeed, within a given state, a federal award may cover some workers whereas a state award covers others doing the same work: this occurs if some employers are not made parties to the dispute whereupon the federal award is founded. Differences between awards and between the principles observed by the different tribunals can generate unrest and cause efforts to manoeuvre between jurisdictions. For much of the history of conciliation and arbitration there was little communication or cooperation and some tension between the federal and state tribunals. In this respect there have been major changes in recent times. There are now regular meetings of the heads of tribunals. Amendments to commonwealth and some state Acts have allowed members of state tribunals to undertake conciliation and arbitration on behalf of the Australian Commission and vice versa; and have also permitted joint sittings of federal and state tribunals. Recommendations of the Hancock Committee, if implemented, will carry still further the trend toward more cooperative relationships. Few members of the tribunals now perceive themselves as operating rival shops.

Over its long history the system has included tribunals of diverse forms. A major distinction exists between the adversarial format, wherein arbitrators make their decisions after hearing the submissions of the contending interests (and those of any interveners), and the committee format, which involves representatives of the two sides meeting under a neutral chairman who may exercise a casting vote. The latter format has been popular in some of the states, but an attempt made in 1930 to graft it on to the federal system was aborted by a High Court decision to the effect that proceedings within a committee were neither conciliation nor arbitration. A second important source of diversity has been the concept of arbitral tribunals as courts of law. In general it may be said that by uneven steps the court-of-law model has lost ground, but remains influential. On p.183 we note the complaint that the system is tainted by excessive legalism.

The predominant structure in both the commonwealth and the states now involves a tribunal which does not purport to be a court. The Australian Conciliation and Arbitration Commission comprises a President and twelve Deputy Presidents (the Presidential Members) plus thirty Commissioners. Within it are ten panels with responsibilities for specified industries, each panel comprising a Presidential Member and several Commissioners. The more mundane matters which arise from day to day are dealt with by single members of the appropriate panels. Some issues, however, are handled by 'Full Benches'. The members of a Full Bench are chosen by the President, but must number not fewer than three and include at least two Presidential Members. National Wage Cases – perhaps the most publicised function of the Commission – are the responsibility of Full Benches which have included as many as seven members of the Commission. Subject to certain tests being satisfied, appeals can lie from decisions of single arbitrators to Full Benches. Not being a court, the Commission cannot enforce its own awards. This function belongs to the Industrial Division of the Federal Court of Australia. The responsibility of ensuring that the Commission acts according to law rests, in the final analysis, with the High Court.[14] In some respects the structure and procedure of the state tribunals differ from those of the federal Commission. We do not intend to describe the state systems in detail. It is noteworthy, however, that in some of the states there are significant roles for committees (variously described).

Although the arbitral functions of the tribunals attract most notice, conciliation occupies much of their time. Their response to notification of a dispute is often to arrange discussions between and with the parties directed toward agreement on all or some of the subject matter of the dispute and also to identify the area where arbitration is likely to be required. The members of the tribunals seek to assist the parties in various ways, including the making of recommendations to them. Agreements reached between the disputants – with or without the tribunals' help – may be given the force of awards by registering the agreements or by securing consent awards in terms of the agreements. Alternatively the parties may resolve some, but not all, of the issues in a dispute but leave the residue for arbitration. In practice most of the terms of awards are agreed upon. This level of agreement, however, does not demonstrate the unimportance of arbitration. First, agreement tends to concentrate on less fundamental issues. Second, discussions and negotiations take place in the shadow of arbitration: very often, the parties have views about the outcomes likely to emerge in arbitration and their perceptions of what is achievable affects their willingness to settle issues on non-arbitrated terms.

A duty of the tribunals is to be alert to the outbreak of 'bushfire' disputes, involving strikes or other limitations of work (such as overtime bans). The first endeavour of the relevant tribunal member will be to identify the source of difficulty. In many instances he or she will try to resolve it by informal means – perhaps recommending a course of action to one or both of the disputants. Quite often the convening of a hearing or a conference will achieve a sufficient movement in the parties' positions for the interruption of work to cease. The tribunals have some reluctance to arbitrate under duress and often refuse to arbitrate while direct action persists. Ultimately, but by no means automatically, steps may be taken to penalize a party to direct action. In the commonwealth system, this requires preliminary and discretionary measures to be taken by the Conciliation and Arbitration Commission before a complaining party has access to the processes of the Federal Court. The penal procedures were frequently invoked by employers in the 1950s and 1960s, but have since fallen into disuse.

GOVERNMENT AND INDUSTRIAL RELATIONS

Government is involved in industrial relations in many ways. The most important involvements are as follows:

(1)   Governments are major employers. Some 30.4 per cent of the employee labour force (excluding members of the defence forces) work for governments and their instrumentalities.[15] The partial isolation of the public sector from the chill winds of market competition and employers' profitability has given rise to standards of employment and attitudes which affect behaviour and expectations within the private sector.

(2)   The conciliation and arbitration authorities function in accordance with the relevant federal and state Acts of Parliament and the regulations made thereunder. Moreover the legislation also deals in some detail with the constitutional requirements of trade unions and employers' associations who have standing in the system. The frequency of amendments to these laws is evidence of the active interest of governments in the operation of the system.

(3)   Governments are entitled to be heard as interveners by the conciliation and arbitration tribunals. They often exercise their rights, especially in cases of major economic consequence.

(4)   There are frequent discussions and negotiations between governments and the 'peak' organizations of labour and employers. Since 1983, the links between the ALP and the ACTU have had an important bearing on economic management. (See the discussion of trade unions and politics, pp.170–1).

(5)   Industrial disruption often causes formal or informal intervention by governments who are concerned about the economic ill-effects of lost production, inconvenience to the public and political damage to themselves.

(6)   As was noted above (p.174), state Parliaments and, to a limited extent, the federal Parliament may legislate directly about the terms of employment.

(7)   Australia is a member of the International Labour Organization and the Commonwealth Parliament has ratified many of its conventions. Traditionally, the division of industrial power between the commonwealth and the states caused delays in the ratification of conventions while the agreement of the states was sought; and, in some instances, the withholding of that agreement prevented ratification. The decision of the High Court in the *Tasmanian Dams Case*, however, has lent force to the view that the commonwealth may be able to ratify and enforce conventions without the states' concurrence (as an exercise of commonwealth authority for external affairs).[16]

There is a commonwealth Department of Industrial Relations (headed by a senior Minister) and counterpart departments (under various names) in the states. These administrative arrangements reflect the extent of governmental concerns about industrial relations.

The public services and, to a degree, statutory authorities have been distinguished by a greater level of job security, superior superannuation and greater emphasis upon seniority in promotions than are typical in the private sector (though there are companies which resemble the public services in these respects). At the highest levels the salaries of public-sector employees are below those of senior executives in private companies: top-level private salaries are apparently raised by forces of competition which are more muted in government employment. At lower levels there developed in the early years of the Whitlam government (that is, in 1973–74) a concept of the public service as a 'pace-setter' in terms of employment. This notion lost favour in 1974–75. An important occurrence which co-incided roughly with the pace-setter principle, and probably owed something to it, was an upgrading of superannuation schemes to levels of generosity which were quite out of line with private-sector standards: most private-sector workers were not superannuated at all and those benefits which were provided were generally parsimonious. There is now no apparent support among federal and state governments for 'pace-setter' terms of employment, although legacies of the earlier benevolence remain. Reversals have been more numerous in the state public services than in the commonwealth service, possibly reflecting a greater degree of budgetary crisis in the states. Trade union militancy in the public sector has in recent years encountered increased employer resistance. The resistance has taken the form chiefly of a preparedness to endure direct action rather than capitulate to union demands. This is not to deny that governments have been willing to resolve disputes by negotiation and to make concessions in the process. The concessions, however, have been less readily forthcoming and have fallen further below union demands since 1983 or thereabouts than in earlier periods.

Foremost among those areas of unrest within the private sector which have caused governmental concern has been the building industry. The source of greatest difficulty for some years was the Australian Building Construction Employees' and Builders Labourers' Federation (BLF), which had developed techniques of 'guerilla' militancy (to use the union's own term), such as ceasing work while concrete pours were under way. After unsuccessful attempts to get the union to be less turbulent, the commonwealth government in 1985 initiated steps leading to its deregistration from the commonwealth system; and parallel action was taken by the state governments in New South Wales and Victoria. This action by no means converted building into a scene of industrial tranquillity. Other unions absorbed former members of the BLF; and the position of some union leaders seemed to be under challenge. In these circumstances federal and state governments were sometimes willing to acquiesce in union claims rather than risk the defeat of such leaders and the reappearance of the BLF leadership in a new guise.

Governments have been perturbed, too, by industrial unrest in the coal industry. The impact of disputation on the flow of coal for export to Japan gives rise to fears about the loss of the market to alternative suppliers and the undermining of Australia's capacity to bargain about price. During 1987, a worsening market for coal and Japanese insistence on lower prices caused a conflict between the commonwealth government and the miners' union, marked by recurrent direct action. The union tried to link acceptance of job losses and other concessions to the establishment of a marketing authority for export coal. For its part, the government was prepared to offer financial support (or reduced burdens of taxes and charges) to the industry; but it was unwilling to impose a marketing authority, discounting the miners' contention that competition between Australian suppliers forced export prices below the level which the Japanese market would bear.

Late in 1986, there was an increase in attention by governments to restrictive work practices. This subject was brought to the forefront of current debate by the chief executive of Peko Wallsend Ltd, Charles Copeman. The company operates a mine at Robe River in Western Australia, and took unilateral action (bypassing conciliation and arbitration) to eliminate many allegedly unwarranted practices at the mine. Peko Wallsend was criticized for a somewhat defiant attitude toward the Western Australian Industrial Commission. Nevertheless, in the climate of heightened interest in restrictive practices, the common-wealth government encouraged union-employer discussions about them. Removal of restrictive work practices was subsequently encouraged by the terms of the decision in the National Wage Case given in March 1987.

We referred earlier (p.169) to the Industrial Relations Bill, which was introduced in the Commonwealth Parliament in May 1987 but lapsed with the dissolution of the Parliament. Late in 1987, it seemed likely that a modified form of the Bill would be brought forward in 1988. Because we do not know the terms of the new legislation, we refer to the matter in broad terms only. It will give effect to many, but not all, recommendations of the Hancock Committee; and in some areas it will go beyond the Committee's proposals. Instead of the Australian Conciliation and Arbitration Commission there will be an Australian Industrial Relations Commission, with similar functions and (presumably) membership. An area of uncertainty is whether the government will proceed with its earlier intention (embodied in the lapsed Bill) to establish an Australian Labour Court (in lieu of the Industrial Division of the Federal Court), whose judges would include suitably qualified members of the Indus-trial Relations Commission. There will be provisions to facilitate closer interaction with the state tribunals. Union amalgamations will be encouraged and made easier. The obligation of the Industrial Relations Commission to take account of the economic effects of its decisions will be greater than that now resting upon the Conciliation and Arbitration Commission. It appears, however, that those provisions contained in the 1987 Bill which would have strengthened the sanctions against direct action will not be proceeded with; nor will those restricting access to the courts for the award of damages and the granting of injunctions against unions involved in certain kinds of direct action. The government, apparently, has responded to employer criticisms of the latter provisions by maintaining the status quo with respect to penalties.

INDUSTRIAL DISPUTATION

The subject of this section is 'direct action'. Strikes and lockouts are its most conspicuous and most easily measured manifestation, strikes being more common than lockouts. But strikes and lockouts are not the only forms of direct action. Another form, which does not lend itself to measurement, is the selective ban. Limitations on the working of overtime are one example. Another is bans on the performance of specific duties. That is, the employees attend work at the prescribed times but refuse to carry out designated tasks. If the employer acquiesces in the employees remaining at work, the normal wages and salaries must be paid, so that the ban is (to the employees) a costless form of direct action.

Statistics of stoppages – the only available measure of direct action – lend some support to the perception of Australia as a strike-prone country. A study by Creigh compares the records of twenty countries in the period 1962–81.[17] In terms of days lost per employee, Australia's record was the fifth-worst. The average Australian worker lost less time than workers in Iceland, Italy, Canada and the Irish Republic, slightly more than those in the United States, and rather more than those in the United Kingdom, New Zealand, Japan and most of Western Europe. The Australian pattern of stoppages was unusual. Only one country – Italy – had a higher proportion of workers involved in stoppages. However, the duration of Australian stoppages was low. That is, Australia had frequent strikes which were typically of short duration.

The international comparison of time lost must be interpreted with caution. In particular it does not necessarily indicate the success or failure of systems of dispute resolution. This caution gains force from the differences which exist between the states in respect of time lost. For the years 1966–86, the time lost per employee (in days per year) was: New South Wales, 0.59; Victoria, 0.53; Queensland, 0.45; Western Australia, 0.34; Tasmania, 0.32 and South Australia, 0.21. The states are similar in the role played by conciliation and arbitration in dealing with disputes. It must be inferred that factors other than the 'system', such as differences of industrial structure and local history, affect powerfully the levels of industrial unrest. These differences are likely to be even more important between countries than between states. Moreover the factors likely to affect the level of disruption include the macro-economic condition of the country. A study of international differences taking this influence into account has been carried out by Beggs and Chapman.[18] We cannot discuss this study in detail, but it suggests that, in a rank-order of countries 'corrected' for differences in macro-economic conditions, Australia's relative position is rather better than in the crude comparison.

A matter of current interest is whether there was a step down to a lower level of disputation as a result of the Accord and the consequent developments in wage determination. These developments included commitments given by unions to 'no extra claims'. That is, unions wishing to secure for their members increases granted in National Wage Cases and related state cases have been called upon to renounce the right to pursue claims outside the principles of wage adjustment set out by the tribunals in those cases. All but a few unions gave the commitments. Having done so, they had fewer occasions to involve their members in direct action. Undoubtedly the amount of time lost per head in the post-Accord years has been exceptionally low; and the present government has claimed credit for this. Beggs and Chapman, in another study, ask whether the time lost has been less than could have been expected if the economic conditions of the recent period were taken into account.[19] They find that some of the reduction can indeed be attributed to the state of the economy. Much of it, however, cannot be so explained. This analysis suggests, therefore, that the Accord and associated developments have effected a reduction of days lost through strikes.

Whatever Australia's standing in international comparisons of stoppages, we must stress that time lost is a flawed indicator of the state of industrial relations. One weakness – the occurrence of other forms of direct action – has already been noted. There are also manifestations of poor industrial relations which are not forms of direct action – absenteeism, high labour turnover, restrictive work practices and indifferent on-the-job performance. The fundamental objection to relying upon statistics of stoppages to measure the quality of industrial relations is that at any time only a minute fraction of the labour force is on strike or locked out. In assessing the health levels of a community, we might take some note of the size of the hospital population. We should be conscious, however, that this would be a dubious index of the condition of the vast majority of people who are *not* in hospital. Participation in stoppages is similarly deficient as an index of industrial relations.

ISSUES IN THE DEBATE

1: Labour costs and economic policy

The macro-economic consequences of decisions about wages and related costs have been the subject of debate since the 1920s. That debate has occurred in different contexts, ranging from deep depression to vigorous boom. Underlying it has been a realization that the principal arbitration tribunal has, alongside its other responsibilities, a role in the determination of national economic policies. Since the mid-1970s the economic effects of labour costs have been assessed against a background of serious unemployment and inflation. In more recent years there have also been concerns about the balance of payments, the level of overseas debt, the value of the Australian dollar in other currencies and the competitiveness of Australian industry.

In the early 1970s there had been a de-emphasis of wage policy and a permissive attitude, on the part of the wage-setting tribunals, toward wage increases negotiated 'in the field'. This stance ceased in 1975, with the introduction of indexation and a set of guidelines intended to limit severely wage increases secured outside the national wage cases. That system continued, with modifications as time progressed, until 1981, when the Conciliation and Arbitration Commission judged that there was insufficient commitment to the post-1975 system for it to be sustainable. Consequently it abandoned the 'orderly' adjustment of wages and acquiesced in a return to collective bargaining akin to that of 1974 and immediately preceding years. The new era lasted until late 1982 when the Commission, responding to arguments advanced by the Fraser government, introduced a 'wage freeze'. After the election of the Hawke government, the 'freeze' gave way to a new centralized system similar to that of 1975 but differing in specific contents. It embodied both a qualified commitment to index award wages to the Consumer Price Index and various rules designed to inhibit other increases. The limited opportunities which this system left for unions to pursue benefits for their members caused problems. One relaxation approved by the Commission in 1986 allowed unions to seek employer contributions (up to 3 per cent of wages and salaries) to superannuation funds. In December 1986 the Commission gave its approval in principle to a 'two-tier' system, and in March 1987 the details of this arrangement were spelt out in a national wage case decision. The first tier would consist of a flat-rate increase of $10 (about 3 per cent of average ordinary-time earnings) and a possible later increase of 1.5 per cent. A second tier would accommodate further increases of up to 4 per cent. The most important of the available grounds for second-tier increases is 'restructuring and efficiency'. Wage increases granted in terms of this criterion should be offset – preferably more than offset – by alterations in work arrangements which raise productivity or otherwise reduce costs.

There is little disagreement that restraining the growth of labour costs facilitates national adjustment to the adverse economic conditions of recent times. Such disagreements as have been aired concern, rather, the degree of wage restraint actually achieved by the Conciliation and Arbitration Commission. In the period between 1982 and the earlier half of 1987, wages rose proportionally less than prices: prescribed wage rates grew by 3.6 per cent per year, earnings by 5.5 per cent and consumer prices by 6.3 per cent. The severest critics have stressed the high growth rates of *money* wages. These critics note that money wage rises tend to maintain the momentum of inflation; assert that they erode Australia's international competitive position, contributing to the adverse balance-of-payments situation; argue that they militate against the survival of businesses (especially in the rural sector); and allege that they 'price workers out of jobs'. The point is frequently made that the rate of increase of wages exceeds significantly the rates of increase recorded by Australia's trading partners. Judgements of performance which emphasize *real* wages are more diverse. This diversity arises from a division of opinion about the 'sacrifice' which must be borne by wage and salary earners on account of national economic problems. Foremost among the factors recognized as necessitating *some* sacrifice is the adverse movement of the terms of trade. This is, in principle, a fairly non-contentious matter, though there are disagreements about the extent of the wage 'discounting' warranted by it. More division surrounds the suggestion that real wages should be reduced to curb inflation or to enhance profit margins (the latter being perceived by some as a strategy conducive to high employment). The objections imply a concern about the equity of reductions of real wages. They are reinforced by assertions that businesses have failed to reinvest the higher profits which many have earned.

It is not possible in this paper to discuss the macro-economic aspects of wage policy in the detail required for a well-founded set of conclusions. Some of the issues currently debated are ephemeral, and the relative importance of others varies. The issue whether wage policy should be judged by reference to the movements of money wages or those of real wages is, however, one of enduring importance. It goes to the question of how a wage-fixing tribunal can and should 'break into' the inflationary process. Various answers are possible. Perhaps the most telling argument for disregarding real wages is their long-term dependence on forces (notably productivity and the terms of trade) other than money wage levels. The less dependent are wage-earner living standards on money wages, the weaker is the case for raising wages so as to protect real wages and the stronger the justification for giving priority to other goals such as stable prices and a more encouraging climate for investment. Against this the point may be made that inflation is a process embracing the generality of prices; and that to use one set of prices – those of labour services – as a brake on the others, has adverse short-term effects on the recipients of the controlled prices. The measure of restraint, it may be said, is the extent (if any) by which wage increases are retarded relative to the general movement of prices. A sensible comparison between Australian wage behaviour and wage movements in other countries would, therefore, pertain to real rather than money wages. The case for attending to the behaviour of real wages often alludes to 'industrial relations realities'. Industrial tribunals, it may be argued, cannot disregard the expectations of the parties. Not only must they try to prevent and settle industrial disputes: they must also accept that their own authority is less than absolute. That authority may support the use of wage policy as a restraining mechanism, but fall apart if more drastic measures (such as ignoring the cost of living) are attempted.

If the justification *in principle* for equating wage restraint with acceptance of lower real wages were accepted, a difficulty would remain in measuring that restraint. The wage-setters influence directly the level of money wages; but because consumer prices may change to offset movements in money wages, the tribunals' control over real wages is tenuous and uncertain. If we find that real wages rise less (or fall more) in one period than in another, the reason is not *necessarily* a difference in the degree of wage restraint: the statistics may simply be registering economic realities. The degree of restraint must then be a question of subjective judgement. If this is a correct interpretation of the matter, the case for attributing restraint to the tribunals must be based on an examination of their actual decisions. It would include:

the tribunals' acquiescence in some of the fall in real wages that occurred during the 'wage freeze' of 1982–83;

the determined efforts of the tribunals to curb 'back-door' increases in particular wage rates such as might have been achieved by invoking the principles of 'work value' and 'comparative wage justice';

substantial delays which have occurred in translating CPI increases into national wage adjustments; and

the absence for many years of any decision taken with the intent of increasing real wages (whereas previously a steady growth of real wages was regarded as normal).

A remarkable feature of industrial relations in 1987 was an acceptance by the ACTU of the contention that price increases were not a sufficient justification for wage increases. This acceptance – perhaps limited to the circumstances of 1987 – took the form, not of renouncing wage increases, but rather of supporting their linkage to steps which would enhance economic performance. The 'restructuring and efficiency' criterion, mentioned above, accorded with this concept, and was supported by the ACTU. Toward the end of 1987 the government, the ACTU and the CAI were discussing the 'next phase' of wage policy, anticipating a National Wage Case scheduled for May 1988. The discussion focussed on other means of relating wage increases to economic performance, such as profit-sharing. At the time of writing, it is hard to foresee how the agenda of the debate and its outcome will be affected by the collapse of share values which occurred in October 1987. The collapse appears, however, to exacerbate the tension between stability and equity. Arguments that the adverse consequences of events in the share-market necessitate greater wage restraint collide with the judgement that wage-earners ought not to 'suffer' on account of financial speculation. (After all, earlier rises in the share-price index were not translated into larger wage increases).

We have, in this section, concentrated on the explanation of issues without asserting our own opinions about them. This reflects our judgement that the issues are complex, requiring fuller analysis than is possible here. It is, however, relevant to the tenor of the whole chapter for us to record our opinion that macro-economic management would be more difficult and the outcomes less favourable if there were no centralized wage policy.[20]

2: The law and 'legalism'

In no country are industrial relations exempt from extensive legal regulation. This is not surprising, in that a purpose of the law is to regulate conflicts of interest, and conflicts between employers and employees are among the most obvious and important of those which confront all modern societies. The question at issue, in Australia as elsewhere, is not whether there is a place for the law, but just what that place is; what sort of law and what sort of legal institutions are appropriate to Australian industrial relations at the end of the twentieth century?

In retrospect it is clear that the founders of conciliation and arbitration were too ambitious in their vision of the role of law. The new courts simply lacked the authority which was accorded to the 'ordinary' courts of the land. No court or other tribunal can be effective unless there is a general willingness in society to follow its rulings, even if they are unfavourable. The trade unions especially, but not they alone, were not prepared to accord the early arbitration courts this type of allegiance. In those circumstances the mere existence of heavy penalties on the statute books is worth little. An attempt to impose them irrespective of the powers of the parties or whether they will be seriously aggrieved, which is the way a court should act, would be a cure worse than the disease. Much of this was recognized in 1930 when, to general approval, the commonwealth Act was stripped of its majestic provision making all strikes and lockouts illegal.

By then, however, the Commonwealth Court and its state equivalents had acquired many supporters as well as critics. They might not be able to behave much like courts in many circumstances; but they were certainly performing socially useful tasks and many people and institutions had come to depend on them. Hence they successfully resisted powerful attempts to abolish them or to restrict their activities, and survived into the 1930s and beyond as courts – rather odd courts, certainly, but courts nevertheless. There has been a great deal of further modification since the 1930s; but some of the dilemmas and inconsistencies remain. Since 1956 there has no longer been a Commonwealth Conciliation and Arbitration *Court*. The work of conciliation and arbitration at the federal level is in the hands of the Australian Conciliation and Arbitration Commission. Its procedures would often seem to a layperson indistinguishable from those of a court, especially when, as is often the case, the parties are represented by barristers. Hearings are often prolonged, although the Commission can also act with speed when an industrial situation requires this.

It has often been suggested that a tribunal which has many of the characteristics of a court is an unsuitable venue for the resolution of conflict in industrial relations because of its emphasis on the adversarial character of such proceedings. Though this contention has some force, it needs to be qualified in two rather different ways. One is that to a large extent industrial relations *is* an arena of conflicting interests and that this will be true whatever the precise character of the institutions set up to deal with that conflict. The other is that the operation of the Commission has many aspects which are quite unlike those of a court. It makes great use of conferences, conducted informally and in the absence of the press and the media, in a way which would be quite unsuitable, and indeed scandalous, in a court. 'Legalism' in the Commission is only one aspect, and a minor one, of the role of the law in Australian industrial relations. More important is the role of 'real' courts, both in association with the commonwealth conciliation and arbitration system and independently.

The two areas in which the courts have recently extended their role have been in the application of Sections 45D and 45E of the Commonwealth Trade Practices Act, involving the Federal Court of Australia, and the revival of actions at common law against the 'industrial torts' of inducement of breach of contract and intimidation. Both of these are complex and controversial matters and the second, in particular, remains unclear.[21] Two points are to be made about them. First, it is in these areas, rather than before the Commission, that the really important aspects of the role of the law in Australian industrial relations will be resolved. Second, they illustrate that what can be achieved by the law, for better or worse, will be confined to particular actions against specific examples of industrial action rather than the fantasy, which underlay the early arbitration systems, that all forms of industrial action could be rendered illegal and punished accordingly. We return briefly to the subject of 'regulation' by courts in section 5 below.

3: The 'balance of power'

A common complaint in Australian history during this century has been that trade unions have 'too much power'. It is not surprising that this has been, and remains, a view to be found among employers and in the non-Labor parties. It is more notable that it appears to have been held by most Australians, including many trade unionists. Evidence to this effect needs to be considered with caution. When a sample of the population is asked 'Do you think that the trade unions in this country have too much power, or not too much?,[22] this is obviously, in itself, a limited and ambiguous type of inquiry. But the answers do tell us *something*, especially if, as in this case, the question is combined with a corresponding question about the power of 'big business'. In 1967, 47 per cent of a national sample of Australian voters said that the unions had 'too much power'; but rather more (52 per cent) said the same of 'big business'. This suggested a generalized suspicion of major economic institutions rather than a particular hostility to trade unions. By 1979, there had been a significant change. Seventy-eight per cent then said that unions had 'too much power', whereas 63 per cent said this of 'big business'.[23] While there had been an increased tendency to see both groups as too powerful, the unions were now more likely to be so perceived. Nearly ten years later it is natural to ask whether there have been further changes in opinion. Unfortunately it is not so easy to find an answer. This once common question, especially as regards trade unions, seems to have dropped out of the repertoire of the pollsters.

There are, of course, wider arguments about the present power of unions. Unions – more specifically the ACTU – have greater access to the present commonwealth government than to any of its predecessors. Consultation with unions not only on narrowly 'industrial' matters but on budgetary strategy, education policy and many other issues of domestic and even foreign policy is not new; but it has been formalized and consistently applied to a greater extent than ever in the past. In these respects the unions have been given a greater apparent opportunity to exercise power. Whether their real power has increased is a more complex matter. If power consists of the capacity to oblige others to act otherwise than they would wish to do, has this really been a characteristic of the Accord years? These have been marked by 'packages' of negotiation and agreement, wherein the unions have experienced both gains and losses. Let us grant, for example, that unions have secured from unwilling employers improvements in superannuation, in occupational health and safety and in provision for redundancy; and that during the same time they have experienced, and tacitly acquiesced in, an overall decline in real wages. Is such a period one of union power or union weakness?

Responses to such questions turn in part on whether employers are prepared to accept the legitimacy of a system in which such deals can be made. If such a framework is accepted, then the record of the unions has been a mixed one and certainly illustrates their limited power. But, of course, there are those to whom the very existence of a system in which the unions have an officially recognized place shows that they have 'too much power'. They object to the rules of the game rather than the scores of the players. To these critics, the entrenched position assumed by the unions is symbolized by *Australia Reconstructed*, a report on a mission to European countries by a joint delegation from the ACTU and from a section of the commonwealth Department of Trade published in 1987. The report, much influenced in particular by Swedish experience, advocates (among other things) greater union involvement in management as well as in public policy. All this may indeed suggest growing trade union power; but it occurs at a time of union vulnerability in other respects, of which the apparent decline in the unionization of the workforce is only the simplest example. Employers are undecided whether to continue to acquiesce in an increased range of union influence, as long as that influence is used 'responsibly'; or to campaign actively against unionism and reverse the long-term trend towards greater union participation in industry. The future of Australian industrial relations may depend largely upon which of these tendencies characterizes employers and managers during the next decade.

4: Workplace relations

The conciliation and arbitration system deals with trade unions and employers or their associations. With exceptions it does not have direct relations with individual workers. The grievances of individual workers do come before the tribunals, but this is because they are taken up by unions or because the unions respond to employer initiatives; and unions, for the most part, are not specific to single enterprises. These facts, it is said, militate against the resolution of workplace problems to the satisfaction of the employers and employees who are directly affected. The further claim is made that bad industrial relations within enterprises depress both the level and rate of growth of productivity. Taken together these assertions are drawn upon in support of a contention that the conciliation and arbitration system is largely to blame for Australia's allegedly poor economic performance.

We do not here explore the determinants of Australia's long-run economic performance, limiting ourselves to the observation that the topic cannot be disposed of simply by identifying one feature of the society which (in the critic's mind) leaves something to be desired and leaping to the conclusion that this is the source of pervasive economic ills. Beyond this we confine ourselves to the simpler (though still difficult) issues whether the formal system does cause bad relations at the workplace and whether any weaknesses of this kind are inherent in the system or can be overcome by reforming it.

The high incidence of short-term stoppages in Australia (see pp.178–80) is sometimes seen as a symptom of the system's failure to avert 'niggling' workplace difficulties. It is argued that long-lasting strikes and lockouts, of which Australia has few, represent less of an industrial relations 'problem'; and economies are more capable of taking them in their stride. Lack of communication and understanding between managers and employees is the specific fault attributed to the resolution of disputes within the framework of conciliation and arbitration. Employers are prone to consult the provisions of the awards rather than investigate and remedy particular grievances; workers are apt to refer grievances to union representatives rather than take them up with management; and there is little or no joint endeavour to foresee problems, to devise solutions and to innovate. Moreover the conciliation and arbitration system tends to emphasize uniformity, whereas good workplace relations require solutions tailored imaginatively to the circumstances of different establishments.

The assertion that the system has these ill-effects is, at best, the result of intelligent speculation. So far as we know it is not the outcome of empirical analysis. Equally we know of no empirical study which supports a contrary view. Speculating ourselves, we make the following points:

(1)   The 'level' of dispute resolution, which is allegedly 'too high', may well reflect the level at which disputes tend to occur. Australian trade unions are, with few exceptions, non-enterprise unions. Some are industry unions; some are occupational; and others are conglomerates. This being so, it is difficult to imagine there being no major disputes transcending individual enterprises. The fact that the tribunals commonly operate at a level above the enterprise may therefore accord with the need for their services.

(2)   Despite this the tribunals do very often address problems within particular plants. Much of the tribunal members' time is taken up with such disputes. Many awards are single-employer awards. An area of work for the tribunals which has burgeoned in recent years is disputes about dismissals and reinstatements. At the federal level this is mainly an informal jurisdiction: because there is a technical impediment to the Commission's making orders about reinstatements and like matters, it depends upon the parties consenting to abide by its decisions.[24] Consent is frequently given. At the state level there is no similar complication, and the tribunals are actively engaged in the resolution of these enterprise-level disputes.

(3)   There may be scope for enhancing the grievance procedures available when problems arise at the workplace. The Hancock Committee recommended that such procedures be incorporated in awards. Until this step is taken, and the effects are known, it is premature to suppose that there is an inevitable hiatus in the system.

(4)   An obstacle to cooperation at the workplace is authoritarian managerial techniques. The conciliation and arbitration system does not prescribe these techniques. Historically, however, it has recognized areas of 'managerial prerogative'. Indeed the federal tribunals have been constrained to do so by decisions of the High Court which excluded various managerial decisions from the permissible scope of 'industrial disputes'. Indirectly the support given to managerial prerogative may have encouraged managers to persevere with prescriptive forms of workplace control. Recent decisions of the High Court, however, have responded to changing customs and attitudes and the scope of managerial prerogative has been significantly reduced. It is unlikely that in future the arbitral tribunals will impede the development of more collaborative workplace relations.

If participative and consultative arrangements enhance productivity and profits – as is frequently suggested – firms which implement them will benefit whether they operate under conciliation and arbitration or under other systems, and the key to change in this respect is likely to be management training. Associations of employers such as the CAI and the BCA are increasingly affirming the benefits of participative workplace relations and measures, such as profit-sharing, which strengthen employees' commitment to the well-being of the enterprises for which they work. They resist, however, governmental interference which might be construed as imposing participation on them.

5: Deregulation
'Deregulation' of economic activity has gained support with remarkable rapidity. To some degree this support may justifiably be termed 'ideological', resting upon the premise that government and its regulatory agencies normally produce results which are inferior to those likely to emerge from an unconstrained 'market'. There is also a more pragmatic school which calls only for the critical assessment of regulation on a case-by-case basis, leading to the abandonment of measures which fail to achieve the intended results or have unforeseen and undesired side-effects. The call for deregulation of the labour market has come more from the former than from the latter school. The case made by proponents of deregulation has indeed included specific complaints against the Conciliation and Arbitration Commission – for example, that the Commission has prescribed excessive rates for juveniles; but it has taken for granted the inference that such 'errors' can be avoided only by dismantling the system of regulation or greatly restricting its role. Not all critics of the Commission are

advocates of deregulation; but all who call for deregulation of the labour market are critical of the Commission. We do not attempt here to discuss the in-principle merits of 'free' markets. To do so we should need to embark on the large task of analysing the properties of competitive systems and the consequences of imperfections which would remain in a deregulated labour market. These are issues beyond the scope of this chapter. The ensuing paragraphs deal with aspects of the deregulation proposal which are industrial, practical or political in character.

'Regulation' includes, presumably, the following:

the network of awards, determinations and registered agreements which are made or approved by the Commission, its state counterparts and specialist authorities such as the Coal Industry Tribunal;

legislation which is ancillary to this system – for example, that which has to do with the registration of trade unions and relations between unions and their members; and

laws (chiefly of the states) which prescribe terms of employment directly rather than leaving them to be settled by the processes of conciliation and arbitration.

If this body of law were somehow swept away there would remain the common law, which would control employment relations and the conduct of industrial relations in different ways. In general common law is more favourable to employers than the system of regulation now in existence. As Sir Otto Kahn-Freund said, 'the common law knows nothing of a balance of collective forces'.[25] This gives rise to the question whether supporters of deregulation really wish to 'free' the labour market from state intervention or rather to alter the balance of industrial power. A fully deregulationist programme would incorporate a provision along the lines of the British Trade Disputes Act of 1906, which proscribed actions for tort brought against trade unions and employers' associations if the alleged torts were related to trade disputes (such as strikes). The Trade Disputes Act substantially deregulated the British labour market. Industrial relations were left to employers and employees and their organizations; and the courts, along with other arms of the state, would not interfere.[26] To the best of our knowledge no protagonist of Australian deregulation has noted – let alone accepted – this implication. Indeed ostensible advocates of 'deregulation' commonly support statutory 'regulation' in the form of Sections 45D and 45E of the Trade Practices Act. 'Deregulation', then, is selective.

The ambiguities of the concept of deregulation were noted by the Hancock Committee, which also suggested an interpretation that seemed practical, if not desirable. In comparison with dismantling the conciliation and arbitration system,

a less fanciful form of 'deregulation' would involve a change in the *style* of conciliation and arbitration, with the tribunals adopting more passive stances than hitherto – facilitating compromises between parties to collective bargaining and de-emphasizing broader policy considerations. This change would be encouraged by removing from the legislation the requirement for Full Benches to have regard to the public interest and especially the direction to take account of the economic consequences of their decisions. A more emphatic step would be the enactment of a prohibition upon the Commission's making general orders, as in *National Wage* cases. Such proposals do not have the 'either/or' connotations of abolishing arbitration – the tribunals can be more or less policy-oriented and conversely more or less accommodative to bargaining pressures.[27]

One of the grounds upon which the report has been criticized is its failure to recommend 'deregulation'; but, in the main, the critics have failed to take up the challenge to specify such a programme.

Blandy and Sloan, however, have made concrete proposals directed toward deregulation.[28] These include the cessation of general policy-making, such as occurs in national wage cases. Australia, in short, would cease to have a wage policy. This might be defended on either or both of two grounds:

> that wage policy is not a worthwhile constituent of the existing set of techniques of macro-economic management; and

> that the constraints of a wage policy (for example, the uniformity of treatment which it requires) have adverse side-effects.

Blandy and Sloan may agree with the former contention; and they certainly agree with the latter. Their view is that the degree of centralism required in the operation of a wage policy militates against better relations in the workplace. The issue of wage policy is too large to be discussed adequately here. We do observe, however, the paucity of answers to the questions: What changes in other components or macro-economic policy would be required to contain the inflationary pressures generated by or transmitted through the labour market; and what would be the consequences (especially for unemployment) of relying exclusively on these other measures? The near-silence of the critics of the Hancock Committee about these questions is the more surprising because of the Committee's portrayal of wage policy as a significant and beneficial product of the centralized system.

A form of 'deregulation' which has gained some support involves voluntary opting-out of the official conciliation and arbitration system. This possibility was considered sympathetically by the Hancock Committee. The Committee recognized that, to be effective, legislation providing for opting-out must envisage alternative forms of conciliation and arbitration. It is beyond the commonwealth's power to legislate (for example) for a general right of collective bargaining. Accordingly, the Committee proposed a legislative entitlement for employers and unions to agree on their own forms of conciliation and arbitration. In the event, the Committee's proposal was not accepted. The Minister, Mr Willis, said that it entailed too serious a threat to an orderly wage policy. Unions frustrated by the limitations imposed on them and their claims by the centralized system might use the opting-out facility to avoid these restrictions. The Committee was conscious of this danger, but thought the risk worth taking. It is no surprise that the government saw the matter otherwise.

6: Conclusion

The debate about industrial relations which has arisen in recent years has, to a significant degree, involved a division between those with a detailed knowledge of the current system (whatever their professional allegiances) and those, without this familiarity, whose attitudes owe more to broad principle. Of course there are exceptions to this rule; but they are remarkably few. David Nolan, the Director of the Industrial Council of the CAI, makes the point in trenchant terms. The debate, he says, is 'between those on one side who are deeply and regularly involved in industrial relations, against those on the other side who strike ideological positions but who do not have an extensive background in dispute resolution. It is a debate between those who are involved in industrial relations and those who are not'.[29]

The critics of the current system do not speak with a single voice. We referred in the previous section to the use of the term 'deregulation' to describe both a greater reliance on competitive markets and a shift in the balance of industrial power from unions to employers. Thus a similarity of language tends to conceal a diversity of views. Another source of critical ideas is the assumption that industrial relations would be more harmonious if decentralized to the enterprise level. This is the principal message of a *Policy Statement* – subtitled, *Toward an Enterprise Based Industrial Relations System* – which the BCA published in March 1987. The BCA seeks a fundamental reorientation of the system

> away from one largely focussed outside the enterprise, adversarial in nature, and conducted by intermediaries positioned between management and other employees–

> towards one which is centred on the enterprise, develops a high degree of mutual trust and interest, and strengthens the direct relationships between employers and employees.

The statement notes the existence of 'pressures to move the industrial relations system in the opposite direction to that proposed by the Business Council', referring to High Court decisions and the views of the Hancock Committee as implying further growth in the role of the Conciliation and Arbitration Commission.[30]

The BCA's statement – for all of its constructive intent – is lacking in concrete proposals. This is perhaps conceded in the foreshadowing of a study commission (subsequently appointed) 'to examine what legislative and institutional changes are required to enable our favoured system to be developed further'. By implication there would cease to be a centralized system of wage determination complementing other arms of macro-economic policy. The document is silent about wage policy except for a single sentence which recognizes only the social role of minimum standards: 'National wages policy could play a role to ensure that enterprise negotiations take place against a backdrop of minimum acceptable wages and conditions'. Enterprise negotiations, which the BCA advocates, must not be assumed to have any remarkable power to transform the industrial climate. Devolution of negotiations to the firm or the workplace characterizes British industrial relations;[31] and the United Kingdom coalminers' dispute of 1984–85 was a prime example of enterprise bargaining.

Those who engage in the debate about industrial relations need to bear in mind two realities. One is the historical legacies which impinge upon present structures and practices and restrict the options for changes to be imposed by legislation. The federal system of government, the level of unionism, the nature of the unions now in existence and the acclimatization of major parties to the processes of conciliation and arbitration are among those legacies. The other reality is the system's own fluidity. It changes in response to such influences as alterations in the industrial composition of the labour force, the level of education of workers, the sophistication of trade union leaders and the state of the economy. There is likely to be more profit in studying these inherent processes and adapting them than in relying on blueprints of 'new orders'. Those new orders are probably inaccessible; and, if they were attained, would not yield the anticipated benefits.

189

Notes

[1] Members of the Committee were K.J. Hancock, C.H. Fitzgibbon and G. Polites. For the Committee's views and analysis (the Hancock Report), see *Australian Industrial Relations Law and Systems: Report of the Committee of Review*, 1985 (3 vols.) Canberra, AGPS.

[2] *Industrial Relations Policy*, announced by the Hon. Neil Brown MP, 11 May 1986.

[3] D. Rawson 1983. State Controlled Union Ballots. In Bill Ford and D. Plowman (eds.), *Australian Unions: an Industrial Relations Perspective*. South Melbourne, Macmillan, p.234.

[4] Australian Bureau of Statistics (ABS). Trade Union Members, Australia, August 1986. Catalogue No. 6325.0.

[5] ABS. Trade Union Statistics, Australia: June 1986. Catalogue No. 6323.0.

[6] Australian Council of Trade Unions (ACTU). Executive Report for consideration by the Congress of the Australian Council of Trade Unions . . . September 1987, pp.92-100.

[7] The principal exception to this is the work of D. Plowman 1987. The Role of Employer Associations. In G.W. Ford, J.M. Hearn and R.D. Lansbury (eds.), *Australian Labour Relations: Readings*. (4th edn), South Melbourne, Macmillan.

[8] See the chapter by D. Plowman, *op.cit.* p.234.

[9] *Australian Industrial Law Review (AILR)*, 1986, p.257.

[10] *AILR*, 1986, p.27.

[11] The data reported in this paragraph are taken from ABS, Incidence of Industrial Awards, Determinations and Collective Agreements May 1983. Catalogue No. 6315.0.

[12] The commonwealth's power to make laws about conciliation and arbitration for the *prevention* of disputes has not been generously interpreted by the High Court. There have been suggestions of a possible reconsideration of this interpretation. If the tribunals could act to prevent interstate disputes by arbitrating upon intrastate matters, their powers would be enhanced.

[13] R v *Coldham and Others; ex parte The Australian Social Welfare Union* (1983-1984) 153, *Commonwealth Law Reports*, p.297.

[14] The Commission does not have a monopoly of commonwealth conciliation and arbitration. There are a Coal Industry Tribunal (created jointly with New South Wales) and a Flight Crew Officers Industrial Tribunal which operate, within defined areas, instead of the Commission. An Academic Salaries Tribunal came into being because of the limitations on commonwealth power which obtained before the *Social Welfare Union Case*. The Hancock Committee recommended that these specialist tribunals cease to exist and that their duties be transferred to the proposed Industrial Relations Commission.

[15] Calculated from data in ABS, Employed Wage and Salary Earners Australia, Catalogue No. 6248.0, December quarter 1986. The 30.4 per cent comprises 7.8 per cent working for the commonwealth, 19.9 per cent working for the states and 2.7 per cent in local government. Public administration (including civilian defence employment) accounted for 5.5 per cent; other services (mainly education and health) 13.7 per cent; and business activities, 11.2 per cent.

[16] (1983) 57 *Australian Law Reports*, p.450.

[17] S.W. Creigh 1986. Australia's Strike Record: The International Perspective. In R. Blandy and J. Niland (eds.), *Alternatives to Arbitration*. Sydney, Allen and Unwin.

[18] J.J. Beggs and B.J. Chapman 1987. Australian Strike Activity in an International Context: 1964-85. *Journal of Industrial Relations* 29, pp.137-49.

[19] See J.J. Beggs and B.J. Chapman 1987. An Empirical Analysis of Australian Strike Activity: Estimating the Industrial Relations Effect of the First Three Years of the Prices and Incomes Accord. *Economic Record* 63, pp.46-60. See also the same authors' Declining Strike Activity in Australia 1983-85: An International Phenomenon? *Economic Record* 63, 1987, pp.330-9.

[20] Arguments suporting this view may be found in the Hancock report, *op.cit*, vol.2, pp.144-62.

[21] They are briefly discussed in D.W. Rawson 1987. Law and Politics in Industrial Relations. In G.W. Ford *et al.*, *op.cit.*, pp.63-6.

[22] The question is taken from D. Aitkin 1982. *Stability and Change in Australian Politics* (2nd edn). Canberra, ANU Press, p.363.

[23] See G.J. Bamber 1987. Conciliation, Arbitration and Human Resource Management: A British Perspective. *Human Resource Management Australia* 25, pp.384-5.

[24] A decision given by the High Court in December 1987, *Re Ranger Uranium Mines Pty Limited*, suggests that the impediments to the involvement of the Conciliation and Arbitration Commission in matters of dismissal and reinstatement may be less significant than was formerly supposed. Further clarification of the law is required, because the Ranger case pertained to the Northern Territory, where the constitutional requirement that disputes be 'interstate' in character does not apply.

[25] O. Kahan-Freund, 1972. *Labour and the Law*. London, Stevens, p.165.

[26] This, of course, has not been a philosophy consistently adhered to in the United Kingdom. The Thatcher government, in particular, has introduced laws to control the behaviour of unions. A British scholar of industrial relations has written: 'Although Mrs Thatcher mouths the rhetoric of deregulation, her government has aimed to

regulate industrial conflict and unions, in particular, to a greater extent than any twentieth-century peacetime British government.' G.J. Bamber 1987. *op.cit.*, vol.25.

[27] See the Hancock report, *op.cit.*, vol.2, para.4.6.

[28] R. Blandy and J. Sloan 1986. *The Dynamic Benefits of Labour Market Deregulation*. ACC/Westpac Economic Discussion Paper No. 3.

[29] Industrial Relations and the Economy. Paper delivered to the Industrial Relations Society of Tasmania, 5 April 1987, p.1.

[30] The BCA made no submission to the Hancock Committee.

[31] An analysis is given in: Royal Commission on Trade Unions and Employers' Associations 1965-68 (Chairman, the Rt Hon. Lord Donovan), *Report*, Cmnd. 3623. London, HMSO, 1968.

9

Australian Law After Two Centuries

James Crawford

A review of the whole of Australian law, whether over 200 years or the past fifty, is impossible, at least in a single essay. The law's subject matter is vast; so is the body of legal materials developed to deal with it. The law as a subject of social scientific study is almost equally vast, though much less explored, requiring as it does an account of underlying tendencies and impacts, causal relationships and links with other social sciences.

Law has always had an ambiguous role among the social sciences, and the position is no different in Australia. In part this is because of the overtly prescriptive or normative function of law. In part it arises from the tendency of legal scholars to concentrate on the 'professional' study of law – law as subject matter (but paradoxically, law in the books rather than in practice). Even legal scholars who seek to put their work within a wider frame of reference sometimes appear to be suspended awkwardly between the world of professional legal practice and that of the social sciences. Quite apart from problems of sheer size, this dichotomy presents real difficulties in the focus of any review. The only choice is to be selective and impressionistic, and in this chapter three questions will be discussed: first, the main historical factors that influenced Australian law; second, the things that enable us, geography or nationality apart, to talk about Australian law as a distinct phenomenon; and third, and very tentatively, some possibilities for the future.

THE HISTORICAL LEGACY

The phenomenon, 'law', has always been intimately related to history. So too 'law' as a subject of study. The historicity of law is enhanced within the common law tradition since its basic doctrines, its methods of procedure and the organization of its legal profession were all deeply affected by a continuous English development, beginning in the twelfth century and undergoing only a partial and internal revolution in the century after 1645. Legally and constitutionally Australia may not be a 'frozen continent'[1] – but it is certainly a country without even an inherited revolution.

Historical factors thus profoundly influenced Australian law – in particular, English law, the experience of colonization and federalism. Another factor – Aboriginal Australia – signally failed to have any influence, itself a profound phenomenon. Something should be said about each of these.

English law
Australian law was once English law, transposed to a new continent. Particular doctrines and rules are, in almost all cases, English in origin. Deliberate Australian variations are

notable, and noted, for being so: they are not always persisted in.[2] Equally important is the underlying structure of thought – the notions of 'law' and 'equity', of causes of action and the individualistic assumptions of the law of contract; in public law, the notion of judicial power and its independence, the relationship between executive discretion and the requirements of 'due process' imposed by the courts and the idea of a 'superior court' – still the organizing conception, despite federal overlays, of the court system.

I do not suggest that this is a bad thing. Legal traditions have their virtues and take a long time to mature. The common law tradition was tolerant in the mode of liberal individualism, resisted codification, gave considerable power to the individual judge both in the appreciation of facts and the application of previous decisions, avoided – except for half a century at the height of the influence of positivism – any rigid or absolute doctrine of precedent and allowed for a considerable degree of 'open texture' in legal reasoning. Except for a period from 1943 to 1963 (one which, curiously, coincided with the emergence of full Australian independence), the Australian common law was similarly tolerant, and the tolerance extended to variations from the English norm, even though these variations might be justified as furthering a perceived 'purity of doctrine'.[3]

English influences are no longer as dominant as they were, but they remain by far the most important non-Australian influences. For example, of the foreign cases listed as 'judicially considered' in the Australian Law Reports in 1983–87, 397 were English, 16 Canadian, 7 USA and 6 New Zealand. All these legal systems are within the same broad tradition. By contrast there was little reference to the case law of continental Europe and none to that of third world countries.

Colonialism

Rather than constituting a political entity, Australia began as a collection of British colonies common to a continent. The colonists brought with them a body of British law, common law and 'received' statute law. Subsequent impositions of legislative authority were relatively limited in scope and tended to be confined to certain fields – for example, shipping. Once the initial impetus of British colonial government had passed the occasions for paramount legislative intervention from Westminster were few, and some of the most important of these were in the cause of freedom. The Colonial Laws Validity Act 1865, for example, was enacted to make it clear that the colonies were not fettered by general principles of English law or by any statutory rules other than those imposed in terms by the Imperial Parliament. The occasion was a series of aberrant decisions by an aberrant judge in South Australia. The fact that the Colonial Laws Validity Act remained binding on the commonwealth until 1931, and on the states until 1986, testifies to its limited practical effect, as well as to the lack of concern of most Australian politicians for symbols of dependence.

As a result the legacy of colonialism as such, in the sense of compulsive elements in Australian law, was limited: the English legacy was the product of influence rather than control, emulation rather than paramountcy.

Federalism

The key political event in the emergence of the Australian nation, federation, required a certain stepping outside the English model, a model in theory strictly unitary. Probably the references made by the 'founding fathers' of the Constitution to Swiss and German experience were rhetorical flourishes rather than serious attempts to assimilate foreign models. But many aspects of the United States Constitution were adopted, if for somewhat different reasons. Hugh Collins has argued that the Australian version of federalism:

> is a product of convenience rather than of conviction. Unlike Switzerland, or French and British Canada, Australian federalism is not a means of preserving the integrity of linguistically distinct communities within a single polity. Nor, as in the American case, is it traceable to the normative assumption that, even within a relatively homogeneous community, power should be divided between levels as well as branches of government. Rather, the constitutional framework chosen in Australia in the 1890s was a practical adjustment to circumstance. Faced with small communities separated by great distances but already endowed with political institutions, those seeking a limited range of cooperative action in matters like defense, trade, and immigration found a federal scheme expedient. There continues to be a lively interest in federalism in Australia, but it remains focused upon the practical working-out of fiscal, constitutional, and administrative arrangements between the states and the Commonwealth. Political appeals to 'states' rights', like declarations of 'new federalism', are typically and realistically understood as claims to particular shares of the federal pie rather than as articulations of normative principle.[4]

There is much truth in this. The Australian 'founding fathers' were concerned with political and economic unity in the face of potential external threats and with the need for increased freedom of trade internally. As experienced state politicians, they had little reason to distrust state governments – let alone government, within accepted modes, as such. Thus most individual rights originally contained or subsequently included in the United States Constitution were rejected. The British model of the 'rule of law', a method of protecting rights by seeming to ignore them,[5] was influential in the rejection or watering down of 'rights' in the Australian Constitution. Nonetheless in key respects the United States model was adopted, with its principles of judicial review of the constitutionality of legislation, a similar structure for the distribution of powers and similar federal guarantees. Australian courts were thus committed to an involvement in public and political disputes which was different in kind from that of British courts, and which emphasis on 'strict and complete legalism'[6] failed to conceal.

Aboriginality

By contrast Australian law was specifically not influenced or affected by the Aboriginal societies which the colonists encountered, or by the laws and institutional traditions of those societies. One reason was the decision not to treat with those societies as collective entities at all. Aborigines were, after initial brief uncertainty, classified as British subjects, that is, as individuals subject to British law. The Australian colonies were classified as 'settled', with no relevant pre-existing legal system. Aboriginal laws were not legally recognized, even in relation to the affairs of Aborigines among themselves. And, although this did not follow from the classification of Australia as a 'settled' colony or of Aborigines as British subjects by virtue of settlement, no individual or collective Aboriginal rights to land were recognized at common law.[7] When issues of Aboriginal rights were raised in later years these were usually dealt with by executive action. Legislation on Aboriginal matters was limited in amount and effect until the latter half of the nineteenth and the early twentieth century, when legislation implementing the policy of 'protection' came to be passed. This legislation restricted still further the formal legal rights of Aborigines – rights which, in most cases, they were not aware they had.

In the result Australian law remained wholly uninfluenced and unaffected by Aboriginal laws and traditions – a situation which continued unmodified until very recent times and which has now been modified only to a slight extent. There is now a considerable amount of legislation on certain Aboriginal issues, especially land rights, local government and Aboriginal heritage issues, race and sex discrimination and protection of heritage areas. But on most matters the established techniques of executive discretion and accommodation of cultural difference through exercises of flexibility under the general law (for example, sentencing discretions) continue to hold sway.[8]

'AUSTRALIAN' LAW?

The configuration of Australian law which resulted from English influence, British control, federation and the perception of a mono-cultural society remained basically unchanged until the 1970s. Such variation as there has been from this pattern has resulted from legislative innovation – in the nineteenth century often influenced by European or North American ideas which were not yet embodied in law there (for example, universal suffrage, juvenile courts and industrial arbitration); and more recently influenced by legislative models, increasingly North American (for example, trade practices, consumer protection and consumer claims, freedom of information and administrative review). Other influences have been international, in provenance if not origin (for example, race and sex discrimination and protection of natural and cultural heritage). But in what sense is the law so influenced 'Australian', other than in the obvious sense of being the law of the nation state, Australia?

The search for 'autochthony'

'Autochthon' is a word of respectable ancestry: its rather more recent derivatives 'autochthonous' and 'autochthony' are used by lawyers to indicate that a legal system or (more rarely) a particular rule are of local derivation, and were not imposed from outside (in particular, by a former colonizer). In modern times the demand for autochthony has led to deliberate, if momentary, legal discontinuity in the process of a state's becoming independent and establishing its independence constitution.

Nothing of the kind happened in Australia. Indeed it is still unclear when, and by exactly what process, Australia became independent in international law. Australia and New Zealand remained 'dependent' in their own law for more than a decade after they were generally regarded as internationally independent, a curious reversal of the normal course of events. The best known use of the term 'autochthonous' in relation to Australian law was the label 'autochthonous expedient' applied by the High Court in the *Boilermakers' Case* (1956)[9] to the provision in the Constitution which enables the Commonwealth Parliament to vest federal jurisdiction in state courts. The context was inglorious, but the passage has, unfortunately, been much cited since, to the confusion of law students. Its use in that context revealed a characteristic unconcern on the part of the High Court – characteristic, that is, of most Australian lawyers – for any deeper form of autochthony.

Lack of concern to distance oneself from one's ancestors may be a mark of maturity. But it is also important to understand in what respects we are different, particularly when the difference takes the form of nationhood at the other end of the world. In Australia's case, the foundation for autochthony has – at last – been firmly laid. There is (in the case of state courts exercising state jurisdiction, only since 1986) no longer any appeal to the Privy Council. It is now established that no Australian court is bound as a matter of precedent by non-Australian decisions, however influential they may be. Other Australian courts are of course bound by decisions of the Full High Court, but they retain considerable freedom to depart from their own previous decisions. So too does the High Court itself.

These rules establish only the preconditions for an 'Australian' jurisprudence. The substance will take longer, especially since there is little indication of anything approaching judicial nationalism.[10] The dominant feature is an adherence to independent reasoning within the received technical mode, but it is combined with a considerable degree of openness to decisions and developments in other jurisdictions. An Australian jurisprudence may well be the outcome of such an approach, but it is not its object.

Distinctive institutions

There are, however, many distinctive legal institutions providing the material structure of Australian law and significantly affecting the emphases and context of the substantive law. Again it is only possible to discuss some examples: four of particular interest are the Constitution, the industrial tribunals, the Family Court and the system of federal administrative tribunals.

The Constitution

Drafted at a series of intercolonial conventions during the 1890s, and enacted by the British Parliament with a single (and, as it has proved, insignificant) change, the Constitution remains central to an understanding of the Australian polity. One reason for its influence has been the great difficulty in changing it: thirty of thirty-eight constitutional referenda since 1900 have failed. It is unlikely that this indicates general public support for the document, as distinct from electoral conservatism, suspicion or indifference. Recent research suggests that nearly 50 per cent of Australian electors are unaware even of the existence of the Constitution (although most know at least that much of the United States Constitution).[11] Faced with such ignorance, one cannot praise the constitutional draftsmen for a memorable text, although the text is, as to fundamentals, workmanlike and economical, unlike some recent amendments to it.

There is a continuing debate about the constitutional achievement on matters of substance. The key problem the draftsmen faced was the combination of responsible government (members of the executive being also members of one or other House of Parliament, and responsible to it) with federalism, requiring both guarantees of the rights of the states and provision to secure their interests, in particular through equal representation in the Senate. The problem was only partially resolved, leaving a crucial uncertainty about a government's right to supply (and thus to continue in power) when faced by a hostile Senate. That uncertainty led directly to the crisis of 1975, when the Prime Minister was dismissed by the Governor-General on the basis that he had failed to obtain supply from the Senate. Much has been written about this incident, and much controversy generated as to the legality and propriety of the actions of the participants. Sawer's conclusion, in a masterly study, is that the Governor-General's failure to advise the Prime Minister of his intentions and to give him the opportunity to advise and, if supply could not be obtained, to go to an election as Prime Minister, was unconstitutional, but not strictly illegal.[12] That conclusion is, I think, clearly right: it cannot be permissible for a Governor-General to ambush a Prime Minister. But the setting for that ambush was provided by the Constitution itself.

Since 1975 a number of steps have been taken to prevent a recurrence of the problem but, short of constitutional amendment, the basic weakness remains: a Prime Minister, to be sure of a full term, needs at least the acquiescence of both Houses of Parliament.

The debate over the events of 1975 has tended to overshadow other, perhaps more fundamental, issues about the Constitution. One relates to what might be described as the 'standard' political science critique, expressed by Jaensch in these terms:

> The planners designed the constitution to be long-lasting and inflexible. The product must be seen in the environment of those who produced it. The planners sought to create a structure and process of government which reflected their dominant interests: of agricultural and commercial elites in the colonies which viewed the inauguration of a national government and parliament in some senses as a threat. As a political statement, then, the constitution established a national government with strictly limited powers and functions, and with very restricted authority to affect, let alone intervene in, the states. As a social document, the constitution was, and is today, 'permeated by the conservatism, parochialism and pettiness that characterised the Australian colonies at the end of the nineteenth century'.[13]

I do not think this is fair either to 'the planners' or to the Constitution as it has evolved. There have been rigidities, certainly: one of the most significant is the federal system of industrial arbitration which, for want of adequate alternative sources of legislative power, is very nearly a constitutional inevitability and which therefore imposes a high degree of rigidity, equality and (perhaps to a lesser extent) legalism in the processes of fixing wages and conditions of work. But the 'planners' can hardly be blamed for the difficulty of amending the Constitution, a difficulty they seem not to have foreseen. To vest the constituent power in the federal electorate, without involvement of any kind by state parliaments or governments,[14] was a remarkable act of faith, and of nationalism. The most doubtful aspect of Section 128 was its requirement of a popular majority in a majority of states, but so far this requirement has defeated only four referendum proposals: in only one case have the smaller states overridden a proposal with really widespread popular support.

To describe the national government as one with 'strictly limited powers' is also hardly accurate. The federal list of powers in Australia originally contained thirty-nine matters, many of great potential significance and many not contained in the United States Constitution. It was equally significant that the Constitution contained no list of reserved state powers similar to the list of exclusive provincial powers in the Canadian Constitution Act of 1867. That left little basis for a secure doctrine of state powers under the Constitution. Not only was it possible to predict the coming financial dominance of the commonwealth, as Deakin did in 1906,[15] but it was also possible for Isaacs and Higgins, by 1908, to establish the doctrine of the interpretation of powers which prevailed in the *Engineers case* in 1920[16] and which underlies all the major developments in the interpretation of powers since then.[17] There is no basis in the Constitution for the notion of an illicit 'intervention' in state affairs, and little more for any implied protection of state agencies or instrumentalities.

Thus the High Court has been able since 1920 to establish a consensus on basic principles of interpretation of powers which has inevitably seemed to favour the commonwealth, but only because of the (deliberate or accidental) absence of countervailing guarantees of state power. Even in the area of nationalization, where the case for a 'conservative Constitution' is strongest, there is considerable potential for governments to act. The failure of bank nationalization in 1949 was the result more of a failure of nerve or support than of an unbreachable constitutional barrier. Today the more flexible approach taken to Section 92 would increase the opportunities for success in a carefully planned programme of nationalization – although the trend to deregulation and sale of government enterprises seems to have rendered the issue irrelevant, at least for the time being.

The industrial tribunals

One of the most distinctive aspects of the Australian legal system is its industrial tribunals. Operating both at federal and state levels, they play a central – and centralized – role in determining wages and conditions of work and in settling industrial disputes. The tribunals are discussed in another essay in this volume (see Chapter 8), and only a few comments need be made here.

Unlike the idea of a Labour Court in some other countries, the Australian industrial tribunals are not primarily concerned with the enforcement of industrial laws but with establishing wage and labour standards binding on employers and employees. Indeed at the federal level most of the strictly enforcement functions are required to be vested in a federal court, whereas the 'non-judicial' function of making industrial awards and settling industrial disputes cannot be vested in a court.

Attempts have been made from time to time to impose 'penal' sanctions on trade unions in respect of breaches of awards (especially unauthorized strikes or other industrial action), but, except in extreme cases of non-compliance, with very limited success. One 'extreme case' involved the Australian Builders' Labourers Federation: the penalty amounted to exclusion from the industrial system altogether by way of deregistration (effected in 1986). But the legal and practical obstacles encountered in the process of deregistration suggest that it is unlikely to be attempted very often.

The setting of industrial conditions by a quasi-adversary, quasi-judicial process involves a pronounced degree of legalism. This occurs both at the level of the Australian Conciliation and Arbitration Commission, where hearings on major issues have a pronounced forensic character, and also in the High Court and the Industrial Division of the Federal Court, which hear challenges to the jurisdiction or procedure of the Commission, based in particular on the somewhat restrictive requirements of an 'industrial dispute extending beyond the limits of any one state'.

The establishment of industrial tribunals in Australia and New Zealand in the fifteen years after 1896 was heralded as a 'new province for law and order'.[18] Now enthusiasm has dwindled, and proposals continue to be made that the industrial arbitration systems should be abandoned, converting to some form of collective bargaining (such as in the United Kingdom or the United States). In particular the period from 1966 to 1975 was a troublesome one for the industrial tribunals. Penal sanctions against unions were discredited; the capacity of the tribunals to maintain 'industrial peace' was challenged by a large increase in strikes; and there was a distinct move towards collective bargaining. The consensus among industrial relations writers was of the undesirability, and lack of realism, of industrial arbitration. In England judicial settlement of labour disputes was tried and failed. Higgins' 'new province for law and order' was repeatedly debunked, seldom defended.

But the inflation, industrial troubles and recession of the 1970s led to a gallop back to arbitration. In 1974–75 only 21.2 per cent of the average weekly wage increase was attributable to the national wage case: in 1975–76, with indexation, the figure was 88.5 per cent. Similar high figures have been maintained since, except for the period 1981–82 when wage indexation was temporarily abandoned. In a sense collective bargaining was never really tried, because the arbitration system retained its role as guarantor of minimum standards for the employed – passing on what the strong had earned to the industrially humble and meek. Real collective bargaining would cause pronounced changes in wage relativities which have always been extremely difficult to achieve in Australia. Some critics of industrial arbitration have accepted the point, proposing mixed forms of bargaining and arbitration with the tribunals acting only in a secondary role. Indeed that is not far from Higgins' own conception (the problem of penal sanctions against trade unions apart). At the same time many of the supposed defects of the system have been reassessed in more favourable terms — the 'legalism' of the Australian Commission, for example.

These 'revisionist' interpretations culminated in the endorsement of the principles of conciliation and arbitration by the Hancock Report, which concluded that:

> In the submissions we received, no strong case for radical change by way of abolition of conciliation and arbitration was apparent.... After an examination of all the material before us, we reached the conclusion that no substantial case had been made that industrial relations would improve if conciliation and arbitration were abandoned in favour of some other system, such as collective bargaining. Thus, we have concluded that conciliation and arbitration should remain the mechanism for regulating industrial relations in Australia.[19]

On the basis of this somewhat unenthusiastic conclusion, the Report went on to propose substantial re-enforcement and centralization of the arbitration machinery under a new Act. This would involve an Australian Industrial Relations Commission with comprehensive authority over federal industrial disputes, an Australian Labour Court, with judges holding joint commissions as presidential members of the Commission and provision for joint proceedings with state industrial authorities and other forms of cooperation. (Those recommendations were embodied in the Industrial Relations Bill 1987, which was withdrawn when the 1987 federal election was announced, but is likely to be reintroduced in some form.) Whatever the details of the new system the underlying structure is likely to remain very much the same as that developed since 1904, with a continuing need for the industrial tribunals to balance their role as settlers of industrial disputes with their role as central economic agencies – independent arms of government. Short of fundamental constitutional change (always unlikely), that dual role seems destined to continue – an 'established' province for law and order, perhaps for want of a better.

Family law

The movement to establish specialist family courts was by no means limited to Australia, but the 'family court ideal' has been carried to considerable lengths under the Family Law Act 1975. The family court ideal envisages a unified court with as wide a jurisdiction over family matters as possible, a 'helping court', which provides counselling facilities to persons with family troubles whether or not they are litigants, a specialist court, with judges who are aware of and responsive to its special needs, and one which functions with a minimum of formality and delay. A Senate Committee Report in 1974 strongly supported the family court ideal, predicting that 'the establishment of a Family Court and the simplified substantive provisions in the Bill will reduce the scope for legal disputation'.[20] This view was accepted, and the principal judicial agency under the Family Law Act 1975 was a new specialist court, the Family Court of Australia. The Act also established a comprehensive divorce law with divorce based on a single ground – irretrievable breakdown of the marriage, evidenced by a year's separation, without regard to the fault of either party.

The Act sought to achieve the ideal of the family court in a number of ways. A prospective judge must be 'by reason of training, experience and personality . . . a suitable person to deal with matters of family law'.[21] There was extensive provision for counselling and reconciliation with court counsellors appointed as officers to the Court's staff and welfare officers also available.

Since its establishment the Family Court has attracted a vast case-load. For example in the years 1980–84 it averaged, in round figures, 42,000 dissolution applications, 9400 custody applications, 4600 applications for access, 9400 maintenance applications, 12,300 property applications and 4800 applications for injunctions. The numbers of dissolution applications have remained fairly steady – after the initial rush in the first year or so after the Act came into force. But there have been significant increases in maintenance and especially property cases since 1980. To cope with the workload the Family Court has 46 judges, making it by far the largest superior court in Australia. Apart from this enormous pressure of work there have been real problems with the operation of the Court. Indeed attacks on the Family Court in the 1980s have created the impression, and to some degree the reality, of a court under siege. In the period 1980–84 three bomb attacks (one on a court building, two on judges' homes) and a shooting resulted in the death of a judge and a judge's wife. The physical security of Court personnel and buildings has become a major problem.

The prestige and professionalism of the Court has also been questioned, for example in these extrajudicial comments of Chief Justice Gibbs in 1985:

It may have been a mistake to establish a separate court to administer the Family Law Act . . . [T]he creation of that Court has made it difficult to maintain the highest standards in the making of judicial appointments . . . Although many judges of considerable ability have been appointed . . . it would be hypocritical to pretend that the jurisdiction of that Court, which is limited in scope and likely to be emotionally exhausting, is such as to attract many of the lawyers who might be expected to be appointed to the Supreme Courts or to the Federal Court. The consideration which I have had to give to judgments of the Family Court has led me to conclude that . . . there is a present need to provide a new and more effective avenue of appeals from its decisions.[22]

Within the legal profession there is a tendency to segregate family law from other areas of legal practice and to regard family law as a 'less prestigious' area of practice. The poor quality of many Family Court buildings and facilities, and the lower salaries of judges, have contributed to this tendency.

The Court has also experienced major jurisdictional problems, to a considerable degree caused by the limitations on federal legislative power over family law under the Constitution but also by a rather narrow approach adopted by some members of the High Court to the interpretation of the relevant powers. Problems have arisen with the extent of jurisdiction over custody of ex-nuptial children, the effect of Family Court orders (especially property orders) on third parties and the relationship of federal to state law and jurisdiction.

The Family Court has had its successes: these include the provision of counselling, simplified procedures for dissolution, the reduced formality of proceedings and, perhaps, the growth of a specialist judiciary and legal profession. The defects are equally clear: excessive delay in some registries, jurisdictional gaps and uncertainties greater than in any other Australian court and marked unevenness of operations between states. Despite these difficulties there is still strong support, within the Court and outside it, for the family court ideal. The commonwealth government also appears to remain committed to the ideal, and has undertaken a programme of 'renovation' of the Court with improved facilities and buildings, greater delegation of cases to registrars and magistrates and measures to resolve many of the jurisdictional problems which have dogged the Court. It remains to be seen whether these reforms will resolve the problems, or whether they are of a more basic, structural kind.

Administrative review

Like other common law courts, Australian courts can review the legality of administrative decisions and grant appropriate relief: the massive expansion of statutory executive powers in this century has been accompanied by a similar expansion of administrative law decision-making by the courts, applying and extending common law principles. Although there are important differences in jurisdiction and in the remedies provided by statute, both within Australia and as compared with other common law countries such as the United Kingdom, Canada and New Zealand, substantive doctrines of review are very similar, and have tended to be expanded along parallel lines in the various countries with a good deal of mutual reinforcement and citation. Important though it is, the area of judicial review of administrative action is not, with minor exceptions, distinctive to Australia.

There have, however, been important experiments with non-judicial review of administrative decisions, especially through the federal Administrative Appeals Tribunal (AAT), established in 1975. The AAT's function is not, or not primarily, to determine the legal validity of a federal administrative decision, but to 'review' it on the merits, as an independent authority. Although it will take note of administrative policy in particular areas it is not bound by such policies (unless they are given statutory force). What it has to determine is whether the decision made is the preferable one, all things considered. It can review the facts of the case, and in many instances much more information becomes available through the arguments and investigations of the parties. It can also review the correctness of the application of the law to the facts, although as a non-judicial body it cannot decide questions of law or jurisdiction conclusively.

As at 30 June 1986 the AAT had jurisdiction to review decisions under a total of 236 Acts, regulations and ordinances,[23] a steep increase from 93 in 1980. The matters over which it has jurisdiction vary in importance, but they include decisions to deport persons under the Migration Act 1958, appeals in federal tax matters, decisions of the Director General of Social Services which vary decisions of a Social Security Appeals Tribunal, and so on. In its first three full years of operation the AAT averaged 288 applications for review annually. For the three financial years from 1983–84 to 1985–86, that average had grown to 2160, an enormous increase, due in large part to new areas of jurisdiction.

Despite the conferral of jurisdiction over social welfare cases and taxation cases in 1980 and 1986 respectively, the AAT's jurisdiction still falls short of the original proposals made in the Kerr Report in 1971.[24] It is possible that the rather formal approach taken by the AAT in many cases, with a strict adversarial method and frequent use of legal representation, may deter further substantial increases in jurisdiction. Within federal government departments, different views are held as to the value of the AAT at a time of financial restrictions in the public sector. Perhaps the main argument against an AAT is that it leads to excessive legalism and formalism in administration and tends to assimilate administrative to judicial decision-making. According to this view it is better to concentrate resources on improving primary administration rather than on providing a more elaborate apparatus of appeals. Such criticisms have to meet the point that tribunals continue to be established in a diffuse and disorganized way, in which case what is at issue would seem to be not the 'tribunal' form of decision-making so much as the independence or lack of it of tribunals. But on any view the AAT is an important experiment in public administration.

Conclusion

Any proper study would require a far more comprehensive account of the similarities and differences between the Australian legal system and cognate systems abroad – and even then the assessment would be markedly subjective. What is clear is that the original heritage has been added to, principally by legislation, with the addition of a considerable number of institutions and structures distinctive either in conception or in the relatively thorough-going way in which they have been applied. Moreover the range of influences is now considerably wider. New developments are as likely to come from Canada, the United States or continental Europe as from the United Kingdom. Examples adopted in the past fifteen years include the ombudsman, small claims courts, a judicial commission charged with 'judicial training' and exercising certain disciplinary powers and community justice or mediation centres. There have also been advances in the monitoring of new or existing laws through standing governmental bodies such as the Administrative Review Council or the Family Law Council, or through semi-governmental organizations such as the Australian Institute for Judicial Administration. Whether all this amounts to an autochthonous, distinctively Australian legal system is perhaps not very important (there is certainly an 'Australian blend'). The degree of communication and borrowing between legal systems has increased markedly, as has the quantity of international legislation in the form of treaties regulating a wide variety of questions and requiring to be implemented as part of Australian law. A more important question is whether the system meets the needs of the community and, in particular, whether it allows effective democratic control to be exercised whenever necessary over powerful groups – foreign corporations, local conglomerates controlling particular sectors (mining, the media), the professions and so on. Those issues, still inadequately investigated, are among the most important areas for socio-legal study.

TRENDS AND PROSPECTS

One thing more difficult than reviewing the development of Australian law (whether as subject matter or social science) is predicting the future. But something can at least be said about some trends and prospects.

Centralism and the accommodation of regional difference

I have argued that the High Court is on firm constitutional ground in refusing to imply 'protected' state rights or powers into the Constitution, and that it is this consistent refusal, rather than any change in the composition of the Court, which has led to the present position of extensive federal legislative power. But the balance of political power in a federation is not wholly or even mainly a matter of the interpretation of a written document: to have legal power does not resolve the question whether or how it should be used. Claims made after the *Tasmanian Dams* case that 'federalism is dead', are thus not merely exaggerated but unfounded.[25] While state institutions remain, so will federalism, however muted, and the shape of federalism will be more the result of the interplay of those institutions and of public opinion than the product of legal doctrine.

Nonetheless the 'dynamics' of federalism do point towards a greater use by the common-wealth of its legislative powers, particularly in the area of corporate law and regulation. The uniform cooperative companies scheme is widely seen as inefficient and cumbersome and is ripe for replacement by a unified federal Act. Similar moves for greater federal regulation are likely to occur in the area of the control of organized crime. But in many areas the case for federal involvement may be principally one of standard setting, as distinct from day-to-day administration, which may be more sensibly devolved to or left with the states. It should be noted that the external affairs power, which has been at the heart of much of the debate about the 'demise of federalism', is substantially a power to set minimum standards in accordance with international treaties rather than a plenary power to regulate and administer the subject in question.

Legalism and its alternatives

One important theme in political science literature in Australia is that of 'legalism'. It is argued that the Australian polity turns to legalistic methods in order to solve essentially political or social problems. The debate is as much concerned with quasi-legal or para-legal bodies as with the ordinary courts. It relates to the use of quasi-legal tribunals to resolve industrial issues, or of administrative tribunals to resolve policy or administrative issues for which governments should take responsibility themselves. It concerns also the role of *ad hoc* commissions of inquiry, which may be used not so much in a genuine search for 'the facts' as in an attempt to postpone political responsibility for decision-making. (Incidentally there is also a continuing and lively controversy among judges as to when it is proper to accept extra-judicial roles of this kind, although that debate has been conducted largely in terms of judicial prestige and the separation of powers.)

It is not easy to reach any overall assessment of these arguments. Federalism has often been equated with legalism, and it certainly means duplication. Judging by numbers of lawyers per unit of population, Australia ranks reasonably high on any international scale (though, of course, far behind the United States). But such comparative figures are relatively crude indicators given the large number of variables, which includes the differing roles lawyers are called on to play in different societies.

An apparently inevitable trend which Australia shares with other developed countries is the trend towards increasing complexity of laws and legal disputes, especially in the areas of corporation law but also in certain areas of crime. This is giving rise to law cases of a size, complexity and cost which remind one of the famous and endless case of *Jarndyce* v *Jarndyce* in Dickens' *Bleak House*, and which cast almost equal doubt on the capacity of the system to cope. This aspect of 'legalism', much less commented on, requires more attention to methods of judicial administration (until recently neglected in Australia) and willingness to experiment with new procedures. It is, for example, hard to see how the jury system can continue to work in criminal trials lasting nine months. More is needed than merely tinkering with the rules for the composition of juries: some form of interlocutory procedure in criminal cases, provision for formal admissions of fact and reform and simplification of the law of evidence, are among the changes needing to be explored.

To some extent the increased length, cost and complexity of legal proceedings may be an inevitable result of technological changes and of the growth of corporatism in the private sector. If so it is unlikely to be affected by developments such as plain English legislative drafting, or alternative dispute resolution, however valuable these may be in themselves. The alternative dispute resolution movement is a good example of the way in which new initiatives, often presented as ways of stemming the tide of legalism and reducing the cost of legal proceedings, may be extending the 'legal domain' to areas of dispute not previously covered by it. But another danger with such developments is that they may transfer cases which require adjudication into a forum where 'mediation' leads to a compromise of rights in favour of the more powerful party. The New South Wales community justice centres were specifically designed to avoid this, and have apparently succeeded in doing so. If this is so it is because they have excluded from their scope most disputes which presently come before courts or tribunals.

One function of law is to confer rights in situations of relative inequality of bargaining power. Increasingly those rights – especially against governments – are of a procedural character, rights to due process. It seems likely that there will be a growth of similar kinds of rights in the corporate sector, which (especially with 'deregulation' and 'privatization') is likely to take on still further the role of a 'private government' in certain fields. But a characteristic of procedural rights is that they usually require specific adjudication: whether a particular opportunity to present a case amounted to a 'hearing' and whether 'irrelevant considerations' were taken into account are questions which do not lend themselves to decision by rule. Individual decision-making, which is the focus of most administrative law and which the rules of administrative law tend to reinforce and extend, requires individual consideration on appeal or review. Whether it is not more efficient to settle some kinds of cases by rule, even at some cost to individual cases, may be a real issue – it is one reason for the adoption of no-fault compensation schemes for personal injury. Either way lawyers are likely to be called on, in courts or tribunals, to apply the alternative structures. In short it is difficult to see an end to 'legalism' – a by-product of a process of conferring and extending rights (including rights to individual consideration or due process) which shows no sign of stopping.

Law reform

A cynic would define 'law reform' as the process of seeking to change the law as described by those with an interest in change. A substantial point underlying the cynicism is that, in considering proposals for law reform, it is essential to look at indirect costs and effects as well as the more obvious or substantive arguments for change. Standing law reform agencies in Australia appear to be well aware of this, but the techniques of legal cost-benefit analysis are still rudimentary and the law and economics movement, itself under-represented in Australia, has tended to get bogged down in ideological debates having little to do with 'efficiency'.

What the enthusiast would describe as the law reform agenda still contains many items, despite the 'first wave' of law reform which began in the early 1970s. Considerable attention has been given, for example, to the possibility of constitutional reform, first through the Australian Constitutional Convention (1973–85), and, from 1985, through the Constitutional Commission. The failure of the Convention, which combined the deliberations of politicians and quite extensive preparatory work by sub-committees with expert assistance, only reinforced stereotypes of Australian constitutional inertia. It remains to be seen whether the Constitutional Commission, a smaller body assisted by five specialist committees, will have any greater success. Certainly any proposals for change are likely, after the combined work of Convention and Commission, to be well considered.

Less spectacular but equally important is the work of the increasing number of law reform agencies established in the last fifteen years. They will no doubt continue to deal with substantive subjects but, as suggested, perhaps their most important role in the next decade – whether or not it is dignified as a 'second phase' of law reform – should be to examine the whole range of legal and administrative procedures and structures in the interests of effectiveness and efficiency. To some extent this is happening already, with work on criminal procedure, judicial administration and plain English drafting. But much more needs to be done, for example, in the area of comparative cost-benefit analysis of different methods (judicial, quasi-judicial and administrative) of dispute resolution and the avail- ability and effect of legal-aid programmes. The old reproach – that the law, like the Ritz, is open to all – is increasingly justified for litigants without legal-aid or other sources of legal assistance. As the costs of litigation are increasingly met, directly and indirectly, from public funds, so the public interest in procedural efficiency increases.

An area of 'law reform' which has so far had limited acceptance is the proposal for a Bill of Rights. Three different federal Bills, each based substantially on the International Covenant on Civil and Political Rights of 1966, were introduced in 1973, 1984 and 1985. In each case the proposal has been repulsed, amid much invective in a debate which has seemed less well informed as successive Bills have been watered down. The only area of change has been that of discrimination, with federal legislation on race (1975) and sex (1983) discrimination, and with equal opportunity legislation in some states. In addition there have been not one but two versions of a federal human rights commission, with the function of educating about human rights and conciliating complaints, but without any enforcement powers.

Apart from these institutional arrangements the courts retain important responsibilities for law-making and thus for 'law reform'. Indeed some topics may be more appropriate for 'gradual' reform through the judicial process than for legislative change, especially of a detailed kind. For example, in one case where the High Court refused to extend the standing of a conservation group to challenge non-compliance with statutory procedures, Justice Stephen commented that:

> If the present state of the law in Australia is to be changed, it is pre-eminently a case for legislation, preceded by careful consideration and report, so that any need for relaxation in the requirements of locus standi may be fully explored and the limits of desirable relaxation precisely defined. Just such an investigation is at present being undertaken by the Australian Law Reform Commission.[26]

But the Australian Law Reform Commission report which resulted from this inquiry, and which did recommend a substantial extension in the law of standing, has not been implemented: the Commission's recommendation is seen as politically too controversial.[27] By contrast in England an almost identical outcome was achieved by a series of judicial decisions based on an apparently slight change in wording in the Rules of the Supreme Court. Evidently there are more ways than one of extending rights.

CONCLUSION

An account of two centuries of Australian law should, no doubt, come to a resounding conclusion, with far-reaching prophecies as to the future. The great American academic lawyer and judge, Felix Frankfurter, commented that 'to give shape and visage to mysteries still in the womb of time ... requires poetic sensibilities with which judges are rarely endowed and which their education does not normally develop'.[28] Judges are lawyers well-promoted, but otherwise fairly characteristic of the breed. When asked to predict the future, a lawyer's characteristic response is to look for a precedent!

The habit of searching for and relying on precedents itself ensures that the legal issues and problems of the future will tend to be addressed through the received array of concepts and terms. And there are other reasons why legal change in Australia is likely to be gradual, with the future emerging by osmosis – apparent on reflection rather than through revelation. They include the failure of the movement for an enforceable bill of rights, the unlikelihood of other major constitutional, or indeed institutional, changes, and the increasing interpenetration of the Australian economy and polity by international influences and institutions which, without world war or economic collapse, will continue to work in an evolutionary, diffusely-organized way. If the future holds a 'big bang', it is unlikely to be produced by the lawyers, however much they may claim to control it afterwards.

Notes

[1] Geoffrey Sawer's concluding words in *Australian Federalism in the Courts*. Melbourne, Melbourne University Press, 1967, p. 208.

[2] e.g., the High Court's recent return to an objective element in self-defence: *Zecevic v DPP* (1987) 71 ALR 641, not following its previous decision in *Viro v R* (1978) 141 CLR 88 and preferring *Palmer v R* [1971] AC 814.

[3] As in *Parker v R* (1963) 111 CLR 610 (which marked the decisive modern break from English precedent).

[4] H. Collins 1985. Political Ideology in Australia: The Distinctiveness of a Benthamite Society. In S.R. Graubard (ed.), *Australia: The Daedalus Symposium*. Sydney, Angus & Robertson, pp. 147, 152-3.

[5] Classically expressed by A.V. Dicey 1959 (1885). *Introduction to the Study of the Law of the Constitution* (10th edn). London, Macmillan. Especially chs. 4, 13.

[6] Dixon CJ's famous words on being sworn in as Chief Justice of the High Court: (1952) 85 CLR viii.

[7] R v *Jack Congo Murrell* (1836) 1 Legge 72; *Cooper v Stuart* (1889) 14 App Cas 286, 291; *Milirrpum v Nabalco Pty Ltd* (1971) 17 FLR 141; *Coe v Commonwealth* (1979) 24 ALR 118.

[8] See Australian Law Reform Commission 1986. Report 31, *The Recognition of Aboriginal Customary Laws*. Canberra, AGPS, chs. 4, 6. The public and official silence that greeted that Report testifies to the unlikelihood of change.

[9] R v *Kirby, ex p Boilermakers' Society of Australia* (1956) 94 CLR 254, 268.

[10] The main exceptions have been the two High Court judges in recent years who were former politicians and federal ministers, Barwick CJ and Murphy J. See, e.g., their views in *Cullen v Trappell* (1980) 29 ALR 1; *McInnis v R* (1979) 27 ALR 449 respectively. The two cases demonstrate that 'nationalism' may not provide much guidance as to outcomes.

[11] According to research conducted for the Constitutional Commission by Newspoll (April 1987), 53.9 per cent of voters knew Australia had a written constitution. But of respondents in the 18-24 age group, 70 per cent did *not* know this. (This was presumably the cohort which had not yet had the chance to vote 'no' in a referendum!)

[12] G. Sawer 1977. *Federation under Strain*. Melbourne, Melbourne University Press, chs. 8 and 9. On the events of 1975 see the three apologias, G. Whitlam 1979. *The Truth of the Matter*. Ringwood, Penguin; J. Kerr 1978. *Matters for Judgment*. South Melbourne, Macmillan; G. Barwick 1983. *Sir John did his Duty*. Wahroonga, Serendip Publications. See also G. Winterton 1983. *Parliament, the Executive and the Governor-General*. Melbourne, Melbourne University Press, pp. 149-60; B.J. Galligan 1980. The Kerr-Whitlam Debate and the Principles of the Australian Constitution. *J. Cth. and Comp. Pol. 18*, p. 247.

[13] D. Jaensch 1981. Remaking the Australian Constitution. *Current Affairs Bull.* 58, pp. 14-15, citing S. Encel 1977. The Constitution as a Social Document. In S. Encel, D. Horne and E. Thompson, *Change the Rules!* Bedford Park, Australasian Political Studies Association, p. 43.

[14] Moreover under s. 128 the Senate, intended as a states House, can be by-passed by the House of Representatives. In the US and Canada, by contrast, state or provincial legislatures have a key role in the amending process.

[15] In a *Morning Post* letter of 1906, cited by G. Greenwood 1976. *The Future of Australian Federalism* (2nd edn). St Lucia, University of Queensland Press, p. 64.

[16] *Amalgamated Society of Engineers v Adelaide Steamship Co. Ltd* (1920) 28 CLR 129. The basic positions were established by Isaacs and Higgins JJ in dissenting and separate opinions in cases such as *R v Barger* (1908) 6 CLR 41.

[17] The doctrine of broad interpretation of granted powers and the rejection of any implied prohibition on the Commonwealth 'entering state fields of power' underlie the perceived 'expansion' of federal power in areas such as trade and commerce (*Murphyores Pty Ltd v Commonwealth* (1976) 136 CLR 1), corporations (*Strickland v Rocla Concrete Pipes Ltd* (1971) 124 CLR 468) and external affairs (*Commonwealth v Tasmania* (1983) 158 CLR 1). The only exception, and that a partial one, is the marriage power, which after an expansive beginning (*A-G (Vic) v Commonwealth* (1962) 107 CLR 529; *Russell v Russell* (1976) 134 CLR 64) has been the subject of an erratic and unconvincing jurisprudence: e.g., *R v Lambert ex p Plummer* (1980) 146 CLR 447; *Gazzo v Comptroller of Stamps (Victoria)* (1981) 149 CLR 227.

[18] H.B. Higgins 1922. *A New Province for Law and Order*. London, Constable.

[19] *Australian Industrial Relations Law and Systems, Report of the Committee of Review,* 1985 (Chairman, K.J. Hancock). Canberra, AGPS. Summary, pp.1-2.

[20] Senate Standing Committee on Constitutional and Legal Affairs, *Report on . . . the Family Law Bill, 1974* (Parliamentary Paper 1974/133) 29.

[21] Family Law Act 1975 (Cth) s.32(2)(b).

[22] H. Gibbs 1985. The State of the Australian Judicature. *ALJ 59*, p. 522.

[23] Listed in Administrative Review Council, *Tenth Annual Report 1985-86*. Canberra, AGPS. Appendix 4.

[24] Commonwealth Administrative Law Committee, *Report*. Canberra, AGPS. pp. 86-92.

[25] *Commonwealth* v *Tasmania* (1983) 158 CLR 1. See G. Samuels 1984. The End of Federalism? *Aust. Q.* 56, p. 11.

[26] *Australian Conservation Foundation* v *Commonwealth* (1980) 146 CLR 493, 540.

[27] ALRC 27, *Standing in Public Interest Litigation*. Canberra, AGPS.

[28] F. Frankfurter 1956. *Of Law and Men*. New York, Harcourt, Brace, p. 39.

10

Democracy Untrammelled: The Australian Political Experience Since Federation

Don Aitkin and Francis G. Castles

If any country and its government were to be selected as showing the course which a self-governing people pursues free from all external influences and little trammelled by intellectual influences descending from the past, Australia would be that country. It is the newest of all the democracies. It is that which has travelled farthest and fastest along the road which leads to the unlimited rule of the multitude. In it, better than anywhere else, may be studied the tendencies that rule displays as it works itself out in practice.[1]

THE TRAJECTORY OF AUSTRALIAN DEMOCRACY

Australian democracy today is undoubted, but also unremarkable. Contemporary texts on government and politics describe its institutions and practices, and chronicle its peculiarities, in terms of categories common to advanced liberal democracies. Australia has its own history and political culture, of course, but these have not produced notably distinctive arrangements of government. Australian government and politics belong to that broad class of polities of the twentieth century which have sought to reconcile the potentially conflicting imperatives of individual private ownership and political rule for and by the people. Australia is a nation of representative and responsible government; it possesses a welfare state and a mixed economy in which state intervention to protect the disadvantaged is tempered by a disinclination to interfere with property rights. In all these things, Australia is as other Western democracies. The contrasts offered are usually ones of quantity – Australians are, perhaps, more 'over-governed' than other nations, pay rather less in taxes or possess a somewhat less generous welfare system – rather than of the quality or distinctiveness of Australian democracy. For the most part, we are content to think of ourselves as similar to other advanced nations. Some see us as being a bit better, in that what is most familiar is most comfortable. Others, less cheerful, find the contrast less pleasing, perhaps because other pastures always look somewhat greener. Few would argue that we are in a position to offer a blueprint of democratic self-realization to others or believe that we require any fundamental reappraisal on our own part.

But Australian democracy was not always unremarkable. A reasonably convincing case can, indeed, be made that Australia, subject to marginal caveats about potential racialist exclusions under Section 25 of the Constitution and the long delay in granting the federal vote to the Aboriginal population, was the first truly democratic state in the modern sense of fully representative government based on free, equal and universal suffrage. Using that criterion, we find that Australia became a democracy in 1903, New Zealand in 1907, Denmark and Norway in 1915, with the remainder of today's liberal democracies becoming so in the aftermaths of World Wars I and II. Moreover, whereas the post-1918 impetus to full achievement of democracy clearly owed much to either defeat in war or the imperatives of national mobilization, Australia's emergence as a democracy was almost exclusively a result of internal political development.[2]

Australia was remarkable not merely in achieving democracy early and achieving it independently. It was equally remarkable – or so it seemed to contemporaries – in what the democratic achievement seemed to imply about the character of self-government in the modern state and the policy ends to which it would naturally lead. To most foreign commentators and to the majority strand of political opinion at the turn of the century, the fulfilment of the democratic imperative was identified with social progress. Australia was seen to be in the democratic vanguard, especially with respect to political influence for the working man and legislation embodying his interests. By 1930, however, with the publication of W.K. Hancock's *Australia*,[3] there had been a subtle shift in evaluation. While an appreciation of the distinctiveness of Australian democracy remains, the belief that Australia served as an example to the rest of the world is much less apparent. Indeed, in Hancock, the 'social liberal' identification of democracy and progress is overlaid by a growing ambivalence about the possibly corrupting influence of rule by the democratic masses.[4]

From the 1930s onwards Australian democracy began to be seen less as remarkable than as parochial, and contrasts with the rest of the world were often focussed on Australia's need to catch up with progressive policies already adopted elsewhere.[5] After the Second World War scholars notably refrained from sweeping contrasts between Australia and other democracies; and there was even some questioning of aspects of the distinctiveness of the earlier democratic experience.[6] For political practitioners with a reformist penchant – first in the period of post-war reconstruction and with still more vehemence in the Whitlam era – the imperative for change and the focus of international comparison had ceased to be the self-evident virtue of being in the democratic vanguard and now became an increasing anxiety about ending up in the democratic rear.

There are reasons, therefore, for believing that the developmental trajectory of Australian democracy in this century has been different from those of most other Western nations. From being a radical exemplar in the years after Federation, Australia has become a nation with no special political lessons for the rest of the world. Depending on the way one looks at things, others have caught up where Australia once led, or Australia has fallen behind on the democratic road. Either way a focus on the relative trajectory of Australian democracy does suggest a degree of distinctiveness in the unfolding of the democratic process. Understanding what made Australian democracy different is essential to comprehending the character of the political reality confronting Australia as she starts out into her third century of national existence. It is not the ephemera of contemporary political conflicts that will shape our future but the choices made about the basic form and content of our democracy. Those choices are focussed on contemporary issues, but are much shaped by our democratic past. With a view to locating the character of Australian politics today, we shall attempt to describe the nature of Australian democratic distinctiveness and speculate as to its causes.

AUSTRALIAN DEMOCRACY AS RADICAL EXEMPLAR

Louise Overacker, in a seminal work on the Australian party system written in the late 1940s,[7] cited Lord Bryce's opinion 'that Australia was the most interesting spot politically in the world'.[8] Bryce, whose major treatise on Australian democracy was based on the political experience of the first two decades after Federation, was following in the footsteps of many previous commentators. Even before Federation Australia was seen as a democratic pioneer, with Sidney Webb arguing that, in contrast to Britain, 'you have here a genuine Democracy, the people really getting what it wishes to get',[9] and Albert Metin taking very seriously Australia's description as 'the workers' paradise'.[10] Both Webb and Metin were socialists, but Bryce, writing twenty years later in a far more academic vein, saw the claim for Australian distinctiveness in much the same light: for good or evil, it was the country in which the rule of the masses had proceeded furthest and in which that will was most fully expressed in progressive legislation.[11]

The empirical basis for such an assessment of Australian exceptionalism could scarcely be contested in the early years of the new century. Throughout continental Europe social democratic labour parties expressed radical, sometimes revolutionary, opposition to the bourgeois state; but in Australia the Labor Party influenced the policy of the state, either by holding the balance of parliamentary power or through its own parliamentary majority. The world's first labour government took office in Queensland in 1899; throughout much of the first decade of the century, Labor Party support was the linchpin of the creation of a viable majority at the federal level, and in 1910 the Party, having secured 50 per cent of the popular vote, formed the world's first majority government committed to the workers' cause. Moreover the rise of the Labor Party brought with it a change in the character of democratic party organization. Party discipline, as manifested in the pledge and caucus control, exemplified a new conception of the parliamentary arena as a battleground on which disciplined armies fought to realize the aims of contending platforms. The Australian Labor Party, no less than Michels' German Social Democratic Party, showed clearly that the character of mass democracy was to be very different from the models offered by Burke or John Stuart Mill. To Bryce the implications of the new party discipline, particularly as exemplified in the power of caucus to name ministers and require their resignation, was 'in effect a supersession of Cabinet government, and largely of Parliamentary government itself'.[12]

It was not only the rule of the working masses and the novel character of mass democracy which impressed commentators, but also the achievement of higher material standards than elsewhere.[13] Australia was not merely a prosperous country, but one wherein the workers shared the fruits of prosperity. 'It may safely be said that there is no country in the world where the material prosperity and substantial comfort of the working classes are so assured as in Australia', wrote Henry Turner in the pages of the *Melbourne Review* in 1882,[14] and, despite the long depression of the 1890s, such remained the general view for three or four decades thereafter. Prosperity obviously owed much to general economic conditions in the Australian colonies, but it was clear to all observers that government in Australia saw itself as having a very positive role in fostering the continuance of prosperity and its equitable distribution. The role of the state in late nineteenth and early twentieth century Australia was manifestly much greater than in Europe and America, and its primary task was conceived as intervention to procure the preconditions for national economic development. The result was a 'colonial socialism' in which, circa 1901, the state's expenditure amounted to around 20 per cent of GDP and public employment was approximately 8 per cent of the total workforce.[15]

Building the basis of a self-reliant community in a land far from the European centres of capital and manpower required an activist stance by central government to procure and guarantee foreign loans, to build an infrastructure for further development and to foster the immigration of those who would labour to build the New Jerusalem. Under such circumstances the rhetoric of laissez-faire was unlikely to appeal to practical men whether they were manufacturers crying out for protection from foreign competition, pastoralists demanding the necessary investment of social capital to take their produce to markets at home and overseas or trade unionists concerned to prevent the dilution of labour by migration from low-wage countries. To most sections of organized political opinion, the state was an instrument to be used rather than a power to be feared; and big government was the natural consequence of the democratic expression of such a view.[16]

A secondary priority before the emergence of a Labor parliamentary presence, but one which vied with the development imperative thereafter, was the use of legislation to determine working conditions and wages. Acts to control sweated labour, to regulate hours of work and to establish wages boards were the beginning of this process. Its apotheosis was the federal arbitration system which, under Mr Justice Higgins, set out to establish a *New Province for Law and Order*.[17] The minimum wage was to be dictated by 'the normal needs of the average employee regarded as a human being living in a civilized community',[18] and the payment of such wages was to have priority over the rate of profit.[19] Arbitration was itself only the most directly welfare-relevant aspect of a package of reforms enacted in the first decade after Federation, constituting an historic compromise between emergent classes. Other crucial components, which were to distinguish the public policy pattern of the next half century, were protective tariffs designed to bolster manufacturing and maintain high wage levels and an exclusionary policy in respect of coloured migration. The latter was designed to maintain full employment and to create a barrier behind which might thrive a democracy for the white aristocracy of labour.[20]

As we shall later argue, it is possible to attribute the emergence of this pattern of policy to the early democratization that gave the working masses a genuine say in the shape of their society, but it is important to emphasize that we are not suggesting that the pattern was in any sense an inevitable product of youthful democracy. At every stage choices were made – the founding fathers' choice to build arbitration into the federal constitution, Higgins' choice to articulate the notion of a 'living' wage, Deakin's choice to link the manufacturing tariffs with fair wages and, later, the labour movement's choice to put its faith in all of these. Although those choices were constrained by the alternatives existing at the time, there always were alternatives – the alternative not to establish a federal court of arbitration, not to enunciate general wage norms, not to buy tariffs at the cost of interfering with employers' wage-setting prerogatives and, for the trade unions, not to accept wage settlements at a level inferior to those produced by free collective bargaining. Once choices were made they, in turn, served as constraints on future options, shaping the alternative structure for succeeding generations. Much which seems strange in the developmental trajectory of Australian democracy is to be explained by the choices made in the decade after Federation and institutionalized in the decades immediately thereafter.

This applies as much to the shape of the future welfare system as to the compromise on wages and tariffs. Although by no means as radical a departure from practice elsewhere, the early years after Federation saw the introduction of a variety of explicit welfare-state measures, including age pensions and invalidity and maternity benefits, which sought to alleviate poverty in sections of the population unprotected by the wages system. Certainly such welfare reforms were hardly as contentious in Australia in that period as they were to become later. Writing of the parliamentary debate in New South Wales on that state's pension scheme, Pember Reeves noted: 'seldom, indeed, has a striking, novel and expensive social reform been adopted with so little hesitation and amid so harmonious a chorus of blessings and good wishes'.[21] These measures provided flat-rate, subsistence-level benefits on a means-tested basis financed from the general revenue, a pattern of provision which has characterized Australian welfare to the present day. That pattern, arguably, contributes to the lack of generosity of the modern welfare state[22] but, at the time, the reforms marked a major step forward in society's willingness to provide for the disadvantaged. Whether or no Australia could be aptly described as the 'workers' paradise' in the decades following Federation, it stood out clearly as an exemplar of the fact that the democratic state could be used to aid the weak and the helpless.

In many of the accounts of this period there is a fascinating, and by no means fully resolved, contradiction between the form and the content of the emergent democracy. On the one hand the reforms enacted appeared to serve the interests of the working masses and to be enacted, at least in part, as a consequence of their organized and disciplined participation in democratic politics. To many the explicitness of a class conflict based on material interests distinguished Australia from other contemporary Anglo-Saxon democracies where the democratic temper cut across entrenched economic interests. On the other hand the vast majority of the reforms were in content of a 'social liberal' character, either welcomed unreservedly by all sections of opinion, as in the case of age pensions and much of the infrastructural development, or involving compromises between class interests, as in the case of conciliation and arbitration, which to some held out the promise of higher wages and for others offered the prospect of industrial peace. If this augury of Australian democracy were to be believed, the advent of the working class in politics seemed to promise class collaboration in the name of social progress, rather than class conflict and the usurpation of the capitalist system.

With hindsight the paradox seems easier to resolve. Much of the confusion of contemporary observers was a direct consequence of their unfamiliarity with organized mass politics and the notion of disciplined mass action to achieve political objectives. The idea of a Labor Party offering 'Support in Return for Concessions', with the aim of making and remaking social conditions implied a radical vision, along the lines of some of Marx's earlier writings, of universal suffrage leading to the victory of the working class. Today it implies nothing of the sort: democratic politics is almost everywhere dominated by the confrontation of mass-based parties espousing diverse platforms largely constituted of material demands. The form of the democratic class struggle has been transformed by the advent of mass participation. In this Australia was certainly ahead of the rest of the world in the decades after Federation, but has long since become as other democratic nations. The content – or outcome – of the democratic class struggle was quite another matter, and here Australia maintained her distinctiveness for much longer.

If the emergence of a new working-class politics was the topic which interested virtually all observers of late nineteenth and early twentieth century Australia, the reasons for its emergence seemed more or less self-evident. It could not be merely a consequence of the prosperity of the colonies leading to a greater willingness to make concessions to the working classes, for in per capita terms the USA was arguably almost as rich but by no means as socially progressive. Nor could it be simply the intellectual influence of democratic ideas, for these had been conspicuously unsuccessful in their lands of origin. What seemed to make the difference was the existence of democratic institutions and the absence of entrenched interests opposing democratic reform. The contrast between Australia (and New Zealand, which, in the accounts of *Webbs' Australian Diary*,[23] Metin,[24] Pember Reeves[25] and Bryce,[26] was bracketed with the Australia as the only other exemplar of radical democracy of the masses) and the rest of the world was quite clear. Elsewhere the landed classes fought to preserve aristocratic privilege – and as tenaciously in the New World as the Old, as was demonstrated by the war between the North and the South in the United States.[27]

But in Australia 'the privileged, unshielded by any acceptable sanctions, were forced to defend themselves by entrenching in the positions of strength remaining to them'.[28] Already by the 1850s and 1860s, responsible government and universal male suffrage had been demanded and conferred, with the last bastion of privilege to be found in the upper houses of the colonial parliaments. Even with respect to male democracy these developments were far in advance of their time, and with them went other features of democratic practice, today taken for granted but then considered as radical innovations, such as the secret ballot (called 'the Australian ballot' in America) and payment of members of parliament. A cynic might argue that the strength of Labor in the Federal House of Representatives in the first decade of this century was a function of parliamentary salaries of around four times the average wage; a radical of the day might have responded that it was a vindication of the old Chartist demand, achieved so much more readily in Australia than in the Old World.

Australia at the turn of the century could be seen as a radical exemplar because it was the country in which the working masses first made an organized impact in politics, and that impact was itself attributable to the early emergence of democratic institutions. For those who observed the Australian scene this was a situation of great portent, for if Australia was 'democracy untrammelled', if it showed the tendencies democratic rule displayed 'as it works itself out in practice', then might not the great wave of democratization heralded by the twentieth century mean that Australia was the wave of the future?

THE PORTENTS OF AUSTRALIAN DEMOCRACY

Where might Australian democracy have gone, given its progress by, say, 1901? The ordinary citizen of that time, asked to express an opinion on the shape of Australian democracy in the late 1980s, might not have pitched his answer much in terms of political institutions or practices. Women already had the vote in some states, and would acquire it in commonwealth elections very soon. The common man had the vote and no-one had more than one vote, MPs were paid a decent salary and elections were honestly conducted and frequent. What more could be sought there? The urge was rather for a decent wage (perhaps, in the short term, the restoration of the customary seven shillings a day for unskilled labour, but, for the distant future, possibly 'ten bob a day' for all), a roof over your head and some kind of security against sickness and old age: social rather than political democracy. Told that Australia was a world leader in democracy, and asked to look ahead, he might have had two possible sorts of reaction. The optimistically inclined might have imagined that leadership in political democracy would be transformed into leadership in social democracy. The less sanguine might (since it is hard to visualize what has not yet existed) have settled for a familiar picture. Its base would have consisted of the already existing institutions of political democracy. Its superstructure would have been a kinder economic order: high and secure wages, insurance against unemployment due to sickness, cheap and available housing, accessible schools and hospitals and some provision to guard against poverty brought on by too many mouths to feed. The latter dream was by no means an impossible one, and much of it eventuated; the optimist's dream, however, was not to come to pass.

What, by contrast, might the educated observer have envisaged as the likely developmental path of Australian democracy? One obvious possibility was a continuation of the apparent trend to working-class domination. Bryce cites a French writer (M. Voisson, author of *La Nouvelle Australia*, written at the turn of the century) as predicting the total usurpation of capital, the wholesale destruction of the entrepreneurial spirit and eventual revolution.[29] Others, perhaps with a clearer appreciation of the ideological character of the Australian working-class movement, were less sanguine about the existence of any real revolutionary potential, for, as Lenin put it, 'the leaders of the Australian Labor Party are trade union officials, an element which is everywhere most moderate and "capital-serving" '.[30] Lenin, however, predicted that with time the existing *liberal* Labor Party would give way to a *socialist* Labor Party. A closer reading of the realities of post-Federation politics could suggest a very different scenario. To Deakin, Labor strength was a function of party disunity to the Right and, as he saw it, 'once the fiscal issue is settled a union of the two other parties will ensue, putting the Labor Party in a comparatively small minority'.[31]

But before utilizing hindsight more extensively to say what did happen to Australian democracy in the twentieth century, let us ask one more hypothetical question. What would social science theorizing – both that extant at the time and that of more recent provenance – have suggested might be the future of Australian democracy as seen from a turn of the century vantage-point?

Voisson's view of an ineluctable march to working-class domination may be taken as representative of all those theories which posit a developmental logic to the unfolding of history, and particularly to the working out of the democratic imperative. Strangely enough, Marx, in some of his writings, may be classified among the democratic determinists, for he had written of the Chartist demand for the vote that 'where the proletariat forms a large majority of the population' and where 'it has gained a clear consciousness of its position as a class', the inevitable result of universal suffrage would be the political supremacy of the working class.[32] Surely, then, a radical socialist future for Australia might reasonably be predicted on the basis of its early adoption of democratic institutions and the concomitant rise of the Labor Party. A less apocalyptic vision, but one nonetheless suggesting a progressive future for Australian democracy, was the dominant 'social liberal' strand of opinion of the times which, resting on the idealist theory of the state, believed that democracy was simultaneously the working out of a doctrine of progress and a process of emergent societal consensus, and saw Labor as the torch-bearer of an enlightened liberalism.[33]

These theories rest on notions of the immanent logic of democratization. In contrast, Lenin's view may be taken as representative of more empirically based theories linking the progress of democratization with the nature of social structure and economic conditions. To Lenin, as to Marx in his later years, the crucial determinant of progressive development was the emergence of a proletarian mass and a political leadership expressing its interests. Labor's *liberal* character in Australia was, hence, a natural reflection of the virtual absence of large-scale factory production and the petit-bourgeois nature of trade union leaders who might, at best, be expected to espouse short-term economistic demands against employers. Only if Australia's economic development took the normal capitalistic course could she progress beyond the mundane limits of petit-bourgeois liberalism.

A not wholly dissimilar conclusion might be derived from an analysis linking the conditions of democratic emergence and its subsequent dynamic to the social determinants of political cleavages. To Therborn, a modern neo-marxist theorist, what distinguished the early democracies – Australia, Denmark and New Zealand – was the existence of an independent class of small proprietors together with divisions within the ruling class.[34] These factors made the achievement of democracy relatively simple but, quite possibly, retarded the independent dynamic of the labour movement, which elsewhere had to develop the greater organizational and ideological cohesion required to scale the barriers protecting established political privilege. Seen in this light, Australia's early democratic achievements become readily comprehensible, but the probability that it might continue in the democratic vanguard is diminished. The Australian working class had been given power by default, but lacked the internal resources to move forward to greater victories.

Predicted outcomes are of course a function of the factor or factors presumed to be of causal significance, and the marxist and neo-marxist emphasis on class structure is not the only social science approach to the economic determinants of democratic development. Much sociological theorizing of the post-war era has stressed the links between measures of economic modernity on the one side, and democratic stability[35] and progressive welfare provision[36] on the other. High per capita incomes, economic growth and urbanization are, according to this influential strand of theorizing, conducive to democratic legitimacy and to an effort by all parties to preserve that legitimacy by building an extensive structure of state welfare. Here, then, is a theory of democratic progress which rests, not on the immanent logic of the democratic process, but rather on the economic prerequisites of democratic success. Applied to the conditions of Australia in the early twentieth century, it would have predicted a rosy future of continued democratic progress and welfare innovation. Whilst Australia remained amongst the richest and most urbanized nations in the world she might expect to remain in the democratic vanguard. The only cloud on the horizon was the rate of economic growth which had fallen dramatically in the depression of the 1890s, but a renewed spurt of economic growth in the first decade of the new century could have been interpreted as suggesting that even that impediment to progress was only temporary.

Theories of the immanent realization of the democratic imperative and those which posit the sociological determination of political development leave little room for the contingency of historical events and the working out of political conflicts. Deakin's argument that the fate of Labor rested on the settlement of the fiscal issue raises questions of this latter kind. But arguments from contingency suggest a rather limited capacity for forecasting the future. Everything depends on how things pan out; Australia's continued status as a radical exemplar might rest on the capacity of Labor to become the natural party of government or on choices of political strategy made by Labor or its opponents or, indeed, by political actors outside parliament. Thus social science theories which highlight contingency and choice tend to be open as to outcomes. Rustow, for instance, has argued that the transition to democracy depends on the willingness of political actors to resolve major substantive conflicts by instituting decision-rules which allow consensus around 'second-best' solutions and the subsequent habituation of those rules as they prove capable of resolving subsequent disputes.[37] In these terms one might see the constitution-making of the 1890s as the decision phase of Australian national democracy and the inclusion of working-class interests as a pertinent consideration in the solution of the fiscal issue as the beginning of the habituation phase. But, looked at in this way, the future of Australian democracy becomes unpredictable, depending for its very continuance on the capacity to use those decision-rules to resolve new disputes and for its content on the substance of those resolutions.

FREEZING THE FORM OF AUSTRALIAN DEMOCRACY

Finally embracing the advantages of hindsight, we can see that those theories which are least optimistic about the inherent progressive dynamic of democratization and the onward march of the working-class movement are those which fit the Australian case best. G.K. Chesterton, in one of his novels, tells of the game called 'Cheat the Prophet', in which the people listen carefully to all that the clever men have to say about what is to happen in the next generation, wait until all the clever men are dead, and then go and do something else. Chesterton uses this device to preface a story in which, contrary to all predictions, the London of a hundred years hence is exactly as London is now. Given that by far the prevailing tenor of Australian political commentary in the years after Federation was the democratic optimism of the progressive 'social liberals', one is inclined to think that 'Cheat the Prophet' must have been the overwhelming national pastime throughout much of this century. Little of the essential form and content of Australian democracy has been altered in the twentieth century, although it is possibly true that the past decade has seen more questioning, more searching for new directions, than in any other period since Federation.

That is not, of course, to say that the way we look at the functioning of Australian democracy is similar to the way we would have looked at it some eighty years ago. What was striking then – the emergence of the popular will as a force to be reckoned with – is now old hat; the notion that party discipline constituted an illegitimate challenge to the tenets of representative democracy has faded into the background as we have reshaped our justifications of democratic practice in terms of a theory of 'party government',[38] and the novelty of big government and social policy intervention have disappeared as both have become commonplaces of twentieth-century democratic government. Moreover, in much the way suggested by Rustow's concept of a habituation phase of democratic development, many of the solutions originally accepted as second-best by the contending parties and groups of the post-Federation era became, as the century progressed, simply a part of the intellectual baggage with which all responsible Australian policy-makers confronted their world. Thus what had once been seen as contentious by domestic politicians, and as constituting Australia's claim to democratic leadership by many outside commentators, gradually became accepted orthodoxy. It was the Australian way of doing things and, at the same time, the democratic way of doing things, but no longer the radical way of doing things.

The Australian way of practicing democracy has not changed very greatly in the twentieth century and, in the light of the rigid character of its federal constitution and the rather advanced character of Australian democratic forms circa 1900, that may be neither surprising nor particularly dismaying. Admittedly we have preserved a reputation for being ready to experiment with new electoral rules from time to time[39] but it can scarcely be argued that these changes have been introduced as part of any radical vision for improving the quality of democratic participation. Certainly very little has been done to transform *de jure* rights of representation into *de facto* rights of citizenship, where that might have involved major constitutional change. The right of women to vote, granted exceptionally early, has not been, with some recent exceptions in the Senate, transformed into the actuality of a substantial female legislative presence and, in this respect, Australia falls far behind most contemporary European practice.[40]

More usually motives have involved some balance of partisan advantage, as, most conspicuously, was the case with the introduction of preferential voting in 1918.[41] Moreover what experimentation there has been has remained within the confines of the British traditions of territorial representation and strong government; the Single Transferable Vote was acceptable in those terms; list systems of proportional representation, as practiced in all contemporary West European states, were not. Thus, for good or evil, Australian democracy continues to be tied to the idea of the representation of the individual, rather than to the more modern European notion of accurate representation of political parties.[42] Nor can it be truly said that individual representation, so relatively advanced in Australia at the turn of the century, moved forward very rapidly thereafter. The Aboriginal population had to wait until 1962 for the federal vote, and in the states, which retained their nineteenth-century constitutions after the Federation came into being, progress toward 'one vote, one value' and the democratization of upper chambers was slow and uneven. South Australia, the first state to introduce female suffrage in 1896, had to wait a further seventy-seven years until it became almost the last of the states to confer universal suffrage for its Legislative Council (Tasmania was last of all in 1983); Queensland, a lone innovator in abolishing its upper house, perhaps not coincidentally, is famous for an egregious system of rural overweighting for elections to its unicameral parliament.

If there has been little fundamental change in the electoral arena, there has been still less in terms of the formal division of powers. What Whitlam's dismissal in 1975 demonstrated was not so much that Australia did not possess truly responsible government,[43] but that the current Australian version of responsible government was dated in the extreme. Whereas parliamentary government has almost everywhere been made progressively compatible with party rule by a shift to unicameralism or by a diminution in the powers of the upper chamber,[44] Australia possesses a system in which a democratically elected majority can be frustrated in the exercise of its power by a body unrepresentative of the demographic majority of the voting population. At a formal level, too, the division of powers between the commonwealth and the states has been notoriously difficult to alter – indeed, the failure of Fisher's first majority Labor government to extend the economic powers of the commonwealth through the amending procedures of the Constitution represents the first major setback in the labour movement's triumphal march. The 1946 social services amendment was the first and only time that Labor surmounted this constitutional barrier on a matter concerning powers of economic intervention. In this area, at least, changes did come about through less formal means – in particular, through agreements between the commonwealth and the states from the 1940s onwards which made income taxation a commonwealth responsibility and facilitated uniform service provision across the states. Without such informal changes, it seems probable that Australia's laggardly post-war welfare performance in comparison with the other Western democracies would have been even worse than it was.

Not only have the forms of Australian democracy remained relatively unchanged; so too have the major protagonists, although sometimes, on the non-Labor side, with cosmetic changes of name. Admittedly the decade following the New Protection compromise was one of flux. Deakin's prediction of a union between the parties opposed to Labor came true with the 'fusion' of Liberal Protectionists and Free Traders into the Liberal Party, but the resulting two-party configuration was to last only until the debut of the Country (now National) Party on the federal stage in 1919. Since then the basic configuration of party competition has been a three-party contest between the Labor, Liberal and Country parties. Deakin's prediction nevertheless was prescient in so far as preferential voting served to provide a kind of functional equivalent to union – to such an extent that one eminent observer of political parties has described the Liberal and Country parties as 'symbiotic' and their coalition as, effectively, a 'coalescence'.[45] Within that coalescence the rural interests espoused by the Country Party have always had the minority voice, although one which has effectively constituted a minority veto on novel departures in policy-making. Thus had Sir Joh Bjelke-Petersen succeeded in his 1987 bid to become Prime Minister, and still more if the National Party had in the process assumed anti-Labor leadership, it would clearly have involved a real departure from the previous form of Australian democracy.

Moreover the balance of power between the major protagonists also remained remarkably stable, although, if anything, Labor's potential to influence policy outcomes slipped somewhat. The Labor Party's rapid growth in electoral support came to an end at just that point when it first acquired a majority in its own right; thereafter, support has fluctuated generally between 45 and 50 per cent of the popular vote. In the European multi-party systems of proportional representation that would have been enough to guarantee an almost perpetual tenure of governmental office. In Australia the coalescent unity of the Right and preferential voting, combined with the obvious symptoms of recurrent disunity within the Labor Party – factionalism, party splits and leadership defections – served to condemn Labor to long periods in the political wilderness.

The country in which Labor had first obtained power through the will of the democratic electorate was to become the one in which there was the greatest discrepancy between democratic socialist electoral support and office-holding. Nearly half the popular vote did not translate into anything like nearly half the office-holding. When Labor was in office it might succeed in hurrying the pace of reform – as did the Curtin, Chifley and Whitlam governments – but such governments were few and the periods between them long. The strategic dilemma for Labor has always been the same: how to combine ameliorative social reform, the economic stability by which Australians appear to judge their governments of all political complexions and the need to maintain office. In recent years that dilemma has been addressed in two different ways. The Whitlam emphasis was to hope that building a constituency of support on the basis of radical social reform would win the electoral battle. Whitlam was frustrated by a combination of Australia's poor economic performance, world economic forces and Australia's conservative constitutional structure. The Hawke strategy appears to be a watered-down version of the 'inevitability of gradualism', with gradualism replaced by immobility or retreat when the economic or electoral going gets tough. Labor's unique third consecutive win in the election of July 1987 showed that the strategy worked for retaining office but, possibly, at the cost of relegating social reform to the status of a subordinate objective for the foreseeable future.

Arguably, then, the form of Australian democracy and its chief protagonists have not changed appreciably since the first decade after Federation. The question is whether we should be surprised at the slowdown in the rate of change in Australia in these respects; and the answer is that we should not. Certainly democratization continued its forward march in much of the rest of the Western world for several decades longer than in Australia. Party alignments also continued to change, but that, as we have already intimated, was almost entirely because Australia was, at the turn of the century, already several decades ahead. In fact in all the emergent democratic states there was to be a 'freezing of party alternatives' at roughly that point at which mass political mobilization and mass suffrage became a reality.[46] Party organizations grew up around current social cleavages and sought to establish mass organizations to extend and consolidate their support bases, and in the process froze the character of the party system at that point where the electorate was largely attached to one or other of the contending parties. In a similar way, the rules of the democratic game were similarly frozen at that point where the established parties had some assurance that they could maintain a level of representation and access to decision-making commensurate with their support base in the society.

In these respects, differences in democratic forms and party alignments depend on choices made under circumstances of a given conjuncture of cleavage structures and the timing of democratic mobilization. Thus Australia's Constitution might well have been changed to provide a form of responsible government more consonant with party government if Labor had confronted an upper house based on privilege; Australia might possibly have adopted a form of proportional representation for the lower house if territorial separation of rural and urban producers had not already ensured a reasonably low threshold of representation for existing organized interests; and Labor's own growth pattern might have been very different if its opponents had not been initially divided, and subsequently found common cause. But differences of these kinds between modern democracies rest on choices made by political actors many decades ago, and those choices, once the outcome of victorious political struggle, come to serve as constraints on subsequent generations. As Schumpeter put it, 'social structures, types and attitudes are coins that do not readily melt'.[47] Much the same goes for political institutions and arrangements, and Australian democratic forms have been no more impervious to change than those of other countries. In that sense, we have no reason to think Australians more prone to play the game of 'Cheat the Prophet' than the peoples of other democracies; only that they began to play somewhat earlier.

THE MECHANISM OF AUSTRALIAN DEMOCRACY

To argue that there was little change in the substantive forms of Australian democracy in the period since Federation does not mean that Deakin and his contempories would have found the character of contemporary democratic practice at all familiar or congenial. Australian commentators at the turn of the century had, in a sense, not caught up with the changing reality that already surrounded them. Like most nineteenth-century liberals they hoped that the future would bring the century of the common man; but, although the realities of party government were already with them, they did not visualize that the political influence of the masses would be exercised almost exclusively through organized party channels. That failure of cognition can perhaps be partially excused – despite the obvious qualitative change in the character of party brought about by the rule of caucus and the pledge the Labor Party in its first few years on the federal stage appeared to be behaving in accord with liberal assumptions. The prevailing assumption was that once the people were enfranchised, politicians would do what the people wanted in order to stay in power: political parties as such would have little part to play. Labor's willingness to trade support for concessions, its readiness to let others implement its policy rather than seek power in its own right, could be interpreted as a fulfilment of that expectation.

We see now that this was a transitional period. By 1910 the parties had regrouped into two, Labor and Liberal. Very quickly the mechanism of party became the established gatekeeper of political activity: the parties monopolized politics by controlling entrance to parliament itself and by controlling the behaviour of the politicians once they had arrived there. Ever since, the policy options of Australian politics have been in the hands of the major parties, and attempts to break this monopoly have been quite unsuccessful. In 1988, as in 1910, an aspirant for parliamentary power must obtain the endorsement of a major party for a winnable seat if he or she is to have any realistic expectations of success, and an organization seeking to have a given policy implemented must gain the support of a major party for it. Individuals and groups outside the party system can, from time to time, achieve temporary veto power, but that is all.

The consequence has been that the role of the citizen in late twentieth-century Australian politics has been in some ways much less pivotal than the liberal thinkers of the nineteenth century would have anticipated, given that what they saw as the institutional building-blocks of political democracy – universal adult suffrage, payment of members of parliament, honestly conducted elections – were firmly in place. Moreover none of this could have occurred without the consent and cooperation of the citizens themselves. Once again, like the peoples of other democratic states, Australians played 'Cheat the Prophet', but this time by departing from what they initially regarded as the essential character of democratic practice. To understand the nature of contemporary Australian politics and the mechanism by which the policy content of Australian democracy is shaped, we must ask what happened to divert the attention of citizens from policies to parties, and then to keep their attention diverted.

The answer has several parts.[48] First, it is political aspirants who provide the opportunity for citizens to vote. Once aspirants saw that party endorsement was critical in securing organizational and financial support, they flocked to obtain it. By and large, from 1910 to the present, parties have had the pick of candidates who were genuinely on offer. Second, and Aristotle notwithstanding, it is probably true that, in democracies, most people most of the time place active participation in politics rather low on their order of priorities: a division of political labour is for most a sensible approach to life. Third, the complexity of politics has increased very markedly in the twentieth-century, and citizens would have had to provide themselves with some kind of simplifying mechanism to make sense of the dozens, hundreds or thousands of issues dealt with in the modern political arena. But, fourth, the political party has proved to be an extraordinarily useful invention, as important in the world of politics as the limited liability company is in the world of business, and for the same reason: both deal effectively with the unfortunate mortality of individual humans. Political parties serve as political simplifiers in the further sense that they present political choices to the electorate in a special blend of rationality and ideology. In the beginning, citizens chose parties because the party's view of the world was satisfactorily akin to their own, and its policies were therefore to be trusted. Citizens became partisans of their parties – meaning for some it was their party, right or wrong, for others that they would vote for its candidates, whoever they were, for still others that they were more likely to vote for it than for its rivals.

In time people passed down their partisanship to their children, not by precept but by example. The transmission of party loyalty through the generations has been, perhaps, the single most important factor in closing off other political options and thereby freezing the form of Australian democracy. The Country Party has been the only successful entrant into Australian party politics since 1910, and it was able to survive only because it hived off a substantial section of the Liberal Party's electoral support in 1919, maintained its territory throughout the 1920s by vigorous defence and coalition, and then profited from the transmission of Country Party loyalty through succeeding generations. Name changes in the 1970s and early 1980s have not affected that loyalty, in part because the party has been able to protect its territory, in part because its voters 'know' that the old party is there embodied in the new.

The parties themselves have also been careful to insulate themselves against the citizens, or against a sudden wave of citizen participation which might threaten party dominance. The establishment of compulsory enrolment (1911) and compulsory voting (1924), the latter supported by all the parties, reduced the need for parties to have large memberships. Ironically compulsory voting has also been widely supported by the citizens – who correctly believe that elections are the foundation of modern democracy, and go on, rather less soundly, to assume that all, including themselves, should be compelled to vote. In similar fashion, post-war moves to change to more proportional forms of representation for federal and state upper houses have occurred within the context of tight party control of endorsements. Certainly new choices have been made, but always within the constraining context of established party government.

It would be easy, but wrong, to tell the story of Australian democracy in the twentieth century as that of the dwindling power of the citizen in the face of the monolithic accretion of power by the political parties. It is not simply that citizens have acquiesced in the dominance of parties. Here is an area in which, perhaps, there really was no alternative, in the sense that party rule might well be considered an intrinsic feature of modern mass democracy. In all countries that can reasonably claim to be democratic, in which the citizenry can, however indirectly, be said to rule, the political party is the crucial institutional form. Australia did not copy its parties or its party system from anyone else; least of all from Britain, whose modern party system came afterwards. The party system developed here in response to Australian circumstances, and its strong similarities with party systems in the rest of the industrialized world are to be explained by the fact that the other nations in that world all have had mass communication systems and mass electorates for nearly half a century or more. Thus the developmental trajectory of the form of Australian democracy has been influenced not merely by the freezing of the alternatives structure but also by the fact that it started down much the same track as other Western political systems.

Today the resulting democratic structure is under some intellectual challenge. That, too, is a universal of Western political democracy in the late twentieth century. The complexity of decision-making in a progressively post-industrial society is seen as too great for even the simplifying structure of the party system to cope with adequately. Diagnoses vary. Major organizations have a vast impact on policy and exercise power without responsibility. Could a solution be to move from party government as we have known it to corporatist modes of decision-making, of which, perhaps, the Hawke government's Accord with the ACTU might be a prototype? Parties rather than citizens have been the active agents of twentieth-century democratic practice, but has that not led to fiscal irresponsibility on the part of parties seeking to bribe the electorate? To those who answer yes, big government is attributable to democratic party competition, and solutions range from constitutional limitations on the size of the deficit to dramatic populist interventions to cut-back expenditure and taxation. Sir Joh Bjelke-Petersen's push for national power in 1987 was only one instance of this populist phenomenon. The lesson of similar attempts overseas suggests that the established structures of party government have the resilience to shrug off the challenge. Giving power to parties rather than leaving it in the hands of citizens inevitably leads to the accretion of power at the centre, where party politicians have the greatest leverage. Should we not self-consciously turn away from such developments and give power to individual citizens as individual consumers through a deregulated and free market system?

These alternatives and others are the common coinage of intellectual dissent from the outcomes of modern mass democracy. There are other questions we might ask of the

Australian democratic system with a more local and perhaps more radical flavour. We might ask whether the system has given the parties of reform and the status quo an equally 'fair go'. Labor, having achieved an electoral share of 45 per cent or greater in 24 of 32 elections since 1910 – a record comparable to that of the Swedish Social Democrats, and better than that of any other democratic socialist party in the world – would certainly answer no. We might ask whether the Australian system led to undue preoccupation with the concerns of party rather than those of policy. That has been a frequent criticism levelled at Labor, not least by its own more radical supporters; but, perhaps in this respect, Australia is not greatly different from other nations. As party government has become institutionalized it has everywhere become a force of inertia, diverting energy from programmes of reform to the immediate needs of party self-preservation. We might ask whether, in the Australian environment, the party system, for all its dominance, was strong enough to counteract the enormous conservative pressures supplied by the federal provisions of the Constitution and of a citizenry made cautious by early wealth and democratic achievement. Certainly the lesson of more than eight decades of Australian democracy is that the disjointed incrementalism that results from the federal system has blunted the enthusiasm of most politicians for sweeping or comprehensive policies: life is too short for such utopianism.

Having said all this, we must emphasize that the mechanism of party government developed under Australian conditions has had many virtues, not least that of satisfying most citizens most of the time. Australian democracy has been civil and orderly. Its temper is cool; its elections are honest, and beaten governments vacate the seats of power without demur; the public sevices are competent enough, hard-working and not known for taking bribes; and politicians are respected for their work as individuals, if not admired as a collectivity. Since there are many other societies in which governmental forms can hardly be said to have so beneficent an effect, it may be argued that Australians have much to be thankful for. Indeed neither general intellectual or local Australian concerns about the quality of the democratic system relate to explicit disquiet about democratic forms as such, but rather to the policy content of Australian democracy. It is to that topic that we now turn our attention.

AUSTRALIAN DEMOCRACY AT THE CROSSROADS

Had this chapter been written two decades earlier – as a retrospect, say, on the Menzies era – our analysis of the public policy content of Australian democracy would have been essentially similar to the account we have offered of the freezing of democratic forms. Naturally, in the case of policy, we would not have been arguing that there had been little change, but rather that the change which had occurred had taken place within parameters established in the first decade of the century. Moreover, taking a comparative viewpoint, we would have noted that, despite change along a trajectory largely marked out by political choices made more than a generation previously, Australian democracy – once a leader in respect of big government and social policy innovation – had, by the 1960s, long since been caught up and, in many cases, overtaken by other Western democratic states.

What had emerged as the distinctive goals of Australian public policy – its emphasis on national development and on distributional equity – had not changed but rather had shifted focus in such a way that they did not translate into rapid growth of the state on the scale common in most of the post-war capitalist democracies. Since real growth in the public sector there certainly was, that is not how Australians perceived the situation at the time, but it is a picture readily apparent when one examines cross-national comparisons of public expenditure and public employment expansion in the 1950s and 1960s. Developmentalism had been the initial impetus for Australia's early start in big government, taking the form of direct public action to procure the capital and labour required for national expansion. As a strategy it tied Australian fortunes to Britain, whence most of these resources came. The Great Depression was a turning point, marking not only the drying up of traditional sources of capital inflow, but a revulsion against such wholesale reliance on the outside world. What took its place was an ever-increasing dependence on tariff protection as a means of sheltering the growth of those sections of the Australian economy vulnerable to fluctuations in the world market. In a process which transformed the New Protection into John McEwen's 'all-round' protectionism, and the Tariff Board from a minor agency into one of the pivotal institutions of Australian macroeconomic policy-making, developmentalism ceased to mean primarily the 'colonial socialism' of direct state ownership and, instead, took on a more regulatory cast. As was true also of the post-war reconstruction turn to Keynesian macroeconomic policy management, the state interfered more, but intervened less directly. The change in focus was never complete. And the Snowy Mountains Scheme and a massive programme of post-war assisted migration seemed to spell a reassertion of the older approach to development. But, under Liberal-Country Party aegis, the strategy for national growth quickly assumed the character of a regulated partnership between state and private ownership.

A regulatory focus was already central to the wage control strategy that was a crucial component of the post-Federation settlement. Arbitration was to procure social justice and wage equity by requiring employers to pay a living wage. This was Australia's alternative to state redistribution to compensate for market-based inequalities. Such a strategy could only serve as an instrument of social amelioration where, as in Australia, wage levels were relatively high, but could, under those circumstances, become for the working class 'a rallying point in the class war, a trench to man against the attacking forces of capitalism'.[49] But in so far as the living wage became a symbol of the working class's successful resistance to exploitation, it militated against trade union and Labor pressures for social amelioration through state welfare intervention.

Herein lies the essential clue to the weakness of welfare-state development in Australia since quite early in the century.[50] Throughout Europe the labour movement was an ally of those who sought on humanitarian and other grounds to extend the scope of social citizenship. In Australia, under the pressure of wartime national mobilization, Labor was certainly impelled to adopt schemes already commonplace elsewhere, but it remained ideologically attached to a belief in selectivity which was lauded for its more redistributive impact for the few unfortunates who fell outside the protective ambit of the wages system. Certainly the fact that in Australia Labor was rarely in office contributed to the weakness of the welfare imperative, but what was at least equally significant was the absence of a party fully committed to the expansion of the social rights of citizenship through income maintenance programmes and social wage entitlements. In Europe, whether in or out of office, the labour movement was a force for greater generosity in the welfare system, but in Australia that could scarcely be so, since, whether welfare financing came from contributions or from general taxation, it obviously competed for resources with what really mattered: namely, the size of the living wage. Throughout Europe the extent of the state, as measured by expenditures, taxation and personnel, grew almost exponentially, especially in the two and a half decades following World War II. In Australia the state grew far more slowly, and by 1970 was, as it remains today, one of the smallest amongst the advanced democracies. Throughout Europe the motive power for the expansion of the state was inter-party competition for the democratic vote on an agenda of welfare amelioration, which meant that labour movement programmes for social amelioration could have a policy impact even when Labor was not in power. In Australia the democratic agenda was not so much about welfare as about wages, which reduced that impact when in office and rendered it nugatory in opposition.

In both Australia and Europe the advent of mass democracy and of a distinct working-class presence in politics were as crucial in shaping the subsequent content of public policy as they had been in determining the form of democratic institutions. Social conditions and timing were again the crucial determinants of growth trajectories. An Australian accommodation or historic compromise between the emergent classes of capitalism occurred earlier than in Europe because the major protagonists of divergent sectional interests were politically mobilized some decades earlier. But, by the same token, the historic compromise which emerged in Australia reflected the special circumstances of its time and place. In Australia sectional conflicts between employers and employees were superimposed over the older cleavage line between the primary and secondary economy, creating a situation in which a class alliance between labour and manufacturing could win the day with a policy of New Protection – offering tariffs for the one in return for wage guarantees for the other. For most of the European states no such compromise was available at the time when social democracy finally overcame the barriers to full political representation. The European economies, and most particulary the smaller ones, reflected the prior resolution of the conflict over the role of manufacturing in favour of free trade coupled to a wages structure which henceforth had to conform to the exigencies of international competition. Under these circumstances the basis for an accommodation, where it was possible to arrange one, was the corporatist trade-off between a labour movement guarantee of the industrial peace required for competitive manufacturing and a degree of social wage enhancement sufficient to compensate those most disadvantaged by the wages structure.[51]

Australia's initial push towards big government was largely a consequence of developmentalism of a 'colonial socialist' character, later augmented by the adoption of welfare schemes designed to cater for those who fell outside the protective ambit of a controlled wages system. The subsequent slowdown in state growth resulted from a shift towards a regulatory mode with respect both to the developmental and equity objectives of Australian public policy. In contrast big government came later to those countries in which infrastructure development was a lesser priority, but followed a steeper trajectory as welfare redistribution became the accepted strategy of compensating for the inequalities generated by the capitalist rewards structure. A regulatory strategy was not appropriate for the European welfare states: relying as they did on the export of finished manufactured goods, protection would have been for them a recipe for economic suicide.

It is, perhaps, less clear why Australia did not opt for a compensatory strategy once it was apparent that this was the favoured solution elsewhere. Indeed there were steps in such a direction, first in the 1920s and 1930s, when the non-Labor parties attempted to introduce contributory social insurance, and later under Whitlam, with an attempted shift to greater universalism and generosity; but the early proposals met implacable opposition and the later ones were never completed. Here, yet again, choice plus a freezing of alternatives rather than complete determinacy is the appropriate perspective. The 1938 National Health and Pensions Act, had it been implemented, would have changed the entire face of the Australian welfare system. More than a generation later, when Whitlam sought to make a radical change to welfare and other policy parameters, the possibilities were still more constrained by the past. Already by the 1920s the Australian way of doing things was becoming an accepted part of the political culture, a taken-for-granted conventional wisdom hallowed by a generation of familiarity and hedged around with the encrustation of established interest coalitions that always lock into place around functioning institutions. Moreover the Australian way of doing things was, until well into the 1960s, a seemingly successful way of doing things. As the Menzies era ended, Australia, despite protection, was experiencing economic growth unprecedented in the twentieth century, and full employment was combined with low inflation. Moreover, whilst academics might point to a degree of poverty in the midst of plenty, there was absolutely no evidence that the strategy of social amelioration based largely on wages control had resulted in greater poverty or inequality than elsewhere.[52] Six decades after Federation the distinctive inheritance of the Australian public policy settlement was no longer such as to make Australia a radical exemplar, but it was hardly such as to imply the need for wholesale change.

Two decades further on, that conclusion no longer holds. In democratic content, if not democratic form, recent years have seen an unfreezing process beginning to occur. That unfreezing is by no means complete or coherent: much of it is going on below the exposed surface of the public policy iceberg in the form of new ideas and greater conflict about the appropriateness of established policy priorities. In terms of outcomes, it is represented in cracks and scars on the surface of the ice. Whitlam's welfare reforms represent one such crack, and the retreat from universality represented by the assets test a scarring of the surface. The drift to free collective bargaining in the late 1960s, and the reimposition of wage indexation and the subsequent emergence of a two-tier bargaining system, manifest a similar process in the arena of wage control. The same phenomenon is apparent in trade policy, with a 25 per cent cut in tariffs and the subsequent imposition of import quotas in industries threatened by overseas competition. There are even signs that dissolving certainties in policy directions may translate into questioning of democratic forms and a search for new institutional mechanisms for democratic conflict resolution. The Accord between the Labor Party and the ACTU, apart from its specific policy proposals, proposed mechanics for its implementation – the creation of EPAC (the Economic Planning and Advisory Council) as a representative tripartite body – which pointed in just such a direction. These developments reflect conflicts and uncertainties generated by serious changes in Australia's economic and social environment.

The option of wholesale change is now on the welfare agenda – when increasing unemployment and the transformation of the family structure have created a situation in which one child in five is reported to be living in poverty. Arbitration no longer commands universal acceptance. On the Left it is seen as an instrument of wage restraint,[53] and on the Right it is seen as a major cause of inflation.[54] Protection and economic regulation are regarded no longer as defences for high wages, full employment and an extended manufacturing base, but rather as an impediment to successful competition in world markets.

The historic compromise of the post-Federation era appears to be breaking up without there being any obvious coherent and consensual alternative. In the late 1980s we have competing visions of a new content for Australian democracy – whether in the shape of a corporatist polity designed to foster economic growth and social amelioration by social partnership as envisaged in the Accord, or in the shape of a deregulated economy and a much limited state as propagandized by the enthusiasts of the H.R. Nicholls Society.

Neither vision as yet appears to offer the basis for a fundamental compromise between the established interests of contemporary Australian society, and both implicitly challenge the present form of Australian democracy: the Accord, by attacking the primacy of the parties as the sole legitimate source of authoritative decision-making, and the rightist vision, by its redefinition of the scope of legitimate political action. That is why, Australian democracy is at the crossroads.

The direction that Australia will take in decades to come is far from clear, and we do not intend to tempt others to play 'Cheat the Prophet' by predicting what it might be. But what is apparent from all that has gone before is that the process of democratic development in Australia and elsewhere is not a matter of the unfolding of some predetermined blueprint, but rather of the choices made by political actors in circumstances constrained by their social structure, economic conditions and historical experience. If the early advent of democratization in Australia was less trammelled by its inheritance from the past than was the case in most countries, that will not be true of the choices Australians may now make about the future shape and content of their democracy. We can only hope that any new direction taken remains strongly influenced by what was most hopeful in the post-Federation historic compromise: the concern that all Australians would have an equitable share in their country's future.

Notes

[1] J. Bryce 1921. *Modern Democracies*. Vol.II. London, Macmillan, p.181.
[2] See C.T. Therborn 1977. The rule of capital and the rise of democracy. *New Left Review*, No.103, pp.3-41.
[3] W.K. Hancock 1930. *Australia*. Brisbane, The Jacaranda Press.
[4] See B. Brugger and D. Jaensch 1985. *Australian Politics: Theory and Practice*. Sydney, Allen and Unwin, p.32.
[5] See, for example, C.H. Grattan 1949. *Introducing Australia*. Sydney, Angus & Robertson, pp.129-34.
[6] See H. Mayer 1956. Some conceptions of the Australian party system 1910-1950. *Historical Studies* 7, p.27.
[7] L. Overacker 1952. *The Australian Party System*. New Haven, Yale University Press.
[8] *ibid.*, p.vii.
[9] See A. Austin (ed.) 1965. *The Webbs' Australian Diary 1898*. Melbourne, Sir Isaac Pitman & Sons Ltd, p.115.
[10] A. Metin 1977. *Socialism Without Doctrine*. Chippendale, NSW, Alternative Publishing Cooperative Ltd, pp.177-91.
[11] J. Bryce 1921. *op.cit.*, p.189.
[12] J. Bryce 1921. *op.cit.*, p.229.
[13] See N.G. Butlin 1964. *Investment in Australian Economic Development*. London, Cambridge University Press; for a revisionist view, see J. Lee and C. Fahey 1986. A boom for whom? Some developments in the Australian labour market, 1870-1891. *Labour History*. May.
[14] See I. Turner 1968. *The Australian Dream*. Melbourne, Sun Books, p.105.
[15] See N.G. Butlin *et al.*, 1982. *Government and Capitalism*. Sydney, Allen and Unwin, p.5-6.
[16] See D. Aitkin 1983. Big government: The Australian experience. *The Australian Quarterly* 55(1), pp.10-11.
[17] H.B. Higgins 1922. *A New Province for Law and Order*. London, Constable & Co.
[18] *ibid.*, p.3.
[19] *ibid.*, p.7.
[20] See S. Macintyre 1985. *Winners and Losers*. Sydney, Allen and Unwin.
[21] W.P. Reeves 1902. State experiments in Australia and New Zealand. Vol.II. Grant Richards, p.289.
[22] See F.G. Castles 1987. Trapped in an historical cul-de-sac: The prospects for welfare reform in Australia. In P. Saunders and A. Jamvozik (eds.), *Social Welfare in the Late 1980's: Reform, Progress or Retreat?* Sydney, Social Welfare Research Centre, pp.91-101.
[23] See A. Austin (ed.) 1965. *op.cit.*
[24] A. Metin 1977. *op.cit.*
[25] W.P. Reeves 1902. *op.cit.*
[26] J. Bryce 1921. *op.cit.*
[27] B. Moore, Jr 1966. *Social Origins of Dictatorship and Democracy*. Boston, Beacon Press, pp.111-55.

[28] See R. Gollan 1960. *Radical and Working Class Politics*. Melbourne, Melbourne University Press, p.50.

[29] See J. Bryce 1921. *op.cit.*, p.286.

[30] V.I. Lenin 1952. In Australia. *Sochineniya*, Gosoz-polit, Moscow, 19, p.188.

[31] J.A. La Nauze 1968. *Federated Australia: Selections from Letters to the Morning Post*. Melbourne, Melbourne University Press, p.196.

[32] See K. Marx 1852. The Chartists. *New York Daily Tribune*, 25 August.

[33] See T. Rowse 1978. *Australian Liberalism and National Character*. Victoria, Kibble Books, pp.37-76.

[34] See G. Therborn 1977. *op.cit.*, pp.23-8.

[35] See S.M. Lipset 1960. *Political Man*. London, Heinemann.

[36] See H.L. Wilensky 1975. *The Welfare State and Equality*. Berkeley, University of California Press.

[37] See D.A. Rustow 1970. *Transitions to Democracy: Towards a Dynamic Model*. Comparative Politics, No.2, pp.337-63.

[38] See F.G. Castles and R. Wildenmann 1986. *Visions and Realities of Party Government*. Berlin, De Gruyter.

[39] See L. Overacker 1952. *op.cit.*, pp.27-9.

[40] See M. Simms 1981. Australia. In J. Lovenduski and J. Hills, *The Politics of the Second Electorate*. London, Routledge and Kegan Paul.

[41] See B.D. Graham 1966. *The Formation of the Australian Country Parties*. Canberra, ANU Press, p.129.

[42] See V. Bogdanor 1981. *The People and the Party System*. London, Cambridge University Press, p.212.

[43] Compare D. Horne 1976. *Death of the Lucky Country*. Victoria, Penguin Books, pp.27-33.

[44] See G. Pasquino 1986. The impact of institutions on party government: Tentative hypotheses. In F.G. Castles and R. Wildenmann, *Visions and Realities of Party Government*. Berlin, De Gruyter, pp.128-9.

[45] G. Sartori 1976. *Parties and Party Systems*. London, Cambridge University Press, pp.187-8.

[46] S.M. Lipset and S. Rokkan 1967. *Party Systems and Voter Alignments*. New York, The Free Press.

[47] J. Schumpeter 1947. *Capitalism, Socialism and Democracy*. New York, Harper & Brothers, p.11.

[48] For a fuller exposition see D. Aitken 1982. *Stability and Change in Australian Politics* (2nd edn). Canberra, ANU Press.

[49] W.K. Hancock 1930. *op.cit.*, p.157.

[50] For an elaboration of this argument see F.G. Castles 1985. *The Working Class and Welfare*. Sydney, Allen and Unwin.

[51] See P.J. Katzenstein 1985. *Small States in World Markets*. Ithaca, Cornell University Press.

[52] See R.F. Henderson, A. Harcourt and R.J.A. Harper 1970. *People in Poverty: A Melbourne Survey*. Melbourne, Cheshire.

[53] See F. Stillwell 1986. *The Accord . . . and Beyond*. Sydney, Pluto Press.

[54] See P.A. McGavin 1987. *Wages and Whitlam*. Melbourne, Oxford University Press.

11

Australia in the World

J.D.B. Miller

Australia's place in the world alters with time, because of changes in itself and in its international environment. At various periods Australians have been exhorted to think of themselves as being in the British Empire, as belonging to the West, as having a special place in 'our region' and as part of Asia. Foreign policy has to take account of assertions like these; it also has to work out how the actions of foreigners are likely to affect Australia. This chapter attempts to see the country's present situation in terms of how its attitudes and policies have developed in the past.

A suitable point of departure is the chapter on 'Foreign Policy' in W.K. Hancock's *Australia*,[1] published in 1930 when Australia had no Department of Foreign Affairs and no ambassadors abroad; when the United States still regarded it as part of Britain; when there was no Statute of Westminster; and when the dominant political attitude in Australia was to regard an independent foreign policy as disloyal. Hancock had no wish to be disloyal; indeed, he made clear his belief in the value of the British Commonwealth. What he did was to show that Australia was committed to a particular view of the world by what it did at home. Its social policies, he pointed out, had effects abroad: a restrictive immigration policy had implications for foreign countries, as did the other 'settled policies' about which he wrote. He indicated how insistent had been W.M. Hughes' demand at the Paris Peace Conference that Australia should have control of the islands to its north, and showed that this proprietary attitude was in no sense new, having been often expressed by the Australian colonies in the nineteenth century. Australians then, he suggested, had seen themselves as part of the world as a whole, but only sometimes: 'Their attitude to the outside world was one of indifference, shaken by occasional spasms of alarm'. In the twentieth century, in deciding to have a navy of their own, they had accepted burdens as well as benefits in terms of defence. They knew that 'Australia's future is, to a considerable degree, bound up with the future of the Pacific'; but a good deal of nonsense was being talked about 'that rather over-rated ocean', and for the time being their future lay very much with Britain and not with the United States. 'Economically, Australia still remains joined to Europe, where her best markets lie. This economic interest implies some sort of a political interest in the affairs of Europe, of the Mediterranean and of Egypt'. Hancock thought the commonwealth bond would persist, partly because of Australia's 'strong feeling of racial individuality. America has too many foreigners and hybrids!' Australians were still 'passionately convinced of their rightness in keeping themselves "ninety-eight per cent British" '.

This is a fair picture of how things stood in the 1930s. It does not describe the situation in the late 1980s. In particular there have been changes in the nature of Australia's dependence on other countries, in the forms of expression and the content of Australian nationalism, and in the approaches taken by Australian policy and public opinion towards particular countries and groups of countries. For many years Australia has had an active foreign policy, expressed through many international agencies and by a variety of means. Instead of acting as part of the British Empire – and latterly of the British Commonwealth – it has operated as a sovereign state with relationships often closer and more cordial with foreign countries than with the original 'mother country'. The claim to be 98 per cent British has long been discarded. The White Australia Policy is dead. Many young Australians have names that recall continental Europe, even though they speak and act like those whose names recall the British Isles. It is a different country; but how different?

DEPENDENCY

It is still a dependent country. All countries depend to some extent on others: the United States and the Soviet Union, which are superpowers, depend on their allies for space and military manpower, on their customers for trade and on what is vaguely called 'world opinion' – selectively chosen – for approval of their policies. Neither is self-sufficient in every important respect. Middle powers such as Canada, India and Iran can hardly be called entirely independent, and neither can those of Western and Eastern Europe. But there are degrees of dependency, and one form of dependency can be more significant than another. We can still speak of independence, while recognizing that some states have more of it than others. Independence for a state means freedom of action in situations in which freedom is desired. Any state's independence is exercised within a system of more or less interdependence with others. Australia has experienced interdependence from its very beginnings; the nature and extent of this interdependence, and the degree of one-sidedness which it has involved, have decided the extent to which it can be called dependent or independent.

Australia was dependent on the United Kingdom for the first century and a half of white settlement. In political terms, this first involved direct dependence in the sense that British policies could be imposed upon the Australian colonies whenever the British authorities wished. That initial political dependence, modified from the 1850s onwards, was augmented by direct dependence in terms of defence: throughout the first century of Australia's existence Britain was Australia's shield, known and valued as such by the colonists. Federation did not change the situation. Until World War II that dependence on Britain for defence was seen in terms of the global operations of the Royal Navy, in spite of Australia's contribution by way of its own navy, justly celebrated by Hancock. Thereafter it was the United States on which Australians believed their defence depended. A totally independent Australian defence has been suggested from time to time, but has never gained majority support, and has never been adopted by any federal government. A major protector is still important.

Australia has also been a dependent economy, in the sense that its national wealth has continued to be drawn very largely from the sale of commodities overseas in spite of the fact that these commodities (e.g., wool, wheat, meat, sugar, minerals) have been produced by a steadily decreasing proportion of the population. Its manufacturing industry, developed to a great extent under the shadow of tariffs and other restrictive practices, has been largely the result of investment from abroad by multinational corporations, first from Britain and later from the United States and Japan. Australian domestic investment has gone into houses and land, government bonds and to a considerable extent into farming; it has gone into retail trade, banking and insurance; it has established some factories, and has been important in the oil industry and in the development of iron ore and coal. Nevertheless there is a constant demand for investment from overseas, especially by multinational corporations.

This has made Australia heavily dependent on others in industrial research and development, in spite of the high level of scientific capacity in such fields as medicine and physics, and the rural research of the CSIRO. The markets that mattered to Australian exports began to change in the 1950s and 60s, moving from Britain to Japan, the United States and Western Europe, and involving Southeast Asia and to some extent China; but the kinds of exports remained the same, except that minerals assumed a larger place in the 1960s. When commodity prices fell in the 1980s, and seemed likely to stay low, Australian manufacturers were unable to make up the deficit in the balance of payments: their factories were designed to serve the home market behind the tariff, to export a little to neighbouring countries like New Zealand and Papua New Guinea, and to do their part in the worldwide operations of the multinationals which owned them, but they were in no position to expand exports or display the high technology of the contemporary world. This state of things, true of automobiles, chemicals and oil, was less true of steel; but the lessening importance of heavy industry made steel exports difficult, even if BHP had wanted to expand them. In its non-steel operations BHP was still dependent on foreign corporations' cooperation.

Dependence in trade has been paralleled throughout Australian history by dependence in investment. This is most obvious in manufactures and mining; but it was evident throughout the nineteenth and early twentieth centuries in respect of public works, and continues to be so in the 1980s in regard to the balance of payments, which has been kept in some sort of order by extensive borrowing to cover the deficit. When the Australian dollar was at last allowed to float in 1986, after many decades of central bank management of its value and that of its predecessor the Australian pound, international investors proved to be highly sensitive to such indicators as the degree of inflation and unemployment in Australia, and the extent to which its wage system was responsive to the country's capacity to earn abroad.

Australia has also been dependent in its culture. Writers and artists have constantly attempted to find effective Australian images and to picture those aspects of the landscape and society which could be regarded as distinctively Australian; but they have done so as elements in a worldwide pattern of English-speaking countries in the one case and artistic fashion – starting with Paris and now extending to New York – on the other. Interdependence is clearer in the arts than elsewhere. Australia has found that any attempt to base the whole of its art on indigenous themes, like that of the Jindyworabaks of the 1940s, is doomed to failure. Music, painting, the novel and the drama have all found increasingly Australian subjects, but the thrust of each activity has been greatly affected by international models.

Looking at the problem of dependence in defence, trade, investment and culture, one can see that while the location of the source of dependence has altered with time – from Britain in defence, trade and investment to Japan and the United States, from strictly British models in the arts to continental European and American – the fact of dependence has remained. One should recognize, however, that to a considerable extent it has been merged in that of interdependence. In defence, for example, the situation of complete dependence on Britain before World War II has turned to one in which the United States, while acknowledged as Australia's ultimate protector, is glad that Australia responds by providing room for electronic installations that enable the United States to defend itself more securely

230

against the Soviet Union, while Australia's influence amongst the small states of the South Pacific assists with acceptance of policies which might not be so easy to sell if the United States itself were pushing them. In trade, while Australian dependence is accentuated by the vulnerability of its commodities in world markets, Australia is attractive as a market for other rich countries' goods. The Australian need for other rich countries' money is paralleled by those countries' desire to profit from the prodigality of natural resources available for exploitation in Australia. At times of general recession the incentive to invest is low; but when conditions change Australia provides more opportunities than many competing countries. In culture there was until recently little interdependence, since Australia, in spite of Dame Nellie Melba, Joan Sutherland, Percy Grainger, Henry Handel Richardson and others, was a taker rather than a giver; but in the 1970s and 80s Australian films have shown that in mass culture Australia can give as well as receive.

Interdependence, then, is more of a fact than in the days when Australian nationalism was formed; but this in itself has created problems for those who think of themselves as Australian nationalists.

NATIONALISM

Articulate nationalism is normally a reaction against actual or supposed domination: it is an assertion of indigenous values and ways against those of a foreign superior, a statement of a local position which stresses local virtues and insists on the right of local people to live their lives in their own way, as against a regime imposed from outside. It can also be a mere statement of patriotic pride. The expression of nationalism can be through cultural means, through political action, through the cultivation of sentiment which exalts local symbols; it can operate through the exclusion of people or goods from other countries, through the assertion of national uniqueness, and through such tangible symbols as service in war and prowess in sport. Australia has experienced all of these in expressing indignation about others and simple pride in local virtues.

Australian nationalism began as a reaction against British control. Wentworth's complaints about autocratic rule in the 1820s, Daniel Deniehy's attack on the idea of a 'bunyip aristocracy' in 1854, Parkes' ideal of a continent for a nation and a nation for a continent in the 1890s and Daniel Mannix's refusal to accept conscription for a 'sordid trade war' in World War I were all protests against the assumption that Australia was simply an extension of Britain – whether the protests were made in terms of 'the rights of Englishmen' abroad or not. In Sydney *The Bulletin*'s attacks on 'Fat', the British investor, and its railings at the monarchy were part of the same tendency, like Higinbotham's contempt for 'a person named Rogers' who presumed to give directions to the elected government of Victoria in the 1860s. In the late nineteenth century Australian nationalists were prone to cite the example of the United States, which, at a time when its people were overwhelmingly British in origin, had 'cut the painter' because of overbearing British policies.

In World War I Australian nationalism gained something of a new face (though one which had fleetingly made its appearance during the Boer War) because of dissatisfaction at the ineptitude of British commanders and the waste of Australian lives. The Easter Rebellion of 1916, and the attempt to impose conscription on Australia, gave Australian nationalism an especially Irish tinge. The split in the Labor Party over conscription left the field of radical nationalism clear for those who were Irish and Catholic in origin, and anxious to identify the wrongs of their mother-country with those of Australia. It also kept Labor out of office.

This set of circumstances largely explains the decline of vehement Australian nationalism between the two world wars, at least at the governmental level. The men who governed Australia in the 1920s and 30s were mostly British and Protestant in origin; they and their parties, the Nationalist, Country and United Australia parties, delighted in their Britishness and proclaimed their undying loyalty to the flag and throne. This did not prevent them from driving a hard bargain with Britain when trade questions came up, or from giving tacit approval to the anarchic nationalist image of the first AIF; nor did it prevent an Australian government from being fussily arrogant about the 'bodyline' controversy of 1932–33. It did, however, largely discredit the nationalist image of an Australia essentially independent and indigenous in its attitudes and policies. Hancock's 1930 statement should be seen against this background.

The aggressively conservative approach to Australia's connection with Britain did not survive the Pacific War, because of Britain's failure to provide the protection which Australians had been taught to assume was their right. The events of 1942 gave a new impetus to Australian nationalism. Ironically this occurred in the process of transferring to a new protector, the United States, but the new protector could not (and did not wish to) claim the same ethnic relationship with Australia as Britain, and did not carry on its politics in a similar way. This time people could exalt the achievement of Australian troops without having to identify them with the protector. Instead the sense of having been temporarily isolated and then rescued by the United States caused Australians both to value the continued link with the new protector and to cultivate their own sense of national individuality.

The events of the post-war world have accentuated this tendency. It has no longer been necessary to express Australian nationalism as a reaction against another country, except by those to whom the other country is anathema. Threats have been perceived on the part of external powers – the Soviet Union, China, Indonesia – often with no more basis than the Australian belief that such a desirable country as their own must inevitably be the target of other peoples' designs. These 'threats', however, have been so lacking in substance that none has provided anything like the same impetus to national feeling as the Japanese threat in World War II. Instead the main force of Australian nationalism has gone into the cultivation of local myths – centred on such diverse symbols as the Aborigines, the bushrangers, the Anzacs, the unsuccessful explorers, the sporting heroes and the campaigners for women's rights – intended to show that Australians are a distinctive people. The symbols have been heavily employed by advertising agencies and by leftist propagandists for protest against the United States, but their principal effect has been to build up a national consciousness, often badly astray in its history and poorly expressed by its images, though perhaps appropriate to a society attempting to persuade large numbers of immigrants from the Mediterranean, the Middle East and Southeast Asia that there was something distinctive for them to embrace.

What has been the effect of this enhanced nationalism upon Australians' attitudes to the outside world? It must be remembered that it has appeared at a time when the characteristic impulse of Australians – an overwhelmingly petit-bourgeois people – has been to cling to the Western alliance in order to avoid attacks from forces which might destroy the kind of society to which they were accustomed. This has meant that nationalist sentiment, always at its strongest when directed against some supposed or actual dominance, has needed to find room for the connection with allies and associated countries. Australian nationalism has had to accommodate itself to dependence on the United States, a situation which has proved impossible for the Left in politics. Leftist sentiment seems now to equate nationalism, republicanism and anti-Americanism.

From the 1950s onwards, Australians have learnt more about the outside world than ever before. Restrictions on travel imposed by depression and war which isolated the country in the 1930s and 40s were removed, and a variety of influences came into play. These included television supplementing radio and newspapers; the satellite taking over from the telegraph wire; and jet planes and the cheap holiday enabling people to overcome the limitations of time and space which the steamship and the railway train had imposed on them. In addition knowledge of other countries has increased with the appearance of many thousands of migrants from non-English-speaking countries. Again the greater ease of travel has co-incided with a period in which the contacts of Australian businessmen, academics, journalists, officials and others with foreign countries have greatly increased. Compared with the 1920s, 30s and 40s – periods in which very few Australians travelled, and then largely to Britain – the 1950s, 60s, 70s and 80s have been decades of constant movement, involving the discovery of Japan, Southeast Asia and the United States.

In this period of intensified foreign travel and contact with peoples from other societies, Australian national sentiment has come to terms with a different view of the world economy from that which prevailed until some years after World War II. The earlier view had emphasized the importance of Australian self-reliance in manufacturing and foodstuffs, the means to ensure this being protective tariffs in the one case, and subsidies and the search for sheltered markets in the other. The outside world provided investment and markets, but the markets were seen as risky; the development of an industry at home was preferred to letting foreigners compete in the local market.

In the late 1980s the situation is very different. Even the most strident nationalist is reluctant to maintain that Australia should aim at self-sufficiency. Protection for manufactures has been under siege for many years. Primary products compete in the world market without subsidy. Australian spokesmen lecture the United States and the European Community for their agricultural protectionism. There are preferences in the Australian market for products from under-developed countries. Calls for import restrictions and higher tariffs – as in the balance of payments crisis of 1986 – are answered by the government in terms of the need for reciprocity with major trading countries, and for competition in the local market. This is a long way from Hancock's Australia, with its indifference to the outside world and occasional spasms of alarm. Alarm, when it occurs, is now supposed to be met by different remedies.

The conventional Australian nationalism which has emerged from these various influences, and which can be detected in official policy, is more sophisticated about the world at large, though perhaps more gullible about the character of the Australian people than that which it replaced. It is the product of a more cosmopolitan Australia in which far more people know at first hand about the world outside than was the case in earlier periods, when that knowledge was confined largely to the British Isles and to the battlefields of France and the Middle East. It is replete with local symbols and gives as much significance as ever to sporting triumphs; but it shows more understanding of the world economy and is discriminating in its approach to particular foreign countries. It has, for example, accommodated itself not only to the United States as a protector, but also to the former enemy Japan as a principal market and source of investment, and to Southeast Asia and the South Pacific as areas of prime importance. It is still inclined to blame foreigners for the country's woes, but not with such stridency as before. The notion of interdependence in both economics and politics is more widely understood.

However there is more than one strand of nationalism in the Australian political system. That which has just been described can be said to stretch from somewhere on the centre Right to the centre Left, with less disagreement on the extreme Right of the spectrum than on the extreme Left. People on that end of the spectrum (including some of those who inherit the political values of the once monolithic Communist Party of Australia, together with those to whom radical ideas are attractive as such, and those who are deeply troubled by the possibilities of nuclear war) reject much of this view of the world. They would dispute that the United States, Japan and Western Europe are the places with which Australia should be closely associated; they are suspicious of notions of interdependence when these seem to imply that Australia's dependent position must be accepted; and they emphatically reject an alliance with the United States. In all these respects their sense of nationalism is offended. Instead of the rich capitalist countries, they regard the countries of the Third World as those which a truly independent Australia would recognize as its natural associates. They view interdependence as more of a moral than a political or economic imperative: Australia has an obligation to assist countries less well-off than itself. Above all they think that Australia should free itself from dependence on the United States in foreign policy and defence. Self-reliant neutral countries such as Sweden and Switzerland are often held up as examples to be followed. Australia's past readiness to welcome US installations and to allow nuclear-armed US naval ships into its ports is regarded as weakness and foolishness, since US defence of Australia in an emergency is by no means assured, and the installations would be likely to attract nuclear attack from the Soviet Union in the event of a war between the superpowers.

Those who adopt the more conventional view would argue that their sense of nationalism is no less genuine than that of the Left, but is distinguished by a greater realism and a greater awareness of Australia's interests. They would maintain that a country is not necessarily any less independent because it freely cooperates with others or because it recognizes its own lack of power and comes to terms with strong allies. They would also say that Australia's need for imports to keep up its standard of living requires that it export to other rich countries, and that any attempt to tie Australia's fortunes to those of the Third World would soon lead to a drop in standards in Australia itself.

Probably Australian nationalism will continue to display two aspects, one which stresses the country's need to accept the requirements of complex interdependence, and the other which puts independence first and judges all policies by the extent to which they seem to limit Australia's possible freedom of action. Almost certainly governments of all political complexions will adopt the first of these stances. The notion of independence first, come what may, is attractive to oppositions, especially to those elements of opposition which are unlikely to be called upon to govern. It is much harder to translate into practical policies; public opinion shows no sign of accepting it as a majority viewpoint.

To some extent the two aspects of Australian nationalism are embodied in the two sides of Australian politics, though to identify Labor too closely with the radical aspect, and the Liberal and National parties with the conventional, would be a mistake. Labor must, it is true, somehow incorporate or temporarily satisfy the demands of its Left wing; but this process is largely symbolic and rhetorical when Labor is in office, and its leaders stick fairly closely to the conventional line. Similarly a Liberal-National coalition government will give much less support to South Africa in practice than its more conservative members might wish. There is normally considerable agreement between the front benches, especially evident in their combined defence of Indonesia against the hostility often found on both back benches. The parties do differ on details from time to time and tend to magnify their differences for electoral purposes; but their performance in office is often much the same.

A similar situation occurs with defence. Here, however, performance may well diverge more between the two sides, although basic attitudes remain the same. Both are committed to an effective local defence and to support for the ANZUS alliance. Labor is likely to give more emphasis to the first and the Liberal-Nationals (especially in opposition) to the second. Labor's history emphasizes either opposition or scepticism towards 'forward defence' (i.e., the use of Australian forces in other countries); the other parties have a history of ardent support for the wars in which Britain and the United States were senior partners. In practice, however, the United States' movement away from wars in Asia in the 1970s and 80s, together with the very real difficulties of defending the Australian coastline against small or substantial incursions, has meant that local defence has become a first priority. There is still the prospect of rhetorical disagreement between the parties.

In the execution of both foreign affairs and defence, the influence of officials is of considerable importance. Australia now has a substantial bureaucracy in both areas. It is big enough to allow for a certain amount of difference of opinion about where the emphasis in policy should fall: ministers are somewhat more tolerant towards heterodoxy than in the 1940s and 50s, when departmental staffs were smaller and ministers more dictatorial. All the same, the departments of Foreign Affairs and Defence do tend towards 'departmental lines', which change slowly. 'Forward defence' was common to both for many years, along with the conviction that Australian security required an armed American presence in Southeast Asia. Both were slow to recognize the importance of the Pacific islands; both tended in the 1960s and 70s to exaggerate Australia's importance to the countries of ASEAN. Neither knows as much as it should about the United States. In any case the primary concern of both is not policy but what might be called housekeeping – the preservation and enhancement of establishments, posts, bases, equipment and careers. The same is true of such departments in many other countries. Policy becomes a preoccupation in time of crisis, but otherwise precedent is the normal guide.

THE BRITISH CONNECTION

Having seen how dependence and national sentiment have altered under the pressure of events since Hancock wrote, we can now look at contemporary Australian policy and attitudes towards particular countries.

It is natural to begin with Britain. Australians live in a society characterized by the English language, the English legal system, a monarch shared with the British, table manners which come directly from Britain, television programmes which often do the same, vehicles which drive on the left, and churches, professional organizations, trade unions, universities and armed forces which derive from Britain. The cultural heritage is strong, and is reinforced by the occasional political group, such as the Returned Servicemen's League, which puts great weight upon the monarchy and the memories of united action in war. Yet three major influences have been at work to reduce the British connection to less significance than it has ever possessed before: the change in immigration, the change in trade and the change in foreign policy.

The change in immigration began in the 1950s when migrants were actively sought from continental Europe, in contrast with the previous practice of looking exclusively to the British Isles. It has continued in a diversified fashion, so that now Australia's population is recruited from a very wide range of countries – still including Britain, but with much less prominence than in the past. The lack of emphasis upon recruitment from Britain is paralleled by a lack of mention of the interests of British immigrants once they come to Australia, in comparison with the stress upon the interests of other ethnic groups.

Non-British migrants are confronted by, and have to adjust to, a society in which the main institutions are British in origin. This in itself does not lead to hostility towards Britain, but it does engender a determination that British people should not gain special opportunities in a society in which their background gives them a built-in advantage, if only in language. Thus there was pressure to abolish the advantages which 'British subjects' possessed in obtaining citizenship and employment in public services. Governments have responded to pressure of this kind, as they have to that which called for various forms of assistance to non-British ethnic groups. The result has been to devalue the British connection from its previous high state, and to encourage the belief that a British monarch and a flag with the Union Jack in the corner are unsuited to a multicultural Australia. Whether these assertions are true or not, they tend in the long run to reduce the general Australian concern for Britain. The sense of emotional unity – so strong in 1914 when Andrew Fisher expressed it, and in 1939 when Robert Menzies gave it voice – is now difficult to arouse, except in highly specialized company.

The change in trade has been massive and has had major effects on opinion. It can be briefly stated: in the late 1940s Britain took over 40 per cent of Australian exports, while in 1982–83 it took just over 5 per cent. The fall in imports from Britain was not quite so spectacular but was of the same order. In addition the preferences which Australian exports of foodstuffs enjoyed in the British market from 1932 onwards were withdrawn when Britain entered the European Community. Today it is the right of entry of Australian goods into the EEC that matters, not whether the British will buy them or not. Britain is only one member of a community, the entry policies of which are set, in respect of agricultural produce, very largely by the interests of continental countries with farmers who produce much the same things as Australia produces. In the Australian market Britain still sells quality goods such as woollens, whisky and certain types of machinery, but there is no sentiment about the sale. 'Buy British' now seems to have much the same appeal in Australia as 'Buy French' or 'Buy Italian', or even 'Buy Japanese'. It was different in the 1930s and 40s.

The effect of the change in trade upon Australian attitudes towards Britain is much the same as that of the change in immigration: to make Britain less visible, to decrease the degree of sentiment and the influence it may have, to merge Britain in a larger entity (Europe in the case of trade, the world in respect of immigration) and to remove Britain from the sphere of what might be thought of as Australia's vital interests. In the 1930s and 40s the sense of dependence on Britain in culture and defence was powerfully augmented by a belief that only Britain could be counted on to buy Australia's exports.

The change in foreign policy was not a matter of disagreement about fundamental issues (Australia, like Britain, continues to support alliance with the United States against possible attack from the Soviet Union and its associates), but of the effects of geography. Britain's withdrawal from East of Suez, and its concentration upon Europe, have meant its disappearance from those parts of the world which Australian governments have come to regard as the most important. In the 1960s, while Britain retained its interest in Malaysia and was still a colonial power in the Pacific, it was possible to think of the British effort in these areas as being complementary to the American and as serving Australian interests in something like the same way. The major divergence occurred with the Vietnam War, although there had been an irritating split in respect of Communist China.

When the United States decided to send troops in force to Vietnam in 1965, and Australia did the same, Australia was embarking for the first time upon a war in which Britain played no part. Britain's continued abstention from the conflict meant that Australia was denied much of the emotional support – and, to some extent, the diplomatic support – which it had experienced in the two world wars and the Korean War of the 1950s. Continued British reluctance to be involved in Asian affairs in the 1970s and 80s has meant that the two countries' activities have taken different paths. It is now difficult to find an issue of practical concern – apart, that is, from the expression of 'democratic' aims – upon which they could combine in positive action.

There would have been more concern in Australia about this divergence if the ground had not been laid by the changes in immigration and trade. It is now far more difficult than in the 1950s to think of Britain and Australia as indissolubly united. When their similarities are discussed, the emphasis is necessarily upon the past. With social composition and patterns of trade grown so dissimilar, it is easy for Australians to accept the idea that Britain has little relevance to their future – especially since the EEC is continually represented by Australian governments as adopting policies which strike at the root of Australia's prosperity.

THE AMERICAN CONNECTION

It is quite otherwise when one turns to Australian attitudes and policies towards the United States. This is a question of much greater importance to the Australian government, and to articulate public opinion, than any issue relating to Britain. Whether one is thinking in terms of defence, foreign policy, economic advantage or cultural connection, one becomes aware of the prime importance of the United States. To Australian governments (as to those of so many of the associates of the United States) there is nothing more important than the American approach to major questions. The same is true of Australian radicals, though in the opposite direction.

As already indicated, the association with the United States in defence is a divisive issue amongst Australians who think and talk about foreign policy. The problem is heightened by the fact that, as in many other countries, the question of whether to be allied with the United States is complicated by attitudes towards America as a society, and concern about the place of the United States in the world economy. The United States bulks so large in most countries' lives that it cannot be regarded as simply a factor in international politics. Through television, movies, books and magazines, through investment and the activities of multilateral corporations and through its nuclear strength and economic prominence, it cuts a figure that can nowhere be ignored, but about the significance of which peoples can find themselves deeply divided.

This said, it should be stated that no Australian government is likely to court the displeasure of a US administration, although it is normal for Australian governments to complain about the activities of the US Congress when these threaten Australian export income. An administration which became hostile to Australia would not need to go to war in order to create alarm and despondency. Its influence with investors, its tacit word to

Congress that discrimination against Australian exports would meet with no presidential opposition and its pressure upon countries in Asia and the Pacific, would be quite sufficient. Whether Australia would deserve such attention, or would receive it if deserved, is another question. Australian governments are aware of the possibility and it effectively prevents them from hasty or tendentious statements about basic American policy.

It is not only this fear, however, that causes Australian governments to be so favourable towards the United States. It is also the recognition that most Australians value the US alliance and are attracted by the glitter and the evident promise of American life. The social differences between the two countries – especially the former Australian belief, to which Hancock referred, that 'America has too many foreigners and hybrids!' – have become much less obvious with the passage of time. The Australia of 1930 had relatively few contacts with the United States apart from the movies. The prevailing image of the United States was largely that which Australia got by way of Britain – one which was suffused by the conviction, common in British official circles between the wars, that the United States was an upstart society striving to suborn Britain's dependencies and to replace Britain as a power, especially in the world economy. This kind of popular image has been replaced by one which combines the superpower with the mixture of folksiness and street smartness characteristic of American television programs. The many Australians in business, government and education who have been able to see the United States at first hand have supplemented the popular image by one of more accuracy in circles in which an understanding of American attitudes has been important.

Above all, however, it is the sense of dependence in defence that counts in Australian consideration of the United States. Although it is common to attribute this to American support in World War II, it would be better to regard that experience as the beginning of the sense of dependence rather than as a single cause. The wartime experience has been fortified (and to a large extent replaced) by the events of the post-war period, and by the Australian belief that defence is needed against possible attack from either the Soviet Union or a hostile Asian power, or both. From the desire for protection against attack has grown an acceptance of a large-scale system of mutual cooperation which connects with the United States' alliances in Western Europe and East Asia. The American installations in Australia are defended by governments as contributing to a world-wide system of deterrence of the Soviet Union. While ANZUS is recognized as committing the United States to at least moral support of Australia in the event of some local conflict distinct from the global contest between the superpowers, it is considered naive in Australian government circles to believe that moral support would be accompanied by military activity: Australia must defend itself in local conflicts, but is part of a world-wide network in support of the overall American position. Australia's 'dependence' is thus indirect to a considerable extent, is accepted as such by Australian governments, but may not be understood so widely within the community as a whole. Nevertheless the fact that Australia is a junior partner in the overall US operation is probably acceptable to most Australians, whose basic anti-Communism has never been seriously in dispute.

EQUIVOCAL CONNECTIONS

Approaches to the other superpower, the Soviet Union, are not difficult to describe or explain. Since the beginning of the Cold War Australian governments have taken a stern view of the aims and practices of the Soviet Union, and have acted accordingly at the United

Nations and in other international forums. In this they have been supported by Australian public opinion. Labor governments have been hardly less sceptical about Soviet intentions than coalition governments. In economic terms, Australia has been happy to sell wheat and other commodities to the Soviets, but never with a belief that the sales would continue: windfall gains are all that could be expected. Whether official hostility has gone too far is debatable, but it shows little sign of lessening. Anti-Communism in Australia has a solid basis in the country's petit-bourgeois traditions. This has been reinforced in recent times by the determined anti-Soviet beliefs of many immigrants from east and central Europe, and by the Jewish community's reaction to Soviet policies in the Middle East and towards Soviet Jews.

The most significant changes in Australian attitudes and policies have taken place towards Asia. Those relating to Britain, the United States and the Soviet Union have been developments or contractions in previous approaches; in regard to Asia, however, there have been major reversals.

To speak of 'Asia' in this way is to invite rebuke, since there is no single Asia, and those parts of it which form distinctive regions have little respect or sympathy towards one another. Similarly Australia has had varying policies towards them; but Australians do customarily speak of Asia as a unity. This is perhaps an outcome of their traditional vagueness about places which are now said to be Australia's neighbours, but is more likely to result from their longstanding belief that 'Asia' constitutes a threat to Australia. This notion, applied at different times to Japan, China and Indonesia, is a kind of guilt-ridden consequence of Australians' traditional view that they inhabit a highly desirable continent which millions of Asians wish to live in, and that the comparatively small size of the Australian population provides an opportunity to these Asians which can be nullified only by Australia's obtaining a protector with massive strength. For many years one means of dealing with the so-called problem was the White Australia Policy, but this served only to keep Asians at arm's length, not to deter their governments from what were presumed to be their designs on Australia.

Japan's advance towards Australia in 1942, together with the bombing of Darwin and the minor attempts on Sydney and Newcastle, was seen at the time as confirmation of the traditional Australian belief that a dominant Asian power would attack the country. 'He's Coming South!' shouted the propaganda posters of the day, depicting a ferocious figure more generally Asian than specifically Japanese. Yet in the post-war period this attitude has disappeared under the pressure of Japan's becoming Australia's most important trading partner. The same has been true of the anti-Chinese attitudes and policies which were so evident after the Communist takeover of China in 1949, and which lasted for a quarter of a century. It is not quite true of the popular approach to Indonesia, which continues to be one of doubt, in spite of the attempts of one Australian government after another to assure people that Indonesia is a good neighbour. But the general change in attitude is unmistakable: Asian countries, even when they have been viewed as threats in the past, can become valued 'neighbours' in Australian thinking. The movement of policy is towards much closer association with them.

Japan and China provide striking examples of this tendency, but much the same applies to changes in Australian approaches to Southeast Asia. Before World War II countries such as Thailand, Malaysia and Singapore – together with the Dutch East Indies, now Indonesia – were treated as insignificant, since they were under European control or influence and had only a slight trading connection with Australia. Their peoples were lumped in with other

Asians. It is now commonplace to regard the ASEAN countries as highly important to Australia and to try to expand contact in such sophisticated fields as investment while valuing their people as students and settlers in Australia. Australian tourists throng to them. In this case, as in those of Japan and China, the images which formerly strengthened Australian nationalism have been adjusted to take account of inescapable aspects of politics and economics. Australian do not need to think of themselves as 'part of Asia' in order to recognize that in future they may have more connection with East and Southeast Asia than with Europe. The fact that Australia fought an unsuccessful war in Vietnam, along with the occasional criticism by ASEAN countries of Australian trade, airline and education policies, may dampen Australian enthusiasm about Southeast Asia, but will not extinguish the sense of closeness and concern.

One other area that can be linked with Asia when thinking about Australian approaches to other countries is the South Pacific. This is the one part of the world in which Australia looks like a major power. To the island states of the South Pacific, of which Papua New Guinea and Fiji are the most important, Australia and even New Zealand appear to be important places which provide not only trade but also aid and advice, countries which can be cultivated with advantage and which can provide support when the small states have to confront the superpowers and others of consequence. Australians may not yet be fully conscious that the islands have become sovereign states; but Australian governments have become very much aware of the position which their country holds in the South Pacific Forum.

Australian foreign-aid policy began in the 1950s with an emphasis upon the Indian sub-continent and Southeast Asia. It is now aimed at countries near to Australia. The independence of Papua New Guinea in 1975 meant that the previous Australian subventions to its former colony had to be converted into aid to another sovereign state if Papua New Guinea's development schemes and administrative structure were to be preserved. The growing salience of other, smaller states in the South Pacific – subject to economic difficulties, population problems and natural disasters – indicated the need to extend the aid programme to these. At the same time the ASEAN states were either increasing in prosperity, like Malaysia, Thailand and Singapore, or falling into economic and political disarray, like the Philippines; in either case, opportunities to provide significant Australian aid were decreasing. The island states were the beneficiaries – although budget cuts in Australia have to some extent reduced their advantage.

Relations with other states in the South Pacific are amongst the most important aspects of the connection between Australia and New Zealand. There is considerable agreement between the two, in spite of the disturbance to their relations caused by the Lange government's refusal in 1985 to allow nuclear-armed and powered ships into its ports, and the consequent withdrawal of American defence cooperation from New Zealand. Australia and New Zealand have continued with bilateral defence arrangements. Both are prominent in the South Pacific Forum. Australia's special concerns are with Melanesian countries such as Papua New Guinea and Vanuatu, New Zealand's with the Polynesian states such as Fiji and Western Samoa; but both agree that they should coordinate policy as much as possible towards such matters of importance to other members as French nuclear testing and the future of New Caledonia.

*   *   *

FURTHER ISSUES

The countries considered so far represent direct and continuing interests on the part of Australia. It is easy to see why they seem important to the Department of Foreign Affairs, even if the importance may be declining, as in the case of Britain, or a matter of prospects rather than achievement, as with China. But global political interdependence means that problems are created for countries such as Australia by having to take account of the situation of others with which they may not be directly connected. It is notable, for example, that questions involving South Africa have become much more immediate to Australian governments in the 1970s and 80s, not because of any particular connection between South Africa and Australia, but because *apartheid* in South Africa is a matter of moment to the forty or so other African states, and these have made the issue one of significance to the Third World at large. Developed countries such as Australia have taken increased notice of South Africa because of the clamour of opposition to its racial policies. Similarly the position of Israel which has been of some significance to Australian authorities for forty years because of the interest taken in it by the Jewish community, has lately become a major issue because of Third World agitation about the Palestinians. Even Latin America, an area almost entirely distinct from previous Australian interests, has intruded upon both policy and opinion because of the policies of the United States towards Cuba, Chile and Nicaragua, and because of the indignation of Australian radicals and some Third World governments.

The prominence of issues such as these in the eyes of Australian interest groups, editorialists, television interviewers and the like is a reflection of increased interdependence. They bring into question the relations which Australia has with countries of more direct concern, especially the United States. Australian approaches to them are a test of both nationalism and dependence: is there a distinctive Australian contribution to the solution of the problems involved, and how is such a solution likely to be affected by the degree of dependence in which Australia stands to the United States and, to a lesser degree, to regional associates such as Indonesia? These are continuing tests of diplomacy, as are global questions of arms control, the regime of the seas and the control of commodity prices.

FUTURE PROSPECTS

Australia's position in the world is thus one in which dependence and nationalism sometimes create conflict, but are more often balanced by an official policy which attempts to recognize the limitations which global interdependence places on Australia's freedom of action and tries to get the best deal it can in both political and economic negotiation. The issue of defence remains one in which Australian opinion and Australian policy unite in adherence to the notion of a protector; but in this sphere there is articulate opposition from a minority which asserts that Australian independence should come first in any formulation of official policy. Australia has become one of the notable countries of the Pacific, no longer 'that rather over-rated ocean', and its influence in the South Pacific is considerable, though it is unlikely to repeat those spurts of proprietorship over the islands which were a feature of colonial politics in the nineteenth century. It is still buffeted by the international economy, and may be seen as more dependent than ever upon foreigners' propensity for trade and investment.

It is tempting to peer ahead. Complex interdependence means that the future rests largely upon what other countries do. Some of it, however, has implications within Australia. It is likely, for example, that a consequence of the immigration programme will be an increasing influence in foreign policy by the ethnic groups which at present are not yet of major political importance. Forty years ago the Jews were the only recognizable ethnic group with a keen interest in foreign affairs: they were concerned to influence the Australian government about the formation of Israel. Today there are said to be as many Muslims as Jews in Australia, perhaps more; and all governments are inclined to tread warily. Similarly both Greeks and Turks have been prominent in post-war immigration, which means that there are two constituencies to satisfy over the Cyprus issue. The future of Lebanon is of great importance to Lebanese immigrants; Tamils in Australia are concerned about what happens in Sri Lanka; Vietnamese demonstrate over events in Indo-China; Chinese students from Malaysia keep in close touch with educational and economic developments there; Poles, Hungarians, Ukrainians, Croatians and Estonians are often passionate about the policies current in their former homelands. It can be expected that ethnic groups will continue to organize in pursuit of foreign policy objectives.

The extent to which Australia will be able to control its economic environment is highly problematical. It will presumably continue to be concerned about its balance of payments. This concern, so evident in the 1930s and 40s, became much less pressing in the 1960s and 70s; it returned in the 1980s. Clearly the shape of the Australian economy, and the extent to which governments can influence its transformation into one with more acceptable exports and less need for imports of goods and capital, are matters to some extent under Australian control; but the terms of trade are not decided in Canberra, and international investors have fashions and prejudices which are more affected by what happens elsewhere than by what is done in Australia.

Perhaps the most teasing question is whether Australia can in future make itself fully responsible for its own defence, and whether this would be worthwhile even if it were practicable. Certainly the future holds little prospect of an Australian government which would enthusiastically embrace the idea of neutrality, or of total independence. The sense of interdependence is too strong, even if, in this case, it expresses itself through an obvious form of dependence. Which country to identify as embodying the direct threat and whether that perception might change with the passage of time – as views of China and Japan have done – are questions too difficult for most politicians and a great many electors to attempt.

Yet Hancock, fifty-one years after his *Australia* was published, made a plea for independent defence to a conference in Canberra, saying that he looked forward 'to the advent of a government that will lead us once again on the road to national self-respect and self-reliance'.[2] The coupling of self-respect with self-reliance indicated that he thought Australia had reached the point of maturity at which its national sentiment required that it look after itself in the world. The contrast with his conviction in *Australia* that in 1930 the country needed the kind of interdependence represented by the British Commonwealth of Nations is noteworthy. Perhaps the way of the future is towards complete independence in defence, but, if so, it will need to be linked with a degree of independence in economics which the Australia of the late 1980s shows little sign of achieving.

Notes

[1] W.K. Hancock 1930. *Australia.* London, Benn, ch XII.
[2] W.K. Hancock 1982. Our interests and obligations in peace and war. In R. O' Neill and D.M. Horner (eds.), *Australian Defence Policy for the 1980s.* St Lucia, University of Queensland Press.

Select bibliography

ACTU (Australian Council of Trade Unions) 1987. Executive Report for Consideration by the Congress of the Australian Council of Trade Unions, September 1987, Melbourne.

ACTU and Trade Development Council 1987. *Australia Reconstructed*, Canberra, AGPS.

Adler, D. 1965. Matriduxy in the Australian family. In A. Davies and S. Encel (eds.), *Australian Society: a sociological introduction*, Melbourne, Longman Cheshire.

Administrative Review Council 1986. *Tenth Annual Report 1985–86*, Canberra, AGPS.

Aitkin, D. 1982. *Stability and Change in Australian Politics* (2nd edn), Canberra, ANU Press.

   1983. Big government: the Australian experience. *Australian Quarterly*, 55(1).

   1983. Where does Australia stand? In G. Withers (ed.). *Bigger or Smaller Government?*, Canberra, Academy of the Social Sciences in Australia.

Alexander, F. 1967. *Australia Since Federation: a narrative and critical analysis*, Melbourne, Nelson.

Alford, R. 1963. *Party and Society: the Anglo-American democracies*, Chicago, Rand McNally.

Allen, P. 1983. Poverty policy issues. In R. Mendelsohn (ed.), *Australian Social Welfare Finance*, Sydney, Allen and Unwin.

Austin, A. (ed.) 1965. *The Webbs' Australian Diary*, Melbourne, Pitman.

Australian Committee on Technical and Further Education (Chairman: N. Kangan) 1974. *TAFE in Australia*, Canberra, AGPS.

Australian Council for Educational Research 1964. *Review of Education in Australia*.

Australian Education Council Taskforce on Education and Technology 1985. *Education and Technology*, Melbourne, AEC.

Australian Law Reform Commission 1985. *Standing in Public Interest Litigation*, Canberra, AGPS.

   1986. *The Recognition of Aboriginal Customary Laws*, Canberra, AGPS.

Australian Schools Commission 1981 Report for the Triennium 1982–84, Canberra, Union Offset 1955–62, Melbourne, ACER.

Baird, C., Gregory, R. and Gruen, F. (eds.) 1981. *Youth Employment, Education and Training*, Canberra, Academy of the Social Sciences in Australia.

Bamber, G. 1987. Conciliation, arbitration and human resource management: a British perspective. *Human Resource Management Australia* 25.

Barcan, A. 1980. *A History of Australian Education*, Melbourne, Oxford University Press.

Barwick, G. 1983. *Sir John Did His Duty*, Wahroonga, Serendip Publications.

Bean, P. *et al.* 1985. *In Defence of Welfare*, London, Tavistock.

Beggs, J. and Chapman, B. 1986. Australian strike activity in an international perspective. *Journal of Industrial Relations* 29.

   1987. Declining strike activity in Australia 1983–88: an international phenomenon? *Economic Record* 63.

   1987. An empirical analysis of Australian strike activity. *Economic Record* 63.

Bernard, J. 1973. *The Future of Marriage*, New York, Bantam.

Better Health Commission 1986. *Report*, Canberra, AGPS.

Beveridge, W. 1943. *Pillars of Security*, London, Allen and Unwin.

   1944. *Full Employment in a Free Society*, London, Allen and Unwin.

Birrell, R., Hill, D. and Nevile, J. (eds.) 1984. *Populate and Perish: the stresses of population growth*, Sydney, Fontana.

Select bibliography

Blandy, R. and Sloan, J. 1986. The Dynamic Benefits of Labour Market Deregulation, ACC/Wespac Economic Discussion Paper.

Bogdanor, V. 1981. *The People and the Party System*, London, Cambridge University Press.

Bolton, G. 1984. The image of Australia in Europe. *Journal of the Royal Society of Arts*, February.

Borrie, W. 1949. *Immigration, Australia's Problems and Prospects*, Sydney, Angus and Robertson.

1980. British immigration to Australia. In A. Madden and W. Morris Jones (eds.), *Australia and Britain*, Sydney, Sydney University Press.

Boserup, E. 1970. *Women's Role in Economic Development*, London, Allen and Unwin.

Bouma, G. and Dixon, B. 1986. *The Religious Factor in Australian Life*, Melbourne, MARC Australia.

Bowman, M. and Halligan, J. 1983. *Victorian Local Government's Role in Human Services*, Department of Political Science, University of Melbourne.

Brennan, D. 1983. *Towards a national child care policy*, Melbourne, Institute of Family Studies.

Briggs, A. 1961. The welfare state in historical perspective. *European Journal of Sociology* 2.

Brugger, B. and Jaensch, D. 1985. *Australian Politics: Theory and Practice*, Sydney, Allen and Unwin.

Bryce, J. 1921. *Modern Democracies*, London, Macmillan.

Bryson, L. 1974. Men's work and women's work: occupation and family orientation. *Search* 5.

1983. Thirty years of research on the division of labour in Australian families. *Australian Journal of Sex, Marriage and Family* 4.

1984. The Australian patriarchal family. In S. Encel et al. (eds.), *Australian Society: Introductory Essays* (4th edn), Melbourne, Longman Cheshire.

Buchanan, W. and Cantril, H. 1953. *How Nations See Each Other: a study in public opinion*, Urbana, University of Illinois Press.

Bureau of Labour Market Research 1983. *Youth Wages, Employment and the Labour Force*, Canberra, AGPS.

1985. *Labour Market Efficiency in Australia*, Canberra, AGPS.

Burns, A. 1980. *Breaking up: Separation and Divorce in Australia*, Melbourne, Nelson.

1986. Why do women continue to marry? In N. Grieve and A. Burns (eds.), *Australian Women: New Feminist Perspectives*, Melbourne, Oxford University Press.

1987. Attitudes to marriage among young tertiary educated women. Paper presented to the SAANZ Conference, Sydney, 14–18 July 1987.

Burns, A. and Goodnow, J. 1985. *Children and Families in Australia*, Sydney, Allen and Unwin.

Butlin, N. 1964. *Investment in Australian Economic Development*, London, Cambridge University Press.

1983. Yo ho ho and how many bottles of rum? *Australian Economic History Review* 23.

Butlin, N., Barnard, A. and Pincus, J. 1982. *Government and Capitalism*, Sydney, Allen and Unwin.

Callan, V. 1982. Australian, Greek and Italian parents; differentials in the value and cost of children. *Journal of Cross-Cultural Psychology* 11.

Calwell, A. 1945. *How Many Australians Tomorrow?*, Melbourne, Reed and Harris.

Carmichael, G. 1986. Australian divorce rate: is real decline at hand? In D. Barnard (ed.), *Making Marriage and Family Work*, Melbourne, Marriage Education Institute.

Carter, M. and Maddock, R. 1984. Working hours in Australia. In R. Blandy and O. Covick (eds.), *Understanding Labour Markets in Australia*, Sydney, Allen and Unwin.

1987. Leisure and Australian wellbeing 1911–1981. *Australian Economic History Review* XXVII (1).

Castles, F. 1985. *The Working Class and Welfare*, Sydney, Allen and Unwin.

1987. Trapped in an historical cul-de-sac: the prospects for welfare reform in Australia. In P. Saunders and A. Jamrozik (eds.), *Social Welfare in the Late 1980s: Reform, Progress or Retreat?*, Sydney, Social Welfare Research Centre.

Castles, F. and Wildenmann, R. (eds.) 1986. *Visions and Realities of Party Government*, Berlin. De Gruyter.

Caves, R. and Krause, L. (eds.) 1984. *The Australian Economy: a view from the north*, Sydney, Allen and Unwin.

Chapman, B. and Miller, P. 1985. An appraisal of immigrants' labour market performance in Australia. In M. Poole, P. de Lacey and B. Randhawa (eds.), *Australia in Transition: culture and life possibilities*, Sydney, Harcourt Brace Jovanovich.

Chapman, B. and Mulvey, C. 1986. An analysis of the origins of sex differences in Australian earnings. *Journal of Industrial Relations*, December.

Chiswick, B. and Miller, P. 1985. Immigrant generation and income in Australia. *Economic Record* 61.

Clemenger Network 1986. *Home Truths: how Australian couples are coping with change*, Melbourne, John Clemenger Pty Ltd.

Collins, H. 1985. Political ideology in Australia: the distinctiveness of a Benthamite society. In S. Graubard (ed.), *Australia: the Daedalus symposium*, Sydney, Angus and Robertson.

Committee of Review of Australian Industrial Relations Law and Systems 1985. *Report* (the Hancock Report), Canberra, AGPS.

Committee on the Future of Tertiary Education in Australia (Chairman: L. Martin) 1964. *Tertiary Education in Australia*, Melbourne.

Commonwealth Administrative Law Committee 1971. *Report*, Canberra, AGPS.

Commonwealth Tertiary Education Commission 1982. *Learning and Earning*, Canberra, AGPS.

Connolly, J. 1983. *Stepfamilies*, Sydney, Corgi Books.

Conway, J. 1985. Gender in Australia. *Daedalus* 114. Special issue of the Proceedings of the American Academy of Arts and Sciences, titled: *Australia: Terra Incognita?*

Conway, R. 1972. *The Great Australian Stupor*, Melbourne, Sun Books.

Cowan, R. 1983. *More Work for Mother: the ironies of household technology from the open hearth to the microwave*, New York, Basic Books.

Creigh, S. 1986. Australia's strike record: the international perspective. In R. Blandy and J. Niland (eds.), *Alternatives to Arbitration*, Sydney, Allen and Unwin.

Crittenden, B. 1981. *Changing Ideas in Australian Education*, Melbourne, ACER.

1981. The identity crisis in secondary education. *Australian Journal of Education* 25 (2).

1982. *Cultural Pluralism and Common Curriculum*, Melbourne, Melbourne University Press.

1984. Secondary education: reshaping the pattern. *Current Affairs Bulletin* 69 (9).

1986. Education after Year 10: the role of the secondary school. In I. Palmer (ed.) *Melbourne Studies in Education 1986*, Melbourne, Melbourne University Press.

Crowley, F. 1945. The British contribution to the Australian population 1960–1919. *University Studies in History and Economics*, University of Western Australia.

Curthoys, A. 1986. the sexual division of labour; theoretical arguments. In N. Grieve and A. Burns (eds.), *Australian Women: New Feminist Perspectives*, Oxford, Oxford University Press.

Danziger, S. and Smolensk, E. (eds.) 1985. Income transfers and the poor: a cross-national perspective. *Journal of Social Policy* 14.

Degler, C. 1980. *At Odds: Women and the Family from the Revolution to the Present*, New York, Oxford University Press.

Department of Immigration and Ethnic Affairs, National Population Council 1987. What's happening to the Australian family? *Population Report 8*, Canberra.

Department of Labour and National Service 1968. *Equal Pay: some aspects of Australian and overseas practice* (3rd edn), Melbourne.

Dicey, A. 1959. *Introduction to the Study of the Law of the Constitution* (10th edn), London, Macmillan.

Dickey, B. 1980. *No Charity There: a short history of social welfare in Australia*, Melbourne, Nelson.

Donnison, D. 1979. Social policy since Titmuss. *Journal of Social Policy* 8.

Dorwick, S. and Ngyen, T. 1987. Australia's economic growth performance: measurement and international comparison. *Discussion Paper no 160*, Centre for Economic Policy Research, Australian National University.

Economic Planning Advisory Council 1986. Growth in Australian social expenditures. *Council Paper No. 17*.

Edwards, M. 1982. Financial arrangement made by husbands and wives: findings of a survey. *Australian and New Zealand Journal of Sociology* 18.

1985. Individual equity and social policy. In J. Goodnow and C. Pateman (eds.), *Women Social Science and Public Policy*, Sydney, Allen and Unwin.

Encel, S. 1977. The Constitution as a social document. In S. Encel, D. Horne and E. Thompson (eds.), *Change the Rules!*, Bedford Park, Australasian Political Studies Association.

Evans, M. and Kelley, J. 1986. Immigrants' work: equality and discrimination in the Australian labour market. *Australia and New Zealand Journal of Sociology*, December.

Falding, H. 1957. Inside the Australian family. In A. Elkin (ed.), *Marriage and the family in Australia*, Sydney, Angus and Robertson.

Select bibliography

Feather, N. 1975. *Values in Education and Society*, New York, Free Press.

Fisk, E. 1985. *The Aboriginal Economy in Town and Country*, Sydney, Allen and Unwin.

Forsyth, W. 1942. *The Myth of Open Spaces*, Melbourne, Melbourne University Press.

Frankfurter, F. 1956. *Of Law and Men*, New York, Harcourt Brace & Co.

Freebairn, J., Porter, M. and Walsh, C. (eds.) *Spending and Taxing*, Sydney, Allen and Unwin.

Frost, L. (forthcoming). *The New Urban Frontier*, Melbourne, Cambridge University Press.

Galligan, B. 1980. The Kerr–Whitlam debate and the principles of the Australian Constitution. *Journal of Commonwealth and Comparative Politics* 18.

Gibbs, H. 1985. The State of the Australian Judicature. *Australian Law Journal* 59.

Gleezer, H. 1984. Antecedents and correlates of marriage. In *Social Change and Family Policies*, Melbourne, Institute of Family Studies.
   1984. *Changes in marriage and sex-role attitudes among young married women.* Proceedings of Institute of Family Studies Conference, Melbourne, Institute of Family Studies.

Golder, H. 1985. Divorce in 19th Century New South Wales, Sydney, University of NSW Press.

Goldthorpe, J. 1984. The end of convergence. In J. Goldthorpe (ed.), *Order and Conflict in Contemporary Capitalism*, Oxford University Press.

Gollan, R. 1960. *Radical and Working Class Politics*, Melbourne, Melbourne University Press.

Goodman, P. 1964. *Compulsory Mis-education and the Community of Scholars*, New York, Vintage Books.

Goodnow, J. (in press). The nature and function of children's household tasks. *Psychological Bulletin.*

Goodnow, J. and Burns, A. 1985. *Home and School*, Sydney, Allen and Unwin.

Goodnow, J., Burns, A. and Russell, G. 1986. The family context of development. In N. Feather (ed.), *Australian Psychology: review of research,* Sydney, Allen and Unwin.

Graham, B. 1966. *The Formation of the Australian Country Parties*, Canberra, ANU Press.

Gray, A. and Smith, L. 1983. *Australian Aboriginal Studies* 1.

Grbich, C. 1987. Primary care fathers – a role study: some preliminary findings. *Australian Journal of Sex, Marriage and Family* 8.

Greenwood, G. 1976. *The Future of Australian Federalism* (2nd edn), St Lucia, University of Queensland Press.

Gregory, R. and Duncan, R. 1981. Segmented labour market theories and the Australian experience of equal pay for women. *Journal of Post Keynesian Economics* 3.

Gregory, R. and Foster, W. 1983. A preliminary look at some labour market dynamics in Australia, Japan and North America. In K. Hancock *et al.*, (eds.), *Japanese and Australian Labour Markets: a comparative study*, Australia–Japan Research Centre Monograph, Australian National University.

Gregory, R. and Ho, V. 1985. Equal pay and comparable worth. *Discussion Paper No. 123*, Centre for Economic Policy Research, Australian National University.

Gregory, R., Daly, A. and Ho, V. 1986. A tale of two countries: equal pay for women in Australia and Britain. *Discussion Paper No. 147*, Centre for Economic Policy Research. Australian National University.

Grimshaw, P. 1983. The Australian family. In A. Burns *et al.* (eds.) *The Family in the Modern World*, Sydney, Allen and Unwin.
   1987. Marriage. In C. Davidson and J. McCartney (eds.), *Australians in 1988*, Sydney, Weldon, Syme & Co.

Gruen, F. 1982. The welfare state debate: economic myths of the Left and the Right. *Economic Record* 58.
   1985. The Federal budget. *Discussion Paper No 120A*, Centre for Economic Policy Research, Australian National University.

Haig, B. 1982. Sex discrimination in the reward for skills and experience in the Australian work force. *Economic Record* 58.
   1984. Gambling in Australia 1920/21 to 1980/81. In G. Caldwell *et al.* (eds.), *Gambling in Australia*, London, Croom Helm.

Hamilton, A. 1981. *Nature and Nurture: Aboriginal Child-rearing in North-Central Arnhem Land*, Canberra, Institute of Aboriginal Studies.

Hancock, W. K. 1930. *Australia*, London, Benn.

Harper, J. 1980. *Fathers at Home*, Ringwood, Vic., Penguin.

Harper, J. and Richards, L. 1979. *Mothers and Working Mothers*, Ringwood, Vic., Penguin.

Harreven, T. 1982. *Family Time and Industrial Time*, Cambridge, Cambridge University Press.

Harrison, D. 1984. The impact of immigration on a depressed labour market. *Economic Record* 60.

247

Henderson, R., Harcourt, A. and Harper, R. 1970. *People in Poverty: a Melbourne Survey*, Melbourne, Cheshire.

Hicks, N. 1978. *This Sin and Scandal: Australia's population debate 1871–1911*, Canberra, ANU Press.

Higgins, H. 1922. *A New Province for Law and Order*, London, Constable.

Hirst, J. 1983. *Convict Society and its Enemies: a history of early New South Wales*, Sydney, Allen and Unwin.

Hogan, M. 1984. *Public versus Private Schools*, Ringwood Vic., Penguin.

Home, A. and Burns, A. 1985. Through a child's eyes: quality of neighbourhood and quality of life. In I. Burnley and J. Forrest (eds.), *Living in Cities*, Sydney, Allen and Unwin.

Horne, D. 1964. *The Lucky Country: Australia in the sixties*, Ringwood Vic., Penguin.

    1976. *Death of the Lucky Country*, Ringwood Vic., Penguin.

    1980. *Time of Hope: Australia 1966–72*, London, Angus and Robertson.

Horsburgh, M. 1976. Child care in NSW in 1870. *Australian Social Work* 29.

Hughes, H. 1985. *Australia in a Developing World*, Sydney, Australian Broadcasting Corporation.

    1985. Australia and the world environment: the dynamics of international competition and wealth creation. In J. Scutt (ed.), *Poor Nation of the Pacific?*, Sydney, Allen and Unwin.

Hugo, G. 1986. *Australia's Changing Population: trends and implications*, Melbourne, Oxford University Press.

Inglis, P. and Strombak, T. 1986. Migrants' unemployment: the determinants of employment success. *Economic Record* 62.

Interim Committee for the Australian Schools Commission (Chairman: P. Karmel) 1973. *Schools in Australia*, Canberra, AGPS.

Jaensch, D. 1981. Remaking the Australian Constitution. *Current Affairs Bulletin* 58.

Jones, E. 1971. Fertility decline in Australia and New Zealand, 1861–1936. *Population Index* 37.

Jones, F. 1984. Income inequality. In D. Broom (ed.), *Unfinished Business: social justice for women in Australia*, Sydney, Allen and Unwin.

Kaspar, W. 1983. The market approach to social welfare. In R. Mendelsohn (ed.), *Australian Social Welfare Finance*, Sydney, Allen and Unwin.

Kaspar, W. *et al.* (eds.) 1980. *Australia at the Cross Roads: Our Choices to the Year 2000*, Sydney, Harcourt Brace Jovanovich.

Kaspura, A. and Weldon, G. 1980. Productivity trends in the Australian economy 1900–01 to 1978–79. *Working Paper No. 9*, Department of Productivity, Canberra.

Katlenstein, P. 1985. *Small States in World Markets*, Ithaca, NY, Cornell University Press.

Kemp, D. 1978. *Society and Electoral Behaviour in Australia: a study of three decades*, St Lucia, University of Queensland Press.

Kendig, H. (ed.) 1985. Contributions of the aged. *Proceedings of the 19th Annual Conference of the Australian Association of Gerontology*, Sydney.

    (ed.) 1986. *Ageing and Families: A social networks perspective*, Sydney, Allen and Unwin.

    1986. Social relations: networks and ties. In H. Kendig (ed.), *Ageing and Families: a social networks perspective*, Sydney, Allen and Unwin.

Kenyon, P. and Dawkins, P. 1987. *Explaining Labour Absence in Australia*. Working Paper No. 1, Economic Programme, Murdoch University, August.

Kerr, T. 1978. *Matters for Judgment*, South Melbourne, Macmillan.

Kewley, T. 1973. *Social Security in Australia 1900–1972* (2nd edn), Sydney, Sydney University Press.

Khoo, S. 1987. A profile of cohabitation in Australia. *Journal of Marriage and the Family*, 49.

Kingston, B. 1977. *The World Moves Slowly: a documentary history of Australian women*, Sydney, Cassell.

Kreigler, R. and Stendal, G. 1984. *At Work: Australian experiences*, Sydney, Allen and Unwin.

Lake, M. 1985. Helpmeet, slave, housewife: women in rural families 1870–1930. In P. Grimshaw *et al.* (eds.), *Families in Colonial Australia*, Sydney, Allen and Unwin.

La Nauze, J. 1968. *Federated Australia: Selections from Letters to the Morning Post*, Melbourne, Melbourne University Press.

Lee, J. and Fahey, C. 1986. A boom for whom? Some developments in the Australian labour world 1870–1891, *Labour History*, May.

Lenin, V. 1952. In Australia. *Sochineniya*, Moscow, Gosozpolit.

Lewis, D. 1983. The Measurement and interpretation of segregation of women in the workforce. *Journal of Industrial Relations*, September.

Lewis, R. and Spanier, G. 1979. Theorizing about the quality and stability of marriage. In W. Burr *et al.* (eds.), *Contemporary Theories About the Family*, New York, Free Press.

McDonald, P. 1984. *Can the Family Survive?* Melbourne, Institute of Family Studies.

McDonnell, W. *et al.* 1956. *Review of Education in Australia 1948–1954*, Melbourne, ACER.

McEwen, E. 1985. Family history in Australia: some observations on a new field. In P. Grimshaw *et al.* (eds.), *Families in Colonial Australia*, Sydney, Allen and Unwin.

McGavin, P. 1987. *Wages and Whitlam*, Melbourne, Oxford University Press.

McGregor, C. 1966. *Profile of Australia*, London, Hodder and Stoughton.

Macintyre, S. 1985. *Winners and losers*, Sydney, Allen and Unwin.

Macintyre, S. 1986. The short history of social democracy in Australia. In D. Rawson (ed.), *Blast, Budge or Bypass: Towards a Social Democratic Australia*, Canberra, Academy of the Social Sciences in Australia.

McKay, I. *et al.* 1971. *Living and Partly Living*, Melbourne, Nelson.

McLean, I. 1987. Economic wellbeing: living standards and inequality since 1900. In R. Maddock and I. McLean, *The Australian Economy in the Long Run*, Melbourne, Cambridge University Press.

McLean, I. and Pincus, J. 1983. Did Australian living standards stagnate between 1890 and 1940? *Journal of Economic History* 43.

McNab, K. and Ward, R. 1962. The nature and nurture of the first generation of native-born Australians. *Historical Studies, Australia and New Zealand* 10.

Maddock, R., Olekalns, N., Ryan, J. and Vickers, M. 1984. The distribution of income and wealth in Australia 1914–80. *Source Paper No. 1*, Source Papers on Economic History, Australian National University.

Madgwick, R. 1969 (1937). *Immigration into Eastern Australia* (reprint), Sydney, Sydney University Press.

Manning, I. 1985. *Incomes and Policy*, Sydney, Allen and Unwin.

Marklund, S. 1986. The Swedish model – work and welfare. *ACOSS Impact* 16 (18), December.

Markus, A. 1984. Labour and immigration 1946–9: the displaced persons program. *Labour History*, November.

Mathews, R. 1976. *Making Federalism Work*, Canberra, ANU Press.

Matthews, J. 1984. *Good and Mad Women*, Sydney, Allen and Unwin.

Mayer, H. 1956. Some conceptions of the Australian party system, 1910–1950. *Historical Studies* 7.

(ed.) 1961. *Catholics and the Free Society: an Australian symposium*, Melbourne, Chesire.

Mendelsohn, R. 1979. *The Condition of the People: social welfare in Australia 1900–1975*, Sydney, Allen and Unwin.

Metin, A. 1977. *Socialism Without Doctrines*, Chippendale NSW. Alternative Publishing Cooperative Ltd.

Miller, P. 1982. The economic position of migrants: facts and fallacies. *Australian Bulletin of Labour* 8(4).

1982. The rate of return to education – the evidence from the 1976 Census. *Australian Economic Review*, 3rd Quarter.

Milligan, V. *et al.* 1984. Non-government welfare organisations in Australia. Social Welfare Research Centre, *Reports and Proceedings No. 51*, Sydney, University of NSW.

Mills, S. 1986. *The New Machine Men: polls and persuasion in Australian politics*, Ringwood Vic., Penguin.

Ministerial Review of Postcompulsory Schooling (Chairperson: J. Blackburn) 1985. Melbourne, Government Printer.

Ministry of Education, Victoria 1986. *Taking Schools into the 1990s*, Melbourne, Government Printer.

1986. *The Government Decision on the Report of the Ministry Structure Project Team*, Melbourne, Government Printer.

Mistilis, N. 1984. Explaining partisan patterns amongst immigrant electors. In J. Jupp (ed.), *Ethnic Politics in Australia*, Sydney, Allen and Unwin.

Mitchell, W. and Sherrington, G. 1985. Families and children in 19th century Illawarra. In P. Grimshaw *et al.* (eds.), *Families in Colonial Australia*, Sydney, Allen and Unwin.

Mol, H. 1985. *The Faith of Australians*, Sydney, Allen and Unwin.

National Population Inquiry 1975. *Population and Australia*, Vol. 1, Canberra, AGPS.

1978. *Supplementary Report*, Canberra, AGPS.

Neilson, P. (ed.) 1986. *The Penguin Book of Australian Satirical Verse*, Ringwood Vic., Penguin.

Nevile, J. 1975. Inflation, company profits and investment. *Australian Economic Review*, 4th Quarter.

1979. *The Root of All Evil: essays on economics, ethics and capitalism*, Sydney, Australian Council of Churches.

Nevile, J. and Warren, N. 1984. Inflation and personal income distribution in Australia. *Australian Economic Review*, 4th Quarter.

Nevile, J. *et al.* 1988. Inflation, anti-inflationary policy and the distribution of income in Australia. *Centre for Applied Economic Research Working Paper*, Kensington, University of NSW.

Norman, M. 1980. *Small Schools Study*, Canberra, Australian Schools Commission.

Norman, N. and Meikle, K. 1985. *The Economic Effects of Immigration on Australia*, Melbourne, Committee for Economic Development of Australia.

Oeser, O. and Hammond, S. (eds.) 1954. *Social Structure and Personality in a City*, London, Routledge & Kegan Paul.

Overacker, L. 1952. *The Australian Party System*, New Haven, Yale University Press.

Pappas, Carter, Evans and Koop Ltd 1985. *Victorian Football League Study*, Melbourne, mimeograph.

Partridge, P. 1968. *Society, Schools and Progress*, Oxford, Pergamon Press.

Patience, A. and Scott, J. (eds.) 1983. *Australian Federalism: future tense*, Melbourne, Oxford University Press.

Peterson. N. and Langton, M. (eds.) 1983. *Aborigines, Land and Land Rights*, Canberra, Australian Institute of Aboriginal Studies.

Pettman, B. (ed.) 1977. *Equal Pay for Women: progress and problems in seven countries*, Washington, Hemisphere.

Piggott, J. 1984. The distribution of wealth in Australia: a survey. *Economic Record* 60.

Plowman, D. 1987. The role of employer associations. In G. Ford, J. Hearn and R. Lansbury (eds.), *Australian Labour Relations: Readings* (4th edn), South Melbourne, Macmillan.

Portus, G. 1937. *Free Compulsory and Secular*, London, Oxford University Press.

Price, A. 1924. *The Foundation and Settlement of South Australia 1829–1845*, Adelaide, F. W. Preece.

Price, C. 1984. *Birthplaces of the Australian Population 1961–1981*, Canberra, Department of Demography, Australian National University.

Pringle, J. 1965. *Australian Accent*, London, Chatto and Windus.

Quality of Education Review Committee (Chairman: P. Karmel) 1985. *Quality of Education in Australia*, Canberra, AGPS.

Radford, W. (ed.) 1953. *The Non-governmental Schools of Australia: a descriptive and statistical account*, Melbourne, Melbourne University Press.

Ravitch, D. 1984. The continuing crisis: fashions in education. *The American Scholar*, Spring.

Rawson, D. 1985. State controlled union ballots. In B. Ford and D. Plowman (eds.), *Australian Unions: an Industrial Relations Perspective*, South Melbourne, Macmillan.

1987. Law and politics in industrial relations. In G. Ford, J. Hearn and R. Lansbury (eds.), *Australian Labour Relations: Readings* (4th edn), South Melbourne, Macmillan.

Reeves, W. 1902. *State Experiments in Australia and New Zealand*, London, Grant Richards.

Report of the National Estate 1974. Canberra, AGPS.

Reynolds, P. 1974. *The Democratic Labour Party*, Brisbane, Jacaranda.

Robinson, J. and Griffiths, B. 1986. *Australian Families: current situation and trends, 1969–1985*, Social Security Background Paper No. 10, Canberra, Department of Social Security.

Robson, L. 1965. *Convict Settlers in Australia*, Melbourne, Melbourne University Press.

Rolfe, P. 1979. *The Journalistic Javelin: an illustrated history of The Bulletin*, Sydney, Wildcat Press.

Ross, E. 1985. *Living in Poverty: social need in NSW*, NCOSS Issues Paper No.3, Sydney, Council of Social Service of New South Wales.

Rowland, D. 1979. *Internal Migration in Australia*, Canberra, Australian Bureau of Statistics.

Rowley, C. 1971. *Outcasts in a White Australia: Aboriginal policy and practice, Vol. 2*, Canberra, ANU Press.

Rowse, T. 1978. *Australian Liberalism and National Character*, Melbourne, Kibble Books.

Royal Commission on the Decline of the Birth rate and on the Mortality of Infants in New South Wales: Vol. 1, *Report and Statistics*, Sydney, NSW Government Printer.

Russell, A. 1987. Mother–child and father–child relationships in middle childhood. *Child Development* 58.

Russell, G. 1983. *The Changing Role of Fathers?* St Lucia, University of Queensland Press.

Rustow, D. 1970. Transitions to democracy: towards a dynamic model. *Comparative Politics* 2.

Ruth, E. 1984. The south-west Aboriginal and family law. *Proceedings of the First Australian Family Research Conference*, Melbourne, Institute of Family Studies.

Ruzicka, L. and Caldwell, J. 1977. *The End of Demographic Transition in Australia*, Department of Demography, Australian National Unversity.

Ruzicka, L. and Choi, C. 1981. Recent decline in Australian fertility. *Yearbook Australia*, No. 65, Canberra.

Samuels, G. 1884. The end of federalism? *Australian Quarterly* 11.

Sarantakos, S. 1984. *Living Together in Australia*, Melbourne, Longman Cheshire.

Sawer, G. 1967. *Australian Federalism in the Courts*, Melbourne, Melbourne University Press.

1977. *Federalism under Strain*, Melbourne, Melbourne University Press.

Scotton, R. and Ferber, H. 1978, 1980. *Public Expenditure and Social Policy in Australia*, Vol. I 1972–75, Vol. II 1976–78, Melbourne, Longman Cheshire.

Scutt, J. (ed.) 1985. *Poor Nation of the Pacific? Australia's future*, Sydney, Allen and Unwin.

Secretariat to the Committee to Advise on Australia's Immigration Policies 1987. *Understanding Immigration*, Canberra, AGPS.

Senate Standing Committee on Constitutional and Legal Affairs 1974. *Report on ... the Family Law Bill*, Parliamentary Paper 1974/133.

Serle, G. 1963. *The Golden Age*, Melbourne, Melbourne University Press.

Seymour, I. 1980. *OPEC: Instrument of Change*, London, Macmillan.

Shaver, S. 1983. Sex and money in the welfare state. In C. Baldock and B. Cass (eds.), *Women, Social Welfare and the State*, Sydney, Allen and Unwin.

Shaw, A. 1966. *Convicts and the Colonies*, London, Faber.

Sheehan, P. and Stricker, P. 1984. Welfare benefits and the labour market. In R. Blandy and O. Covick (eds.), *Understanding Labour Markets in Australia*, Sydney, Allen and Unwin.

Simms, M. 1981. Australia. In J. Levenduski and J. Hills (eds.), *The Politics of the Second Electorate*, London, Routledge & Kegan Paul.

Sinfield, A. 1978. Analysis in the social division of welfare. *Journal of Social Policy*, Vol. 7.

Smart, D. 1978. *Federal Aid to Australian Schools*, St Lucia, University of Queensland Press.

1986. The financial crisis in Australian higher education and the inexorable push towards privatisation. *Australian Universities Review* 29(2).

Smith, R. 1984. Estimating the impacts of job subsidies on the distribution of unemployment: reshuffling the queue? *Discussion Paper No 95*, Centre for Economic Policy Research, Australian National University.

Social Science Data Archives (SSDA) *Bulletin* No 11. August 1987.

Social Welfare Commssion, Family Services Committee 1978. *Families and Social Services in Australia*, Vol. 2, Canberra, AGPS.

Soltow, L. 1972. The censuses of wealth of man in Australia in 1915 and in the United States in 1860 and 1870. *Australian Economic History review* XII(2).

Spearitt, A. 1983. The electrification of the home in New South Wales. Unpublished thesis, University of Sydney.

Stillwell, F. 1986. *The Accord and Beyond*, Sydney, Pluto Press.

Storer, D. (ed.) 1985. *Ethnic Family Values in Australia*, Sydney, Prentice Hall.

Swain, S. 1985. *A refuge at Kildare: the history of the Geelong Female Refuge and Bethany Babies Home*, Geelong, Bethany Child and Family Support.

Throsby, D. and Withers, G. 1979. *Economics of the Performing Arts*, Melbourne, Arnold.

1984. *What Price Culture?*, Sydney, Australia Council.

Turner, I. 1968. *The Australian Dream*, Melbourne, Sun Books.

Twopenny, R. 1973 (1883). *Town Life in Australia*, Ringwood Vic., Penguin.

United Nations Economic Commission for Asia and the Pacific 1982. Country Monograph Series No. 9, *Population of Australia* (2 vols), New York.

Victoria, Inquiry into Prostitution 1984, 1985. *Options Paper* (2 vols.), *Final Report*, Victorian Government Printer.

Select bibliography

Walker, R. *et al.* 1984. *Responses to Poverty: lessons from Europe*, London, Heinemann.

Ward, R. 1978. *The Australian Legend* (rev. edn), Melbourne, Oxford University Press.

Waring, B. 1984. *The Ideology of Motherhood*, Sydney, Allen and Unwin.

White, J. P. and Mulvaney, D. (eds.) 1987. *Australia to 1788*, Sydney, Fairfax Syme and Weldon Associates.

Whitlam, G. 1979. *The Truth of the Matter*, Ringwood Vic., Penguin.

Winterton, G. 1983. *Parliament, the Executive and the Governor-General*, Melbourne, Melbourne University Press.

Wison, R. 1978. Urban and regional policy. In R. Scotton and H. Ferber (eds.), *Public Expenditures and Social Policy in Australia*, Melbourne, Longman Cheshire.

Withers, G. 1985. Television viewing and ABC program policy: an econometric study. *Australian Journal of Management* 10(2).

1987. Labour. In R. Maddock and I. Mclean (eds.), *The Australian Economy in the Long Run*, Melbourne, Cambridge University Press.

Withers, G. and Pope, D. 1985. Immigration and unemployment. *Economic Record* 61.

Wright, J. 1985. Landscape and dreaming. In S. Graubard (ed.), *Australia: the Daedalus Symposium*, Sydney, Angus and Robertson.

Young, C. 1984. Leaving home and returning home: a demographic study of young adults in Australia. *Proceedings of the Australian Family Research Conference*, Melbourne, Institute of Family Studies.

1986. *Selection and Survival: immigrant mortality in Australia*, Canberra, AGPS.

1987. *Young people leaving home in Australia*, Canberra, ANU Press.

Zagorski, C. 1985. *Social Mobility into Post Industrial Society*, Canberra, Sociology Department, Research School of Social Sciences, Australian National University.

Index

For EU product safety concerns, contact us at Calle de José Abascal, 56–1°,
28003 Madrid, Spain or eugpsr@cambridge.org.

www.ingramcontent.com/pod-product-compliance
Ingram Content Group UK Ltd.
Pitfield, Milton Keynes, MK11 3LW, UK
UKHW030856150625
459647UK00021B/2781